BYRON AND THE RUINS OF PARADISE

BYRON

AND THE

RUINS OF PARADISE

by Robert F. Gleckner

The Johns Hopkins Press, Baltimore

Library of Congress Catalog Card No. 67-25071

This book has been brought to publication
with the generous assistance of a grant
from the Carl and Lily Pforzheimer Foundation.

The frontispiece photograph was provided
by Brown Brothers.

For Susan and Jeff

ACKNOWLEDGMENTS

Apart from my many debts to Byron scholars and critics, which I have acknowledged, however inadequately, in the notes, I am pleased to record special thanks to the University of California, for its several generous travel and Intramural Research Fund grants which made much of this book possible; to The Miriam Lutcher Stark Library of the University of Texas, whose patient, courteous, and helpful staff made available to me its splendid Byron manuscript collection and, in particular, to the Librarian, June Moll, and to the Manuscript Committee of the Library, for permission to quote from the manuscripts; to the staffs of the Henry E. Huntington, University of California at Los Angeles, and University of California at Riverside libraries, for invaluable help; to Sir John Murray, for his several courtesies; to Herbert Cahoon, curator of Autograph Manuscripts at the Pierpont Morgan Library, and to the British Museum, for their help in locating and microfilming certain material; to Mr. and Mrs. Allen Becker and Willis W. Pratt, for their many kindnesses during my stay in Austin; to Clarence L. Cline, for his special efforts at a critical time; to Mr. and Mrs. John R. Bickley, for helping to provide the place and time for much of my writing; to my colleagues Stefan Fleischer and Stanley N. Stewart, for several critical suggestions; to Pat Mayhew, for advice on the title; to Caroline Kirkpatrick, whose typing left nothing to be desired; to Barbara Parmelee, for her enthusiasm and encouragement; to Jean Owen, for her efficient and sensitive editing of the manuscript; and to my wife and children, who ever cheerfully let me steal my time from them to complete this work.

R. F. G.

Grand Terrace, California
May 1, 1967

CONTENTS

CONTENTS

INTRODUCTION

Even at this late date, a case must still be made for Byron as poet if one chooses to concentrate his attention on those poems in which his greatness is not assured (as it is in *Don Juan, The Vision of Judgment,* perhaps *Manfred*) but in which his own age saw a dazzling talent. The judgment of the age, however, was in a sense purchased in coin of the realm—a universal melancholy that awaited only a silver tongue to give it voice. Curiously, this judgment has produced a contrary verdict in our age. More enlightened, and rather self-righteously freed from nineteenth-century *Weltschmerz,* we have been strangely blind to all but the rampant "Byronism," as we parrot-like continue to call it, of *Childe Harold's Pilgrimage,* the Turkish tales, many of the lyrics, most of the plays—indeed, to all of the poems which are neither satiric nor antic. Nourished in the atmosphere of Swinburne's devastating attacks upon Byron's sloppiness,[1] most modern critics perpetuate the fashion of disdaining to comment on the poetry written prior to 1816, or of dismissing it with appropriate condescension: they are almost apologetic in their discovery of the same bright spots in the last two cantos of *Childe Harold* (but not enough to redeem Cantos I and II), of an occasional lyric or two that beggars criticism, and of a few passages of grandeur and force in the tales. Even such

---

[1] See especially *Miscellanies* (London, 1886), which contains the savage essay "Wordsworth and Byron," originally published in *The Nineteenth Century* (April–May, 1884). A more tempered appraisal may be found in *Essays and Studies* (London, 1875), and it is worth noting that although Swinburne insisted that Byron "can only be judged or appreciated in the mass," he did publish *A Selection from the Works of Lord Byron* in 1866.

aperçus are accompanied by painfully little evidence, analysis, or discussion.

Now in these days of the *Variorum Don Juan* we have been taught to be a bit more careful about accepting the slap-dash habit of composition Byron himself is to blame for projecting upon the forefront of our critical minds. Yet, if *Don Juan* cost him so much effort, this fact has only served to "prove" that his genius was essentially satiric and that his imagination responded as any great poet's should to his characteristic stimulus. More important, perhaps, than this critical half-sightedness—not to mention the depths to which biographizing has plunged the general state of Byron criticism from his day to ours—is an apparent inability to see his so-called "romantic" poetry as other than a cheap appeal to a debased public taste. In their narrow staginess and contrived melodrama, these works are tolerated as dated amusements or dutifully pointed to as curiosities of literary history, artifacts of an "ism" that said little to Byron's own time and says nothing to ours. Because of his inveterate self-contradiction, his pooh-poohing of his own serious poetic purpose, modern criticism has all too often surrendered its normal and healthy critical curiosity to an easy understanding of content and a rather smug rediscovery of Byronic character or his "power" or "presence." Thus in judging only the surface of the poetry, we have found Byron, as a major non-satiric poet, seriously wanting. But we have taken the obvious to be all, unwilling to probe beneath the admittedly forbidding surface of his language and prosody to essential form and structure, essential theme and style. We have seen the kinship among Childe Harold, the heroes of the Tales, Manfred, Cain, and Don Juan, but, cowed by Byron's deliberate—and undeliberate—contradictions, we have rather uncritically denied the remarkable coherence of the vision that provides these figures their landscape and their continued vitality.

I should like to speak, initially, then, of four recent critical studies of Byron, not because they are the only good ones (though in some ways they are) but because corporately they augur well, I think, for the future of Byron criticism, while separately they exemplify the curiously fragmented nature of even our most informed and sensitive criticism today. The first of these, Paul West's *Byron and the Spoiler's Art* (New York, 1960), almost defies categorization. Hailed by most reviewers who deplore the paucity of good criticism on Byron's poetry, it has also been rightly attacked for its flamboyant writing, West's self-conscious fascination with his own penchant for sententious aphorism, and the sheer monotony of its unrelieved stylistic brilliance. Yet it is a book with abundant critical insights into Byron's total creative effort and, more important, a book which conceives of that effort as a studiable whole. But West was unable to escape from the man: with far less finesse than Charles du Bos,[2] he sees all the poetry motivated by a psychological drive—for West, the need for elimination. As such, Byron's poetic efforts, achievements, and failures become manifestations of the fluctuations of his psyche, their "coherence" dependent upon the relative success of their eliminatory aspects.

More quietly brilliant than West is George Ridenour's *The Style of "Don Juan"* (New Haven, 1960), perhaps the best single critical work on the poet yet done. Ridenour also sees Byron's poetry whole (his Yale dissertation on *Childe Harold* is an important preliminary study to this book),[3] informed by a coherent vision of man's Fall and its consequences and sustained by a metaphorical technique tantamount to myth-making. Yet, as the book's title signifies, Ridenour, for whatever reasons, limits his perceptions and sense of Byron's wholeness to the world of *Don Juan*, thus vitiating to some extent his all-important claim to Byron's consistency of *Weltanschauung*: ". . . as violence and disorder lurk behind the most winning manifestations of tranquillity and harmony, the tranquil and harmonious are fated inevitably to dissolve again in the violent and chaotic. This is an apparently immutable law of Byron's world" (p. 45). In a review of Andrew Rutherford's and Doris Langley Moore's recent books on Byron, Ridenour makes his point again in a slightly different way: ". . . unless the terror of Byron's universe

---

[2] *Byron et le Besoin de la Fatalité* (Paris, 1931), translated by Ethel C. Mayne as *Byron and the Need of Fatality* (London and New York, 1932).
[3] "Byron and the Romantic Pilgrimage: A Critical Examination of the Third and Fourth Cantos of Lord Byron's *Childe Harold's Pilgrimage*" (unpublished Ph.D. dissertation, Yale University, 1955).

is grasped we miss the significance of his successes in dealing with it, and the pathos of his failures."[4] Exactly. Although I can sharply disagree, then, with many aspects of Ridenour's work, and although my own sense of Byron's coherence of view was arrived at before I knew that work, his approach is clearly the right one and I am happy to acknowledge my debt to him.

The third book is Andrew Rutherford's *Byron: A Critical Study* (Edinburgh and London, 1961), judicious, beautifully written, convincing, yet representative of the very half-sightedness I spoke of above. Rutherford's gentlemanly contempt for the first cantos of *Childe Harold* and for all the tales, his seeing in them a "strong element of silly self-dramatization" (p. 45), precludes a vision of the whole Byron or a significant departure from earlier judgments made on the same basis. Divorced from each other, except in their central characters or overlapping themes, the poems are read and judged with a critical acuteness long lacking in Byron criticism; but the resultant total estimate must be seen as suspect, because its basis is the anthologist's disjointed critical vision.

The final book, William H. Marshall's *The Structure of Byron's Major Poems* (Philadelphia, 1962), is perhaps the most disappointing when one measures its accomplishment against the promise of the title. Structure often becomes story, criticism and analyses more often explication by summary. Yet Marshall's aim is clearly right, to see the poem in terms of a structure rather than an "ism," a self-portrait, or a meandering meditation. Until we can accommodate such a view within our current critical stance, the discrepancies between Byron's attempt and his achievement will be blurred, his relative successes unrecognized in our haste to condemn the language or versification or grammatical horrors. If my own stance leans lopsidedly in the direction of structure, then, I owe a considerable debt to Marshall's corroboration of my own long-held suspicions, though I absolve him of any blame for my own willingness to lean in an attempt to redress the prevailing imbalance.

What I ask here, and hope in some measure to answer,

---

[4] "Byron: Criticism and Fact," *Yale Review*, series 2, LI (1961–62), 323.

is that Byron's non-satiric poetry be given its critical day—that we approach it with due regard for its integrity as poetry and without apology for considering seriously what perhaps may immediately strike our sensibilities as unworthy of such attention.[5] What Byron calls *"minute* or *verbal* criticism"[6] I eschew as common knowledge. My purpose is not to agree or disagree with those who have established beyond doubt the infelicities, crudeness, bad taste, sloppiness, bad grammar, overwriting, and absurdity of segments of Byron's poetry, and who have with equal diligence pointed out the frequent brilliance, power, lyric grace, control, mobility, savagery, and humor that constitute its greatness. Rather, I seek to see the poetic canon as indeed canonical, as elements in a fascinating history of struggle for form (for what Ridenour calls "style," a "characteristic way of meeting and shaping experience"[7]), as hammer strokes (some firm and ringing, some hollow and glancing) forging a frighteningly dark and coherent vision of man and life, of the human condition not merely "circa 1811," as David Erdman suggests,[8] but throughout human history. Such a struggle presupposes, of course, a self-consciousness in Byron the poet capable of being dissociated from the flippancy and poses of Byron the man and legend. In a sense, I suppose that my aim is to give Byron the poet *his* day despite his own indifference (genuine or feigned) or reluctance to have precisely this kind of day. Some of this self-

---

[5] Although our conclusions differ substantially, W. W. Robson's approach in his Chatterton Lecture of 1957 I applaud, especially for its rarity: "The assessment of Byron's poetry . . . must begin and end with the poetry" and therefore his lecture is only for those "whose interest is in poetry and not, primarily, in *Kulturgeschichte*, psychopathology, or scandal," or in Byron as a "human force" ("Byron as Poet," *Proceedings of the British Academy*, XLIII [1957], 30, 25–26).

[6] Ltr. to William Bankes, 6 Mar. 1807, in *The Works of Lord Byron: Letters and Journals*, ed. R. E. Prothero (6 vols., rev. ed.; London and New York, 1902–4), I, 121. All future references to this work will be noted as *LJ*, followed by volume and page number.

[7] *The Style of "Don Juan,"* p. xi. See also Edward E. Bostetter's chapter on Byron in *The Romantic Ventriloquists* (Seattle, Wash., 1963), in which he too deals with Byron's "style" in this sense. Bostetter's essay is one of the best yet done on the poet, despite the fact that it is limited almost completely to *Childe Harold, Manfred, Cain,* and *Don Juan*.

[8] Unpublished essay on Byron and Shelley.

INTRODUCTION

consciousness is occasionally apparent in the letters and journals, though in general those documents we must recognize as written not by the poet but by the public as well as the private man, the one who consistently contrasted the profession of poetry with *any* other activity of the mind or body. If, as has often been asserted, the letters and journals offer a suggestive commentary on the poetry, the nature of that commentary is severely qualified by the tone and particular occasion and by the eagerness of the man to dissociate himself from poetry as a serious occupation. On the contrary, the most revealing commentary on the poems is the poetry itself, and particularly the evaluation therein of the poet as a crucial, central character, whose prophetic view of the past and of his own time develops gradually into the myth of man's eternal fall and damnation in the hell of human existence, the myth of what I choose to call the ruins of paradise and the consequent human condition.

Early intimations of this vision can be accepted as such only with the greatest caution, and even here interpretation runs the considerable risk of a blind narrowness born of Freudian eagerness to find in juvenile utterances and experiences the seeds of mature idea. The problem is especially complicated in the study of Byron by the peculiarities of his childhood and adolescence, which intensified in him the normal trauma of this stage of life. His ancestry, his incorrigible father, his well-meaning but stupid mother, his lameness, his precipitate and early elevation to the peerage, the parochialism of his early tutoring and schooling, his inflammable yet warmly kind and sensitive nature, his early exposure to sexual experience, his many youthful acquaintances and few real friends all contribute to the formation of his character and the general contours of his life; but they are slippery counters for reckoning the origins of a coherent vision, even for the experienced Freudian. Finally, all of this may be overshadowed by Byron's early-formed habit of keeping his letters-and-journal voice and his poetic voice separate, a habit that even antedates the embodiment of the latter in verse. The voice we hear, particularly in the letters, is one I should like to call the public-private voice, conscious of its own revelation and of a form which, in its very privacy, encourages yet discourages the whole truth. For the letter is, however private, a kind of publication after all, a self-consciously wrought autobiography (at least for Byron), in which the facts as they are seen by the subject-object (both of which are Byron) are conveyed with as much exactness as possible, where a state of mind, attitude, or point of view is conveyed explicitly or implicitly, but also where certain facts, attitudes, and states of mind are withheld by the human reluctance to bare all of the heart and mind.[9] In the poetry, on the other hand, we hear a private-public voice,[10] broadcast across the land, yet in its very publicness capable of a peculiar kind of intimate revelation. The two urges, the urge to reveal discreetly and the urge to articulate fully one's essential being, are the same urge—to reveal, to give vent, to proclaim, above all to create a world. Neither world, for Byron, is more real than the other, but that was not a conclusion he came to easily or quickly. After his earliest volume, *Hours of Idleness*,[11] he still had to discover that the feignings of the poet were but fictionalized reality after all, and that the poet *manqué* became a poet only when he understood that lesson. But I shall turn to those early lyrics in a moment. Here I wish rather to focus on that risky evidence of the early letters and journals to suggest, with no claim of conclusiveness, no assurance of conviction, and no intention of Freudian prediction, the faint clues and indirections which seem to me to have a bearing upon the mature co-

---

[9] It is worth noting in this regard that Byron early wanted his letters retained by his correspondents, clearly as a record of how he saw himself, how he was, how he would like others to see him.

[10] I am acutely conscious of the awkwardness of these terms, but since neither voice is unalloyed by the accents of the other, the hyphenations do express the kind of shifted emphasis that is the essence of their difference.

[11] Actually Byron's earliest poems appeared in a series of issues: *Fugitive Pieces*, anonymous, in 1806; a second edition, also anonymous (lacking two poems of the original but including twelve new ones), entitled *Poems on Various Occasions* (1807); *Hours of Idleness* (later in the same year); and *Poems Original and Translated* (1808). Since the 1831 edition of Byron's poetic works, published by John Murray, *Hours of Idleness* has been the aggregate title given to the poems contained in all four of the above volumes. See *The Works of Lord Byron: Poetry*, ed. E. H. Coleridge (7 vols., rev. ed.; London and New York, 1903–5), I, xi–xiii, for a full bibliographical account. All future references to this edition will be noted as *P*, followed by volume and page numbers. All line numbers cited correspond to Coleridge's.

herence of Byron's grim poetic vision of the world and the human condition.

On June 25, 1809, at Falmouth waiting to embark on his grand tour, Byron writes to Hodgson: "I leave England without regret—I shall return to it without pleasure. I am like Adam, the first convict sentenced to transportation, but I have no Eve, and have eaten no apple but what was sour as a crab;—and thus ends my first chapter."[12] Byron was 21. From such evidence as this, and there is a good deal of it throughout his writings, critics have come to see Byron as plagued by the idea of original sin, of man's inherited damnation. The description is, I think, too heavily loaded with theological overtones to be exact. As the letter to Hodgson suggests, Byron's emphasis is not so much upon Adam's, and hence man's, sin as it is upon a world that renders man's propensity to good (however small) nugatory and sentences him to eternal exile, alone, without whatever compensatory affection an Eve embodies. Man's fall, then, and his consequent expulsion from Eden is not totally understandable in terms of a sin, the commission of some forbidden act; rather, for Byron, man's fall is the paradoxically providential act of a God who punishes as evidence of his love. As Ridenour shows, and Lovell before him,[13] the idea of man's fall is ever before his eyes but, as the former cautions us, only as "a *metaphor* which Byron uses to express his own personal vision."[14] But that vision, I suggest, has not so much to do with the Fall itself, metaphor or reality, as it does with the consequences of the Fall, whatever the reasons for it may have been. It is a vision from within, not from without, the vision of an Adam condemned *before* he has become Cain, bewilderingly asking why and eliciting no response to his desperate cries. In other terms, man is born into the Eden of innocence, childhood, home, love, security, only to be awakened early to the facts of life which deny that Eden ever existed except in man's mind, in the remotely dim past, or in fiction and "romance." And in that life, although man's evil and perversion

---

[12] *LJ*, I, 230. Francis Hodgson, clergyman and poet, was a lifelong friend of Byron.

[13] Ernest J. Lovell, Jr., *Byron: The Record of a Quest* (Austin, Tex., 1949).

[14] *The Style of "Don Juan,"* p. 21.

perpetuate his own wretchedness, what Byron called later his "innate though secret tendency to the love of Good in his Mainspring of Mind"[15] also leads, paradoxically, to death and destruction. Thus man's vision of his own sin is in a sense a more comfortable vision than that of his own goodness gone awry. Religion may console us for the former, but our own mind is the last resort of possible understanding of, as well as refuge from, the latter.[16] To blame Adam is easier than throwing bricks at a temple that is not there.

We are told, by Byron himself as well as others, that he was fascinated early by the drama of the Old Testament, not the New, which struck him "as a task";[17] he took particular delight, he tells us, as young as eight years of age, in the story of Cain and Abel, the catastrophe of which he interprets later as due not to natural depravity but at least in part to "a fit of dissatisfaction . . . with the politics of Paradise, which had driven them all out of it."[18] At the same time that he was fascinated by a vengeful, punishing God, he also, in the first school to which Mrs. Byron sent him, was drilled to repeat by rote, "God made man, let us love him," his "first lesson of Monosyllables."[19] Yet, if he listened to its meaning, his automaton-like repetition of the sentence did not teach him to read: "Whenever proof was made of my progress at home, I repeated these words with the most rapid fluency; but on turning over the new leaf, I continued to repeat them, so that the narrow boundaries of my first year's accomplishments were detected, [and] my ears boxed."[20] This disturbing juxtaposition of God's love and the divinity of man with the insensitive brutality of one of his created beings is similar to the incident of May Gray, the young Scottish girl who succeeded her sister Agnes as Byron's nurse and continued teaching him the Bible. As Hobhouse wrote of it: "When [Byron

---

[15] From a diary and journal Byron kept in Ravenna in 1821. He entitled it "Paper Book of G. G. B., Ld. B.," but it has been known since as *Detached Thoughts*. The quotation in the text is from *LJ*, V, 457.
[16] Cf. Bostetter's fine analysis of this point in *The Romantic Ventriloquists*, especially pp. 277ff.
[17] Ltr. to John Murray, 9 Oct. 1821, in *LJ*, V, 391.
[18] Ltr. to Thomas Moore, 19 Sept. 1821, in *LJ*, V, 368.
[19] *Detached Thoughts*, in *LJ*, V, 406.
[20] *Ibid.*

was] nine years old at his mother's house a free Scotch girl used to come to bed to him & play tricks with his person."[21] Marchand points out that "if Byron was nine years old when this sex-play began, it must have gone on some time before Byron revealed it to Hanson."[22] Clearly such an experience affected his mature sexual life—or at least his attitude toward sex—and perhaps was, as Marchand says, "in part the foundation of his lifelong hatred of cant and hypocrisy in religious people";[23] but one wonders to what extent the grotesque incongruity of May's teachings and her behavior contributed to the confusing and confused sense he had later of man and life in general.

His other early passion in reading was history, which he called, indeed, his first "grand passion,"[24] a concentration that at once piqued his natural bent toward political freedom and hatred of tyranny, his idolization of the great, proud man, and his sense of the waste of human life, the vanity of human wishes, and the disillusionment of idealism's greatest efforts. At the same time it gave him his first glimpse into Athenian Greece, that fabled land that was to be for him throughout his life the closest man has come to recovering Eden. Whether this immersion in history, or, as he himself would have it, his perusal of all manner of writing from biography to "all the British Poets, both by Johnson and Anderson"—Rousseau, Newton, Blackstone, Montesquieu, Paley, Locke, Bacon, Hume, Berkeley, Drummond, Beattie, Bolingbroke, Blair, Tillotson, Hooker, Cervantes, Fielding, Smollett, Richardson, Mackenzie, Sterne, Rabelais, etc.[25]—whether all of this strengthened or weakened whatever he had of a positive vision of man and life is impossible to determine with certainty. But perhaps there is a clue in the fact that he detested Hobbes, whose views were not calculated to

---

[21] Hobhouse's manuscript notes entitled "Lord Byron," cited in Leslie A. Marchand, *Byron: A Biography* (3 vols.; New York, 1957), I, 57.
[22] *Ibid.*, I, 58n. In 1799 Byron had written to John Hanson, his lawyer, lifelong friend, and financial adviser: "I beg if you meet Gray send her a packing as fast as possible" (*LJ*, I, 10). See also Hanson's letter to Mrs. Byron (*LJ*, I, 10n).
[23] *Byron: A Biography*, I, 58n.
[24] *Detached Thoughts*, in *LJ*, V, 406.
[25] Memorandum book dated "November 30, 1807," cited in *Byron: A Biography*, I, 84–85.

flatter the idealistic visions of youth or the reformers of the world.

In any case, his own experience led him more quickly than most men to a sense of life's disappointments, if not its utter darkness. If in moments of melancholy he saw his lameness as a taint, it was also, more simply, a badge of his isolation, perhaps later a symbol of the insurmountable obstacles to happiness, peace, fulfillment, and love. And if he saw his father, in retrospect, as apparently "born for his own ruin" and himself "predestined to evil,"[26] he was thinking less in terms of universal depravity than in terms of man's only partial responsibility for his own ruin and that of others. When he went to Cambridge theoretical dilemma became a kind of reality, for the university turned out to be not a place to learn but to dissipate: "Study is the last pursuit of the Society," he wrote to Hanson; "the Master eats, drinks, and sleeps, the Fellows *Drink, dispute and pun*; the Employment of the Undergraduates you will probably conjecture without my description. I sit down to write with a Head confused with Dissipation which, tho' I hate, I cannot avoid."[27] This simultaneous intoxication and disgust is no distant forerunner of the mixed emotions with which he endowed the heroes of his tales.

Closer to home than these factors are those involving his relationship with his mother, his early love affairs, and Augusta. As Marchand rightly points out in his biography, we are perhaps too quick to condemn Mrs. Byron without a hearing: Byron's early years with her were clearly as happy as the quackery performed on his foot and Mrs. Byron's volatile temper would allow. Her gaucheries, crudeness, and ill-considered interference in his life and affairs had not yet concentrated themselves upon his inexperienced head. As he matured—and we are reminded again and again with what rapidity his passions, at least, matured—his relationship with his mother deteriorated rapidly. Though it is clear that the fault lay on both sides, the degree of responsibility for this failure in what is, in a sense,

---

[26] Thomas Medwin, *Journal of the Conversations of Lord Byron Noted during a Residence with His Lordship at Pisa in the Years 1821 and 1822* (2 vols.; Paris, 1824), I, 60.
[27] Ltr. to Hanson, 23 Nov. 1805, in *LJ*, I, 84–85.

Byron's crucial human relationship is not my purpose to determine; what is significant is the extraordinary consistency of
his language in describing the deterioration. His first harsh word
about his mother's disposition, in a letter of late summer, 1804,
is "diabolical," which he underlines—and then apologizes for
"staining [his] paper with so harsh a word."[28] In this same letter,
Mrs. Byron is described as a *"hurricane"* threatening to "destroy
everything" and gross in the epithets she applies to him; he is
worse than a "captive Negro, or Prisoner of war." Two months
later he admits that he is at least in part at fault for this situation, but in November he confesses that "so far from feeling the
affection of a Son, it is with difficulty I can restrain my dislike."
To his horror and disgust Mrs. Byron urges him to renew his
friendship with Lord Grey, a relationship Byron had cut short
after he was the victim of improper advances by that gentleman.
Augusta rapidly becomes here "the only relation I have who
treats me as a friend; if you too desert me, I have nobody I can
love but Delawarr. If it was not for his sake, Harrow would be
a desert . . ."; and Mrs. Byron becomes a bitter enemy to whom
he is bound only "by nature's law."[29] Early in the spring of 1805
his mother attacks him with even greater violence for what was
presumably a casual remark about the dullness of Southwell,
where Mrs. Byron was living at the time: "one would really
Imagine, to have heard the *Good Lady*, that I was a most *treasonable culprit*, but thank St. Peter, after undergoing this
Purgatory for the last hour, it is at length blown over. . . ."[30]

There is amusement here as well as anger, and the letters clearly show self-pity as well as restraint, but the repeated attacks, increasing in force, in which he is *"stigmatized* in terms
that the *blackest malevolence* would perhaps shrink from,"[31]
soon lead to this curious mixture of lightness and underlying
gloom: "I return you and Lady G.," he writes to Augusta on
April 25, 1805, "many thanks for your *benediction*, nor do I

---

[28] Ltr. to Augusta, 18 Aug. 1804, in *LJ*, I, 30.
[29] Ltrs. to Augusta, 25 Oct. 1804, 2 Nov. 1804, and 11 Nov. 1804,
in *LJ*, I, 40, 43–44, 46. Delawarr was one of Byron's few close friends
at Harrow.
[30] Ltr. to Augusta, 23 Apr. 1804, in *LJ*, I, 61.
[31] *Ibid.*, p. 62.

doubt its efficacy as it is bestowed by *two such Angelic beings*; but as I am afraid my *profane blessing* would but expedite your road to *Purgatory*, instead of *Salvation*, you must be content with my best wishes in return, since the *unhallowed adjurations* of a mere mortal would be of no effect."[32] The compliment is adroit, graceful, but the theological language springs at least in part from his sense that his mother's maledictions upon him have come now to include a prohibition on his seeing even the one relative he loves, "*the nearest relation*" he has "in *the world both by the ties of Blood* and *affection*."[33] He is now neither son nor brother by edict of a mother whose love for her son ought to have created the paradise of innocence, love, security, warmth, beauty, and good which all children should inherit. On August 6, 1805, then, he writes with perverse elation of the expiration of his minority, at which time he will escape "this *Garden* of *Eden*" at Burgage Manor, where Mrs. Byron's "*meek Lamblike de-meanour*" and his "*Saintlike visage*" form "a *striking family painting*, whilst in the back ground, the portraits of my Great Grandfather and Grandmother, suspended in their frames, seem to look with an eye of pity on their *unfortunate descendant*, whose *worth* and *accomplishments* deserve a *milder fate*."[34] However melodramatic and self-pitying this tableau, whatever the psychology behind Byron's series of actions and reactions, the impression of this series of incidents on his mind and the language he chooses, for whatever reasons, to embody that impression are tantalizing glimpses into what seems to me to be the beginnings of a vision of man in his world.

Whatever Augusta was to him originally, she becomes very quickly his only refuge, his sister, mother, even wife, the embodiment of the only good, somehow sustained by the world. It is not necessary here to go into the psychology of *that* relationship either, or, indeed, into the significance of Byron's later staining of Augusta; as I hope that my analysis of the poems prior to 1816 will show, his vision of the ruins of paradise and

---

[32] *LJ*, I, 63. As in the previous letters quoted, the careful italicization is, significantly, Byron's. "Lady G." is Lady Gertrude Howard, daughter of Byron's guardian, Lord Carlisle.
[33] Ltr. to Augusta, 22 Mar. 1804, in *LJ*, I, 20.
[34] To Augusta, in *LJ*, I, 72–73.

man's curiously partial responsibility for those ruins was all but complete before the great scandal. What is pertinent here, however, before we turn to his first poems, are some brief comments upon his early romantic attachments. Marchand, rightly I think, underscores Byron's own awareness that his passions were developed early, and that this, in Byron's words, "caused the anticipated melancholy of my thoughts—having anticipated life."[35] Marchand relates this to a two-fold development in Byron's mind: (1) the adolescent vision of "the ideally beautiful unpossessed love" (Mary Duff and Margaret Parker, for example), which led him in later life "into love with young girls and boys"; and (2) the sense of physical disgust and disillusionment caused by his premature sexual awakening and "the failure of a real experience to measure up to the ideal," which led him into "the cynical search for 'fine animals' like the baker's wife in Venice."[36] This is certainly correct, but I think it does not go far enough. The melancholy of Byron's thoughts he himself traces directly to his "having anticipated life," not merely love. That his rapid experience of the discrepancy between the real and the ideal constituted this anticipation (his imagination's conception of Mary Chaworth's "perfection," say, and his realistic appraisal of her as "anything but angelic"[37]) I would be the first to agree. But by this time, as I have been trying to show, Byron's vision already encompassed more than the feminine *monde*. Further, his own early-aroused passions gave him a precocious glimpse into the dilemma of man's love: it is often trifled with, it is mercurial, it is easily debased, and, perhaps most of all, even when full and complete it is either rejected and falls short of achieving its perfect goal, or with apparent perversity it leads to sorrow, tragedy, even destruction. One product of this insight, as Marchand says, is obviously cynicism, the self-protecting sneer; but another product is what Byron calls melancholy, deepening slowly into despair, made up of man's utter puzzlement at the mixture of good and evil and the unwilled but apparently inevitable perversion of that good in himself and the world around him.

---

[35] *Detached Thoughts*, in *LJ*, V, 450.
[36] *Byron: A Biography*, I, 61–62.
[37] Medwin, *Journal*, I, 65–66.

BYRON AND THE RUINS OF PARADISE

Chapter I

HOURS OF IDLENESS AND EARLY SATIRES

Although the title, *Hours of Idleness*, was affixed to the third issue of Byron's juvenilia not by Byron but by his printer and publisher, S. and J. Ridge of Newark, it reflects admirably the note struck by Byron in his affected and jejune Preface to the volume. There the writing of poetry is contrasted sharply to more useful employment. "Poetry . . . is not my primary vocation," the pompous young lord confesses: "to divert the dull moments of indisposition, or the monotony of a vacant hour, urged me 'to this sin.' . . ."[1] Despite its mincing tone of conventional apology this relegation of poetry to the idle hour is worth noting as the beginning of Byron's lifelong public attitude toward it. Yet, if we compare the early letters with the poetry written at the same time, we find the poetry in general, whatever the motive for its composition, much more intimate, revealing, and "true" than the public-private utterances intended for particular eyes or ears. Still, in *Hours of Idleness* there are a number of poems which, like the letters, were written on specific occasions, reflecting actual incident, or commenting upon the particulars of experience. In these poems there is discernible a certain protective coating within which Byron wraps his imagination, so that the artistic result is rather a poetizing of prose comment than the creation of poetry; that is, in general the conventions of the poetic tradition as Byron knew them effec-

---

[1] *The Complete Poetical Works of Byron*, ed. P. E. More (Boston, 1905), p. 84. E. H. Coleridge oddly omits the Preface from his edition. The same note is struck in the letters, e.g., ltrs. to J. M. B. Pigot, 10 Aug. and 16 Aug. 1806, in *LJ*, I, 104–6.

1

tively camouflage or overlay the emotion and force it into all too familiar patterns and contours. More often, however, he adopts a distinct fictional point of view or tone or role, a simple strategy (or accident of composition) that enables him to speak out more sincerely and less vulnerably than he can in those straightforward single-voiced utterances which are ostensibly products of his private self. It is as if, by dissociating himself from the speaker of the poem, the living voice of his own deep feelings comes through all the more clearly. And in a letter, that dissociation is impossible. In poetry, then, however much he mocked it, he obviously saw a kind of protection for his mind and heart that the flinty world did not afford to straight prose utterance, direct and irretrievable. The poems to "Thyrza" (John Edleston) are excellent examples of this "protection."[2]

Still, withal, what these early poems show, as T. S. Eliot said of Blake's *Poetical Sketches*, is an immense power of assimilation. Byron himself was aware of his lack of originality:

> I have not aimed at exclusive originality, still less have I studied any particular model for imitation: some translations are given, of which many are paraphrastic. In the original pieces there may appear a casual coincidence with authors whose works I have been accustomed to read; but I have not been guilty of intentional plagiarism. To produce anything new, in an age so fertile in rhyme, would be an Herculean task, as every subject has already been treated to its utmost extent.[3]

---

[2] As Marchand remarks, these poems, now known to have been addressed to the young choir boy at Cambridge whose premature death in 1811 "was perhaps the greatest emotional shock of [Byron's] life, have never been considered as a whole nor given their proper evaluation as poetry" (*Byron's Poetry: A Critical Introduction* [Boston, 1965], p. 118). The Thyrza poems include "The Cornelian," stanzas 9 and 95–98 of Canto II of *Childe Harold's Pilgrimage*, "Away, Away, Ye Notes of Woe!," "One Struggle More, and I Am Free," "Euthanasia," "And Thou Art Dead, As Young and Fair," "If Sometimes in the Haunts of Men," and "On a Cornelian Heart Which Was Broken." Marchand conjectures that three other earlier poems may also have been about Edleston: "There Be None of Beauty's Daughters," "Stanzas to Jessy," and "To E—" (*ibid.*, pp. 118–19).
[3] Preface to *Hours of Idleness*, in More's edition of the *Works*, p. 84.

And so we have what is fashionable, compounded with what all young poets write of—in all their typical exaggeration and sense of finality, simplification of life, and brashness in criticism. To determine to what extent these conventionalities, and their familiar sighs and tears, anger and affection, are distinguishable from the reality of Byron's mind and heart is not my purpose here; rather, I propose to look at the general contours of *Hours of Idleness*, to study what seems to me to be its prevailing mood and tone and attitude (whether feigned or not), and to examine in some detail the rather narrow range of voices Byron essays. What will emerge, I hope, is a sense of his early preoccupation with point of view, with the adopted role or persona, and with an increasingly poignant and powerful sense of loss.

I

Charles du Bos and others have focused our attention upon Byron's preoccupation with death and fatality, but none, I think, has seen that preoccupation in proper perspective, in part because most critics have concentrated upon its recurrence in the poems of Byron's maturity. In *Hours of Idleness* this theme takes several forms, that of horror and disbelief at the death of the young (and often beautiful), of death as a desirable escape from the misery of the world, and of the familiar *carpe diem*. Of these the first two are the most frequent and important. Byron's first poem, so far as we know, was "On the Death of a Young Lady," written about his cousin Margaret Parker (Byron was fourteen or fifteen); and it is significant, I think, that the poem itself does not match Byron's description of it (he called it, on the one hand, his "first dash into poetry" and on the other an "ebullition of a passion" for one he loved[4]). For the poem is not focused on Margaret Parker, its ostensible subject, nor is it in any sense a show of passion. The few phrases of endearment are not only conventional but flat and cold; and they are confined to a few lines at the beginning and end of the twenty-four

---

[4] Both quoted phrases occur in *Detached Thoughts*, in *LJ*, V, 449.

3

line piece. It is a poem that is focused upon himself, *his* sense of loss, *his* reaction to death, and by implication *his* view of the world and its ruling powers.[5] Further, the assumption of a maturity he does not have is less interesting (and certainly less surprising) than the fact that he is both participant and narrator in the poem. The scene is Margaret's tomb (which, as a matter of fact, he never visited); the participant is a pilgrim to the shrine. Thus the fundamental facts upon which the poem is built (his love for Margaret and her death) are extrapolated, so to speak, in such a way that the supposedly personal passion Byron apparently intended the poem to convey is buried in the much more intimate private voice's attack upon heaven for permitting the death. Without the role, we should indeed have an "ebullition"—and we should not have Byron's mind; with the role, we have, paradoxically, a sincerity and conviction Byron seemed unable or unwilling to convey in his own voice, except in a few lyrics and perhaps in the satires.

The implications of Margaret's death and the many other deaths in *Hours of Idleness* are twofold, and Byron's reactions are not always consistent. On the one hand, looked at objectively death was a freedom from the impurities of the world's slow stain, an eternity of beauty, joy, virtue, and love, the regaining of paradise lost. On the other, the point of view taken is more often and more tellingly that of the lover or friend left to struggle with or endure a life made barren and loveless through the death. If there is memory to sustain one in such circumstances, it is a memory that intensifies the loss rather than consoling the bereaved or offering a renewed image of hope. The fact of loss, then, is insisted upon constantly at the expense of almost all else. The reason for this insistence is not difficult to find: for Byron, as for the other Romantics, happiness on earth, the sublunary Eden, consisted of love and friendship sitting high, as Keats wrote in *Endymion*, "Upon the forehead of humanity." Allowing for youthful exaggeration, then, as well

---

[5] Similar responses may be seen in "Epitaph on a Friend" and its earlier version, "Epitaph on a Beloved Friend" (*P*, I, 18–20).

as for the urge to graceful poetic compliment, we still can be impressed by the consistency with which Byron associates heaven and paradise with love and friendship. In "To D—," a poem addressed to his close friend Delawarr, he envisions a rare personal immortality:

> *And, when the grave restores her dead,*
> *When life again to dust is given,*
> *On* thy dear *breast I'll lay my head—*
> *Without* thee! where *would be* my Heaven?

In the "Epitaph on a Friend" even "A father's sorrows cannot equal mine":

> *Time will assuage an infant brother's woe;*
> *To all, save one, is consolation known,*
> *While solitary Friendship sighs alone.*

Such "solitary Friendship" or love Byron sees, in "The First Kiss of Love," as "Some portion of Paradise still . . . on earth"; and the loss of it produces the misanthrope ("Love's Last Adieu"). "To Eliza" makes the identification of love, beauty, and Eden explicit: Eliza's "nature so much of *celestial* partakes" that "The Garden of Eden would wither" without her.

Perhaps the most poignant and revealing of these poems is one in which his relationship with his mother is totally ignored (contrary to his effort in the letters to sustain it through a sense of duty if not affection). In "Childish Recollections" he presents himself as

> *one, who thus for kindred hearts must roam,*
> *And seek abroad, the love denied at home.*
> *Those hearts, dear IDA* [i.e., Harrow], *have*
> *I found in thee,*
> *A home, a world, a paradise to me.*   (*ll. 215–18*)

With studied purpose he lists such things as rank, a guardian, wealth, and title as small consolation for the absence of a father. With no sister or brother, "no fond bosom link'd by kindred

5

ties," he hears the "voice of Love" only in dreams—and awakens "A Hermit, 'midst of crowds . . . / . . . though thousand pilgrims fill the way" (ll. 219–36).

As is apparent from these few selections, the loss of love or paradise need not be through death. All forms of separation, whether permanent or temporary, breed the same sense of aloneness, the same shattering of the dream, the same expulsion from Eden, as Byron called it in "To a Lady"—and the same ultimate focus on self rather than on the ostensible subject of the poem. Closely related is the almost equally strong sense of loss he feels at the waning of youth, the time of love and friendship and careless days, that time seemingly wrapped in protective innocence and shielded from the fallen world's intrusion. Thus in "To a Youthful Friend" Byron castigates the world as "specious" and "corrupt"; in it man, having "bid adieu to youth,"

> *himself is but a tool;*
> *When interest sways our hopes and fears,*
> *And all must love and hate by rule.*
>
> *With fools in kindred vice the same,*
> *We learn at length our faults to blend;*
> *And those, and those alone, may claim*
> *The prostituted name of friend.*[6]

"Such is the common lot of man," he concludes, for "by the fix'd decrees of Heaven" joy cannot last.[7]

> *Once I beheld a splendid dream,*
> *A visionary scene of bliss:*

---

[6] Although it is an early poem, written in August, 1808, "To a Youthful Friend" is not a part of the *Hours of Idleness* volume. It appeared first in John Cam Hobhouse's poetical miscellany, *Imitations and Translations, together with Original Poems*, published in 1809.

[7] The last phrase is from "Pignus Amoris," which Coleridge conjectures to have been written in 1806. It was not included in *Hours of Idleness*.

6

Hours of Idleness, Early Satires

> *Truth!—wherefore did thy hated beam*
> *Awake me to a world like this?*

> *I lov'd—but those I lov'd are gone;*
> *Had friends—my early friends are fled:*
> *How cheerless feels the heart alone,*
> *When all its former hopes are dead!*
> *Though gay companions, o'er the bowl*
> *Dispel awhile the sense of ill;*
> *Though Pleasure stirs the maddening soul,*
> *The heart—the heart—is lonely still.*
>   ("*I Would I Were a Careless Child*")

Then, in the accents of *Childe Harold*, Byron concludes this lament for the loss of childhood, love, friendship, all, with

> *Fain would I fly the haunts of men—*
> *I seek to shun, not hate mankind;*
> *My breast requires the sullen glen,*
> *Whose gloom may suit a darken'd mind.*
> *Oh! that to me the wings were given,*
> *Which bear the turtle to her nest!*
> *Then would I cleave the vault of Heaven,*
> *To flee away, and be at rest.*

In perhaps no other poem in *Hours of Idleness*, are the various threads of Byron's early melancholy vision brought together so succinctly and sharply—the desire to escape earth, but to escape on the wings of love, to be at peace within the turtle's nest, eternally embosomed in a lost heaven of the past.[8] "Lines Written beneath an Elm in the Churchyard of Harrow," "To the Earl of Clare," "To George, Earl Delawarr," "When I Roved a Young Highlander," "To Edward Noel Long, Esq.," "Childish Recollections," "Lachin y Gair," and "On a Distant View of the Village and School of Harrow on the Hill, 1806" all rehearse the same theme, drowning out the rather isolated note of "L'Amitié est L'Amour sans Ailes," in which Byron urges that

---

[8] It is worth noting that, as Coleridge points out (*P*, I, 208n), Byron clearly had in mind David's lament in Psalm 55.

Days of delight may still be mine;
Affection is not dead.[9]

Not quite so consistent as the laments for a lost past, but nevertheless pervasive in *Hours of Idleness,* is Byron's employment of dream to characterize bliss, love, Eden, happiness. This motif is especially important as an early adumbration of his habitual use of the image and idea in his later poems. The clearest statement of the relationship is in one of the poems addressed "To M. S. G.":

When I dream that you love me, you'll surely forgive;
Extend not your anger to sleep;
For in visions alone your affection can live,—
I rise, and it leaves me to weep.

Then Morpheus! envelop my faculties fast,
Shed o'er me your languor benign;
Should the dream of to-night but resemble the last,
What rapture celestial is mine!

They tell us that slumber, the sister of death,
Mortality's emblem is given;
To fate how I long to resign my frail breath,
If this be a foretaste of Heaven!

More bitter in their conviction of irredeemable loss, of the inevitable shattering of dream and illusion, even of the certain perversion of man's few virtues in a Hobbesian world are, in addition to the several poems condemning the deceit of womankind (e.g., "Reply to Some Verses of J. M. B. Pigot, Esq.," "To —," beginning "Oh! well I know your subtle Sex," and "To Woman"), the "Lines Addressed to the Rev. J. T. Becher, on

---

[9] It is interesting that "L'Amitie," although written in December, 1806, is the only one of this group not included in the *Hours of Idleness* volume. It is worth noting also that with the exception of "On a Distant View" all the poems in this group are late additions to the volume. See my point about the late additions on p. 15.

His Advising the Author to Mix More with Society." And in "Thoughts Suggested by a College Examination" Byron turns his attack from the fashionable world to the hollowness and superficiality of education, of the supposedly learned and wise who shape the innocence of youth into the nobility and greatness of man.

Most sweeping of all in its awareness of shattered illusion, of the irredeemability of time, and of the irrevocably lost riches of youth is the long, meandering, frequently revised "Childish Recollections." In a sense it is the controlling poem of *Hours of Idleness*, capturing in its often ungainly lines the typically exaggerated youthful sense of final loss, of the end of a world hardly begun, of the beginning of another, dim, arduous, fearful, forbidding. The hyperbolic melancholy and despair I take to be not merely revelatory of Byron's extreme youth but precisely right to convey the rapidity with which recollection accommodated itself to Byron's growing habit of mind. Thus, while on the one hand the poem is fraudulently pompous in its assumption of ultimate knowledge and even wisdom, it is a genuine confession, in proper voice and tone, of Byron's sense of his own mind at this time. What is also most striking is the unWordsworthian view of childhood and youth: here is no boy bounding over the hills like a roe or wandering lonely as a cloud; rather, here is youth craving another's hand in a time when not merely beauty but love "form'd our heaven." And further, while "The Sun of Memory, glowing through [his] dreams" illuminates his present with the past, its warmth and light diminish until remembrance itself becomes a "curse" and is desperately, if vainly, renounced. Here, then, are some of the most revealing passages of this key poem:

> *Hours of my youth! when, nurtur'd in my breast,*
> *To Love a stranger, Friendship made me blest,—*
> *Friendship, the dear peculiar bond of youth,*
> *When every artless bosom throbs with truth;*
> *Untaught by worldly wisdom how to feign,*
> *And check each impulse with prudential reign;*
> *When, all we feel, our honest souls disclose,*

9

> *In love to friends, in open hate to foes;*
> *No varnish'd tales the lips of youth repeat,*
> *No dear-bought knowledge purchased by deceit;*
> *Hypocrisy, the gift of lengthen'd years,*
> *Matured by age, the garb of Prudence wears:*
> *When, now, the Boy is ripen'd into Man,*
> *His careful Sire chalks forth some wary plan;*
> *Instructs his Son from Candour's path to shrink,*
> *Smoothly to speak, and cautiously to think;*
> *Still to assent, and never to deny—*
> *A patron's praise can well reward the lie.*
> (ll. 55–72)

If we see here a glory passed away from the earth, as Wordsworth and the other Romantics did, the tone is not that of lament or sadness, however; it is the anger of a Blake at the inevitable loss of innocence—and Byron acknowledges his tone by defensively denying, immediately following this passage, that his task is to "tear the hateful mask" from "flattering friends" and the world. He does not yet see clearly that his task as poet throughout his life will be largely just that—to strip off the mask, to present what lies hidden under it, or to mock the universal masquerade.

The poem goes on to recount the mimic wars of youth on the cricket field or in the fray with the grumbling rustics whom they teased (ll. 127–46). Of lasting monuments to these heroic deeds there was abundance, not in "splendid tablets" but engraved rudely on the dusky walls of the school:

> *And, here, my name, and many an early friend's,*
> *Along the wall in lengthen'd line extends.*
> (ll. 163–64)

And now, in turn, their successors "rule, the little Tyrants of an hour," poring over those records of ancient battles and heroic deeds. Yet soon only their names will survive:

> *Yet a few years, one general wreck will whelm*
> *The faint remembrance of our fairy realm.*
> (ll. 183–84)

10

Recall of these scenes is stimulated in afterdays not by a rainbow or anything in nature, but rather by the sudden appearance
of a friend. Then "Fashion's gaudy world" fades quickly into
nothingness, and

> *The woods of IDA danc'd before my eyes;*
> *I saw the sprightly wand'rers pour along,*
> *I saw, and join'd again the joyous throng;*
> *Panting, again I trac'd her lofty grove,*
> *And Friendship's feelings triumph'd over love.*
> *(ll. 204–8)*

Byron then rehearses the particulars of his closest friendships,
with Lord Clare, John Wingfield, John Tattersall, Earl Delawarr,
Edward Noel Long, and closes the poem with a final tribute to
friendship and "the shrine of truth" which is almost submerged
by the bitter cynicism of his "welcome" to the world of maturity:

> *amid the gloomy calm of age*
> *You turn with faltering hand life's varied page,*
> *Peruse the record of your days on earth,*
> *Unsullied only where it marks your birth.*
> *(ll. 401–4)*

Even more negative are the lines which originally preceded these
in the version of the poem included in *Poems on Various Occasions*:

> *Ah! vain endeavour in this childish strain*
> *To soothe the woes of which I thus complain!*
> *What can avail this fruitless loss of time,*
> *To measure sorrow, in a jingling rhyme!*
> *No social solace from a friend, is near,*
> *And heartless strangers drop no feeling tear.*
> *I seek not joy in Woman's sparkling eye,*
> *The smiles of Beauty cannot check the sigh.*
> *Adieu, thou world! thy pleasure's still a dream,*
> *Thy virtue, but a visionary theme;*

11

Thy years of vice, on years of folly roll,
Till grinning death assigns the destin'd goal.

. . . . .

Mix'd in the concourse of a thoughtless throng,
A mourner, midst of mirth, I glide along;
A wretched, isolated, gloomy thing,
Curst by reflection's deep corroding sting.

And here Byron categorically denies that this sting has anything
to do with original sin or any other kind of sin:

No dread internal, haunts my hours of rest,
No dreams of injured innocence infest;

. . . . .

No crimes I mourn, but happiness gone by

—that and, of course, the prospect of no happiness in a world
corrupt—

Thus crawling on with many a reptile vile,
My heart is bitter, though my cheek may smile;
No more with former bliss, my heart is glad;
Hope yields to anguish and my soul is sad.

There is little need to comment here upon this striking adumbration of Childe Harold and the heroes of the tales; but there is
another side to it. Remembrance itself, though here cherished,
becomes in itself something to be forgot, for the days of our
youth are clearly not reality but foolish romantic illusions and
dreams.[10] And Byron will have, even this early, only what he
calls truth.

Thus, in "To Romance," all dreams of beauty, good,
and truth, of the realms of gold inhabited by gods and goddesses,
of "a Sylph in every dame" and "A Pylades in every friend,"
are condemned:[11]

---

[10] Byron's need to erase memory is succinctly expressed in the poem
"Remembrance," written in 1806 but not published until 1832.
[11] Byron's powerful sense, even this early, of the destructiveness of
the world and the consequent impossibility of love or even friendship

> *Parent of golden dreams, Romance!*
> *Auspicious Queen of childish joys,*
> *Who lead'st along, in airy dance,*
> *Thy votive train of girls and boys;*
> *At length, in spells no longer bound,*
> *I break the fetters of my youth;*
> *No more I tread thy mystic round,*
> *But leave thy realms for those of Truth.*

And by putting "Romance" and what has turned out to be only the illusory happiness of childhood behind him, he will also, in "Farewell to the Muse," give up poetry, which in one part of his mind he sees as dealing only with illusion. Yet, as we have seen, the poetry he had already written, with all its youthful exaggeration and obvious flaws, is hardly the poetry of dream and illusion: it is, rather, a candid and essentially truthful record —quite different from the letters and journals of the same time —of his own disillusionment. Implicit in this confusion is his clear conviction that the day-by-day account of his mind and heart entrusted to letters and journals (those peculiarly guarded utterances of his public-private voice) constituted the truth of his being, the essential Byron. Yet, obviously, he did not cease writing poetry in 1807 when "Farewell to the Muse" was composed (it is perhaps significant that it was not published until 1832), recognizing in another part of his mind that the whole world of truth and reality may, finally, best be revealed and explored, paradoxically, in a mode that employs a fictional voice and plot and characters, even a fictional world. Nevertheless the "Farewell" is interesting *in extenso* for its yoking together of poetry, childhood and youth, friends, love, dreams, visions, joy, beauty, magic, and the past in general:

---

is reflected in his own footnote to these lines of "Romance": "It is hardly necessary to add, that Pylades was the companion of Orestes, and a partner of those friendships which, with those of Achilles and Patroclus, Nisus and Euryalus, Damon and Pythias, have been handed down to posterity as remarkable instances of attachments, which in all probability never existed beyond the imagination of the poet, or the page of an historian, or modern novelist" (*P*, I, 175n).

BYRON AND THE RUINS OF PARADISE

Thou Power! who hast ruled me through Infancy's
                                                    days,
    Young offspring of Fancy, 'tis time we should part;
Then rise on the gale this the last of my lays,
    The coldest effusion which springs from my heart.

This bosom, responsive to rapture no more,
    Shall hush thy wild notes, nor implore thee to sing;
The feelings of childhood, which taught thee to soar,
    Are wafted far distant on Apathy's wing.

Though simple the themes of my rude flowing Lyre,
    Yet even these themes are departed for ever;
No more beam the eyes which my dream could inspire,
    My visions are flown, to return,—alas, never!

When drain'd is the nectar which gladdens the bowl,
    How vain is the effort delight to prolong!
When cold is the beauty which dwelt in my soul,
    What magic of Fancy can lengthen my song?

Can the lips sing of Love in the desert alone,
    Of kisses and smiles which they now must resign?
Or dwell with delight on the hours that are flown?
    Ah, no! for those hours can no longer be mine.

Can they speak of the friends that I lived but to love?
    Ah, surely Affection ennobles the strain!
But how can my numbers in sympathy move,
    When I scarcely can hope to behold them again?

It is difficult to deny, in the face of all this, that what I have called the general contours, the prevailing mood and tone and atmosphere, of *Hours of Idleness* describe a disillusionment and sadness that will not take much to deepen into despair. The human condition is at best uncertain, at worst a dreary desert relieved but rarely by oases of man's nobility and goodness. It was something considerably deeper than momentary ill temper, then, that led Byron to inscribe in his copy of Owen Ruffhead's *The Life of Alexander Pope* the following (Ruffhead had just written that Pope's "natural benevolence suggested to him that

14

he could not better serve the interest of society, than . . . by writing a book to bring mankind to look upon this life with comfort and pleasure"): first, he heavily underscored the word "mankind" in the text and then added in the margin, "a malignant race with Christianity in their mouths and Molochism in their hearts."[12] This state of mind is graphically revealed by the changes he made in the *Hours of Idleness* collection when it was reissued by Ridge in 1808 as *Poems Original and Translated.* The Preface and all the lighter pieces were gone, and the five poems that were added intensified further the volume's aura of loss. R. C. Dallas, concerned for Byron's state of mind not long before he left on his grand tour, summed it up this way: "Misanthropy, disgust of life leading to scepticism and impiety, prevailed in his heart and embittered his existence."[13] And Byron himself, writing to his mother just prior to his departure, says he will take Robert Rushton with him: "I like him, because, like myself, he seems a friendless animal."[14]

II

As I have said, though, these early poems have another interest, for they display Byron in his first efforts as a poet whose particular need is a role and a voice to disguise the self, however slightly, and envelop it in the lineaments of fashionable heroes and swains, of the lovesick and the damned, of the sageness of the aged and the carefree rollicking of youth. In a sense, of course, all the voices and roles are the same, for the disguise is thin, the feigned voice a bit too feigned, and the human voice all the more eloquent and moving as it belies the ventriloquistic trick. The voice is almost always that which I have called the

---

[12] Marchand, *Byron: A Biography,* I, 138–39. Marchand comments only that this shows Byron's "care and critical attention" even in his miscellaneous reading. The notation was probably made in 1807, while Byron was still at Cambridge.

[13] *Recollections of the Life of Lord Byron* (Philadelphia, 1825), p. 39, quoted in Marchand, *Byron: A Biography,* I, 177.

[14] Ltr. to Mrs. Byron, 22 June 1809, in *LJ,* I, 225.

private-public voice; and whatever the logical or psychological reasons for its mutations, the fact remains that the fictive speakers are there as immediate and necessary elements in Byron's creative imagination.

With the avowed imitations we can dispense, I think, although it may be worth remarking that all but a few necessitate the adoption of a role or voice not Byron's own. In the very fact of imitation, of course, is inherent a certain ventriloquism, more pronounced perhaps and more frank than that we find in unacknowledged imitations of a mode or manner. Yet this borrowing of a voice can be seen in Byron as something more than merely the young poet's trying his wings in various modes or trying to emulate the masters—for the voices he essays in the translations and imitations are interestingly limited in their range: the sighing lover of Catullus, the epic voice of Virgil (which is not attempted again), the somber bardic chant of Ossian, the disillusioned exile of Euripides, the dying voice of Adrian. That these reflect Byron's taste and preference would be foolish to deny; but they are also the voice of Byron's essential self conveyed indirectly, quasi-dramatically, rather than directly, lyrically.

In general the love poems are the most fruitful source of study of Byron's roles, for on the surface they present us with a totally inconsistent view of love, women, and himself. The particular stance adopted in each poem gives but a partial view of the facts; *in toto*, by means of the variety of roles and points of view he adopts, Byron presents us with a panoramic view of man in love—a view obviously controlled and limited by his own mind. By means of the sighs and defeats, actions and reactions, feelings and thoughts of his speakers, each of whom by himself is not Byron, the living voice of his own heart and mind emerge with greater conviction and poignance for being based on the dramatic evidence at hand. Of course it is probable that no such scheme occurred to Byron, for he makes little or no attempt to relate these voices to each other or to see them as a composite. Still, it is instructive to consider a number of the love poems in groups or cycles, for only in this way, I think,

16

can Byron's fairly impressive manipulation of his own voice, even within a somewhat narrow range, be appreciated.

The four poems entitled "To Caroline," for example, illustrate well Byron's habit of constantly shifting point of view and attitude from poem to poem, each poem of the group supposing a distinct dramatic situation out of which that attitude evolves. The first is a farewell to an impossible love, a situation in which "Our only *hope* is, to *forget*." The second is a charge that Caroline's coldness is a sign that she does not love him, despite her protestations to the contrary. The third takes a tack precisely the opposite of the second, for here Caroline's expression of affection is "so warm" that the speaker cannot doubt her love; while in the fourth the lovers have been torn apart and death is envisioned as perhaps the only place where their relationship can be "unmolested" and lasting. The particular attitudes taken in each poem are finally subsumed under the state of mind that controls and infuses the whole cycle. If one must use the awkward and ill-defined term "Byronic," each poem by itself is Byronic—in its feigned posture of the lover—while the four poems taken together reveal the essential Byron in the process of creating a poetic world that is a faithful reflection of the real world of his mind, a world in which love is all but impossible, where "Our only *hope* is, to *forget*," where deceit is to be expected, and where, if love's ashes glow to momentary brightness, they do so in a "mansion of death" that quickly smothers hope.

Perhaps the simplest example of shifting point of view and dramatic situation is in the two poems addressed to an unknown "Mary." The first of these is a declaration of undying love, sustained in absence by the lover's receipt of Mary's picture. It "Revives my hopes, and bids me live"; it is

> *far more dear to me,*
> *Lifeless, unfeeling as thou art,*
> *Than all the living forms could be,*
> *Save her who plac'd thee next my heart.*

The second poem is as deliberately unromantic as the first is

17

romantic. Indeed it is a sharp and impatient reflection by the practical lover on "all th' unmeaning protestations / Which swell with nonsense, love orations"; more particularly, it is a rejection of his mistress's suggestion that they meet in the garden on a night in December. Why in this way, he cries,

> doom the lover you have chosen,
> On winter nights to sigh half frozen;
> In leafless shades, to sue for pardon,
> Only because the scene's a garden?
> For gardens seem, by one consent,
> (Since Shakespeare set the precedent;
> Since Juliet first declar'd her passion)
> To form the place of assignation.
> Oh! would some modern muse inspire,
> And seat her by a sea-coal fire;
> Or had the bard at Christmas written,
> And laid the scene of love in Britain;
> He surely, in commiseration,
> Had chang'd the place of declaration.

> .   .   .   .   .

> here our climate is so rigid,
> That love itself, is rather frigid:
> Think on our chilly situation,
> And curb this rage for imitation.
> Then let us meet, as oft we've done,
> Beneath the influence of the sun;
> Or, if at midnight I must meet you,
> Within your mansion let me greet you:
> There, we can love for hours together,
> Much better, in such snowy weather,
> Than plac'd in all th' Arcadian groves,
> That ever witness'd rural loves;
> Then, if my passion fail to please,
> Next night I'll be content to freeze.

Which of these speakers is the "real Byron" is impossible to tell, for not only do we not know who Mary was but we know nothing of their relationship, beyond the fact that Byron showed his friends a lock of hair and a picture purported to be hers. And if we say that the Byron of the latter poem, the rakish practical lover, is the one we know best, we are guilty of overzealous biographizing. The essential irrelevance of biographical evidence leads us, therefore, to the contradictions inherent in the several possible guesses as to Byron's real attitude—whether neither poem reflects it, or both, or one and not the other. In view of this, our focus is upon the attitudes rather than on the "reality" of those attitudes—two ways of looking at a blackbird, so to speak. Each attitude, Byron is saying, is not only possible but true, poetically; and further, perhaps by accident, each describes the extremes of the spectrum from idealization to realization. Finally, though the point is not made insistently, Byron seems to me to be showing that neither extreme is fruitful: the first poem describes the woes of separation (however much the picture is a consolation), the second protests against the mistress's imitation of the conventions of romance which tend to deny fulfillment, here intensified by the coldness of the place of assignation (perhaps a reflection of the coldness of the mistress herself). What I have called Byron's overview, then, contains distinct hints of the impossibility, or at best the difficulty, of sustaining love in this world. But even if this were not so, the vigor of the second poem overshadows the conventionality of the first, and thus the possibility of man's maintenance of dream, illusion, romantic fantasy, the garden of love, in the face of the history of lovers from Juliet to the present is called into question. Although she is probably not the same Mary, she of "When I Roved a Young Highlander" personifies the death of all love in a manner similar to that of the "Hills of Annesley":

> *Yet the day may arrive, when the mountains once*
> *more*
> *Shall rise to my sight, in their mantles of snow;*
> *But while these soar above me, unchang'd as before,*
> *Will Mary be there to receive me?—ah, no!*
> *Adieu, then, ye hills, where my childhood was bred!*
> *Thou sweet flowing Dee, to thy waters adieu!*
> *No home in the forest shall shelter my head,—*
> *Ah! Mary, what home could be mine, but with you?*

19

A more extended cycle is that addressed to or concerning Anne Houson: "Lines Addressed to a Young Lady," "On the Eyes of Miss A— H—," "To a Vain Lady," two poems entitled "To Anne," and "On Finding a Fan."[15] The first of these is an elaborate courtly apology by the speaker for frightening her by discharging his pistols in a garden near which she was passing. It is tempting to see in the dramatic scene an image of love in the garden threatened by death and the world, and some of the language of the poem tends to support such a thesis: it was an "envious Demon's force" that sped the bullet near her, some "hell-born guide"; it was "Heaven" that protected her; and the speaker must atone in some way for his sin—by enslaving himself to her, by death, whatever she wishes. The force of the poem, however, lies in its flowery compliment, apology, and protestation of undying love. In the second poem Anne's eyes are likened to a "perpetual Summer," the eternal sun of the garden shining "on *All*," and in "To a Vain Lady" she is seen even in her vanity as the epitome of innocence and a trusting heart, who, by her indiscreet revelations of lovers' confidences (perhaps an example of the openness and honesty of youth), will destroy her repose "And dig the source of future tears":

> *thy ling'ring woes are nigh,*
> *If thou believ'st what striplings say:*
> *Oh, from the deep temptation fly,*
> *Nor fall the specious spoiler's prey.*

> *Dost thou repeat, in childish boast,*
> *The words man utters to deceive?*
> *Thy peace, thy hope, thy all is lost,*
> *If thou canst venture to believe.*

---

[15] Of these, only the first was published originally in *Hours of Idleness*. "To a Vain Lady," both poems "To Anne," and "On Finding a Fan," all written early in 1807, were first published in 1832. "On the Eyes of Miss A— H—," written at the same time, was not published until Coleridge's edition.

Thus, in effect, in this poem the speaker-lover warns Anne against the very duplicity and deception the speaker-lover of "Lines Addressed to a Young Lady" practised. Yet in "To Anne" she herself, the personification of love, innocence, purity, and beauty, is accused by the speaker of deceit, though her smile and her presence woo him back to undying love and rapture in both this poem and the other poem "To Anne." One might paraphrase Keats here: "Aye, in the very temple of delight" veiled Disillusion has her sovereign shrine, with the result recorded by Byron in "On Finding a Fan": "every hope of love expires, / Extinguish'd with the dying embers." "Passion's fires" no longer burn, though "Some careful hand may teach" them to revive; but love

> can ne'er survive,
> No touch can bid its warmth return.
>
> Or, if it chance to wake again,
>   Not always doom'd its heat to smother,
> It sheds (so wayward fates ordain)
>   Its former warmth around another.

Whichever role or voice, if any, is really Byron's in this cycle, once again the over-all feeling is one of loss, an inevitability that assures not only the collapse of dreams but the triumph of the real. The reason for all this is, as usual in Byron, unclear: man deceives woman, but woman also deceives man; love is ideal and yet it is earthy; and "wayward fates" seem to ordain its final demise. But the personal voice of the lyric Byron is once again subsumed in the poetic voice of the essential Byron, that voice which ordains, controls, arranges, and presents the imaginative world within which the other, personal, voice has its being as a reflection of biographical reality. Put another way, the differing attitudes of the speakers in the several poems reflect the variety of human experience, while the aggregate of the experiences and points of view reflects the prevailing pattern of the world; Byron can play the role of the lover in its infinite manifestations and guises while at the same time conveying an

21

overview of the human condition as he saw it (in himself and others) and as he reacted to it. I think it is clear, however, that at this time he was at best only partially aware of his accomplishment: the total pattern of all of the groups and cycles is severely constricted by the exigencies of his own real and imagined experience, and his poetic imagination was as yet inchoate in the face of the demands conventional reality (and poetic conventionalities) imposed on it.

The last poems I wish to look at here are perhaps the most somber, those of the cycle revolving about the figure of Mary Chaworth, whose marriage in 1805 "threw [him] out again alone on a wide, wide sea.' "[16] The exquisite "Hills of Annesley" sets the tone and the symbolic landscape for the entire group:

> Hills of Annesley, Bleak and Barren,
>   Where my thoughtless Childhood stray'd,
> How the northern tempests, warring,
>   Howl above thy tufted Shade!
>
> Now no more, the Hours beguiling,
>   Former favourite Haunts I see;
> Now no more my Mary smiling
>   Makes ye seem a Heaven to me.[17]

---

[16] Quoted by Thomas Moore in The Works of Lord Byron with His Letters and Journals, and His Life (London, 1832), I, 256–57. The allusion to Coleridge's "The Ancient Mariner" is an important one, for throughout his life Byron admired, almost extravagantly, both this poem and "Christabel"; it is significant that they are two of the strongest statements in Romantic poetry of the positive forces of evil abroad in man and the world. On Byron and evil, see Edward E. Bostetter, The Romantic Ventriloquists, especially p. 259: " . . . he saw evil as an intrinsic and possibly dominant factor in human life, dooming man to degradation and death, thwarting his conceptions of and aspirations toward good. . . ."

[17] Written in 1805, these stanzas were first published in 1830 by Moore in his Letters and Journals of Lord Byron: With Notices of His Life (2 vols.; London, 1830). It should be noted that the ultimate focus of the poem is not upon Byron's sense of loss at Mary Chaworth's marriage or even upon a bereaved lover; it is rather upon man, whose world has become like that of Lear on the heath.

"The Adieu," written two years later, is a farewell to life as well as to youth, its point of view that of a man "Deprived of active force"; in it Byron poignantly blends Mary's image into the picture of loss:

> *Yet Mary, all thy beauties seem*
> *Fresh as in Love's bewitching dream,*
>   *To me in smiles display'd;*
> *Till slow disease resigns his prey*
> *To Death, the parent of decay,*
>   *Thine image cannot fade.*

In "Well! Thou Art Happy," written a year later, love's bewitching dream is momentarily made a reality, but only in circumstances which prevent the renewal of even an indication of lingering affection:

> *But now to tremble were a crime—*
>   *We met,—and not a nerve was shook.*
>
> *I saw thee gaze upon my face,*
>   *Yet meet with no confusion there:*
> *One only feeling couldst thou trace;*
>   *The sullen calmness of despair.*
>
> *Away! away! my early dream*
>   *Remembrance never must awake:*
> *Oh! where is Lethe's fabled stream?*
>   *My foolish heart be still, or break.*[18]

---

[18] This poem was written after Byron dined with Mary and her husband at their home. His prose version of the experience, in a letter to Francis Hodgson on November 3, 1808, provides the reader an interesting point of comparison:

> I was seated near a woman, to whom, when a boy, I was as much attached as boys generally are, and more than a man should be. I knew this before I went, and was determined to be valiant, and converse with *sang froid;* but instead I forgot my valour and my nonchalance, and never opened my lips even to laugh, far less to speak, and the lady was almost as absurd as myself, which made both the object of more observation than if we had conducted ourselves with easy indifference. You will think all this great nonsense;

In "To a Lady" and "Stanzas to a Lady, on Leaving England"
the impossibility of this love and the particularity of the circumstances began to shade off into the archetypal farewell to
Eden—man's eternal banishment from his garden of love—and
the curse of memory, by which he is tempted to try to return
and then mocked in those attempts because of the very impossibility of recapturing the past, regaining the lost, or realizing
the dream in this world:

> *When Man, expell'd from Eden's bowers,*
> *A moment linger'd near the gate,*
> *Each scene recall'd the vanish'd hours,*
> *And bade him curse his future fate.*
>
> *But, wandering on through distant climes,*
> *He learnt to bear his load of grief;*
> *Just gave a sigh to other times,*
> *And found in busier scenes relief.*
>
> *Thus, Lady! will it be with me. . . .*

That Byron's love, the marriage of Mary, and the "self-exile"
are all factually true does not in any way invalidate the point
I have been trying to make, for the same subsuming of the
private-public voice under the tones of the public-private voice
obtains. Eternal love is proclaimed, even in the final poem (it
concludes, "His home, his hope, his youth are gone, / Yet still he
loves, and loves but one"), but the total effect of the cycle is to
give an overpowering sense of what has been lost, not what
remains. To put it another way, what remains is only the sense
of loss.[19]

---

if you had seen it, you would have thought it still more ridiculous.
What fools we are! We cry for a plaything, which, like children,
we are never satisfied with till we break open, though like them we
cannot get rid of it by putting it in the fire (*LJ*, I, 198).

[19] Of the Mary Chaworth poems, none were included originally in
Hours of Idleness. "Well! Thou Art Happy," "To a Lady," and
"Stanzas to a Lady" appeared first in Hobhouse's *Imitations and
Translations* in 1809; "Hills of Annesley" was first published in 1830,
and "The Adieu" appeared in Murray's edition of Byron's works in
1832.

Other roles played in *Hours of Idleness,* whether or not they correspond exactly or at all with those of the historical Byron, describe man in a variety of stances toward reality: he is the man who has lost or who tries mightily to retain his one friend ("To D——," "Epitaph on a Friend," "To Edward Noel Long, Esq.," "To George, Earl Delawarr," "To the Earl of Clare," and perhaps especially "Inscription on the Monument of a New-foundland Dog"); he is the man who is the last of his line, a Childe Harold-like ruin amid ruins, heir only to a dead past ("When, to Their Airy Hall, My Fathers' Voice," "On Leaving Newstead Abbey," "Elegy on Newstead Abbey," "To an Oak at Newstead"); he is the poet ("From Anacreon. Ode 3," "Oscar of Alva," "The Episode of Nisus and Euryalus," "Answer to Some Elegant Verses," "The Death of Calmar and Orla," "To a Knot of Ungenerous Critics," "Soliloquy of a Bard in the Country," "Farewell to the Muse"); he is the sage and moral adviser ("To the Duke of Dorset," "To Marion," "To the Earl of Clare," "To a Vain Lady," "To a Youthful Friend"); he is the indignant conscience of the people ("On a Change of Masters at a Great Public School," "Thoughts Suggested by a College Examination," "On the Death of Mr. Fox"); he is the cynic ("To Woman," "Reply to Some Verses of J. M. B. Pigot, Esq.," "To the Sighing Strephon," "To Eliza," "Soliloquy of a Bard in the Country," "To——," beginning "Oh! well I know your subtle Sex," "Egotism. A Letter to J. T. Becher," "Queries to Casuists"); he is the exile ("Translation from the *Medea* of Euripides," "To a Lady," "Stanzas to a Lady, on Leaving England"); he is the man nearing death ("Childish Recollections," "The Adieu," "Fill the Goblet Again"); he is the penitent sinner crying for forgive-ness ("The Prayer of Nature," "The Adieu"). However inexact this categorization, the sum total of these roles is an impressively consistent testament to the prevailing undertone of Byron's private-public voice, coloring throughout the public-private voice of each of the individual speakers and roles. Further, however conscious or unconscious of his own technique Byron may have been, we cannot overlook his easy and ready adoption of a variety of voices, points of view, or speakers to convey both the particulars of individual experience and his own over-riding attitude or reaction to that experience. If *Hours of Idleness* is hardly a distinguished introduction to a major poet, in that volume, if we would only look for it, is the birth of a vision—a presage, as it were, of the full despair of his maturity—and the rudiments of a technique and vehicular structure by which to convey that despair. Finally, the various ways in which Byron is occasionally able to subsume the individual voice or character or point of view under the contours of an archetype clearly served him well in his later efforts to present Childe Harold, the Giaour, Selim, Conrad, Lara, Alp, and the Prisoner of Chillon as Man, not merely a motley assortment of romantic pirates and heroes.

III

In the *Hours of Idleness*, as we have seen, childhood innocence, love, and the human heart were among the elements united by Byron in a vision of paradise momentarily regained through memory, and immediately lost again to the power of the worldly present. With these accumulated and increasingly intensified losses came also his wholesale rejection of his retrospective vision as the "dreams of Romance" and a resolution that his lyre would thenceforth be tuned to truth. Such a reversal is, of course, not extraordinary in late adolescence and early maturity as the world takes its quick toll, exacts its punishment, and cruelly punctures the idealism of youth. Yet one can also see here a pattern repeated again and again in Byron's poetry, one that has a particular relevance to the writing of poetry itself.

However pompous and posed Byron's Preface to the *Hours of Idleness*, much of the volume clearly represents his innermost thoughts and feelings, conveyed indirectly. When it was attacked without charity by Lord Brougham in the *Edinburgh Review* of January, 1808, the very process so lamented in the *Hours of Idleness* became operative in his young career: the hard, mental destructiveness of the world had vented itself upon the vulnerable products of a youthful heart, still enamored, and perhaps even within sight, of the lost Eden. Byron's reaction to the blow is the reaction of all of his heroes: he steels his breast against further onslaughts and retreats into the citadel of mind —in other words, he deals with the world on its own terms, and fights for his very life. Such a retreat, I suggest, is not into what has become known as his characteristic vehicle, satire;[20] it is rather a willful burying of his essential self in a role that is more protective than natural—whether it takes a satiric or non-satiric form. All of his future comments about poetry as something to be indulged in when no other activity is available, as essentially a non-serious preoccupation, as the production of what is merely amusing or entertaining, must be understood in the light of this basic opposition between the heart and the head.

When *English Bards, and Scotch Reviewers, Hints from Horace,* and *The Curse of Minerva*[21] came forth from his brain in quick succession, then, we have quite literally his public-private voice speaking to us, that voice by which he would prefer to be heard because it veils his essential nature. Illusion and innocence, love and paradise, childhood and friendship will no longer be his subjects. Now, "Truth be my theme, and Censure guide my song"; or "Fools are my theme, let Satire be my song."[22] The pen with which he writes will no longer trace the feelings of the heart; it is now the "Slave of my thoughts,

---

[20] It is worth noting that Byron had some 380 lines of a poem entitled *British Bards* written before the publication of Lord Brougham's review of *Hours of Idleness* (ltr. to Elizabeth Pigot, 26 Oct. 1807, in *LJ,* I, 147). Line numbers following quotations from *English Bards, and Scotch Reviewers* in my text refer to the fifth edition, Byron's final revision and the version of the poem he finally suppressed as a "miserable record of misplaced anger and indiscriminate acrimony" (Byron's notes written in his copy of the fourth edition, in *P,* I, 297n).
[21] I have excluded *The Waltz,* which Byron wrote in 1812, since its curious libertine prudery and "prurient Puritanism," as Marchand correctly calls it (*Byron's Poetry,* p. 33), is totally unlike anything else he ever wrote.
[22] The first of these lines Byron rejected in favor of the second for l. 7 of the poem.

obedient to my will" (l. 8), a "mighty instrument" for "little men" (l. 10). In a sense he included himself—along with all the poets, dramatists, and critics attacked in *English Bards*—in that last phrase, except that, unlike the others, his mind is stronger and his victory in the battle for survival assured. That strength Byron then dramatizes by attacking—with "the force of Wit," not poetry[23]—his own scribblings of the heart:

> *I, too, can scrawl, and once upon a time*
> *I poured along the town a flood of rhyme,*
> *A schoolboy freak, unworthy praise or blame;*
> *I printed—older children do the same.*
> *'Tis pleasant, sure, to see one's name in print;*
> *A Book's a Book, altho' there's nothing in't.*
> (ll. 47–52)

The prophecy in *Hours of Idleness* of "Farewell to the Muse" he thus quickly honored, taking the side, ironically, of the kind of dispassionate mind which produced the *Edinburgh Review's* severe injury to his heart and to the poetic products of his sensitive self. Emulating Lord Brougham, he even attacked what he had naively assumed to be the "protection" of his title as well as his youth:

> *Not that a Title's sounding charm can save*
> *Or scrawl or scribbler from an equal grave.*
> (ll. 53–54)

The lines that follow these make clear that the reference is to George Lamb, son of Sir Peniston Lamb, whose wife was the daughter of Sir Ralph Milbanke, but the reference to Byron himself is unmistakable.

---

[23] Byron's confusion on this point in the poem is interesting, as if satire were in his mind associated somehow with prose more than poetry, with the art of the critic-reviewer rather than the creator. Although in the opening lines he refers to his *"Muse"* and to "song," the implication of "but not belong / To me the arrows of satiric song" is that this "poem" is something totally different from his earlier efforts, that it represents not "satiric song" but "A keener weapon, and a mightier hand." *English Bards* will be, thus, his "own review."

As if to complete his attack on himself by pillorying his own early taste in lyric poetry, Byron goes on to attack Thomas Moore in terms that might equally well apply to his own imitations of Moore in *Hours of Idleness*:

> *Who in soft guise, surrounded by a choir*
> *Of virgins melting, not to Vesta's fire,*
> *With sparkling eyes, and cheek by passion flushed*
> *Strikes his wild lyre, whilst listening dames are*
> > *hushed?*
> *'Tis LITTLE! young Catullus of his day,*
> *As sweet, but as immoral, in his Lay!*
> *Grieved to condemn, the Muse must still be just,*
> *Nor spare melodious advocates of lust.*
> *Pure is the flame which o'er her altar burns;*
> *From grosser incense with disgust she turns*
> *Yet kind to youth, this expiation o'er,*
> *She bids thee "mend thy line, and sin no more."*
> > (*ll. 283–94*)

If *English Bards* is a poem of anger and hurt, as it undoubtedly is, it can equally well be read as a curious kind of expiation for the "sin" (as Byron himself described it in his Preface to *Hours of Idleness*) of his early poetry.[24] The poetic path to be followed is the same as that through a world eternally destructive of paradise, "full of thorns," where

> *Vice triumphant holds her sov'reign sway,*
> *Obey'd by all who nought beside obey;*
> *When Folly, frequent harbinger of crime,*
> *Bedecks her cap with bells of every Clime;*
> *When knaves and fools combined o'er all prevail,*
> *And weigh their Justice in a Golden Scale.*
> > (*ll. 25–32*)

---

[24] In this connection, it is worth noting that for the last line of the quoted passage on Moore Byron originally wrote, "Mend thy life, and sin no more"—a further indication that the idea of chastising himself for his early "excesses" in poetry may have been in his mind well before Lord Brougham's review appeared.

For a critic of such an age, as for a critic of poetry, "Care not for feeling" (l. 73) is the proper motto:

> *The time hath been, when no harsh sound would fall*
> *From lips that now may seem imbued with gall;*
> *Nor fools nor follies tempt me to despise*
> *The meanest thing that crawled beneath my eyes:*
> *But now, so callous grown, so changed since youth,*
> *I've learned to think, and sternly speak the truth.*
>
>

(ll. 1053–58)

However wrong the judgments of *English Bards*, then (and Byron of course retracted much of it later, finally even refusing to keep the poem in print), and however indiscriminate his flailing attack, it behooves us not to overlook in the poem that private-public voice sounding beneath that of the hardened, cynical man of the world—the voice of lament, of the sense of loss, of the heart which knows its proper paradise however long-lost. Here that "paradise" is the greatness of past poetry as opposed to that of "these degenerate days" (l. 103); and the fact that Byron does not anticipate Keats's lament in the "Ode to Psyche" for the loss of a world of "happy pieties,"

> *When holy were the haunted forest boughs,*
> *Holy the air, the water, and the fire,*

should not blind us to the fact that for him the past of poetry was indeed a fabled past. And what distinguishes it is not the "Sense and Wit" (l. 105) for which Byron initially singles out the poets in *English Bards* but, curiously enough, their effect on the heart and soul: "Pope's pure strain / Sought the rapt soul to charm," and Dryden "poured [a] tide of song" (ll. 109–10, 113); Congreve's "scenes could cheer, or Otway's melt" (l. 115). To these names Byron adds those of Camoens, Milton, Tasso, and Shakespeare, and before them Homer and Virgil, the work of each of whom

>

appears

> *The single wonder of a thousand years.*
> *Empires have mouldered from the face of earth,*

> *Tongues have expired with those who gave them birth,*
> *Without the glory such a strain can give,*
> *As even in ruin bids the language live.*
>
> (*ll. 193–98*)

Here is an adumbration (taken together with several of the *Hours of Idleness* poems[25]) of one of Byron's favorite image patterns, that of the ruin, the force of which parallels that of memory, as seen in the early lyrics. The ruin is at once the reminder of past greatness, glory, even a kind of Eden on earth, and an assertion, all the more powerful for its immortal associations, that the paradisaical past is irretrievable. Further, in contrast to those splendid ruins, the structures of the modern world are dwarfed and awry, the flawed products of postlapsarian man. In *English Bards* Byron points out that there is no dearth of bards, but that they constitute a "pestilence" which must be driven from the land by "some genuine Bard" (l. 687). Without him even the land itself, like Rome, Athens, and Tyre, "may sink, in ruin hurled."[26]

This same note is equally apparent in the *Hints from Horace*, which Byron publicly and stubbornly persisted in ranking ridiculously high in his poetic canon, despite its watered-down Horatian Aristotelianism and its sensible neoclassic advice. It is a "luckless fate," Byron writes, for the young bard to be read by the "many-headed monster," the public, but if he must rhyme, his subject should be man eternal:

> *study Nature's page,*
> *And sketch the striking traits of every age;*
> *While varying Man and varying years unfold*
> *Life's little tale, so oft, so vainly told;*
> *Observe his simple childhood's dawning days,*

---

[25] Especially "On Leaving Newstead Abbey" and "Elegy on Newstead Abbey."

[26] L. 1005. This modern "pestilence" is obviously related to the theme of such poems as "On a Change of Masters at a Great Public School" and "Thoughts Suggested by a College Examination" in *Hours of Idleness*.

BYRON AND THE RUINS OF PARADISE

His pranks, his prate, his playmates, and his plays:
Till time at length the mannish tyro weans,
And prurient vice outstrips his tardy teens!

(ll. 217–24)

"Fooled, pillaged, dunned," he wastes his college years and is "Launched into life," with early fire and innocence extinct, to ape his sire, to raise his own sons the same, and finally to die "Crazed, querulous, forsaken, half forgot" (ll. 239–61). The speaker in this digression is clearly Byron himself, as he confesses somewhat self-consciously; and, having acknowledged it, he immediately turns the poem back to his theme, literature and its Horatian precepts. This technique of digression and forcible return to the central theme will become a familiar one throughout Byron's works, particularly in *Childe Harold* and *Don Juan*: it is one of his ways of making himself heard through or around or between the public voices he employs.

Of these early satires, *The Curse of Minerva* is the most interesting, for it contains some of the basic image patterns and techniques that Byron continues to develop in *Childe Harold* and the tales. Further, the two voices identified above are more clearly defined here than they have been thus far in Byron's poetry; and there is an ostensible theme, conveyed by the narrative or plot, while the voice of the traveler-narrator enunciates the underlying universalization of the surface facts.[27] In many ways, of course, the poem is crude: it ends abruptly without any real conclusion, its range of tones is excessive and cacophonous, the verse (aside from the lovely opening lyric) is at best undistinguished. Yet in its very crudeness the basic machinery of Byron's characteristic vehicle for his vision of the world and man lends itself more easily to study.

Ostensibly, the poem is an attack upon Lord Elgin for his pillaging of the crumbling Greek monuments and sculpture. He is a "spoiler" worse than ravaging "Turk or Goth," a

---

[27] William H. Marshall sensed something of this skeletal pattern but could make nothing of it (*The Structure of Byron's Major Poems*, p. 22).

Pictish "plunderer," a sacrilegious polluter of shrines, a money-hungry "felon," a "filthy jackal" gnawing on the bones of the prey deserted by lion and wolf. This is the curse of the title

> *on him and all his seed:*
> *Without one spark of intellectual fire,*
> *Be all the sons as senseless as the sire:*
>
> .   .   .   .   .
>
> *Oh, loathed in life, nor pardoned in the dust,*
> *May Hate pursue his sacrilegious lust!*
> *Linked with the fool that fired the Ephesian dome,*
> *Shall vengeance follow far beyond the tomb,*
> *And Eratostratus and Elgin shine*
> *In many a branding page and burning line;*
> *Alike reserved for aye to stand accursed,*
> *Perchance the second blacker than the first.*[28]
>
> (*ll. 164–67, 199–206*)

But the particular figure of Lord Elgin and his piratical plundering also takes on all the aspects of a metaphor—of universal corruption and conflict, of wasteful war and ruin, of past glory, wisdom, and art now decayed and irretrievable. Indeed, the title of the poem might well have been *The Fall of Minerva,* the final defeat at the hands of the world and modern man of an Eden "Sacred to Gods, but not secure from Man" (l. 60). For Byron that was Greece, and the opening description of the sun setting over its ruins and the coming of darkness is but a solemn symbol not only for Elgin's ravishment of its ruined beauties but also for the darkness descending upon England's glory.

Though eternally beautiful, even in ruins, Greece, the land of "The God of gladness," is now a landscape of vain altars and shrines, amid which the ghost of Socrates drinks his hemlock shortly before each sunset (ll. 8–31). "The wreck of Greece" in which the goddess Minerva, fallen, weak, and decayed like the paradise of wisdom over which she once ruled, is circled

---

[28] Eratostratus set fire to the temple of Artemis ("the Ephesian dome") on the night of Alexander the Great's birth (Coleridge's note, in *P,* I, 467n).

33

slowly by her symbolic owlet, now become a mourner over the dead:

> Gone were the terrors of her awful brow,
> Her idle Aegis bore no Gorgon now;
> Her helm was dinted, and the broken lance
> Seemed weak and shaftless e'en to mortal glance;
> The Olive Branch, which still she deigned to clasp,
> Shrunk from her touch, and withered in her grasp;
> And, ah! though still the brightest of the sky,
> Celestial tears bedimmed her large blue eye;
> Round the rent casque her owlet circled slow,
> And mourned his mistress with a shriek of woe!
> (ll. 79–88)

That shriek is quickly extended into the jackal's cry, as Minerva castigates Elgin:

> So when the Lion quits his fell repast,
> Next prowls the Wolf, the filthy Jackal last:
> Flesh, limbs, and blood the former make their own,
> The last poor brute securely gnaws the bone.
> (ll. 113–116)

The fierce intensity of this passage, its sense of waste and utter desolation, looks forward to the similar and extraordinary battle-field scene in *The Siege of Corinth*, in which the universe of death is inherited by wild dogs and other predators.

What should be especially noted here, however, is the limited view taken by the narrator in his attempt to "soothe the vengeance kindling in her eye" (l. 124). Just as the overriding sense of doom and loss seeps through the lines of his lush description of the sunset, in which the emphasis is upon the obvious beauty of the scene, so too here he becomes another aspect of Byron's modern man—not the despoiler but the self-righteous. In both passages, then, the ostensible theme or emphasis is overridden by the larger implications or significance of the speaker's remarks as controlled and directed by the poet's judicious handling of the dramatic context and the tone of the poetry. Pointing out to Minerva that her identification of Elgin as an Englishman was a mistake, the narrator leaps to the defense of "Britain's injured name" and shrilly brands Elgin as a Scot: "Frown not on England; England owns him not." He then goes on in jingoistic fashion to condemn Scotland as a "bastard land" where "Wisdom's goddess never held command,"

> *A barren soil, where Nature's germs, confined*
> *To stern sterility, can stint the mind;*
> *Whose thistle well betrays the niggard earth,*
> *Emblem of all to whom the Land gives birth;*
> *Each genial influence nurtured to resist;*
> *A land of meanness, sophistry, and mist.*
> *Each breeze from foggy mount and marshy plain*
> *Dilutes with drivel every drizzly brain,*
> *Till, burst at length, each wat'ry head o'erflows,*
> *Foul as their soil, and frigid as their snows:*
> *Then thousand schemes of petulance and pride*
> *Despatch her scheming children far and wide;*
> *Some East, some West, some—everywhere but North!*
> *In quest of lawless gain, they issue forth.*
> *And thus—accursed be the day and year!*
> *She sent a Pict to play the felon here.*
>
> (*ll. 133–48*)

The implications of the speech are clear: England is none of these things, is indeed all of their opposites; and the speaker presumes mightily to join his curse to Minerva's. The goddess, however, persists: vengeance will be hers, she says to the speaker, and her counsels will no longer be offered to "lands like thine."

Precisely what this last phrase implies is clarified by Byron in that portion of Minerva's curse aimed at England and, by implication, the world (ll. 210ff.). Minerva, aware of the fall, sees herself as a Cassandra warning in vain,[29] her reign over the world now usurped by the Furies. "But one convulsive struggle still remains"; in it Havoc will reign and "The law of Heaven

---

[29] The speaker in *English Bards, and Scotch Reviewers* also adopted this prophetic stance (ll. 991–1010).

35

and Earth . . . life for life" will guide the world to its final self-destruction. "Look last at home," Minerva concludes—

> *"ye love not to look there*
> *On the grim smile of comfortless despair:*
> *Your city saddens: loud though Revel howls,*
> *Here Famine faints, and yonder Rapine prowls.*
> *See all alike of more or less bereft;*
>
> .   .   .   .   .
>
> *Now fare ye well! enjoy your little hour;*
> *Go, grasp the shadow of your vanished power;*
> *Gloss o'er the failure of each fondest scheme;*
> *Your strength a name, your bloated wealth a dream."*
> *(ll. 239–43, 259–62)*

Thus with England the archetype of tyrant (over Denmark, India, Spain, and itself) and agent of corruption, with Greece the archetype of slavery and ruins, Byron divides the world between the spoilers and the despoiled. The inevitable result is war and slaughter, havoc the only victor, and the jackal the inheritor of the earth.

Although this larger theme and the technique of juxtaposing limited and far-ranging points of view cannot be said to be refined in *The Curse of Minerva*, it is difficult to deny their presence there. What is unusual about the theme is that Byron's standard metaphor for paradise is not wisdom but love. Mind for him rapidly becomes the despoiler that unmans man by steeling his heart in order to man "him 'gainst the coming doom." Here, however, it is the mind that is in a sense steeled against itself, with wisdom crowded out by ambition and lust for power. Perhaps Byron indeed saw in the death of Socrates the fall of Minerva and the rise of Athena, goddess of war—the rise of mind (in its limited sense of opposition to heart) which seals the doom of so many in the tales and plays. In any case, *The Curse* gives us Byron's first categorical condemnation of a world whose law is not love but survival, "life for life." Further, his use of the contrapuntal voices of Minerva and the narrator and the narrowness of vision he deliberately attributes to the latter is a continuation of his already well-established habit of masking his own point of view on the surface only to reveal it in the total conception of the poem, in its characters, action, and setting. Finally, *The Curse* is a fine example of the intimate connection between Byron's "romantic" and satiric voices. In the opening description of the sunset the former is obviously operative; it is a lament or elegy, instinct with the sense of irreparable loss. The rest of the poem is satire, bitter anger at the nature of man and the world that are the very cause of lament. In the former stance the heart lives on brokenly amid the wreck of paradise; in the latter, the mind, armed against tears, berates the corrupters and perverters of wisdom and sense. Both are legitimate responses to loss of the ideal, but Byron not only recognized but compensated for the vulnerability of the former stance by manipulating persona, mask, voice, and point of view in the "romantic" poems and by steeling his own heart to vitriolic bitterness, to contempt, and to laughter in the satiric poems.

It should not be surprising, then, to find in *Childe Harold's Pilgrimage,* begun in October, 1809, and finally completed in 1818, the voices found in *English Bards* (1807–1809), *Hints from Horace* (1811), and *The Curse of Minerva* (1811), as well as some of the voices and roles he had inaugurated, however tentatively, in *Hours of Idleness.*

Chapter II

CHILDE HAROLD'S PILGRIMAGE, CANTO I

Perhaps no other major poem in English literature has fared as badly as has *Childe Harold's Pilgrimage*, at the hands of critics, scholars, students, teachers, anthologists, and even the casual reader of poetry. It is not only fashionable but critically "correct" to dismiss the first two cantos almost as if they never existed, in direct contempt of a reading public and literary world that made Byron famous overnight for writing them; and it is all but impossible to find an anthology which includes even selections from these cantos. While much of this neglect is the result of an overwhelming unanimity of critical opinion about the relative merits of Cantos I and II versus Cantos III and IV, it is also at least in part the result of the somewhat curious critical conclusion that *Childe Harold* is at least two separate poems, and perhaps even three.

Arguments in support of this conclusion are abundant and need not be rehearsed here;[1] but in the face of them I should

---

[1] Arnold was perhaps the first to sound this note, adjudging Byron to be incapable of "the instinctive artistic creation of poetic wholes," his work lacking "a deep internal law of development to a necessary end" (Preface to *Poetry of Byron* [London, 1913], pp. x–xi). Other representatives of this point of view toward *Childe Harold* include Harold Bloom, *The Visionary Company* (Garden City, N.Y., 1961); William J. Calvert, *Byron: Romantic Paradox* (Chapel Hill, N.C., 1935); John Drinkwater, *The Pilgrim of Eternity: Byron—A Conflict* (New York, 1925); T. S. Eliot, *On Poetry and Poets* (London, 1957); Ernest J. Lovell, *Byron: The Record of a Quest*; William H. Marshall, *The Structure of Byron's Major Poems*; Harold Nicolson, *The Poetry of Byron* (English Association Presidential Address, 1943; n.p., 1943); Willis W. Pratt, "Byron and Some Current Patterns of Thought," in

like to suggest, cautiously, that the work is a single entity. I should at least like to argue that we give the poem a chance to demonstrate its unity and continuity—a chance seldom allowed it. That said, I must also say that as a unit, fundamentally coherent even amid its obvious incoherence, the poem emerges as now extraordinary and even brilliant, now uneven, irritating, confused, and at times confusing. In its totality, I find it a major work in all respects.[2] The history of its composition argues mightily against this conclusion, for what is exasperating, inconsistent, and hesitant about it—its apparently erratic fluctuation of tone and point of view—is certainly largely attributable to the span of years (1809 to 1818) during which Byron worked at it only intermittently. During these same years he was also running a remarkable gamut of other literary forms and techniques, experimenting constantly with methods of narration and the manipulation of multiple points of view. Childe Harold alone, even Byron alone, was simply not strong enough or consistent enough to sustain so protracted a scheme.

That the poem does have a recognizable scheme and considerable coherence is remarkable, given the odds against it. Yet perhaps it is not so remarkable if we realize, as we are just now beginning to do, that Byron's protracted and persistent

---

C. D. Thorpe et al. (eds.), *The Major English Romantic Poets* (Carbondale, Ill., 1957); George M. Ridenour, "Byron and the Romantic Pilgrimage"; Andrew Rutherford, *Byron: A Critical Study*; and Paul West, *Byron and the Spoiler's Art*. This parade was certainly encouraged by Byron himself, since Medwin records him as saying, "I know that [*Childe Harold*] is a thing without form or substance,—a *voyage pittoresque* (*Journal*, p. 112). That was in 1821–22. Yet in a letter to Murray of September 15, 1817, Byron wrote flatly, "I look upon *Childe Harold* as my best" (*LJ*, IV, 168). The dissenters are few and not very vocal, with the possible exception of Edward E. Bostetter, in *The Romantic Ventriloquists*; other dissenters include Alfred Austin, *The Bridling of Pegasus: Prose Papers on Poetry* (London, 1910); John Nichol, *Byron* (London, 1890); and Peter Quennell, *Byron: The Years of Fame* (New York, 1935).

[2] I am thus inclined to agree with John Nichol, who rates *Childe Harold*, along with *Manfred* and Scott's *Marmion*, as just missing "being a great poem" (*Byron*, p. 119).

struggle for a form and the fundamental consistency of the vision that he hoped to project in that form are neither unexpected nor illogical in the light of his beginnings as man and poet as presented here. I do not think that I know as yet precisely how to read *Childe Harold* over all, that is, in its minute particularity, as Blake might say. I have a suspicion, for example, that it is Byron's portrait of the artist as a young man, though I am unwilling and unable here to fight for that interpretation.[3] As a gradually evolving index to his main poetic concerns and as the single poem in the canon most revelatory of his search for form, I intend to allow it to reveal itself not only as one poem but as perhaps the most valuable poem Byron ever wrote for the study of him as poet.

I

Aside from the almost bewildering array that is the poem itself, there remains a considerable obstacle, in a book of this kind, to coherent analysis of its structure, form, and themes —once again, the problem of the dates of its composition. Byron's development I see as a continuous struggle, in which the chronology of composition is crucial to understanding— even to seeing—that struggle. To deal with the whole of *Childe Harold* within those confining limits, however, involves risking the very fragmentation of its coherence and achievement I have condemned above. Unfortunately, I can see no other way, for what I shall have to say about *Childe Harold* III and IV is at least in part based upon the development I see in the tales, in *The Prisoner of Chillon*, in "The Dream" and "Darkness," in *Manfred*, and in other poems of 1812 to 1818, as well as in Cantos I and II of *Childe Harold*. However reluctantly, then, I shall comment upon each canto in its proper temporal order,

---

[3] In 1935 Peter Quennell hazarded somewhat the same guess, describing *Childe Harold* as "the autobiographical mythology of a young poet" (*Byron: The Years of Fame*, p. 21). He did not pursue the point either.

reserving the right always to leap ahead as well as to retreat abruptly in my attempt to see the poem whole.

Until very recently *Childe Harold's Pilgrimage* has been read as an account either of Lord Byron's "pilgrimage" (he himself used the term several times to describe his travels[4]) or of Harold's, the focus of all analysis and commentary therefore being upon the character of Harold, or Byron as Harold, or Harold as Byron. Despite Byron's earnest protestations to the contrary, despite his overt condemnation of Harold as "most unamiable,"[5] readers and critics alike have deliberately confused Byron's fictional character with himself; and they have studiously ignored or condemned Byron's simple explanation for Harold's presence—"for the sake of giving some connection to the piece."[6] I see no reason to doubt this. In many instances Harold is simply a vehicle to enable Byron to move the reader from scene to scene, country to country. But, of course, he is more than this—and it is this more that Byron himself perhaps did not ever fully understand and certainly did not at the beginning of the poem. He writes, for example, that Harold was "never intended as an example, further than to show, that early perversion of mind and morals leads to satiety of past pleasures and disappointment in new ones, and that even the beauties of nature and the stimulus of travel . . . are lost on a soul so constituted, or rather misdirected."[7] The voice here is clearly Byron's public-private, letters-and-journal voice: the lesson of the poem will be moral in the true eighteenth-century manner. The days of chivalry were corrupt in any case, "the most profligate of all possible centuries,"[8] and thus a modern knight, the last of his line, suited perfectly this modern version of medieval immorality.

At the same time, I cannot conceive of Byron's being

---

[4] Byron's earliest use of the word is in his ltr. to James de Bathe, 2 Feb. 1808, in *LJ*, I, 176.

[5] "Addition to the Preface" of *Childe Harold's Pilgrimage*, first published in the fourth edition, in *P*, II, 6.

[6] Preface to *Childe Harold's Pilgrimage*, in *P*, II, 3.

[7] "Addition to the Preface," in *P*, II, 7–8.

[8] *Ibid.*, p. 6.

totally unaware of the implications of his choice of hero, the hero's title, and the idea of a pilgrimage. Given the retrospective views of childhood in *Hours of Idleness,* he certainly saw in the appellation "Childe" not merely a modern example of the corruption of chivalry, but also, as his "Addition to the Preface" implies, an example of the decay of love in the world, the love associated in all of the early poems with childhood and early youth. Childe Harold, then, is in a sense modern man, cast out of his Eden (in itself already corrupt and perverted), doomed to wander the universe, between two eternities, as it were, not seeking the goal of fulfillment usually inherent in the romantic quest but rather the nothingness that is relief from the world. The pilgrimage is away from rather than to a shrine, the journey itself a journey of death in life. Harold is the archetypal man, a fallen titan yet a fly "like any other fly," wandering amid the wreckage of the world.[9]

In no sense, then, can I see Harold as Byron's persona. He is instead both an object and a metaphor, individual man in the modern world, with only such particularity of background and experience as will not preclude his symbolizing the wreck of modern man and of the modern world. That he rarely speaks is indicative of Byron's intent, however fuzzy it was initially, to deal *with* him, not *through* him; he is, in a sense, the masks, poses, and roles of the speakers in *Hours of Idleness* now objectified in *propria persona* so that they may be looked at from various angles or points of view, and so that their corporate image may be projected onto the landscape of the world. The main point of view is that of the narrator, which is relatively narrow in that it is finite and in many ways ordinary, yet not so narrow as Harold's vision, warped by his own experience and tending inward rather than outward at the world. The narrator is a traveler also, a storyteller who gathers his facts from a

---

[9] Ridenour seems to see the idea of a pilgrimage as developed only in 1816, in the third canto of *Childe Harold;* there, he says, "the poet speaks as a compulsory exile who is trying to take advantage of his state of deprivation—to turn exile to pilgrimage" ("Byron in 1816: Four Poems from Diodati," in F. W. Hilles and H. Bloom [eds.], *From Sensibility to Romanticism* [New York, 1965], p. 454).

variety of sources, an observer of the particulars of landscape, society, and politics, and a commentator whose view is consistently colored by his patriotism, his fundamental morality, and his orthodox religion. He is a realist, concerned with the truth, which he interprets in the light of the facts as he sees them; he is impatient of fable and poetry and discerning enough to penetrate the veils of appearance, yet capable of generalizing his experience only in a very limited way. He gives advice of various sorts, points lessons (mostly moral), describes the scene or landscape matter-of-factly, without any sense of involvement, and moves us along with him and his fellow traveler Harold throughout the pilgrimage. Basically, he is repelled by Harold, although there are occasional softer notes of understanding and compassion, and he is angry, even bitter, over what he sees and knows of the world; yet he also entertains a hope for improvement in the future.

The other point of view in the poem is that of the poet, whose vision is at once larger and smaller than that of the narrator. He tends almost always to see things in their universality, to see their fuller implications, and of course he manipulates, juxtaposes, and controls the others; but he is also intensely concerned with the poem as poem, with the artistic process of becoming, with the fact as symbolic of larger truth, with the transformation of history into fable. He is a contemplator, neither morally repelled by nor attracted to his characters (the "souls of his thought") but reacting to their particular status as metaphors of reality. In him the pilgrimage exists not as the temporal sequence of events to which the narrator is tied but rather a timeless panorama of the nature of things. His response to this panorama is dictated by the mood of Childe Harold or the scene rather than by the sequential parade of fact.[10]

---

[10] That Byron was at least vaguely aware of two distinct voices in the poem, Harold's and his own, is indicated by an early draft of his Preface to Canto I: "My readers will observe that where the author speaks in his own person he assumes a very different tone from that of 'The cheerless thing, the man without a friend' . . ." (P, II, 4n).

Childe Harold, Canto I

Inevitably, in such a conception the critical problem of the nature, handling, and efficacy of the persona (or voice or whatever) arises, and something must be said of that problem here. With a poet like Byron, a many-faceted character whose ultimate representation of his wholeness is found in the chaotic order of *Don Juan*, it is especially tempting to see the abrupt shifts in tone, point of view, attitude, and the like merely as evidence of the natural mobility of his mind, ineffectively controlled or patterned by the discipline of art. What such a conclusion discounts is Byron the artist, who not only versifies but also structures and formalizes. It is probably true, as Guy Steffan, among others, has said, that all of Byron's characters are partly "like" him because with a kind of Keatsian negative capability he "subconsciously [or] consciously puts *self* into his people . . . not only what he appears and does not appear to be, but what he says he is and what he wants to be without saying it."[11] Yet our proper concern should be, I think, not with what he appears to be or wants to be—or really is—but rather what he does in the poetry. And if that poetry is, finally, the dramatization or exploration of an infinitely varied personality, we cannot begin with the personality to find it in the poetry; we must begin with the poetry in order to discover the personality (a risky procedure indeed if we are biographers), or, better still, we must begin with the poetry to see what is there and the form in which it is embodied.

In my treatment of *Hours of Idleness* I have shown that in many of the poems Byron tends to employ an ostensible theme voiced by the speaker and an underlying, more all-in-

[11] T. G. Steffan, "The Making of a Masterpiece," in Steffan and W. W. Pratt (eds.), *Byron's "Don Juan"* (Austin, Tex., 1957), I, 285. This ability to negate himself has been well established by critics as well as by Byron himself. For example, although they are at best only partially reliable, Lady Blessington's records of her conversations with Byron can be taken as substantially correct on this point. She quotes him as saying, "Now, if I know myself, I should say, that I have no character at all. . . . I am so changeable, being every thing by turns and nothing long . . ." (*Conversations of Lord Byron with the Countess of Blessington* [London, 1834], p. 389).

clusive, theme voiced by the poet. The first theme is limited, specific, particular; the second is universal, general. The first is what T. S. Eliot might have called "the man who suffers," the latter, his "mind which creates."[12] Poetry, Eliot writes, "is not a turning loose of emotion, but an escape from emotion; it is not an expression of personality but an escape from personality."[13] This "escape" Byron accomplishes by means of the various roles, voices, and points of view he adopts for the speaker of his poems, what Proust calls "le personnage qui raconte, qui dit 'Je' (et qui n'est pas moi)."[14] Such a distinction has been made before and since, in different ways, many of them pertinent to my discussion of Byron's technique not only in *Hours of Idleness* but in *Childe Harold* and the later poems.

Leo Spitzer, in distinguishing between the "poetic I" and the "empirical I" in medieval literature, points out the sharp contrast, for example, between Dante as protagonist and Dante as narrator in the *Divina Commedia*: the latter "performs the task of retelling (*redire*) what he has seen," in so doing transcending "the limits of individuality in order to gain an experience of universal experience"; the former is the "individual eye . . . necessary to perceive and to fix the matter of experience."[15] If such a distinction between person and mask or maker inevitably creates what Patrick Cruttwell calls a certain "inconclusiveness," a "kind of wobble,"[16] this is no reason for discounting or ignoring the fact of the distinction. Perhaps it is, as Cruttwell says of

---

[12] "Tradition and the Individual Talent," *Points of View* (London, 1941), p. 30 (first published in the *Egoist* [September–October and November–December, 1919]).

[13] *Ibid.*, p. 34.

[14] Interview with Proust by Elie-Joseph Bois, published in *Le Temps* (November 12, 1913), reprinted in Robert Dreyfus, *Souvenirs sur Marcel Proust* (Paris, 1926), p. 290. I am indebted to Marcel Muller for this reference. For other similar statements, see Professor Muller's *Les voix narratives dans "La recherche du temps perdu"* (Geneva, 1965), pp. 159–60.

[15] "Note on the Poetic and the Empirical 'I' in Medieval Authors," *Traditio*, IV (1946), 416.

[16] "Makers and Persons," *Hudson Review*, XII (1959–60), 490–91.

Laurence Sterne, a matter of "weakness" rather than choice (and it would certainly be difficult to prove deliberate choice in the early Byron), but this possibility should not dissuade us from acknowledging the disparity of styles and viewpoints, and from there beginning our efforts at understanding. Thus, in an excellent article, E. Talbot Donaldson, distinguishes sharply Chaucer the man, Chaucer the poet, and Chaucer the pilgrim, while Robert Jordan, following Donaldson's lead, cautions us to be more fully aware of and "responsive" to the "illusion-making poet" even as we are invited to "surrender to the 'reality' of the journey."[17] Jordan made the point even more explicit in an earlier essay, in his analysis of Chaucer's *Troilus and Criseyde:* "Just as the poem insists upon the distinction between the narrator's level of perception and that of the characters, so does it stress the limitations of the narrator as an agent of the poet's consciousness." *Troilus* has a "vertical organization as a structure of perspective," while at the same time maintaining the "horizontal organization" of narrative.[18] Chaucer's poem is, as *Childe Harold* and Byron's tales will be shown to be, both temporal and atemporal, spatial and aspatial, local and universal. The differences between *Troilus,* and indeed *The Canterbury Tales,* and *Childe Harold* are equally instructive, aside from the obvious surface similarities and differences between Chaucer and Byron. The latter dramatically reverses the proportions of Chaucer's poems so that the narrator usurps the major role, dis-

---

[17] Donaldson, "Chaucer the Pilgrim," *PMLA,* LXIX (1954), 928–36; Jordan, "Chaucer's Sense of Illusion: Roadside Drama Reconsidered," *ELH,* XXIX (1962), 27. If, as Donaldson points out, the pilgrim ("the fallible first person singular") usually "arrives somewhere" at the end of the book, having received "the education he has needed," this does not invalidate in any way the pertinence of his point to the study of Byron's pilgrim, who arrives nowhere. For two other excellent discussions of Chaucer's manipulation of narrator, personae, and point of view—both helpful for an informed reading of *Childe Harold*—see Donald R. Howard, "Chaucer the Man," *PMLA,* LXXX (1965), 337–43, and his *The Three Temptations: Medieval Man in Search of the World* (Princeton, N.J., 1966), pp. 109–46.

[18] "The Narrator in Chaucer's *Troilus,*" *ELH,* XXV (1958), 238–39. Cf. Donald R. Howard, *The Three Temptations,* pp. 109–46.

pelling more often than maintaining the illusion of the poem. In Byron we have greater verticality of organization, with Childe Harold's pilgrimage constantly yielding to and finally blurring into the erratic horizontality of the narrator's travels and mind; and all three of these in turn are absorbed, modulated, and shaped by the poet's overriding vision. The progressive continuity of narrative is constantly collapsing into the dilatory mode and mood of the separate stages of the movement. The focus of *Childe Harold* is upon the narrator's reaction to the scenes and events of a poem which is happening to him, and upon the poet's organization of and attitudes toward that reaction. This forcible focusing on history, then moving, almost immediately, away from history, may be what Robert Langbaum had in mind when he called Byron "the most spectacular representative . . . of sheer assertion of the will,"[19] poetically and in terms of posticonoclastic man's establishing that will as a source of value amid the wreckage of the world.

The concept of *Childe Harold* as a monolithic identifi-

---

[19] *The Poetry of Experience* (London, 1957), p. 20. Langbaum goes on to say that in topographical poetry, the "observer" should not be seen "as the man his friends knew and his biographers write about; we should rather think of him as a character in a dramatic action, a character who has been endowed by the poet with the qualities necessary to make the poem happen to him" (p. 52). Thus to see Childe Harold as Byron "is misleading unless we see that these fictitious characters are related and unrelated to their creators in the same way as the observers" in a romantic lyric (p. 57). Northrop Frye makes essentially the same point in a different way in his fine book on Blake, *Fearful Symmetry* (Princeton, N.J., 1947), p. 113:

all genuine poetry is something quite separate from the person who wrote it. . . . The lyric is no exception to this rule of objectivity. The poet can express himself in a lyric only by dramatizing the mental state or mood he is in, and the imaginative truth of the lyric refers to this state and not to himself. One may pass through state after state with bewildering rapidity: one may experience ten or twelve states of love or passion in as many seconds. But to create one must balance and harmonize one's states, and what one creates takes its unity of tone and mood from that stabilization. The lyric, then, is normally a snapshot or single vision of an imaginative state by a poet who is in but not necessarily of it. . . .

cation of Harold and Byron, a concept which ignores, to all intents and purposes, the artist's controlling hand in the poem, has slowly been losing its supporters. Although it is at least in part correct, it is finally wrong for the critic to assert baldly that Byron "had so many selves to express, that sometimes one of them is uppermost and sometimes another," and that his "many-sidedness as a man was long his weakness as an artist."[20] D. H. Lawrence was more nearly correct, although he did not pursue his idea, in saying that Byron was "a man who is female as well as male, and who lives according to the female side of his nature."[21] However the man lived, the mind of the poet, firm, immensely mobile, all-encompassing, and controlled, constantly exerted the restraint of art upon his emotional responses to man and the world.

As early as 1825, in an almost unnoticed work, J. W. Lake recognized the essential bifurcated vision of *Childe Harold* I and II, the split between Harold himself and the poet; the former, says Lake, ultimately became the teller of the tales and the latter the controlling element in *Childe Harold* III and IV.[22] Although this is an oversimplification of the problem, its core of truth has very slowly emerged at the center of later fragments of critical truth. Even Swinburne, who intended to disparage

---

[20] Calvert, *Byron: Romantic Paradox*, p. 136.

[21] "Study of Thomas Hardy," in *D. H. Lawrence: Selected Literary Criticism*, ed. Anthony Beal (New York, 1956), pp. 70–71. This study was begun by Lawrence in 1914 but was first published posthumously in *Phoenix: The Posthumous Papers*, ed. E. D. McDonald (London, 1936).

[22] *The Complete Works of Lord Byron* (7 vols.; Paris, 1825), I, lxxxvi. Lake's basically acute perception trails off, unfortunately, into a fairly conventional description (p. lxxxvi):

> During the composition of the first cantos of *Childe Harold*, the author had but a confused idea of the character he wished to delineate, nor did he, perhaps, distinctly comprehend the scope and tendencies of his own genius. Two conceptions, distinct from each other, seem therein to be often blended; one of ideal human beings made up of certain troubled powers and passions,—and one of himself, ranging the world of nature and man, in wonder and delight, and agitation, in his capacity of a poet.

Childe Harold even more than he had already done, revealed the sensitivity of his critical ear by describing Cantos I and II of the poem as having been written "in falsetto,"[23] a clear recognition, though he did not know what to do with it, that a voice other than Byron's permeated the work. In 1876 Georg Brandes saw Byron's use of a "mask" in Cantos I and II, a mask that "covers an earnest and a suffering countenance. The mask is that of a hermit; pluck it off, and there still remains a man of a solitary nature! The mask is grandiose melancholy; throw it away; beneath it there is real sadness." Although Brandes saw no interpenetration of mask and maker, he did go on to identify three chief feelings or voices in *Childe Harold*, "solitariness, melancholy, and love of freedom," all of which "gradually become one greater feeling" as the ego expands to encompass all "suffering humanity."[24] His terminology may be confusing and inexact, but his sense of the wholeness and development of *Childe Harold* through its four cantos is refreshingly acute. William Marshall has studied Byron's personae or voices most recently, in his *The Structure of Byron's Major Poems*, and Peter Thorslev specifically identifies "no less than three different poetic characters, none of which is kept clearly distinct from the others" in *Childe Harold* I and II: that of Harold himself, that of "a minstrel-narrator," and that of "Byron's own persona . . . who is not really consistent in voice or character with the other two persons." In Canto IV, Thorslev writes, Byron drops the first two of these and retains only the third, though he does not speculate as to why Byron does this. Even in IV, however, Thorslev distinguishes the persona, as "an achievement of the poet's imagination," from Byron himself.[25]

---

[23] "Byron," *Essays and Studies*, p. 249.
[24] *Main Currents in Nineteenth Century Literature* (6 vols.; London, 1905), IV, 276, 299.
[25] *The Byronic Hero: Types and Prototypes* (Minneapolis, Minn., 1962), pp. 128–31. Andrew Rutherford, in *Byron: A Critical Study*, also distinguishes between the narrator and Childe Harold, but he denies any "significant relationship" between the two: "They co-exist but do not interact . . . they seem simply to reflect the fluctuations in Byron's own mood as he writes" (p. 33).

Such observations are rare and are in general unpursued; and though such a pursuit will not necessarily alter our basic critical judgment of *Childe Harold* I and II, it will, I hope, provide at least an additional, if not a sounder, basis for any such judgment and may lead to a firmer sense of the wholeness of Byron's achievement in the poem. Before essaying this pursuit, however, two other aspects of the total poem deserve comment: it is both a travel poem (and hence a medley of narrative and description) and a kind of unepical modern epic. The traditional travel poem of the Renaissance, especially popular with Continental Latinists, expressed "an appreciation of the world's beauty and the greatness of human achievement together with praise of one's native land."[26] To mix metaphors rudely, it was a kind of choreographic "mingled dish of sauces" (Joseph Warton's phrase[27]) in which a dominant motif was that of the ravages of time. Yet over all it had the optimism of great tragedy as well as local pride. What Byron has done to this traditional conception is to embody it in his narrator's vision, to make that vision a kind of primitive canvas, which is, as Ortega pointed out, "the sum of many small pictures, each one independent and each painted from the proximate view."[28] Unlike such a painting, or a quattrocento catalogue, which forces the eye to travel step by step, pausing wherever the painter himself stopped, Byron's poetry, beginning with *Childe Harold*, provides us with the poet's overarching vision, transcending that of Harold (or any other character) and the narrator, broadening their limited vision into a metaphorical and kaleidoscopic world view. Unlike the traditional pilgrim or traveler, Byron's Harold reaches no goal, indeed has no goal to reach; yet by so wandering in a kind of limbo, he provides the fundamental metaphor for Byron's poet-figure to inhabit, a metaphor (once Byron himself consciously

---

[26] Robert A. Aubin, *Topographical Poetry in Eighteenth-Century England* (New York, 1936), p. 9. See also Eleanor M. Sickels, *The Gloomy Egoist* (New York, 1932), especially pp. 125ff.
[27] Quoted in Aubin, *Topographical Poetry*, p. 55.
[28] Jose Ortega y Gasset, "On Point of View in the Arts," *Partisan Review*, XVI (1949), 827.

accepts it as such in Canto III) that will enable the poet to arrive at a kind of personal salvation in a world of nothingness and wandering.

What must interest us most, then, in the poem is the gradual evolution of the poet as a character and the progressive clarification and coherence of his vision, which becomes explicit rather than implicit. Taken together, these two movements constitute the process through which the poet can dispense with the mechanism of a narrator and construct at first hand what R. A. Foakes calls "a structural image . . . a framework integrating image and value-word, creating a system of symbols, and becoming the vehicle of the poem's final statement."[29] That final statement is ultimately as "modern" as Don Juan, but Byron had no wasteland tradition of disintegrated images, disjunctive history, and cacophonous sound to rely upon for expressing his despair. He wrote, as Lamartine shrewdly saw, "the only epic possible in our day,"[30] one whose dissonant organization Wylie Sypher might call mannerist,[31] one written, as G. Wilson Knight put it with typical élan, "from a vast eternity-consciousness to which historic events, as events, are the negative symbols of its expression."[32]

Since "the primary activity of all communication with the poet is to establish the unity of his poem in our minds . . .

---

[29] The Romantic Assertion (New Haven, Conn., 1958), pp. 49–50. Cf. Earl R. Wasserman, The Subtler Language (Baltimore, 1959), p. 186, and Georg Roppen and Richard Sommer, Strangers and Pilgrims ("Norwegian Studies in English," No. 11; New York, 1964), Preface, passim.

[30] "Vie de Byron," in Le Constitutionnel, III (September 26–December 6, 1865), 22. This life was taken largely from Teresa Guiccioli's account, which she sent to Lamartine in 1856. See Iris Origo's The Last Attachment (New York, 1949), pp. 418–20.

[31] Wylie Sypher, Four Stages of Renaissance Style (New York, 1955), especially pp. 145ff. See also Heinrich Wolfflin's analyses of sixteenth-century German art in Italien und das deutsche Formgefuhl (Munich, 1931).

[32] The Burning Oracle (London, 1939), p. 210.

a unity of words and a unity of images,"[33] let us attempt to see the interanimation of Byron's voices or characters or personae (or whatever) and the tentative, uncertain beginnings of his first great achievement in art.

II

At the outset it must be admitted that no clear and distinct pattern is to be found in *Childe Harold* I; if a pattern exists at all, as I think it does, it is there only in a kind of inchoate state, *in potentio*, waiting, so to speak, for Byron to become aware of it himself. That awareness grows slowly toward the end of Canto II and blossoms in the late prepublication additions Byron made to both cantos, some of which first appear in R. C. Dallas' late fair copy of the manuscript,[34] some not even there. Of these, the dedicatory verses "To Ianthe," the first stanza of Canto I, and the last stanzas of Canto II are most important, providing, as they do, a kind of deliberate thematic frame for the two cantos after the fact. That by themselves they do not succeed in imposing a pattern upon the otherwise erratic organization of the poem is not surprising; but their insistence upon the character of the poet and the gradual darkening of his attitude and point of view represent Byron's first major steps in his struggle to control his own poem. But we must begin at the chronological beginning, the present stanza ii of Canto I, where Byron himself began.

It is at least strange that for all the critical biographizing that has been inflicted upon *Childe Harold*, for all the

---

[33] Northrop Frye, *Fearful Symmetry*, p. 113. That Frye, writing here of Blake, would extend his point to *Childe Harold* is dubious. See his restrained introduction to Byron in G. B. Harrison (ed.), *Major British Writers* (enl. ed.; New York, 1959), II, 149–61.

[34] This is known as the Dallas transcript, now in the British Museum, made after Byron gave the manuscript of the first two cantos of *Childe Harold* to him immediately upon his return from the Mediterranean tour.

scholarly studies of the accuracy or inaccuracy of Harold's pilgrimage in relation to Byron's, no one has thought it odd to find John Cam Hobhouse, Byron's friend and traveling companion, missing from the poem.[35] Ignoring this breach of autobiographical truth, critics have gone on to insist upon the autobiographical elements in the portrait of Harold. I should like to suggest that Hobhouse is indeed very much there; or rather, that the character of the narrator was built out of the complex of attitudes, manner, and point of view that Byron saw continually in his companion. He met Hobhouse at Cambridge and soon grew to admire him and to have a good deal of affection for him. At the same time Hobhouse often acted, occasionally to Byron's irritation, as a kind of moral conscience for him. Marchand describes him accurately as "a tangible embodiment of British conscience and mores . . . despite his veneer of Cambridge sophistication," even a kind of "mirror to [Byron's] shortcomings."[36] Further, Hobhouse was an early advocate of the stoical virtues of the ancients as opposed to the laxity and corruption of modern man, and while at Cambridge he committed these ideas to paper, in an imitation of Juvenal's eleventh satire, which was to be published along with Byron's Popeian satire on all the living authors, British Bards.[37] Such a figure, embodying the conscience of man and responding to the world not only in terms of his knowledge and fondness for ancient Greece but also in terms of a British patriotism dimmed but not extinguished by modern social and political iniquities, was precisely what Byron needed to counter the unresponsiveness of Harold.

Thus both ostensible points of view, or masks, represented for Byron the limitations inherent in the particularity of their characters; and they in turn, especially the narrator, could

---

[35] Only Rutherford, so far as I know, remarks, in passing, upon Hobhouse's absence from the poem, but makes nothing of it (*Byron: A Critical Study*, p. 27).

[36] *Byron: A Biography*, I, 256.

[37] *Ibid.*, p. 140. They were not, of course, published together. Hobhouse's piece became the first poem in his *Imitations and Translations*, published in 1809 (*ibid.*, Notes, p. 14).

reveal through their own limitations the even more limited points of view of others whom they encountered on the pilgrimage. The problem remaining was how to keep these two sets of perceptions in proper perspective, how to control and pattern them. Essentially this was the structural problem Byron himself only gradually became aware of in Cantos I and II, and as such he solved it only sporadically in those cantos and more fully and surely in Canto III, where the voice of the directorial poet emerges as the major note of the poem. Even in Canto I, however, it can be heard if we are willing to bury our preconceptions about the poem and about Harold and forget, for the moment of poetic faith, that Lord Byron is its author.

Part of the distinction is established, perhaps by instinct, perhaps accidentally, but nonetheless firmly in the opening account of Childe Harold himself. The narrator's voice is distinct, clear, personal, and morally biased, indeed so much so that it is tempting to see, as J. D. Symon has, a certain "sardonic mock-solemnity" in Byron's ventriloquistic portraiture.[38] The personal presence of the narrator is immediately established by means of various interjections and phrases ("Oh, me," "it suits me not to say"), as well as by his role as storyteller: he makes guesses as to Harold's past, uses the formula " 'Tis said," speculates about Harold's state of mind with "as if" and "seemed" and "it may be," and flatly denies omniscience in phrases such as "this none knew" and "If friends he had." The moral bias of this voice shows no such tentativeness: Harold is "a shameless wight," "ungodly" (ii),[39] a "sad losel" (iii), one who had run "through Sin's long labyrinth" (v) without a thought for atonement; if his lineage were once great, this last remnant of it is no more significant than "any other fly" living out "his little day" (iv). Further, in notes comparable to Burns's melodramatic

---

[38] *Byron in Perspective* (London, 1924), p. 130. Symon's point, however, is that Byron's intent in *Childe Harold* I is often "burlesque," a "mock archaism," "a recrudescence of undergraduate idiocy."

[39] Quotations will be identified thus by stanza number throughout my analysis of *Childe Harold.*

moral apostrophes in "The Cotter's Saturday Night,"[40] the narrator compliments the one woman Harold loved for escaping his villainous clutches:

> *Ah, happy she! to 'scape from him whose kiss*
> *Had been pollution unto aught so chaste;*
> *Who soon had left her charms for vulgar bliss,*
> *And spoiled her goodly lands to gild his waste,*
> *Nor calm domestic peace had ever deigned to taste.*
>
> *(v)*

Even amid such condemnation, however, there is a certain feeling of sympathy for Harold's desire to flee his "fellow Bacchanals" (vi), for the "Strange pangs" that flashed along his brow (viii), for his deep and profound grief—

> *Ye, who have known what 'tis to dote upon*
> *A few dear objects, will in sadness feel*
> *Such partings break the heart they fondly*
> *hope to heal*
>
> *(x)*

—and for his being at least in part the victim of "flatterers" and "Parasites" (ix), money and women who "might shake the Saintship of an Anchorite" (xi). However sympathetic his tone, though, the narrator accepts the fact as a fact in all its circumscribed substantiality; no flowery rhyme can glaze over the truth to see something different or make of the facts something more[41]:

> *Nor florid prose, nor honied lies of rhyme,*
> *Can blazon evil deeds, or consecrate a crime.*
>
> *(iii)*

---

[40] Curiously, this poem, as hodgepodgy a medley of voices and confused intentions as *Childe Harold* is usually thought to be, is generally admired. For a skillful use of several voices for purposes similar to Byron's, see Burns's "Tam o'Shanter" and Allan H. MacLaine's excellent analysis of it ("Burns's Use of Parody in 'Tam O'Shanter,'" *Criticism*, I [1959], 308–16).

[41] Hobhouse's devotion to fact is well known. Many of his marginal

Childe Harold, Canto I

The portrait of Harold is overdone, overwritten, the moral condemnation repetitive and severe. Is it possible that Byron did this intentionally to accent the limitations of his narrator's vision? Perhaps; but if so we certainly need other evidence to show that the poet's vision is larger, perhaps more generous, certainly not limited to seeing Harold as merely one man. That evidence is scarce, if it is there at all, but I think it important that we consider these possibilities. Whatever Harold is morally or psychologically, he is the last of his line, a man alone, doomed to wander aimlessly, born uncorrupted but soon the corrupter as well as the corrupted, a pilgrim seeking no shrine but escape from a world in ruins, himself a kind of ruin amid ruins traversing the hell within his own heart. He is, or rather in Canto I gradually evolves into, Cain and Ahasuerus, and if he is also, as Thorslev thinks, an eighteenth-century child of nature plus Gothic villain plus gloomy egoist plus man of feeling,[42] he is Byron's adumbration of man the macrocosm as well as the narrator's microcosmic "fly." Perhaps this is why Byron quite deliberately echoes Coleridge's *The Ancient Mariner* early in the canto: that eternal wanderer, we recall, bears Cain's mark, the curse of mankind, destructive of life; but he is also a symbol redolent with Coleridge's sense of evil as a positive force in the world, with or without the agency of man's will, and the incarnation of man as eternal victim. Just as Harold is both right and wrong, or at least sympathetic as well as unsympathetic, so too the Mariner is an ambiguous figure. His "crime" is both an evil deed in its absolute irrationality and relatively bad (killing the bird "That made the breeze to blow"), as well as relatively good (killing the bird "That brought the fog

---

comments and queries on the manuscript of *Childe Harold* reflect this—e.g., his "t. b. [tres bien] but not true" next to stanza lv of Canto II. And, of course, he wrote his own account of the "pilgrimage," *A Journey through Albania, and Other Provinces of Turkey in Europe and Asia . . . during the Years 1809 and 1810* (London, 1813), as well as his *Historical Illustrations to the Fourth Canto of Childe Harold* (London, 1818).

[42] *The Byronic Hero, passim.*

and mist"). Certainly, though, however much Byron sympathized or did not sympathize with Coleridge's interpretation of the crime, he was fascinated by the nature of the Mariner's eternal punishment, death in life, a fate that Byron more and more saw to be all men's. Death thus becomes "a relief from pain," from "the God who punishes in this existence" but who *may* have "left that last asylum for the weary."[43]

Although Harold's wandering has some of the overtones of self-punishment (to "visit scorching climes beyond the sea" and even "seek the shades below" [vi]), Byron sees it clearly as a symbol of the human condition, amoral at its base and thus contrary to his narrator's more narrow, orthodox view. Childe Harold's "Good Night," like the farewells of *Hours of Idleness*, is particular in its detail yet general in its implications, focusing on the loss of native land and life, of "my mother Earth," of friend and lover. The indifferent sun will rise again, but only upon the ruins of the past:

> "*Deserted is my own good Hall,*
>   *Its hearth is desolate;*
> *Wild weeds are gathering on the wall;*
>   *My Dog howls at the gate.*"[44]

What is left is a world with no love, no home, no land, no God, a wasteland of ocean, deserts, caves, comparable to that of Coleridge's Mariner:

---

[43] Ltr. to Hodgson, 3 Sept. 1811, in *LJ*, II, 21. In his *Detached Thoughts* Byron also sees "*material* resurrection" as an abominable continuation of God's punishment and revenge (*LJ*, V, 457). For further comments on Coleridge's possible influence on Byron, see Edwin M. Everett, "Lord Byron's Lakist Interlude," *SP*, LV (1958), 62–75. On Byron's sense of evil, see Edward E. Bostetter, *The Romantic Ventriloquists*, pp. 254ff.

[44] The significance of the dog image here is intensified by Byron's earlier hymn to the only "Friend" he had, his dog Boatswain, who died in 1808. See "Inscription on the Monument of a Newfoundland Dog," first published in Hobhouse's *Imitations and Translations* (1809). On his death, Byron commented to Hodgson, "I have now lost everything except old Murray" (his servant) (*P*, I, 280n).

Childe Harold, Canto I

> *"And now I'm in the world alone,*
>   *Upon the wide, wide sea:*
> *But why should I for others groan,*
>   *When none will sigh for me?*
> *Perchance my Dog will whine in vain,*
>   *Till fed by stranger hands;*
> *But long ere I come back again,*
>   *He'd tear me where he stands."*

The voice is Harold's, the lament for the lost past Byron's.

The narrator, of course, sees more than the figure of Harold, and his reactions to and reflections upon these scenes strengthen both our sense of his provincial orthodoxy and the growing total vision of a wastelandish world instinct with a sense of lost paradise. To the narrator Portugal, and particularly Cintra, is a goodly sight, stirring in him the accents of Coleridge's Mariner:

> *Oh, Christ! it is a goodly sight to see*
> *What Heaven hath done for this delicious land!*
>   *(xv)*

But true to his orthodox Christian bias and to his focus upon fact, the narrator raises his voice in a traditional curse against "impious" man who would mar this pleasant prospect:

> *And when the Almighty lifts his fiercest scourge*
> *'Gainst those who most transgress his high*
>   *command,*
> *With treble vengeance will his hot shafts urge*
> *Gaul's locust host, and earth from fellest foemen*
>   *purge.*
>   *(xv)*

Further, his historical eye sees only the particularity of the scene, "A nation swoln with ignorance and pride" (xvi), a town where "hut and palace show like filthily," a people "dingy" and unclean (xvii). Similarly, Cintra is "glorious," the very epitome of the romantic sublime (xviii), but it is spoiled by the fact that the Convention of Cintra was held there, at which the narrator lashes out savagely in unrestrained satire (xxiv–xxvi).

At the same time that this voice alternately pleases and assails our ears with its exclamations over the beauties or horrors of place and time, we should hear also the clear note of another, calmer voice, that of the poet, whose "lies" the narrator continues to condemn:

> Poor, paltry slaves! yet born 'midst noblest scenes—
> Why, Nature, waste thy wonders on such men?
> Lo! Cintra's glorious Eden intervenes
> In variegated maze of mount and glen.
> Ah, me! what hand can pencil guide, or pen,
> To follow half on which the eye dilates
> Through views more dazzling unto mortal ken
> Than those whereof such things the Bard relates,
> Who to the awe-struck world unlocked
> Elysium's gates.
>
> (xviii)

The extraordinary change from stanza xvii in accent, tone, and diction can hardly be missed—though it can be and has been ignored. The transition from the narrator's minutely detailed picture of the unwashed Portuguese to the softer, more sympathetic, and more universal "Poor, paltry slaves!" is neatly made. The scene shifts, almost imperceptibly, from the glorious beauty of "this delicious land" to the transformation of Cintra into an explicit metaphor of an Eden surpassing even Milton's, from the truth of the narrator's fact to the truth of the poet's vision, a vision so dazzling that his pen is unequal to the task of its description.[45]

The passage continues on for several stanzas, hesitating uncertainly between the two voices until they part over the treatment of Beckford in stanza xxii. For the poet, the author of *Vathek*, secluded from the world, formed his own "Paradise" which now but lingers in "ruined Splendour"; for the narrator, he is an example of the corruption of "wanton Wealth." Yet

---

[45] It is interesting to note that Byron's prose version of this description, in a letter to his mother of 11 Aug. 1809 (*LJ*, I, 236–37), stresses only the beauty of the scene, mentioning the Convention only casually and *en passant*.

even in the treatment of Beckford, we can see illustrated R. A. Foakes's point about disjunctive modern poetry, in which "an episode or story, the whole poem itself, may be a kind of extended subject matter or vehicle, in which the physical events and the landscape portrayed relate to the spiritual state of the hero, or to the state of mankind, or to some aspect of human existence and its problems, only the poet has omitted the connective 'Such seems the human state on earth . . . ,' or whatever it may be, and has left us to make it for ourselves."[46] To the narrator Beckford's individualistic corruption is all; to the poet he is at once an element in the pattern of his total vision and an epitome of that vision of paradise lost, the "fairy dwelling" empty of love, where "giant weeds a passage scarce allow / To Halls deserted, portals gaping wide" (xxiii) and where the specter of Harold and his vacant heritage superimposes itself on Beckford and all "unblest" men. For Harold himself, his vision blunted by his own loss as well as his "satiety," the scene has been merely "A scene of peace" (xxviii) from which he flees just as, in "Mad Song," Blake's frantic madman perpetually flees the light in quest of the comfort of darkness.

The section on Spain following this yields another aspect of the narrator's point of view, his habitual look back at a noble but bloody and warlike past in contrast to a bloody but somehow ignoble present: "Oh, lovely Spain," he cries, after a passing glance at Paynim and Christian crests mixed on Guadiana's "bleeding stream,"

> *Where are those bloody Banners which of yore*
> *Waved o'er thy sons, victorious to the gale,*
> *And drove at last the spoilers to their shore?*
> *Red gleamed the Cross, and waned the Crescent*
> *pale,*
> *While Afric's echoes thrilled with Moorish*
> *matron's wail.*
> *(xxxv)*

After this crimson hymn to "noble" bloodshed, he goes on to

---

[46] *The Romantic Assertion*, p. 35.

condemn the folly of ambition that precipitated the Napoleonic wars, and in a series of brilliantly ironic stanzas castigates the monumental irrationality of mutual slaughter in which havoc and the grave are the only rewards. For the narrator "Red Battle" stamping his foot and shattering nations (xxxviii) is the reality, not the romantic tales told by rhyming liars, the glory that shines "in worthless lays, the theme of transient song" (xliii). But it is still a local reality, a fact of current history, that he speaks of; and the poet, whom he misjudges, sees all, both past and present, as the external, tragic struggle for survival that characterizes the human condition, perverts love and beauty, and leaves both the dream and the reality of Eden in shattered ruins. Even amid the call of the narrator to the "Sons of Spain" to awake and advance upon their oppressors as their chivalric ancestors did (xxxvii), the poet sees defeat in the

> Inevitable hour! 'Gainst fate to strive
> Where Desolation plants her famished brood
> Is vain, or Ilion, Tyre might yet survive,
> And Virtue vanquish all, and Murder cease to thrive.
>   (xlv)

But man is "all unconscious of the coming doom" (xlvi), the "hoarse dull drum" that does not sleep and keeps man from happiness and rest (xlvii).

The reasonable man, whose view the narrator articulates, protests the illogic of it all:

> And must they fall? the young, the proud, the brave,
>   To swell one bloated Chief's unwholesome reign?
>   No step between submission and a grave?
>   The rise of Rapine and the fall of Spain?
>   And doth the Power that man adores ordain
>   Their doom, nor heed the suppliant's appeal?
>   Is all that desperate Valour acts in vain?
>   And Counsel sage, and patriotic Zeal—
> The Veteran's skill—Youth's fire—and Manhood's
>   heart of steel?
>   (liii)

The poet's answer is voiced in the rhetorical nature of the question: for "this" maids are unsexed, art discarded, marriage a perverted union with a weapon, love and beauty and peace lost (liv). The narrator's factual account of the Maid of Saragoza is thus translated by the poet into a parable of the loss of paradise (lix).

Perhaps it is no accident, then, that this section is followed by the poet's hymn to Parnassus, which is out of the chronological and spatial order of the narrative—Parnassus, that eternal symbol of "man's divinest lore" and of a time when men were gods and gods men, when all pilgrimages began and ended there (lx–lxii). But with all the sense of the contrast between the world of Parnassus and the modern world that he has shown us thus far in *Childe Harold,* and will continue to show us with greater and greater intensity, the poet is painfully aware that the mountain is but the splendid ruin of another kind of paradise. Its very reality, which he insists upon—

> *whom I now survey,*
> *Not in the phrensy of a dreamer's eye,*
> *Not in the fabled landscape of a lay,*
> *But soaring snow-clad through thy native sky,*
> *In the wild pomp of mountain-majesty!*
>
> *(lx)*

—mocks modern man's dream of attaining its heights. Not only does the Muse no longer wave her wing from its eminence and Apollo no longer "haunt his grot," but the poet sadly accepts himself as representative of fallen, finite man, trembling merely to "look on Thee" and not daring "vainly . . . to soar." The Muses' seat is now their grave, the mountain a living monument to a dead past, just as the poet, Harold-like, is the last of his line and modern man's heart his own sepulcher. The vision is a grim one, even amidst this archetypal paradise of art; perhaps we are to see the one boon the poet-votary seeks, "one leaf of Daphne's deathless plant," as *Childe Harold's Pilgrimage,* the final vision or fable of man's final degradation and defeat.

The Parnassus passage is also a fine example of

Byron's public-private voice enunciating in clear accents his essential and serious concern for his own poetry, as well as for the particular poem at hand: "Ev'n amidst my strain," he writes,

> I turned aside to pay my homage here;
> Forgot the land, the sons, the maids of Spain;
> Her fate, to every freeborn bosom dear;
> And hailed thee, not perchance without a tear.
>
> (lxiii)

But the pull of the narrative turns him aside, just as Parnassus turned him aside from the narrative; or, to put it in terms of the voices I have been trying to isolate and identify, the narrator is anxious to press on with Harold and the particulars of the pilgrimage while the poet is forcibly detained by the vision of Parnassus and the more universal thoughts it has inspired. Thus the above passage continues:

> Now to my theme—but from thy holy haunt
> Let me some remnant, some memorial bear;
> Yield me one leaf of Daphne's deathless plant,
> Nor let thy Votary's hope be deemed an idle vaunt.

Precisely the same opposition exists in Byron's 1821 diary:

> Upon Parnassus, going to the fountain of Delphi (Castri) in 1809, I saw a flight of twelve eagles (Hobhouse said they were vultures—at least in conversation), and I seized the omen. On the day before, I composed the lines to Parnassus [in *Childe Harold* I], and, on beholding the birds, had a hope that Apollo had accepted my homage. I have, at least, had the name and fame of a poet during the poetical period of life (from twenty to thirty). Whether it will last is another matter; but I have been a votary of the deity and the place, and am grateful for what he has done in my behalf, leaving the future in his hands, as I left the past.[47]

After the Parnassus section, the shift back to the narrator (to whom a vision of eagles is always more correctly

---

[47] *P*, II, 61n.

seen as a flight of vultures), in the stanzas on Seville and Cadiz is properly abrupt: fair, too, is "proud Seville," but it is also the seat of vice, neither Parnassian nor Delphian but rather Paphian, the new shrine of Venus's reveling hordes (lxv–lxvi). The perversion of the imagery used to describe Parnassus thus provides the poet's thematic transition, as does the third juxtaposition in the canto of "Love and Prayer" united in nights of riot and debauchery.[48] Unaware of and unconcerned with such connectives, the narrator launches into an ironic moral condemnation of both English and Spanish Sundays, in which "All have their fooleries," equally corrupt (lxviii–lxxi). It is in this section that the famous bullfight stanzas appear. However accurate they are (and they are indeed well done), however concrete the narrator's particulars, I think we must also see the sequence as a parable not only of man's blood lust and vanity, his perversion of the springs of love and gentleness, but of the game of life in which even the bravest bulls are slaughtered to the cheers of a corrupt and vicious public. Although the narrator declines to see any resemblance between this and an English Sunday ("not alike are thine, / Fair Cadiz"), the poet does see the interrelatedness of the total scene—the hypocrisy of prayers to the Virgin before attending the bullfight (lxxi) and the mock war of love among the spectators (lxxii), which precisely parallels "the worship of the solemn Horn, / Grasp'd in the holy hand of Mystery," the sacred vulgar rite of cuckoldry in England (lxx). The same corruption sits in both societies, and in each it is finally love, the human heart, that is its victim.

It is right, then, for the poet to turn again to his narrator's Harold to close the canto. For in the past Harold had loved, "Or dreamed he loved, since Rapture is a dream" (lxxxii). And even "from the fount of Joy's delicious springs / Some bitter o'er the flowers its bubbling venom flings." Now no longer is love a part of his life; without it, and suffering the miseries

---

[48] Stanza lxvii. The first such juxtaposition was in the passage on Harold's ancestral home (vii), the second in the description of Mafra (xxix).

of vice and pleasure, he abhors life and wanders in "Cain's unresting doom" (lxxxiii). His love song, "To Inez," is perhaps the only love song possible in such a world, one of

> *that settled, ceaseless gloom*
> *The fabled Hebrew Wanderer bore;*
> *That will not look beyond the tomb,*
> *But cannot hope for rest before.*
>
> *What Exile from himself can flee?*
> *To zones though more and more remote,*
> *Still, still pursues, where'er I be,*
> *The blight of Life—the Demon Thought.*

Others may "still of transport dream," of a world of loveliness and peace, of a heart still pure and whole, of a love eternal in a garden of bliss; but the way of the world will out, its force will triumph, and man will awake—to a vision of ruins without and within ("Man's heart, and . . . the Hell that's there").

Byron's decision to replace his earlier "The Girl of Cadiz" lyric with this one was as precisely right as his last-minute decisions on the close of the canto are confusing.[49] In his final words on Spain the narrator laments again its fall and the future waste of more brave men as Napoleon pours fresh legions "adown the Pyrenees" (lxxxix). "Nor mortal eye the distant end foresees" bespeaks perhaps both the narrator's time-bound vision and that note of utter despair sounded with increasing consistency by the poet. But only perhaps. The personal lament of the poet (not the narrator) in stanzas xci and xcii (both appearing for the first time in the Dallas transcript) is also troublesome, a final example of Byron's unclear notion of what he was really about in the poem. Yet at the same time, from the point of view of the complete work, those stanzas are

---

[49] "To Inez" was written in January, 1810, after Byron arrived in Greece and well after he had begun Canto II. "The Girl of Cadiz" was gaily and youthfully cynical about British women and raffishly complimentary to Spanish women (see *P*, III, 1–3). For Byron's difficulties in deciding how to end the canto, see Coleridge's notes in *P*, II, 80–83.

important in further distinguishing the poet's voice from the narrator's (or Harold's),[50] and as the first distinct step, along with the Parnassus passage, in Byron's gradual recognition that the poet's voice is the main one in the poem and that he, not Harold, is the most telling symbol of modern man's sense of loss and his valiant struggle against the tyranny of that sense. In contrast to the at least ostensibly understandable deaths of the warrior in battle, Wingate (the "friend" of stanza xci) "descend[s] in vain," "unlaurel'd" and forgotten in the world's more spectacular melees. It is a senseless, meaningless death, and provokes the poet not to renewed dreams of a paradise where death is not, nor to a future utopia where all is peace, but rather to a vision of the final repose of death, the only boon left to man by a punishing god: "And mourned and mourner lie united in repose" (xcii).

The canto, then, as I have said, is erratic, uncertain, hesitant, with no real center or focus. Yet, as a workshop, as work in progress, it is a distinctive, edifying, and even on occasion fascinating document in any attempt to see Byron the poet at work. A greater sense of self-assuredness, of purposeful manipulation of his three main voices can be logically expected in Canto II, to which we must now turn not with the expectation of emerging from the woods into a sunlit path but at least with the assurance of finding an increasing number of signs pointing the general direction.

---

[50] This distinction is even sharper in the manuscript, where the first two lines of stanza xci juxtapose the poet's "selfish woe" (what I have called his public-private voice, his essential self) and the "lightness" of his "strain" (i.e., the narrator's narrative).

Chapter III

CHILDE HAROLD'S PILGRIMAGE, CANTO II

The manuscript of Canto II of *Childe Harold* was completed, except for a number of late changes and additions, less than five months after Canto I was begun. The time element is important, I think, for it tends to support the theory of some total conception, however inchoate, out of which the two cantos finally emerged. With some hints as to the nature of that total conception discernible in Canto I, especially the growing importance of the poet figure, we should not be surprised to find Canto II opening on that note, with ten important stanzas signaling at least the passing thought in Byron's mind that he might slowly absorb all voices in the poem into that of the poet.[1] At this point, however, it would be folly to press the conjecture, for the poet appears here initially as we have seen him in Canto I.

It is perhaps logical that, after invoking Parnassus as symbolic of the creative mind, as well as of a paradisaical world long lost, at the beginning of Canto II the poet should invoke Athena, the goddess of wisdom, as his Muse; for he will tell no fairy tales nor gloss over reality but, seeing the world in all its factuality and truth, he will present us finally with the totality of its truth, the vision of the wise.[2] In a sense, I suppose, this is "anti-romantic" in its implied antipathy to imagination and

---

[1] See Coleridge's most interesting analysis of these opening stanzas (*P*, II, 99–100n).
[2] For Byron's earlier use of Athena (or Minerva) for essentially the same purposes, see *The Curse of Minerva*, and my analysis of that poem above, pp. 32–37.

dream. The point, however, is not that imaginative vision and conceptions are mere frauds, but rather that in a world where even Parnassus and the Parthenon lie in crumbling ruins, however magnificent, the viability of dream and imagination is a contradiction in terms. The poet is well aware that Athena, in her masculine firmness, her lack of softness and grace, is no Muse—"but Thou, alas! / Didst never yet one mortal song inspire" (i)—and yet her temple of the mind, in its ultimate potentiality (as in its past) and in its present emptiness and desolation, serves as a proper symbol of the final ruin that is the only valid inspiration in the modern world to the poet of such a world. Unlike man, the poet does feel "the sacred glow," urging him to create, if only to create the panorama of ruins that the uninspired cause. In a sense, the poet is the last of a line, for Athena's "grand in soul" are "Gone—glimmering through the dream of things that were" (ii) or, as Byron first wrote, "mingled with the waste of things that were."[3] The waste is the waste of dreams, or, better, so terrible is the waste of what once was that only the fragility and impossibility of dreams can epitomize what has been lost. "Even Gods must yield," the poet says, and little man is but the "Poor child of Doubt and Death, whose hope is built on reeds" (iii). "Unhappy Thing" though he is, his lifting of his eyes to heaven in vain longing for a better—or at least another—life ensures but greater unhappiness and sorrow.[4] For the age is not an age of gods, or even demigods; it is an age of dust and death and vanished hopes, an age brilliantly symbolized by the poet in his juxtaposition of the ruined shrines of the Greek gods, the conglomerate of ruins that he calls "a Nation's sepulchre," with the "defenceless" burial urn and the skull (iii–v). The equation is an extraordinary one, for the elements of each part serve admirably to fortify and amplify the elements

---

[3] P, II, 100n.
[4] For a contrary interpretation of Byron's view of man's aspirations and defeats, see E. D. Hirsch's very interesting essay, "Byron and the Terrestrial Paradise," in F. W. Hilles and H. Bloom (eds.), From Sensibility to Romanticism (New York, 1965), pp. 467–86.

of the other parts. The hymn to the skull, then, is the beginning
of the poet's wisdom—a truth he must now learn to live with—
an eloquent elegy for the death of man, nation, gods, the world:

> *Remove yon skull from out the scattered heaps:*
> *Is that a Temple where a God may dwell?*
> *Why ev'n the Worm at last disdains her shattered cell!*

> *Look on its broken arch, its ruined wall,*
> *Its chambers desolate, and portals foul:*
> *Yes, this was once Ambition's airy hall,*
> *The Dome of Thought, the Palace of the Soul:*
> *Behold through each lack-lustre, eyeless hole,*
> *The gay recess of Wisdom and of Wit*
> *And Passion's host, that never brooked control:*
> *Can all Saint, Sage, or Sophist ever writ,*
> *People this lonely tower, this tenement refit?*

> *Well didst thou speak, Athena's wisest son!*
> *"All that we know is, nothing can be known."*
> *Why should we shrink from what we cannot shun?*
> *Each hath its pang, but feeble sufferers groan*
> *With brain-born dreams of Evil all their own.*
> *Pursue what Chance or Fate proclaimeth best;*
> *Peace waits us on the shores of Acheron:*
> *There no forced banquet claims the sated guest,*
> *But Silence spreads the couch of ever welcome Rest.*
>   *(v–vii)*

Into the vortex of this grim vision, by virtue of the imagery,
are swept Harold's desolate hall, his exile from his native land,
Beckford's "paradise," and the many historical scenes of Canto
I, as well as deserted Parnassus. It is indeed fact on its way
toward myth as it is filtered through the imagination of the
poet.[5]

In the face of this reality, to dream, to imagine para-

---

[5] Of all the Byron critics, only Charles du Bos (aside from Ridenour's
more recent and different point of view) emphasizes this myth-
making faculty. See *Byron and the Need of Fatality,* pp. 159ff.

dise regained or immortality won, friendship renewed and love reborn, wisdom recrowned, is obviously sweet:

> *How sweet it were in concert to adore*
> *With those who made our mortal labours light!*
> *To hear each voice we feared to hear no more!*
> *Behold each mighty shade revealed to sight,*
> *The Bactrian* [Zoroaster], *Samian sage* [Pythagoras],
> *and all who taught the Right!*
> *(viii)*

But in a world where, clearly, whatever is, is not right,[6] to maintain his sanity the poet can live only with a vision of the possible. Thus, in a stanza in the manuscript unfortunately canceled (probably for its too outspoken skepticism[7]), the poet writes:

> *Frown not upon me, churlish Priest! that I*
> *[Dream not of] Look not for Life, where life*
> *may never be:*
> *I am no sneerer at thy phantasy;*
> *Thou pitiest me, alas! I envy thee,*
> *Thou bold Discoverer in an unknown sea*
> *Of happy Isles and happier Tenants there;*
> *I ask thee not to prove a Sadducee;*

---

[6] Of particular interest here, as well as in connection with what I have to say of Shelley's *Queen Mab* later in this chapter, is Ruskin's grouping of Byron, Rousseau, Shelley, Turner and himself, in all of whom "glows the volcanic instinct of Astraean justice . . . which will not at all suffer us to rest any more in Pope's serene 'whatever is, is right'; but holds, on the contrary, profound conviction that about ninety-nine hundredths of whatever at present is, is wrong . . ." (*Works*, ed. E. T. Cook and Alexander Wedderburn [London, 1908], XXXIV, 343).

[7] As Coleridge points out, the deleted stanza "carried the Lucretian tenets of the preceding stanza to their logical conclusion. The end is silence not a reunion with superior souls." Coleridge then goes on to say, perhaps in agreement with Dallas' objection to these sentiments, that "stanza for stanza, the new version is an improvement on the original" (*P*, II, 103–4n). For other examples of Byron's early convictions on religion, see ltr. to Long, 16 Apr. 1807, in *LJ*, II, 19n; ltrs. to Hodgson, 3 and 13 Sept. 1811, in *LJ*, II, 18–23, 34–36.

Childe Harold, Canto II

> *Still dream of Paradise, thou know'st not where,*
> *Which if it be thy Sins will never let thee share.*[8]

Envious of that dream, yet aware that it gives "erring" man no comfort, and certainly aware of his own dream of a lost paradise, the poet must still be wise, stoical, calm—an attitude neatly conveyed in the more personal intimacy of individual loss:

> *There, Thou!—whose Love and Life together fled,*
> *Have left me here to love and live in vain—*
> *Twined with my heart, and can I deem thee dead*
> *When busy Memory flashes on my brain?*
> *Well—I will dream that we may meet again,*
> *And woo the vision to my vacant breast.*[9]
>
> (ix)

The "dream," then, is not really that of the "churlish Priest"—"Of happy Isles and happier Tenants there," a "Paradise, thou know'st not where"—but rather one of love and life entwined in the human heart. Enshrined in the human mind as well, their memory tortures the heart with an ever-present vision of what was lost; and the mind, in turn, steels the heart against further loss. Byron cannot, then, agree with Shelley that one of "the spells by which to re-assume / An empire o'er the disentangled doom" is "to hope till Hope creates / From its own wreck the thing it contemplates."[10] For Byron neither man's will

---

[8] *P*, II, 103–5n. Bracketed material in italics represents Byron's manuscript deletions.

[9] It is significant that this stanza is a late addition. Byron sent it to Dallas on October 14, 1811, for inclusion in the canto. It clearly refers to Edleston's death, about which he had just heard from Edleston's sister. See ltrs. to Dallas, 11 and 14 Oct. 1811, in *LJ*, II, 52–57 and 58, and ltr. to Hodgson, Oct. 1811, in Marchand, *Byron: A Biography*, I, 108. The stanza should thus be read in the context of the other "Thyrza" poems as well as of *Childe Harold*.

[10] *Prometheus Unbound*, IV, 568–69, 573–74. In his diary of 1821 Byron wrote of hope (*LJ*, V, 190):

> and *what Hope* is there without a deep leaven of Fear? and what sensation is so delightful as Hope? and, if it were not for Hope,

nor his imagination have that power. It remains only for the poet to "trace"

> *The latent grandeur of thy* [Jupiter's] *dwelling-place.*
> *It may not be: nor ev'n can Fancy's eye*
> *Restore what Time hath laboured to deface.*
>
> (x)

What is left in a world where "It may not be"? To stand, as the "proud Pillars" of the ruins do, a ruin amid ruins, aware of the irrevocability of loss, yet fortified by the unconquerable mind to die, at least, like a man. Before Byron can fully formulate this idea—a formulation he came to see as involving additional loss —he had to explore its many ramifications in the tales and their heroes as he built toward *Manfred*.

The next set of stanzas is monopolized, with one exception (stanza xv), by the narrator, and the effect of the reversal of the order of speakers in Canto I should not be overlooked. Whereas there we begin with the facts of the narration, with history, which is later guided toward mythologization by the poet's voice, here in Canto II the initial dominance of the poet and his pervading despair tends to further narrow the dimensions and ultimate significance of the narrator's vision. Stanzas xi–xv thus repeat, but in more restrictive terms, the earlier condemnation of Lord Elgin's "plunders." As in *The Curse of Minerva*, the narrator seems more impressed with the

---

where would the Future be?—in hell. It is useless to say *where* the Present is, for most of us know; and as for the Past, *what* predominates in memory?—*Hope baffled.* Ergo, in all human affairs, it is Hope—Hope—Hope. I allow sixteen minutes, though I never counted them, to any given or supposed possession. From whatever place we commence, we know where it all must end.

Cf. ltr. to Moore, 28 Oct. 1815: "What is Hope? nothing but the paint on the face of Existence; the least touch of Truth rubs it off, and then we see what a hollow-cheeked harlot we have got hold of" (*LJ*, III, 232). E. D. Hirsch, in the essay referred to in n. 4 above, quotes only a small portion of the first of these passages and ignores the second in his efforts to establish Byron's consistent and unshakable faith "in the *possibility* of an earthly perfection" (pp. 472–73).

fact that Elgin was not an Englishman than with his despoliation of the Grecian monuments: England, "the Ocean Queen, the free Britannia," shall never be accused of being "happy in Athena's tears" (xiii). As if deliberately intending to dramatize the contrast between this near-chauvinistic satire and his other voice, Byron then has his poet fix the blame in stanza xv on "British hands," although the emphasis of the stanza is upon the heartfelt grief of a lover's loss:

> *Cold is the heart, fair Greece! that looks on Thee,*
> *Nor feels as Lovers o'er the dust they loved;*
> *Dull is the eye that will not weep to see*
> *Thy walls defaced, thy mouldering shrines removed.*

Immediately following these lines Harold is rather rudely re-inserted into the poem, for the first time in the canto. Yet thematically it seems to me right, however abrupt, for, in contrast to both the poet and the narrator, Harold "Little recked . . . of all that Men regret" (xvi). Lost, wandering, with a heart inured against the causes of grief, he remains properly stationary and in a sense dimensionless, Byron's symbol of defeated man with no resource left other than the obduracy of his hardened heart and invulnerable mind.

After the straight, matter-of-fact narration and shipboard description of stanzas xvii–xxii that inaugurate the renewal of Harold's travelogue, the poet's voice once again takes over, the transition accomplished neatly in stanza xxii. This particular transition is typical of Byron's growing consciousness of his two voices, for it involves a shift in mid-stanza from a focus on space and time (the narrative or Harold or history) to an emphasis on mood. The physical vigor of the narrator's story-telling, which requires for continuity that (in xvi) he "urge" Harold "o'er the wave" (the verb is properly forcible), softens to the poet's tones, here especially evident in the almost excessive hushing of consonants and deep-toned vowels:

> *How softly on the Spanish shore she* [the moon]
> *plays!*
> *Disclosing rock, and slope, and forest brown,*

BYRON AND THE RUINS OF PARADISE

> Distinct, though darkening with her waning phase;
> But Mauritania's giant-shadows frown,
> From mountain-cliff to coast descending sombre down.

The meditation this precipitates leaves the fact of Harold's presence and the geographical reality of the Straits of Gibraltar in the shadows, while it cautiously builds Harold's wandering, the ship's track, and the mood into the mythical journey of man.[11] To accent this the poet deliberately uses the first person plural, or "the soul," or "man."

> 'Tis night, when Meditation bids us feel
> We once have loved, though Love is at an end:
> The Heart, lone mourner of its baffled zeal,
> Though friendless now, will dream it had a friend.
> Who with the weight of years would wish to bend,
> When Youth itself survives young Love and Joy?
> Alas! when mingling souls forget to blend,
> Death hath but little left him to destroy!
> Ah! happy years! once more who would not be a
>   boy?[12]

> Thus bending o'er the vessel's laving side,
> To gaze on Dian's wave-reflected sphere,
> The Soul forgets her [dreams] schemes of Hope
>   and Pride,
> And flies unconscious o'er each backward year;
> None are so desolate but something dear,
> Dearer than self, possesses or possessed
> A thought, and claims the homage of a tear;
> A flashing pang! of which the weary breast
> Would still, albeit in vain, the heavy heart divest.

---

[11] For instructive comments on this metaphor of the journey, with particular reference to Byron, see Karl Kroeber, *Romantic Narrative Art* (Madison, Wis., 1960), especially pp. 77–140; Georg Roppen and Richard Sommer, *Strangers and Pilgrims*, Preface and pp. 209–81; and R. A. Foakes, *The Romantic Assertion*, pp. 58ff.

[12] This echo of various poems in *Hours of Idleness* should not be overlooked. W. J. Courthope's suggestion that "Childish Recollections" is an early study for *Childe Harold* deserves more serious consideration than it has received (*A History of English Poetry* [London, 1910], VI, 256).

Childe Harold, Canto II

To sit on rocks—to muse o'er flood and fell—
   To slowly trace the forest's shady scene,
   Where things that own not Man's dominion dwell,
   And mortal foot hath ne'er or rarely been;
   To climb the trackless mountain all unseen,
   With the wild flock that never needs a fold;
   Alone o'er steeps and foaming falls to lean;
   This is not Solitude—'tis but to hold
Converse with Nature's charms, and view her stores
                                        unrolled.[13]

But midst the crowd, the hum, the shock of men,
   To hear, to see, to feel, and to possess,
   And roam along, the World's tired denizen,
   With none who bless us, none whom we can bless;
   Minions of Splendour shrinking from distress!
   None that, with kindred consciousness endued,
   If we were not, would seem to smile the less,
   Of all that flattered—followed—sought, and sued;
This is to be alone—This, This is Solitude!

More blest the life of godly Eremite,
   Such as on lonely Athos may be seen,
   Watching at eve upon the Giant Height,
   Which looks o'er waves so blue, skies so serene,
   That he who there at such an hour hath been
   Will wistful linger on that hallowed spot;
   Then slowly tear him from the 'witching scene,
   Sigh forth one wish that such had been his lot,
Then turn to hate a world he had almost forgot.[14]

Pass we the long unvarying course, the track
   Oft trod, that never leaves a trace behind;[15]
   Pass we the calm—the gale—the change—the tack,
   And each well known caprice of wave and wind;

---

[13] Above this stanza in the Dallas transcript, Hobhouse, true to the nature of the narrator of *Childe Harold*, wrote: "T. t. b. [*tres tres bien*], but why insert here" (*P*, II, 115n).

[14] This stanza was not included in the canto until the seventh edition, published in 1814. Byron alludes to the idea of the hermit in Canto I as well, in his note to stanza xx (*P*, II, 85–86).

[15] Cf. Byron's important modulation of this image in Canto III, stanza iii, and my analysis of it below, pp. 23–32.

Pass we the joys and sorrows sailors find,
Cooped in their wingéd sea-girt citadel;
The foul—the fair—the contrary—the kind—
As breezes rise and fall and billows swell,
Till on some jocund morn—lo, Land! and All is well![16]

(*xxiii–xxviii*)

The smooth return to the narrator in this last stanza is clear; for the poet there is no "jocund morn," no "Land." Nature is finally not satisfying:[17] in its indifferent glory and peace it often remains a mockery of the ruins of a world man must rejoin if he will live. The return is also another indication of Byron's growing ability to shift his focus with precision while maintaining a continuity of theme and universal point of view or attitude; with Eliot-like aptness he, through his narrator, introduces Harold's "love affair" with Florence against the background of the heroic loves of Ulysses-Calypso-Telemachus (xxix–xxxiv). Unlike these lovers of a brighter time, Harold is marble-hearted, incapable of love, unmoved (Byron, incidentally, contrary to G. Wilson Knight's assertion that his affair with Mrs. Spencer-Smith was "purely platonic," was neither unmoved nor incapable[18]). Indeed, so false is love in the modern world that because of it youth is "wasted—Minds degraded—Honour lost,"

---

[16] The anticipation in this entire passage of the Shelleyan-Wordsworthian stanzas in Canto III should be noted. See James Darmesteter (ed.), *Childe Harold's Pilgrimage* (Paris, 1882), and Coleridge's note in *P*, II, 115.

[17] On Byron's fundamentally non-Wordsworthian view of nature, see Ernest J. Lovell, *Byron: The Record of a Quest, passim.*

[18] *Lord Byron's Marriage: The Evidence of Asterisks* (London, 1957), p. 11. Byron wrote several other poems to Mrs. Spencer-Smith: "Lines Written in an Album, at Malta," "To Florence," "Stanzas Composed during a Thunderstorm," "Stanzas Written in Passing the Ambracian Gulf," and "The Spell Is Broke, the Charm Is Flown!," all written between September, 1809, and January, 1810. In the last of these Byron's habit of universalizing an individual loss of love is most clear:

> *The spell is broke, the charm is flown!*
> *Thus is it with Life's fitful fever:*
> *We madly smile when we should groan;*

Shakespeare's "expense of spirit in a waste of shame," as Paul Elmer More aptly suggests.[19]

This section closes with a revealing stanza by the poet (xxxvi), in which his all-inclusive role of director, participant, observer, controller, and philosophizer and his growing absorption of both Harold and the narrator into himself are articulated for the first time. "Away!" he begins, in the accents of his narrator, urging Harold to new scenes; but he concludes the line with a reference to himself and his poem: "nor let me loiter in my song,"

> For we [emphasis added] *have many a mountain-path*
> *to tread,*
> *And many a varied shore to sail along,*

guided not by Harold, by chronology, or by geography, but "By pensive Sadness":

> *Climes, fair withal as ever mortal head*
> *Imagined in its little schemes of thought;*
> *Or e'er in new Utopias were ared,*
> *To teach Man what he might be, or he ought—*
> *If that corrupted thing could ever such be taught.*
> *(xxxvi)*

The purpose of the poem, then, is clearly not to moralize or correct, but rather to project the panoramic vision of the world and the human condition that we have seen slowly taking shape in these first two cantos. Stanza xxxvi is significant in still another way, I think, for the last line reinforces what was said above about the early satires: the satiric poems proceed not from the hope of redemption or correction or betterment, but

---

> *Delirium is our best deceiver.*
> *Each lucid interval of thought*
> *Recalls the woes of Nature's charter.*   *(P, III, 12)*

It is this increasingly consistent universalization in *Childe Harold* that should forestall the charge of offensive "callow self-pity" often leveled against Cantos I and II in particular (see, e.g., Willis W. Pratt, "Byron and Some Current Patterns of Thought," p. 150).

[19] See his edition of the *Works*, p. 1005.

rather from the same despair as do the other poems, the same sense of loss and nothingness, of inevitability and doom, here articulated in bitter comedy or anger instead of compassion and a quiet despair.[20]

In the section on Albania both the narrator's voice and Harold's point of view return, loud and clear, the former detailing with considerable gusto the scenes, customs, character, and history of that "rugged Nurse of savage men" (xxxviii). His commentary is reasonable without full sympathy, moral as always, tinged with a kind of reluctant respect, even awe, for the Albanian's fierce toughness, but always tempered by the cautious English traveler's suspicion, perhaps fear, and ingrained sense of his own superiority. The opening description of the landscape sets precisely the proper mood and tone for the commentary to follow: it is a sublime scene, the hills

> *Robed half in mist, bedewed with snowy rills,*
> *Arrayed in many a dun and purple streak;*

but it is also a scene where

> *roams the wolf—the eagle whets his beak—*
> *Birds—beasts of prey—and wilder men appear,*
> *And gathering storms around convulse the closing*
> *year.*
> *(xlii)*

There is an angry attack, reminiscent of the castigation of religious hypocrisy in London and Cadiz Sundays, upon "Foul Superstition" and the decay of "true Worship's gold" into the "dross" of iconological blasphemy. The scene of the Battle of Actium also leads the narrator to assail bitterly, in the name of God, all

---

[20] On this point see George Gilfillan's neglected essay on Byron in *A Second Gallery of Literary Portraits* (2d ed.; London, 1852), pp. 32–33. For a more sophisticated analysis, with which I am in only partial agreement, however, see Edward E. Bostetter, *The Romantic Ventriloquists*, pp. 254ff.

Childe Harold, Canto II

> Imperial Anarchs, doubling human woes!
> GOD! was thy globe ordained for such to win and
> > lose?
> > > (xlv)

Ali Pasha himself is "lawless law" personified, surrounded by scenery of lush "harmony," gentlest winds, green trees, and peaceful rusticity. Byron's construction here of the sequence from stanza xxxviii to stanza lxiii is worth pausing upon; for while the narrator concentrates upon his close and narrow matter-of-fact observation, that construction, similar to stanzas xxiii and xxviii analyzed above, bespeaks the poet's awareness of the irony of juxtaposing anarchic lawlessness and ferocity with a scene of unqualified grandeur and peace. In one sense my description of the sequence is not quite right, for the reader's final impression is of an Edenic, sublime land surrounded by the awe-inspiring, terrible, and destructive power of the Pasha, a panoramic image of one of Byron's major themes, the ruins of paradise. Finally, near the middle of this imagistic construct is one of three fine late additions by Byron which enable his poet's voice of universal despair to be heard on the scene:

> Oh! where, Dodona! is thine agéd Grove,
> > Prophetic Fount, and Oracle divine?
> > What valley echoed the response of Jove?
> > What trace remaineth of the Thunderer's shrine?
> > All, all forgotten—and shall Man repine
> > That his frail bonds to fleeting life are broke?
> > Cease, Fool! the fate of Gods may well be thine:
> > Wouldst thou survive the marble or the oak?
> When nations, tongues, and worlds must sink
> > > beneath the stroke![21]
> > > > (liii)

---

[21] The fact that this is a late addition is not noted by Coleridge but is pointed out by Robert L. Zimmerman in his most helpful doctoral dissertation, "Manuscript Revision in Byron's *Childe Harold's Pilgrimage*" (Duke University, 1960), p. 230. The imagery of the last line may be found also in *English Bards, and Scotch Reviewers*, ll. 195ff. Coleridge (*P*, II, 133n) suggests Sulpitius Severus' letter to Cicero as a possible source, especially since Byron does quote from it in his note to stanza xliv of Canto IV.

The other two 1811 additions are stanza xv, similar in tone, beginning "Cold is the heart, fair Greece!" (discussed above), and stanza lxxxviii, with its emphasis on the Edenic past when dreams were true, poetry was history, and all life holy in contrast to the present, when "Athena's tower" is a ruin and the monument of death and waste at Marathon paradoxically lives on. The Ali Pasha frame for all this concludes on the same note, though more stridently accented by the narrator:

> But crimes that score the tender voice of ruth,
> Beseeming all men ill, but most the man
> In years, have marked him with a tiger's tooth;
> Blood follows blood, and, through their mortal span,
> In bloodier acts conclude those who with blood began.
> (lxiii)

The narrator recounts the particular instances of Albanian virtue, and Ali's kind treatment of Harold, with an unusual emphasis upon his own function as storyteller; he uses such narrative devices as "It chanced that" and "It came to pass, that," and in the revealing first draft of stanza lxiv, he confirms his own narrow intention:

> Childe Harold with that chief held colloquy,
> Yet what they spake, it boots not to repeat,
> Converse may little charm strange ear or eye.[22]

The entire section closes, properly, with music characteristic of the poet's view of the modern world, the war song "Tambourgi! Tambourgi!"

In contrast to the narrator, Harold is generally unmoved and unexcited by the scenes. The waste of war—at Actium, Lepanto, Trafalgar—repels him, and he will not allow himself to delight "In themes of bloody fray, or gallant fight," for he "loathed the bravo's trade, and laughed at martial wight" (xl). He is at home only in a setting such as "Leucadia's far-projecting rock of woe," where he feels a kinship to the death

---

[22] *P*, II, 140n.

of love epitomized in Sappho's fabled suicide leap (xli). Even this sympathy, however, is but transitory, for habitually, unlike the poet, "His breast was armed 'gainst fate," his heart steeled against compassion and even despair (xliii). More important, Harold sees everything, responds to everything (insofar as he responds at all) in terms of his own lostness, his own mood, without realizing, as the poet does, the significance of the connection between the world outside himself and that within. Thus blinded, he is also inarticulate within the protective shell of his mind-forged fortress. To make him articulate, to transform him from metaphorical object into feeling song, Byron will see in Canto III that he must absorb the accouterments of his metaphorical wanderer into the voice and character of his poet. In Harold there is no salvation, just as for the narrator there is in the end only the slim hope of some improvement sometime, the obstinate optimism of the reasoning man. For the poet, however, "Existence may be borne" (IV, xxi) because however inevitable the fall of man, however desperate the final vision of the world and the human condition,

> The Beings of the Mind are not of clay:
>   Essentially immortal, they create
>   And multiply in us a brighter ray
>   And more beloved existence: that which Fate
>   Prohibits to dull life in this our state
>   Of mortal bondage, by these Spirits supplied,
>   First exiles, then replaces what we hate;
>   Watering the heart whose early flowers have died,
> And with a fresher growth replenishing the void.
>   (IV, v)

It is not that the human heart is elated through art's vision of the ideal, as in Shelley, but rather that it is heartened again and again by the vision of tragedy. In addition, as Byron sees in Canto III, for the artist it is the act of creation itself that is his salvation, and this salvation, untheologically, inheres in the constantly renewed and fresher growth of a feeling heart. Thus out of the unromantic despair of Byron's poet and Harold comes the firmly "romantic" optimism, in a most uncharacteristic form, of course, of the final efficacy of art in human affairs.[23]

But I am some years ahead of Byron's own full awareness of what he himself was doing in *Childe Harold*; the above comments are pertinent here only as an introduction to the confused dialogue between the narrator and the poet, *sans* Harold, that concludes Canto II. It is confused because Byron is hurrying beyond his own present conceptions toward the absorption of the narrator's role into the poet's that will be complete only in Canto IV. Still, in these last twenty-six stanzas we should be struck by the clear beginnings of that process, as seen in the total reversal of the relationship of narrator's voice to poet's voice established in Canto I. Now the poet is dominant, and it is only through him that the accents of the narrator are occasionally heard. The latter's insularity and orthodoxy are thus clearly in the process of being universalized; his solid virtues and sound point of view are being incorporated into the larger scope of the poet's vision. In a sense, Byron is frankly and openly admitting that the richness of the poet's real and imaginative experience and the infinite range of his voice have done away with the need for spokesmen for the several aspects of his role. To put it another way, it is Byron's statement of confidence in his own poetic power, which enables him to objectify the subjectivity of his own world view by means of a single persona instead of a medley of voices.[24]

As the canto began, then, with Greece seen through

---

[23] In its more characteristic form, that optimism is maintained by the poet's repeated creation of a meaningful wholeness and order out of chaos. On the Romantic poet and his peculiar ontological situation, see, e.g., Earl R. Wasserman, *The Subtler Language*, pp. 186ff.; R. A. Foakes, *The Romantic Assertion*, pp. 13ff.; and Georg Roppen and Richard Sommer, *Strangers and Pilgrims*, Preface.

[24] The wrong way to see the transformation is, I think, exemplified by, though by no means limited to, Peter Quennell: ". . . whereas the landscape of the first two cantos is apt to suggest the 'views' cast by a magic lantern—or the slides in an old-fashioned stereoscope—the third and fourth cantos of *Childe Harold* are penetrated, through and through, by the writer's emotion" (*Byron* [London, 1934], p. 87).

the poet's eyes, so this last section of the canto is inaugurated by a somber, funereal scene:

> Fair Greece! sad relic of departed Worth!
>   Immortal, though no more; though fallen, great!
>   Who now shall lead thy scattered children forth,
>   And long accustomed bondage uncreate?
>   Not such thy sons who whilome did await,
>   The helpless warriors of a willing doom,
>   In bleak Thermopylae's sepulchral strait—
>   Oh! who that gallant spirit shall resume,
> Leap from Eurotas' banks, and call thee from
>   the tomb?[25]
>
> > (lxxiii)

The paradoxes are tragic and reflect fully the poet's pessimism and despair, his sense of the futility of the brave hope expressed here. Greece is "Fair," yet finally only a "relic" of what was once fair; it is immortal, alive, yet dead; great, but no more. The fourth line states the problem with simplicity and a hard irony; the once great creatress of the world is now asked to uncreate, and the plea of the last two lines is for the very immortality the wreck of Greece eternally denies. In his mind's eye the poet sees that paradise as if it had never been lost; but the reality of the ruin pricks each dream's bubble at the moment of formation. Only the narrator's mind can formulate a hope— in the martial call of stanza lxxvi and in the spirited attack on bloody, tyrannical, immoral Turkey—in the midst of which the thematic despair of the poet insinuates itself as if unwilled:

> And Greece her very altars eyes in vain:
> (Alas! her woes will still pervade my strain!)
>
> > (lxxix)

Quite in contrast to the narrator's bitterness, the poet

---

[25] Terence J. B. Spencer claims that the first line of this stanza is a "deliberate transference of the Virgilian phrase, *tristes reliquiae Danaum*" (*Byron and the Greek Tradition* [Nottingham, 1960], p. 10).

recalls the fair days of "Stamboul," when the music of the land harmonized with the tunes of the sea, and the rule was love:

> *Oh Love! young Love! bound in thy rosy band,*
> *Let sage or cynic prattle as he will,*
> *These hours, and only these, redeem Life's*
> *years of ill!*
> *(lxxxi)*

Against the backdrop of such a remembrance modern merriment is a sham, a "masquerade," behind which "hearts . . . throb with secret pain" and the sea echoes only enduring sadness and loss (lxxxii):

> *and when*
> *Can Man its shattered splendour renovate,*
> *Recall its virtues back, and vanquish Time and Fate?*
> *(lxxxiv)*

There is no answer—merely the contrapuntal refrain of Greece's sepulcher:

> *And yet how lovely in thine age of woe,*
> *Land of lost Gods and godlike men, art thou!*
> *(lxxxv)*

Now god and man, spirit and temple, no longer live but commingle "slowly with heroic earth, / Broke by the share of every rustic plough" (lxxxv), "feebly brave" like the columns of the Parthenon (lxxxvi). Only nature, indifferent nature, "still is fair" (lxxxvii). The poet's final epitaph for Greece sums up all neatly, trenchantly, movingly—a "consecrated Land," now but a "magic waste" (xciii).

It is not extravagant to see in that phrase, or rather to hear, the voices of poet and narrator joined, the sense of fact combined with the imaginative dream, the wasteland of the world with the Eden it lost, through Fate and time and tide, and man's own perversity of will—a perversity which for Byron is more and more clearly the smothering of his heart, his essential humanity. Here the canto originally ended, but at press time

Childe Harold, Canto II

Byron added six stanzas, the four that close the canto forming the most personal lyric found thus far in *Childe Harold*. The lyric is, properly, a dirge for the death of love and the consequent loss of being, of life. What is perhaps more important technically, it contains a revealing confusion of third and first persons: Harold is clearly no longer necessary to Byron, yet he does not realize that he must let him go. Addressed ostensibly to Edleston, whose death Byron had just discovered, the lines might well be construed as referring, albeit somewhat peculiarly, to Harold:

> *What is my Being! thou hast ceased to be!*
> *Nor staid to welcome here thy wanderer home,*
> *Who mourns o'er hours which we no more shall*
> > *see—*
> *Would they had never been, or were to come!*
> *Would [I] he had ne'er return'd to find fresh*
> > *cause to roam!*
>
> > (xcv)

The so-called Thyrza poems, of which these last stanzas are a part, elaborate upon this death and the poet's consequent despair. The personal grief and the elegies on Greece come together in the first person singular, and this voice now has two major alternatives, which turn out to be no alternatives at all: to "plunge again into the crowd" with laughter and revelry, "False to the heart," and thus "leave the flagging spirit doubly weak," or to allow his smiles to "form the channel of a future tear, / Or raise the writhing lip with ill-dissembled sneer" (xcvii). It is difficult not to refer these alternatives, or two sides of the same emotional coin, to Byron's total poetic canon, the feigned laughter and revelry of the satires so often punctuated by the "ill-dissembled sneer" on the one hand, and on the other, the romantic poet's "spirit doubly weak" for every reach after the lost ideal, the fleeting smile that soon trembles into tears.

These late additions, then, sound no new note, but the note they sound is becoming clearer and more distinct, more moving and more powerful as the poet takes it for his own. The sense of sureness, however, is not yet there,[26] and Byron must experiment further (in the tales) with point of view and narrative technique before the structural solutions are arrived at: the one, in Canto IV of *Childe Harold*, the other, in the plays beginning with *Manfred*. It is instructive to note here, though, that Byron's own sense of the thematic unity of *Childe Harold's Pilgrimage* is strengthened as he moves through the first three of the tales, *The Giaour*, *The Bride of Abydos*, and *The Corsair*: when this last appeared, in 1814, Byron prefixed his stanzas "To Ianthe" to *Childe Harold* (then in its seventh edition). These lines, written late in 1812 as a gallant tribute to eleven-year-old Charlotte Harley but never published, obviously had been dormant in Byron's mind until 1813, when Shelley sent him a copy of *Queen Mab*,[27] which sparked them into life. Although we have no evidence of specific comments by Byron upon the angry, iconoclastic poem (the two poets had not as yet met), part of its theme must have struck a responsive chord in Byron, fresh from the struggles of *Childe Harold*. Within its structured series of visions given to the pure soul of the sleeping Ianthe by Queen Mab, visions of the world past, present, and future,[28] Shelley violently attacks, in crude yet powerful lines, the corruption, misery, waste, crime, lawlessness, violence, religious chicanery, and political licentiousness of the world past and present. But he concludes the poem with a characteristic Shelleyan vision of the attainable ideal future. The imagery and tone of the attack were already familiar to Byron from his struggle to articulate his

---

[26] E.g., Byron explained the shift from "I" to "he" in stanza xcv as a mere avoidance of egotism: "The '*he*' refers to '*Wanderer*' and anything is better than *I I I I* always *I*" (note to Dallas on the manuscript, *P*, II, 161n). A similar note to Dallas caused the rejection of "Though Time not yet hath ting'd my locks with snow" in favor of l. 7 of stanza xcviii as we have it (*P*, II, 162n).

[27] Moore, *Letters and Journals of Lord Byron*, II, 22–23; Marchand, *Byron: A Biography*, II, 621–22.

[28] Byron, of course, made use of a similar scheme later, in *Cain*. Indeed, *Cain* might well be regarded in some ways as a reversal of the *Queen Mab* pattern.

own vision, but it would be peculiar indeed if lines like these did not lend further strength to that vision:

> "Behold," the Fairy cried,
> "Palmyra's ruined palaces!—
>   Behold! where grandeur frowned;
>   Behold! where pleasure smiled;
> What now remains?—the memory
>   Of senselessness and shame—
>   What is immortal there?
>   Nothing—it stands to tell
>   A melancholy tale, to give
>   An awful warning: soon
> Oblivion will steal silently
>   The remnant of its fame.
>   Monarchs and conquerors there
> Proud o'er prostrate millions trod—
> The earthquakes of the human race;
> Like them, forgotten when the ruin
>   That marks their shock is past."
>
> (II, 109–25)

And:

> "Ah! to the stranger-soul, when first it peeps
> From its new tenement, and looks abroad
> For happiness and sympathy, how stern
> And desolate a tract is this wide world!
> How withered all the buds of natural good!
>
> (IV, 121–25)

And, of man:

> ". . . he is formed for abjectness and woe,
> To grovel on the dunghill of his fears,
> To shrink at every sound, to quench the flame
> Of natural love in sensualism, to know
> That hour as blessed when on his worthless days
> The frozen hand of Death shall set its seal,
> Yet fear the cure, though hating the disease."
>
> (IV, 159–65)

Byron would also sympathize with the portrait of the bitter

Ahasuerus, wandering over that world eternally, unable to die (VII, 68ff.), and with Shelley's image of Ianthe's soul, standing in naked purity—

> *Each stain of earthliness*
> *Had passed away,* [and] *it reassumed*
> *Its native dignity and stood*
> *Immortal amid ruin*
>
> (*I, 135–38*)

—with the idea of dream becoming reality through the fairy's vision, with the conception of the "outcast, Man" in a universe seemingly formed for "Peace, harmony, and love" (III, 195–99), and with the idea of the "consentaneous love" (VIII, 108) that inspires all life and creates a new "garden" "in loveliness / Surpassing fabled Eden" (IV, 88–89), a "Paradise of peace" (VIII, 238), a "sweet place of bliss / Where friends and lovers meet to part no more" (IX, 15–16).

Without Shelley's unquenchable hope, but certainly with the horror of Mab's first two visions and the paradisaical beauty of Ianthe's soul in mind, Byron changed the title of his all-but-forgotten tribute from "To the Lady Charlotte Harley" to "To Ianthe"; the poem thus became his hymn to love, beauty, purity, youth, vision, dreams, joy, hope—in short, an epitome of all that *Childe Harold's Pilgrimage*, that "plain . . . tale" and "lowly lay" of truth, asserts again and again to be lost and irrecoverable. "To Ianthe," then, is precisely the right foil for the epigraph from Fougeret de Monbron's *Le Cosmopolite, ou, le Citoyen du Monde*, in which all of the pages of the book of the universe are "*également mauvaises.*" Without the romantic vision of Ianthe, Byron's vision of that universe would have been as shallow and narrow as Childe Harold's.

Chapter IV

THE GIAOUR AND THE BRIDE OF ABYDOS

In 1812 Samuel Rogers, whom Byron had praised in *English Bards, and Scotch Reviewers* and "long viewed with awed respect as the most admirable of the poets who had carried on the tradition of Pope,"[1] published his rambling *The Voyage of Columbus*. Byron certainly read it, although we have no comments from him about it. Whatever his reasons for suspending further writing on *Childe Harold*, his beginning of *The Giaour* in the autumn of 1812, soon after the appearance of *The Voyage*, and his dedication of the poem to Rogers can hardly be coincidental, as Coleridge points out.[2] The poem was an instantaneous success, going into fourteen editions; but since Byron's time, like most of his verse tales, it has not fared well with critics. On the assumption that they were written merely as a sop to public taste for the exotic, the Gothic, the melancholy, the "Byronic," commentators have in general concentrated only on those elements and judged them "nowadays as trumpery and meretricious as extremely bad pictures of the school of Delacroix."[3] In

---

[1] Marchand, *Byron: A Biography*, I, 303.

[2] *P*, III, 76.

[3] Peter Quennell, *Byron*, p. 89. On the other hand, a distinct minority of critics as diverse as J. A. Symonds, T. S. Eliot, Lamartine, and de Vigny thought well of the tales. Symonds, in typical aesthete fashion, thought that "*The Giaour* alone retains sufficient vitality or perfume of true poetry" today—though he also praised *The Prisoner of Chillon* and *Mazeppa* ("Lord Byron," in T. H. Ward [ed.], *The English Poets* [New York, 1903], IV, 247). Eliot, in his essay on Byron (Bonamy Dobree [ed.], *From Anne to Victoria* [London, 1937], pp. 605–7), judged *Childe Harold* to be distinctly inferior to *The Giaour*, *The Bride of Abydos*, *The Corsair*, and *Lara*. With the apparent ex-

so doing they have ignored the interesting and important experimentation found in almost all the tales. It is not difficult, of course, to do this, for the poems tend to sweep the reader along on the momentum of torrential rhetoric, simple plot, melodramatic single-dimensional characterization, and obvious emotion. Further, Byron himself has contributed to the case against the poems by referring to them, as to *Childe Harold*, flippantly and facetiously: his "Harrys and Larrys, Pilgrims and Pirates," he called them;[4] *The Giaour*, he said, is "in foolish fragments," an "awful pamphlet," "but a string of passages";[5] *The Bride of Abydos* he repeatedly denigrated as "the work of a week," "written in four nights to distract my dreams. . . ."[6] And later, when he committed himself strenuously to the reform of English drama by writing correct and regular plays, he condemned his earlier productions almost *in toto* for their "false stilted trashy style, which is a mixture of all the styles of the day, which are *all bombastic*,"[7] for their "rant," and for their "exaggerated

---

ception of Etienne Becquet, who called *The Giaour* "an incoherent fabric of dark and cold atrocities," the French in general responded to the tales enthusiastically: Alfred de Vigny thought *The Giaour* astonishing poetry, Lamartine called it "brilliant," and Villemain agreed with both of these (though he preferred *Mazeppa* as Byron's masterpiece). See William J. Phillips, *France on Byron* (Philadelphia, 1941), for a convenient and excellent summary of French criticism (the above judgments are recorded by Phillips on pp. 39–43).

[4] Ltr. to Moore, 10 Jan. 1815, in *LJ*, III, 169.

[5] Ltrs. to Moore, 1 and 8 Sept. 1813, in *LJ*, II, 257, 262; ltr. to Murray, 29 Nov. 1813, in *LJ*, II, 291.

[6] Ltr. to Gifford, 12 Nov. 1813, in *LJ*, II, 279; ltr. to Moore, 30 Nov. 1813, in *LJ*, II, 293; Journal of 1813, in *LJ*, II, 321. The same defensive mood leads him to aim his classic sneer at his own versifying, the passing thought of "expectorating a romance, or rather a tale in prose" (Journal of 1813, in *LJ*, II, 314).

[7] Ltr. to Murray, 28 Sept. 1820, in *LJ*, V, 82. Actually Byron's attack is aimed at the work of Felicia Hemans, but he adds parenthetically, "I don't except my *own*—no one has done more through negligence to corrupt the language." This confession is perhaps the direct source (if one was needed) of T. S. Eliot's famous charge that "he added nothing to the language, . . . he discovered nothing in the sounds, and developed nothing in the meaning, of individual words" ("Byron," p. 201). Cf. W. W. Robson's more generous presentation of the same

nonsense which has corrupted the public taste."[8]

    To accept these self-slanders as considered judgments, however, is to ignore the well-known peculiarities of Byron's temperament and his prevailing attitude toward the reading public of his day, an attitude which led him, in general, to condemn that work of his own which appealed to the taste of the masses and to champion whatever was severely attacked or ignored. We need only recall, for example, his extravagantly high opinion of *Hints from Horace*, which certainly would have been published in lieu of *Childe Harold* I and II if it had not been for R. C. Dallas' disappointment in the *Horace* and his subsequent "discovery" of *Childe Harold*. When *Harold* turned out to be an instantaneous success, Byron's love of fame dictated postponement of the publication of the *Horace* (it did not appear in full until 1831), while at the same time its worth continued to rise in his estimation. Again, even while condemning his early popular productions in favor of the newly written plays, with their "natural," "regular" style and "common language,"[9] he could also write about his earlier poetry: "the fact is (as I perceive), that I wrote a great deal better in 1811, than I have ever done since," "but that comes of my having fallen into the atrocious bad taste of the times—partly."[10] His feigned facetiousness extended to other favorites besides the tales: *Don Juan* became very quickly "Donny Johnny"; his translation of the *Morgante Maggiore*, which he thought one of the best things he'd ever done, became "Major Morgan"; and *Cain* was written, he said, in his "gay metaphysical style."[11] Of the *Prophecy of*

---

charge—"Byron is the poet and stylist of a linguistic nadir"—in his excellent 1957 Chatterton Lecture, "Byron as Poet," p. 35.

[8] Ltr. to Murray, 20 Sept. 1821, in *LJ*, V, 372; ltr. to Shelley, 20 May 1822, in *LJ*, VI, 67.

[9] See, e.g., ltrs. to Murray, 4 Jan. and 14 July 1821, in *LJ*, V, 217–18, 323.

[10] Ltrs. to Murray, 11 Jan. 1821 and 23 Sept. 1820, in *LJ*, V, 222, 77.

[11] Ltrs. to Murray, 1 Mar. 1820 and 12 Sept. 1821, in *LJ*, IV, 416; V, 361.

Dante he wrote: "I don't know whether the *Danticles* be good or no. . . . for my own part I don't understand a word of the whole four cantos, and was therefore lost in admiration of their sublimity"; and when it fell on indifferent ears, he promptly rated it as "the best thing I ever wrote."[12]

Confusing and erratic as Byron's judgments of his own work were, he did have his more sober and critical moments. However "unlucky" an "affair" *The Giaour* was,[13] he knew that it had merit, that its fragmentary structure was a valuable experiment: "I adhere (in liking) to my Fragment," he wrote in his journal for 1813.[14] *The Bride of Abydos*, even though it was his "first *entire* composition of any length (except the Satire)," he was unsure of because of its hasty composition: "I do not rate [it] in my own estimation at half *The Giaour*," he wrote to Murray; and, in his journal: "I don't think that I shall [like it] long."[15] *The Siege of Corinth* and *Parisina* he did not "feel to be at all equal to my own notions of what they should be," while *Childe Harold*, especially Cantos III and IV, "I look upon . . . as my best."[16] In this chaos of conflicting opinions, attitudes, judgments, and poses (both defensive and belligerent), it is easy to overlook the seriousness of purpose evident in the tales themselves, however problematical their intrinsic worth as poems, however careless, hurried, or gauche, and however fragmentary the evidence of that seriousness. This temptation is especially strong, I think, with *The Giaour*, the first of the series.

That the first two cantos of *Childe Harold* took the world by storm no one will deny. Yet Harold himself is no

---

[12] Ltr. to Hobhouse, 8 June 1820, in *Byron: A Self-Portrait*, ed. Peter Quennell (2 vols.; London, 1950), II, 516; ltr. to Murray, 23 Mar. 1820, in *LJ*, IV, 422.

[13] Ltr. to Murray, 31 July 1813, in *LJ*, II, 242.

[14] *LJ*, II, 372.

[15] Ltrs. to Murray, 29 and 17 Nov. 1813, in *LJ*, II, 291, 285; Journal of 1813, *LJ*, II, 321.

[16] Ltrs. to Murray, 3 Jan. 1816 and 15 Sept. 1817, in *LJ*, III, 251; IV, 168.

Giaour, and to assume that the Giaour's creation was merely a deliberate attempt to capitalize on the taste that, if not created, was at least nurtured by Harold's appearance on the literary scene is to seriously underrate Byron's considerable struggle for a form, a vehicle, a structure suitable to his needs. (What those needs were will, I trust, become gradually apparent in what follows.) Critics also tend to forget that the diversionary tactic which produced *The Bride of Abydos*, Byron's intention to wring his "thoughts from reality to imagination—from selfish regrets to vivid recollections,"[17] is not pertinent to the study of *The Giaour*. What, if anything, is pertinent biographically is almost totally unknown. He had given up *Childe Harold* mainly, as he wrote to Dallas, because he must see the scenes before writing about them: "if I saw them again, it would go on; but under existing circumstances and *sensations*, I have neither harp, 'heart nor voice' to proceed."[18] At the same time, he was not interested merely in pleasing a reading public whose taste he had whetted: he insisted on his own sincerity and integrity as a poet, and "if I am only to write '*ad captandum vulgus*,' I might as well edit a magazine at once, or spin canzonettas for Vauxhall."[19] That he was actually involved in a situation similar to the drowning of Leila in *The Giaour* is at least partially true,[20] but in any case his own travels clearly led him back to, among other things, *Vathek* and D'Herbelot's *Bibliothèque Orientale*.[21]

---

[17] Journal of 1813, in *LJ*, II, 361.

[18] Ltr. to Dallas, 7 Sept. 1811, in *LJ*, II, 28. Byron makes the same point about the necessary stimulation of the "scene" in ltrs. to Moore, 8 Mar. 1816, in *LJ*, III, 274, and to Murray, 17 June 1817 and 25 Oct. 1822, in *LJ*, IV, 139; VI, 157.

[19] Ltr. to Dallas, 7 Sept. 1811, in *LJ*, II, 28.

[20] For a convenient summary of the biographical details, see Marchand, *Byron: A Biography*, I, 257–58. Byron does say in his letter to Professor E. D. Clarke of December 15, 1813, that "our adventure (a personal one) . . . certainly first suggested to me the story of *The Giaour*" (*LJ*, II, 311).

[21] Coleridge, in *P*, III, 76. Byron acknowledges his debt to these works for the first time in a footnote at the end of the second edition of *The Giaour*.

Critically, however, the poem is a crucial document in Byron's search for form, for a "method in arranging my thoughts."[22] Some years after its composition he was "very sorry that I called some of my own things 'Tales,' because I think that they are something better."[23] I think so too.

I

The history of the composition of *The Giaour* is complex, and we do not know all of it. Byron first mentions it in a letter to Murray of May 13, 1813, accompanying a "corrected, and, I hope, amended copy of the lines for the 'fragment' already sent this evening," with instructions to burn the original copy.[24] That original was 407 lines long and is what Byron called some days later "the first sketch";[25] but as the above letter suggests, almost immediately it was added to and refurbished, so that the first published edition ran to 685 lines. This is the edition Byron refers to in his letters to Hodgson of June 6 and June 8, 1813, where he says he added "ten pages, *text* and *margin* . . . which render it a little less unfinished (but more unintelligible) than before"—additions "to the tune of 300 lines or so towards the end."[26] These "ten pages" or "300 lines" constitute the 224-line first version of the Giaour's long speech to the Monk and 54 lines scattered elsewhere in the poem.

---

[22] Ltr. to Hodgson, 13 Oct. 1811, in *LJ*, II, 54. Some hint of that "method," as Byron saw it, can be found in his letter to Murray of May 9, 1817: "my first impressions are always strong and confused, and my Memory *selects* and reduces them to order, like distance in the landscape, and blends them better, although they may be less distinct. There must be a sense or two more than we have, as mortals . . . for where there is much to be grasped we are always at a loss, and yet feel that we ought to have a higher and more extended comprehension" (*LJ*, IV, 119–20). See also ltr. to Mrs. Byron, 12 Nov. 1809, in *LJ*, I, 254.

[23] Ltr. to Moore, 25 Mar. 1817, in *LJ*, IV, 78. See also ltr. to Murray, 25 Mar. 1817, in *LJ*, IV, 85.

[24] *LJ*, II, 204.

[25] Ltr. to Hodgson, 6 June 1813, in *LJ*, II, 215.

[26] *LJ*, II, 214–15.

The former is a significant addition, giving notice immediately that the poem is to be not merely an exciting narrative but a narrative with some sort of commentary.

The basic plot is extraordinarily simple: it is all contained in the original "sketch" of the poem. Byron's main interest, however, was not in the plot (*Childe Harold* I and II should have warned us against this assumption) but rather in the conflicting points of view from which that plot could be viewed. The sketch is, as it were, a piece of sculpture around which the viewer walks in order to see it in different lights and shadows, the eye building up a structure of fragmentary apperceptions, disjointed by virtue of their temporal and spatial discontinuity, but all tending toward a unified imaginative perception of the whole and its "meaning." More exactly, it is like a piece of sculpture surrounded by a number of viewers, each of whom sees it and interprets it in his own light. By focusing not on the sculpture (the plot) but on the beholder or beholders (the speakers) and by juxtaposing their various spatial-temporal views, Byron gradually builds, in the final version of the poem, an interpretation of the "human condition" to which all the viewers contribute, while at the same time he maintains the limited and proper partisanship of each of the separate views.

The first additions to the "sketch," then, provide the initial material for one of the major points of view, that of the Giaour himself, for before this he is represented only at a distance in a third-person narrative, and briefly at the end of the poem in his Manfred-like refusal of aid from the Monk. This basic consistency in Byron's original handling of the Giaour is surely the reason why, in the only other first-edition passage in which he speaks, Byron has him speak of himself in the third as well as the first person (ll. 675–88[27]). It is Byron's early recognition that the Giaour is both an actor in the plot and a commentator on (or an embodiment of a point of view toward) that same plot.

---

[27] All line number references will be to the seventh edition, after which Byron made no further changes in the poem.

The *editio princeps*, then, sketches as much of the plot as we need to know and introduces the several speakers: the poet-traveler (not necessarily Byron), whose point of view is always larger and fuller than the others; the fisherman, a partisan Moslem and storyteller, whose voice carries the bulk of the narrative in which he himself is a sometime participant; Hassan, who speaks only in the drowning scene and in the battle with the Giaour's band; and the Giaour himself. Of these, the fisherman dominates the poem—as participant, narrator, and commentator. Byron's last footnote to the first edition explains the source of this conception: "The story in the text is one told of a young Venetian many years ago, and now nearly forgotten. I heard it by accident recited by one of the coffee-house story-tellers who abound in the Levant, and sing or recite their narratives. The additions and interpolations by the translator will be easily distinguished from the rest by the want of Eastern imagery. . . ."[28] This conscious attempt to distinguish between storyteller and "translator" (what I have called "the poet" above) represents a noteworthy advance over the technique of *Childe Harold* I and II, where the points of view are distinguished only by voice, attitude, tone, and the like. Dissatisfied with that more subtle, difficult, and finally confusing technique, Byron in *The Giaour* attempts the same thing but assigns to the voices, attitudes, and tones a realizable personality and being. Further, rather than merely suggesting vaguely, as he did in *Childe Harold*, that Harold has a companion (or companions) on his tour of the Mediterranean, in *The Giaour* Byron openly announces two narrators, one who speaks the initial, apparently extraneous, lines on Greece and introduces the fisherman, the other the fisherman-storyteller himself. Still, if the poem was not to be merely a narrative with interpolated comments but rather a thematic study of the "human condition" which subsumes all individual and limited views, additional points of view, attitudes, and comments had to be created or enlarged and the role of the controlling poet expanded to the point where he could

---

[28] *P*, III, 145n.

see the fundamental similarity of man's eternal predicament on earth.

That predicament is simply the inevitability of man's fall. I do not speak here of the archetypal Fall, though Ridenour's argument for this in *The Style of "Don Juan"* is persuasive indeed, and it is at least possible that the Calvinistically trained Byron was more fully aware of the analogies he created in his poems than we are willing to give him credit for. I speak rather of the fundamental (and romantic) ironies of man's finite existence, which are nowhere expressed so succinctly as in *Manfred*:

> *Half dust, half deity, alike unfit*
> *To sink or soar, with our mixed essence make*
> *A conflict of its elements, and breathe*
> *The breath of degradation and of pride,*
> *Contending with low wants and lofty will,*
> *Till our Mortality predominates,*
> *And men are—what they name not to themselves,*
> *And trust not to each other.*
>
> (*I, ii, 40–47*)

Or, even better, the Abbot's speech in Act III, Scene i:

> *This should have been a noble creature: he*
> *Hath all the energy which would have made*
> *A goodly frame of glorious elements,*
> *Had they been wisely mingled; as it is,*
> *It is an awful chaos—Light and Darkness—*
> *And mind and dust—and passions and pure thoughts*
> *Mixed, and contending without end or order,—*
> *All dormant or destructive. He will perish.*
>
> (*160–67*)

This pessimism, or "fatalism," as Byron preferred to call it,[29] is

---

[29] Only recently have critics come to see that Byron's "fatalism" is essentially pessimism, neither cynical nor predestinarian. See Ridenour and Bostetter in works already cited, and Alvin B. Kernan's chapter on *Don Juan* in his *The Plot of Satire* (New Haven and London, 1965), Brian Wilkie's chapter on *Don Juan* in his *The Romantic Poets and Epic Tradition* (Madison and Milwaukee, Wis., 1965), and Gilbert Highet's interesting little essay, "The Poet and His Vulture," in *A Clerk at Oxenford* (New York, 1954).

constant in his work and in his life. Man's violence ultimately produces his own defeat or decay, but what is more important is that man's virtues—courage, pride, love, loyalty—also lead him to destruction. As Ridenour says of the Haidée episode in *Don Juan*, "as violence and disorder lurk behind the most winning manifestations of tranquillity and harmony, the tranquil and harmonious are fated inevitably to dissolve again in the violent and chaotic. This is an apparently immutable law of Byron's world."[30] And it is this "immutable law" which Byron seeks to dramatize for the first time in *The Giaour*, whose world is one of love and death, beauty and death, freedom and death, nature and death, man's human and heroic virtues and death. It is not a poem, then, which simply seeks to glorify "the outlaw, the rebel, the renegade, the Ishmaelite, the bold bad man," as Andrew Rutherford[31] and a host of others before him have insisted. Nor is it primarily a poem of self-dramatization (however clearly some of the details of Byron's life seem to obtrude) or an orgiastic indulgence in a vaguely misanthropic melancholy. That these elements, and other similar ones, exist in the poem and in the other tales in varying proportions is obvious; and even if the Giaour is in a distinct *dramatic* and literary tradition, as Bertrand Evans and Peter Thorslev, among others, have shown,[32] what I am concerned with here is Byron's "elaborately coherent" vision of the human condition and his earnest though self-deprecated efforts to achieve a form, a structure, a technique for embodying that vision in his art. The elements repeatedly singled out for critical comment must be seen as the result of partial failures to embody the vision—failures blown out of proportion by the prevailing and almost irresistible penchant of critics (from Byron's day to ours) to read the poems as biography. "My figures are not portraits," Byron cried vainly;

---

[30] *The Style of "Don Juan,"* p. 45.
[31] *Byron: A Critical Study,* p. 43.
[32] Bertrand Evans, *Gothic Drama from Walpole to Shelley* (Berkeley, Calif., 1947), and "Manfred's Remorse and Dramatic Tradition," *PMLA,* LXII (1947), 752–73; Peter Thorslev, *The Byronic Hero.*

and while reveling personally in the notoriety of his figures, he could still attack, with elaborate egotism but abundant justification, those "who, by perversely persisting in referring fiction to truth, and tracing poetry to life, and regarding characters of imagination as creatures of existence, have made me personally responsible for almost every poetical delineation which fancy and a particular bias of thought, may have tended to produce."[33]

That "bias of thought" produced the poet-figure in *The Giaour* as much as the Giaour himself, a vision of human life as well as the fisherman's story—but not without considerable persistence and labor on Byron's part, in which he was perhaps inspired by recalling that his idol, Pope, "*added* to *the* '*Rape of the Lock,*' but did not reduce it."[34] As usual, his own comments on his progress are facetious: it is his "bravura"; it is a "snake of a poem, which has been lengthening its rattles every month"; and twice, with perhaps a wry look at his own snake image, he writes to Murray that he is "bitten again" and has "quantities for other parts" of the poem.[35] The nature of the additions, however, belies this lightness, for almost all of them bolster existing points of view, add others, or elaborate on the overriding themes.

In the second edition, published about a month after the first, the puzzling six lines on Greece that opened the first edition are supplemented in order to introduce that country's Edenic past, "where every season smiles / Benignant o'er those blessèd isles" (ll. 7–8). The poet-speaker then goes on, in another new passage, to elaborate this idea by linking "Nature"

---

[33] Byron's reply to an article in Blackwood's *Edinburgh Magazine*, XXIX (August, 1819), attacking him for *Don Juan*, in *LJ*, IV, 477. See also Byron's complaint in *Detached Thoughts*, in *LJ*, V, 407–8.
[34] Ltr. to Murray, 18 Sept. 1820, in *LJ*, V, 120. This is the famous letter in which Byron describes himself as a "tyger (in poesy), if I miss the first Spring, I go growling back to my jungle. There is no second." This is his general argument for not revising, refurbishing, correcting; but his approval, in the same context, of addition and interpolation is seldom noted.
[35] Ltrs. to Murray, 10 and 26 Aug. and 29 Sept. 1813, in *LJ*, II, 244, 252, 268.

and the "Gods" within "the Paradise" of this "fairy land" (ll. 46ff.). Into this Edenic world "man, enamoured of distress," enters and mars

> it into wilderness,
> And trample[s], brute-like, o'er each flower
> That tasks not one laborious hour;
>
> .   .   .   .   .
>
> Strange—that where all is Peace beside,
> There Passion riots in her pride,
> And Lust and Rapine wildly reign
> To darken o'er the fair domain.
> It is as though the Fiends prevailed
> Against the Seraphs they assailed.
>
> (ll. 51–53, 58–63)

This is followed by the oft-quoted passage beginning "He who hath bent him o'er the dead," which likens present-day Greece to the "mild angelic air" and "rapture of repose" on the face of the newly dead: "Hers is the loveliness in death."[36] The otherwise puzzling six lines that open the poem are thus given a context: the idea of home and safety to the fisherman in his skiff and the beauty and serenity of the land and sea are both shrouded in the gloom of "the Athenian's grave," the grave of the hero set in a land of ruin and death.

The poet's bewailing the loss of this hero (Byron suggests he is Themistocles) is also significant in the light of the presentation of Hassan and the Giaour. They, too, are heroes, but of a different mold somehow: as fallen, finite men, betrayed by their own passions, they destroy rather than create or sustain peace and love and beauty. "Spark[s] of that flame, perchance

---

[36] LI. 68–102. Typical of the praise accorded the lines is that of Ethel C. Mayne (Byron [2 vols.; New York, 1912], I, 262). Her phrase, "that strange, slipshod loveliness," seems to me precisely right. Thomas Noon Talfourd's contemporary criticism sets the style for all later misconceptions of the passage (see William A. Coles, "Thomas Noon Talfourd on Byron and the Imagination," Keats-Shelley Journal, IX [1960], 108).

of heavenly birth" (l. 101), they love intensely—and destroy the object of that love as well as each other. To accent the point, as well as to place the Grecian passages and the narrative in proper perspective through the eyes of the poet, Byron, in another passage added in the second edition (ll. 620–54), has his poet comment on the battle between Hassan and the Giaour. Echoing the juxtaposition of Themistocles' grave and the idyllic Grecian landscape, the battle takes place in a peaceful vale "More suited to the shepherd's tale"; and the personal clash of the two heroic figures is seen, with terrible irony, as an embrace stronger than that of lovers.

Finally, Byron's third addition to this state of the poem (ll. 999–1023) has the Giaour himself comment on the difference between his own finite, "human" heroism that leads to destruction and death and the kind of heroism represented by Themistocles, "The slave of Glory, not of Love." And Hassan was the same, as the Giaour recognizes:

> *Yet did he but what I had done*
> *Had she been false to more than one.*
>
> *(ll. 1062–63)*

What he does not recognize is the waste of it all, the noble passion that miscarries, the irony of his own strength and single-mindedness. "Love will find its way," he persists in thinking,

> *Through paths where wolves would fear to prey;*
> *And if it dares enough, 'twere hard*
> *If Passion met not some reward.*
>
> *(ll. 1048–51)*

Yet almost in the same breath he brands his own brow with the curse of Cain (ll. 1057–59). The point is made again some lines later, when the Giaour describes his love in terms of "scorching vein, / Lips taught to writhe, but not complain" (ll. 1105–6), "bursting heart, and maddening brain" (l. 1106), "daring deed, and vengeful steel" (l. 1107):

103

I knew but to obtain or die.
I die—but first I have possessed,
And come what may, I have been blessed.[37]

(ll. 1113–15)

The irony is double-edged here, for his blessing is Cain's curse and his own death (cf. the "blesséd isles" of the opening passage on Greece); further, the very passion which the poet bewails as missing in present-day enslaved Greece *does* exist, but only to despoil and destroy. The heart of man, "that all / Which Tyranny can ne'er enthrall" (ll. 1068–69), becomes in this world inevitably a tyrant itself. Byron's heroes are consistently slaves of their passions,[38] of love, which presumably in some earlier age led to harmony and peace. Love in this world of men, however, is either destroyed by the world (as Haidée's and Juan's is, for example) or by itself. It is, ironically, as the Giaour says in a fifth-edition enlargement of his final speech,

light from Heaven;
A spark of that immortal fire
With angels shared, by Alla given,
To lift from earth our low desire.
Devotion wafts the mind above,
But Heaven itself descends in Love;
A feeling from the Godhead caught,
To wean from self each sordid thought;
A ray of Him who formed the whole;
A Glory circling round the soul!

(ll. 1131–40)

Yet his experience has also given him a certain wisdom in the ways of the world: "I grant *my* love imperfect" (l. 1141)—and

---

[37] Aside from the passages added in the second edition, all of the passages quoted in the foregoing analysis were present in the first edition.

[38] Bostetter's otherwise excellent analysis of Byron in *The Romantic Ventriloquists* is too heavily dependent on this one point; for example, ". . . under the melodramatic posturings [in *Childe Harold* I and II] there are genuine pessimism and fatalism based on observation of his own sexual nature" (p. 266).

Byron implies continually that all mankind's love is imperfect, and hence lost. That is the human condition.[39]

Conscious of this evolving pattern, in the third edition, issued less than a month after the second, Byron inserts in the poet's opening hymn to Greece a portrait of ideal love in a prelapsarian world:

> there the Rose, o'er crag or vale,
> Sultana of the Nightingale,
>   The maid for whom his melody,
>   His thousand songs are heard on high,
> Blooms blushing to her lover's tale:
> His queen, the garden queen, his Rose,
> Unbent by winds, unchilled by snows,
> Far from the winters of the west,
> By every breeze and season blest,
> Returns the sweets by Nature given
> In softest incense back to Heaven;
> And grateful yields that smiling sky
> Her fairest hue and fragrant sigh.
>
> *(ll. 21–33)*

And, in order to forge more solidly the thematic link between this passage on Greece and the Turkish-Christian narrative, he also adds a passage to the fisherman's account of Leila, "armed with beauty," moving on earth as "The cygnet nobly walks the water" (ll. 512, 504). In the lines prior to these, present in the first edition, the fisherman is willing to swear "By Alla" (l. 481) that her form was more than "breathing clay" (l. 482), "That through her eye the Immortal shone" (l. 492), and that

>   her feet
> Gleamed whiter than the mountain sleet
> Ere from the cloud that gave it birth
> It fell, and caught one stain of earth.
>
> *(ll. 500–3)*

Thus Byron carefully identifies pristine Greece with an unstained

---

[39] This reading of the passage is reinforced by the manuscript version in *P*, III, 137n.

Leila (the flower images in the description of the latter, for example, are precisely parallel to the flower imagery in the Greece passage). But she is also present-day Greece, still lovely but a slave to Hassan, and the Giaour thus becomes an emancipator—paradoxically, in the act of emancipation, her destroyer. As a result, Hassan is dead, his palace and grounds (a refuge of "Courtesy and Pity" afforded to travelers) ruined and decayed, love and beauty and purity dead, and the Giaour left amid these ruins with no faith (in a Moslem or a Christian God), no object, courting death.

The total picture cheers no heroes, advances no cause (private or public), asserts no values. It is a completely depressing, pessimistic, even nihilistic view of man and the world. The only survivors are Hassan's mother (who is fated to greet her son as a corpse rather than a bridegroom), the fisherman (who presumably goes on telling his tale without fully understanding), and the Monk and his brethren (who are helpless to do anything about anything).

With this total picture emerging more clearly in his mind, Byron fills out his presentation of desolation in the fourth, fifth, and seventh editions (only minor verbal changes were made in the sixth) and expands the number of points of view to show more fully the hopelessness of human aspirations and endeavor. In the fourth edition (August, 1813) in a substantial insertion the ruins of Hassan's hall are described at length by the fisherman and contrasted to the idyllic setting it once was (ll. 288–351). Spiders, bats, owls, wild dogs have taken over, and, like the dried-up stream bed on the field of Hassan's and the Giaour's battle, "the stream has shrunk from its marble bed, / Where the weeds and the desolate dust are spread" (ll. 297–98). Luxurious coolness, clear air and stars, music, beauty, childhood innocence, and maternal love have all yielded now to total desolation and death:

> *And here no more shall human voice*
> *Be heard to rage, regret, rejoice.*
> *The last sad note that swelled the gale*
> *Was woman's wildest funeral wail:*

That *quenched in silence, all is still,*
But the lattice that flaps when the wind is shrill.
                                        (*ll. 320–25*)

Equally devastating, perhaps even more so because it is more intimate and movingly human, is the shrewd insertion in this fourth edition of the section recounting the reception by Hassan's mother of the news of her son's death (ll. 689–722). Again, as in the opening passage on Greece and those on Leila's beauty and Hassan's childhood, Byron sets the grimness of death and destruction against an idyllic background:

The browsing camels' bells are tinkling:
His mother looked from her lattice high—
She saw the dews of eve besprinkling
The pasture green beneath her eye,
She saw the planets faintly twinkling.
                                        (*ll. 688–92*)

If it is too much to see the word "lattice" here as a recollection of the ghostly flapping lattice of Hassan's ruined palace, it is clear that from earth to heaven all is peace and beauty, as Hassan's palace once was. Into this scene comes the bloody lone survivor of the battle, bringing death with him in the form of "Hassan's cloven crest" (l. 716). Byron intensifies the blackness of the scene almost unbearably: the mother, expecting her son as bridegroom, about to achieve the fulfillment, joy, and beauty of love, receives the news that "a fearful bride [her] Son hath wed." But perhaps even more horrible is the suggestion that the "gift" he promised to bring in celebration of his attainment of love's heights is the cloven crest of the Giaour. Death as the only "true" bride is insisted upon here, just as earlier the fisherman notes that Hassan, on leaving his palace so hurriedly, was thought to be going "to woo a bride / More true than her who left his side" (ll. 533–34), and then comments later on the horror of the fatal destructive embrace, stronger than that of lovers, of Hassan and the Giaour on the battlefield (ll. 645–54).

The additional point of view of the mother is also of importance, adding as it does another piece to Byron's depressing jigsaw puzzle of the total human predicament of high and low, innocent and guilty alike. That Byron was conscious of his expansion of the range of points of view is evident from his rewriting of the first five lines of the mother's section in order to attribute more clearly to her an angle of vision integrally her own. Originally the passage read (in the fourth edition):

> The browzing camel's bells are tinkling,
> The dews of Eve the pasture sprinkling,
> And rising planets faintly twinkling:
> His Mother looked from her lattice high,
> With throbbing breast and eager eye.[40]

By shifting the order of the lines slightly in the fifth edition, and by avoiding statement of fact without reference to the mother's vision of the scene, Byron establishes clearly a physical point of view that he can then shade off into an attitude or moral point of view. The line beginning "His Mother looked," becomes the second line in the passage, and the phrase "She saw" is added in two different places; the fifth line above is wisely dropped as awkwardly descriptive of an attitude and point of view that it would be more proper to dramatize.

   The fifth edition also establishes the poet fully as the pilgrim-like poet of *Childe Harold*, who, having no heroic themes as in the past "on which the Muse might soar" (l. 144), must make what he can of present desolation set against the memory of what once was, of the "nameless pyramid" or "tomb" from which the "general doom / Hath swept the column" (ll. 129–30) framed by

> The mountains of their native land!
> There points thy Muse to stranger's eye
> The graves of those that cannot die!
>
> (ll. 133–35)

The transition from Greece to the fisherman and his story is

---

[40] Coleridge's transcription of this passage from the fourth edition is inaccurate (*P*, III, 118n).

only superficially mechanical, for it has already been made—from the poet-bard of the heroic, epic past to the fisherman-gossip-storyteller of the modern human condition; from the epic form, stately in its order, which mirrors the artistic control of human passions, to the fragments of a vision, presented with a violent curse, with the need for vengeance, and with only partial understanding.

Finally, in the fifth edition, aside from adding the Giaour's poem to love as "light from heaven" (ll. 1131ff.), which was commented upon above, Byron introduced the friend to whom the Giaour sends a pledge (ll. 1218–56). He is voiceless in the poem, though we should recognize the narrator's reasonable voice of *Childe Harold* I and II in his silent accents. His is the voice of prudence, of reason and restraint, of the prophecy of doom for the passion-directed man. He is the ordinary man, like the chamois hunter of *Manfred*, who pursues his ordinary business, but who also suffers in the general loss. As such, he represents one more point of view, that of the bystander snared in a trap not of his own making, that of the innocent who suffers merely because all men are born to suffer. The Giaour's

> *withered frame, the ruined mind,*
> *The wrack by passion left behind,*
> *A shrivelled scroll, a scattered leaf,*
> *Seared by the autumn blast of Grief!*
>
> *(ll. 1253–56)*

is the same figure, intensified a hundredfold. For Byron's "heroes" are no heroes in the ordinary sense; they are not participants in tragedy, yet they still retain some of the stature of the tragic hero. Like the tragic hero, they are man magnified, macrocosmic, titanic—yet nevertheless small, insignificant, and lost. They are not merely victims, nor are they tyrants; they are a mixture of both, half dust, half deity, at war constantly. The loser, of course, is always self.[41]

---

[41] Pertinent here is Herbert J. Muller's reminder that "the ultimate source of tragedy, historically and psychologically, is indeed the simple fact that man must die" (*The Spirit of Tragedy* [New York, 1956], p. 3).

BYRON AND THE RUINS OF PARADISE

The Giaour is, finally, in an addition appearing first
in the seventh edition, "like the bird whose pinions quake, /
But cannot fly the gazing snake" (ll. 842–43). But only the poet can
see this. The fisherman marvels at his eye and mien, and recalls
in the monastery that

> once I saw that face, yet then
> It was so marked with inward pain,
> I could not pass it by again;
> It breathes the same dark spirit now,
> As death were stamped upon his brow.
>
> (ll. 793–97)

But while death and the mark of Cain are there, the spirit is
not all dark. The glance of the "evil angel" which half frightens
the Friar and leads him to pray to Saint Francis to

> keep him from the shrine!
> Else may we dread the wrath divine
> Made manifest by awful sign
>
> (ll. 909–11)

reveals to the poet the remnants of the whole man, the face of
Greece before the fall into slavery and degradation, the face of
the newly dead

> (Before Decay's effacing fingers
> Have swept the lines where Beauty lingers,)
> (ll. 72–73)

the face of Leila, on whose

> fair cheek's unfading hue
> The young pomegranate's blossoms strew
> Their bloom in blushes ever new,
>
> (ll. 493–95)

the face of "A noble soul, and lineage high" (l. 869). Only to
the poet is it *sad* to trace

> What once were feelings in that face:
> Time hath not yet the features fixed,

110

> *But brighter traits with evil mixed;*
> *And there are hues not always faded,*
> *Which speak a mind not all degraded*
> *Even by the crimes through which it waded:*
> *The common crowd but see the gloom*
> *Of wayward deeds, and fitting doom.*
>
> > *(ll. 860–67)*

If the "common crowd" can see only waywardness and "fitting doom," Byron is careful not to make this mistake. To the Moslem fisherman the doom is just, even if it is not quite the fulfillment of his terrible curse; to the Monk, to Hassan's mother, and to the Moslem and the Christian world, in neither of which the Giaour has a place, his end is fitting and proper. But this is the kind of poetic justice Byron eschews. For him man is "no vulgar tenement / To which . . . lofty gifts were lent" (ll. 872–73), and yet those lofty gifts are given in vain. In imagery that he clearly drew upon for this passage in *The Giaour*, Byron earlier summed up the human condition in *Childe Harold*:

> *Remove yon skull from out the scattered heaps:*
> *Is that a Temple where a God may dwell?*
> *Why ev'n the Worm at last disdains her shattered*
> > *cell!*
>
> *Look on its broken arch, its ruined wall,*
> *Its chambers desolate, and portals foul:*
> *Yes, this was once Ambition's airy hall,*
> *The Dome of Thought, the Palace of the Soul:*
> *Behold through each lack-lustre, eyeless hole,*
> *The gay recess of Wisdom and of Wit*
> *And Passion's host, that never brooked control:*
> *Can all Saint, Sage, or Sophist ever writ,*
> *People this lonely tower, this tenement refit?*
>
> > *(II, v–vi)*

The answer, of course, is no. It is not a matter of refitting or not; the world is simply so. The gifts are real and the tenement is real; but the world and its chaos of destructive passions are even more real.

A final word needs to be said about the method and structure of the poem. I cannot agree with William Marshall that the final version does "not constitute a whole that can be pieced together" and that "any consideration of the structure or imagery of 'The Giaour' should begin with this proposition."[42] That there are inconsistencies of character, an occasional confusion as to the identity of the speaker of certain lines, and perhaps an unnecessary mystery about the whole business one must admit. Yet, having admitted this, we can still admire what Byron has attempted in the structure of the poem—in addition to the converging points of view and the themes I have discussed above.

The narrative itself is carried almost completely by the fisherman, although there are times when a more objective voice is heard to set a scene or "swell a progress." This fisherman is at once a Moslem, garrulous but neither unimaginative nor inarticulate, a collector of gossip and stories, a fierce partisan of Hassan, an eye-witness to several of the scenes and incidents, and, finally, a participant in at least two major events in the story. As such, it is natural for him to blurt out first (to the poet I assume) what he knows best, that is, what he has actually seen—the initial appearance of the Giaour during the Moslem feast (ll. 180–256). That startling sight leads him to jump ahead too quickly, by way of contrast, to the present ruined state of Hassan's palace and its earlier idyllic beauty (ll. 277–351). Immediately following this sequence of death images, he turns naturally, by association, to the scene of death in which he participated, the drowning of Leila (ll. 352–87). From this point to his reappearance at the monastery, the fisherman narrates only what he has gathered from various sources, with the exception of the first-hand descriptions of Leila herself (ll. 473–518) and of Hassan's grave (ll. 723–46).[43] In the first

---

[42] "The Accretive Structure of Byron's 'The Giaour,' " *MLN*, LXXVI (1961), 502. M. K. Joseph is perhaps the only critic to give Byron credit for a serious "concern for the form of the poem"—though he does not say anything about that form other than that it is fragmentary (*Byron the Poet* [London, 1964], p. 37).

[43] One of the most acute comments on the fisherman-narrator is one of the earliest, George Ellis' remark on ll. 288ff.:

this part of the narrative is managed with unusual taste. The fisher-

section of his second-hand narrative (ll. 739–72), he even makes
a point of saying that he does not know everything:

> *Doth Leila there no longer dwell?*
> *That tale can only Hassan tell:*
> *Strange rumours in our city say*
> *Upon that eve she fled away*
> *When Rhamazan's last sun was set.*
>
> *(ll. 445–49)*

From these rumors, from "the tale his [Hassan's] Nubians
tell, / Who did not watch their charge too well" (ll. 465–66),
from what "others say" about that night (l. 467), and from his
own remembrance of the Giaour's mysterious ride into the area,
the fisherman pieces the whole story together—Hassan's sudden
departure "deck'd for war," the battle (obviously told originally
by the lone survivor who reports to Hassan's mother), and the
scene with Hassan's mother.

The fisherman, then, is one of the poet-pilgrim's two
major sources, the other of course being the Giaour himself.
Thus we have the public guesses, so to speak, as to what hap-
pened, the soldier's account, the fisherman's absorption of these
with interpolations of his own first-hand knowledge, the
Giaour's account, the Monk's account of the Giaour—all subsumed under the vision of the poet. To these accounts the poet

---

man has, hitherto, related nothing more than the extraordinary
phenomenon which had excited his curiosity, and of which it is
his immediate object to explain the cause to his hearers; but instead of proceeding to do so, he stops to vent his execrations on
the Giaour, to describe the solitude of Hassan's once luxurious
haram [sic], and to lament the untimely death of the owner, and
of Leila, together with the cessation of that hospitality which they
had uniformly exercised. He reveals, as if unintentionally and un-
consciously, the catastrophe of his story; but he thus prepares his
appeal to the sympathy of his audience, without much diminishing
of their suspense.
Review of *The Giaour* and *The Bride of Abydos, Quarterly Review*,
X (1814), 336–37. See also the intelligent but inconclusive analysis of
the structure of *The Giaour* by Clement T. Goode, "Byron's Early
Romances: A Study" (unpublished Ph.D. dissertation, Vanderbilt
University, 1959), pp. 153–64.

113

adds his own impressions of the Giaour, as well as, by manipulation of their tone and gestures, his impressions of all the other
characters, his interpretation of the story as he pieced it together, and his commentary on its significance in the light of
what he knows of the past and sees in the present. Each of the
other points of view is limited to the bias of the beholder; and
consequently each of these interpretations is incorrect—or at
most only partially correct. For the fisherman, his curse on the
Giaour is deserved, and

> *This broken tale was all we knew*
> *Of her he loved, or him he slew.*
>
> (*ll. 1333–34*)

But it was not all. For Hassan's mother, it meant the
loss of a son; for Hassan's palace and entourage it meant ruin;
for the Monk and the other friars it meant the triumph of evil;
and for the Giaour it meant rage at Hassan, despair and remorse,
enduring his hell within, isolation from the world and mankind
(and, on a shallower level, "one mate, and one alone" man
should take). For the poet, the "broken tale" meant all of these
separately, but corporately it meant the world, man's present,
on which converges a bitter as well as a sweet Edenic past and
a hope (though ultimately a vain one) for the future.

> *And they who listen may believe,*
> *Who heard it first had cause to grieve.*
>
> (*ll. 166–67*)

The basic method by which the poet achieves this
composite is simple: he extrapolates and generalizes upon the
particulars of the story as he receives them, and often comments
on their significance, implications, or connections with scenes,
characters, and events seemingly extraneous to the business at
hand. Thus, after the fisherman's narrative of the Giaour's
mysterious appearance in the beginning of the poem, Byron,
using fundamentally the same technique he used in *Childe*

Harold, slides almost imperceptibly from the fisherman's point of view to the poet's:

> *O'er him who loves, or hates, or fears,*
> *Such moment pours the grief of years:*
> *What felt he then, at once opprest*
> *By all that most distracts the breast?*
> *That pause, which pondered o'er his fate,*
> *Oh, who its dreary length shall date!*
> *Though in Time's record nearly nought,*
> *It was Eternity to Thought!*
> *For infinite as boundless space*
> *The thought that Conscience must embrace,*
> *Which in itself can comprehend*
> *Woe without name, or hope, or end.*
>
> (ll. 265–76)

That Byron was consciously shifting gears here is shown not only by the wide-ranging universalization of this passage (a third edition insertion) but also by a late rewrite, for the seventh edition, of a couplet which precedes it. Instead of the present lines 257–58, he originally wrote, with an eye to his poet-pilgrim's narration,

> *'Twas but an instant, though so long*
> *When thus dilated in my song.*[44]

Precisely where the transition from fisherman to poet occurs is impossible to pin-point, and this problem reflects Byron's continuing difficulty with transitions from voice to voice, as in *Childe Harold*. Yet the total effect is of one voice fading out, as if reflecting its finite limitations, while the other more universal, inclusive voice of the poet grows stronger. Similarly, after the fisherman describes the drowning of Leila (ll. 352ff.), the poet expatiates on the futility of the quest for beauty, the fragility of mortal life, the cruelty of one's fellow man, and the power of remorse (ll. 388ff.)—sentiments which are echoed by

---

[44] *P*, III, 98n.

the Giaour in his death-bed speech. Again, in the battle scene, the particularity of the fisherman's account—

> The foremost Tartar bites the ground!
>   Scarce had they time to check the rein,
>   Swift from their steeds the riders bound;
>   But three shall never mount again:
> Unseen the foes that gave the wound
>
> (ll. 573–77)

—which concludes with the ballad-like choral refrain that Byron used several times, in varying forms, in the fisherman's narrative (ll. 351, 518, 536, 619, 722, 745, 786), yields to the non-partisan objectivity of the poet's account, with its focus on the significance of the battle in terms of the over-all theme of the poem (ll. 620–54). Once more, after the Monk's first speech, in which his fear and bias lead him to say,

> But were I Prior, not a day
> Should brook such stranger's further stay,
> Or pent within our penance cell
> Should doom him there for aye to dwell,
>
> (ll. 818–21)

the poet comments on the decay of the noble soul of man (ll. 832ff.). And in the dialogue immediately following these comments (ll. 883–970), while the Monk sees the Giaour as a creature of neither "earth nor heaven," the poet interprets the plight of man (in the person of the Giaour) in terms of love, bravery, and human passion, seeing the Giaour's particular situation properly in terms of the desolation of Greece, Hassan's palace, and the "vacant bosom's wilderness."

Thus our sense of the whole clearly depends almost entirely on the ability of the poet-pilgrim to maneuver us into the position of seeing all the points of view represented at once. Though "accretive" is a proper word to use in describing the poem's evolution, its structure is more accurately seen as vertical. The tension between the horizontality toward which each segment of the narrative tends and the coinstantaneous thrust of the poet's generalizations, interpretations, and analogies is what gives the poem its peculiar effect and interest. If a modern analogy is not misleading, Faulkner's *The Sound and the Fury*, though a more consummate work of art and more subtly achieved, does very much what Byron was attempting.

After *The Giaour* it is tempting to leap quickly to *Manfred* because that first of Byron's experiments in quasi-dramatic form, where he more clearly separates and distinguishes his speakers and voices (almost to the point of allegorizing them), is so close in conception, theme, imagery, and character to *The Giaour*. Byron himself, however, was not yet ready to take that leap. Preferring to move more slowly in his experiments with form and structure, he tried again several times in a series of tales (or, as he preferred to call them later, "fables"[45]).

II

William Marshall, the only critic to have devoted appreciable attention to *The Bride of Abydos*, sees all the tales as "constructed primarily through the interaction of the elementary themes of Love and Death." In *The Bride*, as in *The Corsair* (Marshall does not deal with *The Giaour* in his book), the characters "tend . . . to assume allegorical dimensions, largely representing either Love, Death, or a fusion of both. . . ." Thus "Zuleika is the Love figure and Giaffir the Death figure. . . . Selim represents the antithesis of Death and of Love in turn, and in the second canto, by his association with Zuleika, the potential for the resolution of the conflict of these motifs through union."[46] This attempt to see all the tales as thematically related rather than as a random collection of vehicles for displaying the "Byronic hero" is eminently commendable. But by, in effect, allegorizing the characters, by assuming that *The Bride* "is almost entirely concerned with action," and by oversimplify-

---

[45] Ltr. to Murray, 25 Mar. 1817, in *LJ*, IV, 85.
[46] *The Structure of Byron's Major Poems*, pp. 40–41.

ing the love-death theme, he misses completely the significance of Byron's experiment in structure as well as theme.

Byron, as usual, depreciated his effort. Again and again, in a series of letters to Moore and Gifford, as well as in his own memoranda, he assured the world and himself that *The Bride* was written only to keep him sane (presumably a reference to his current love affair with Lady Frances Webster), to divert him from himself, to provide himself with some "employment," to wring his thoughts from reality, simply to stay alive.[47] Such a barrage of explanations, all cut from the same cloth (even to the point of self-quotation), suggests a deliberate obscuring, indeed annihilating, of any possible idea in the minds of his correspondents, perhaps even in his own mind, that he was a serious poet beneath the veneer of melodramatic protestant *ad contra*. It may be too early to speculate, but one might suggest here that it is not too much to see Byron the poet, constantly submerged or overwhelmed by Byron the man of the world, as more than fortuitously analogous to the fate of the poet-lover (or man) in the tales. In any case, it is precisely at this time in his life, under whatever pressures that triggered the feverish outpouring of apologies for *The Bride*, that he began to think of the writing of poetry as merely relief, as elimination (to use Paul West's term), or as an escape from self. I should like to suggest, however, that this conception of poetry is more a product of what I called earlier the private-public voice, the one that feigns intimate revelation and in a sense deceives itself, than it is a product of the public-private self's more serious commitment to art and its quieter articulation of powerful feelings and belief through manipulations of plot, character, scene, and image in the poems. To put it more simply, if poetry as elimination appealed to Byron the man, poetry as truth was the concern of Byron the poet.

Very early in his career, probably taking his cue from

---

[47] See, e.g., ltr. to Gifford, 12 Nov. 1813, in *LJ*, II, 278; ltr. to Moore, 30 Nov. 1813, in *LJ*, II, 293; Journal of 1813, in *LJ*, II, 314, 321, 361–62.

his old schoolmaster at Harrow, Henry Drury, Byron wrote in a notebook: "My qualities were much more oratorical and martial than poetical."[48] Yet a year or two later he could see poetry and oratory as being "so nearly similar as to require in a great measure the same Talents, and he who excels in the one, would on application succeed in the other"; he then names Lyttelton, Glover, Young, Sheridan, and Fox as examples of those he "may imitate . . . [but] never equal"[49]—a sentiment that hardly suggests the depreciation of poetry or the feeling that it is unworthy of his efforts. Indeed, the very fact that he will imitate suggests his hope of equaling. Nevertheless, in 1810 to 1811 the letters do begin to give clear evidence of a division in his mind, or better, a specious conflict: poetry, even Scott's, becomes "scribblement" meant only to "amuse," and since he has already done a bit of that (in the volumes of juvenilia), he will publish no

---

[48] *LJ*, I, 29n.

[49] Ltr. to Hanson, 2 Apr. 1807, in *LJ*, I, 126. It is certainly partly because of this conviction that, as Ernest de Selincourt points out, often Byron's "serious verse . . . tended . . . to oratory and declamation, and this may easily, and with him in fact did often, degenerate into rhodomontade" ("Byron," in *Wordsworthian and Other Studies* [Oxford, 1947], p. 121). De Selincourt goes on to argue, however, quite rightly, that this is only one aspect of Byron and that the conception the reader gains from it "has the falsity of a half-truth." The observation is acute, for it tends in its own way to distinguish Byron's public-private voice from his private-public voice, as I have tried to do. S. T. Coleridge put it even better: "Eloquence," he wrote,

> too often is, and is always likely to engender, a species of histrionism. . . . my eloquence was most commonly excited by the desire of running away and hiding myself from my personal and inward feelings, *and not for the expression of them*, while doubtless this very effort of feeling gave a passion and glow to my thoughts and language on subjects of a general nature, that they otherwise would not have had. I fled in a Circle, still overtaken by the Feelings, from which I was evermore fleeing, with my back turned towards them. . . .

Quoted in Donald Davie, *Articulate Energy* (London, 1955), pp. 75–76. W. W. Robson, in his 1957 Chatterton Lecture, was moving toward the same distinction, though he did not develop it, in his analysis of Byron's use of "the histrionic profound" ("Byron as Poet," pp. 40–58).

more.[50] The desire for fame and the fear of failure in the public eye complicate the picture here, but it is still clear that he will continue to write. In a letter to his mother from Athens, immediately after saying that he will "keep no journal, nor have I any intention of scribbling my travels" (in the full knowledge that he had already completed the second canto of *Childe Harold's Pilgrimage*), he writes: "It is true I have some others [i.e., poems] in manuscript, but I leave them for those who come after me; and, if deemed worth publishing, they may serve to prolong my memory when I myself cease to remember."[51] Once Dallas, Murray, and others respond excitedly to *Childe Harold*, however, we hear no further hint of his quitting nor of poetry as a mere outlet for his pent-up emotion. Indeed, it is worth noting here, out of chronological order, his almost Wordsworthian conviction in 1814 that "while you are under the influence of passions, you only feel, but cannot describe them, any more than, when in action, you could turn round and tell the story to your next neighbor! When all is over,—all, all, and irrevocable,—trust to memory—she is but too faithful."[52]

Still, in 1813 to 1814 the notion of poetry as a purgative, as desperate busyness, is prominent in his mind. He says that he even burned the beginnings of a comedy and a novel "because the scene ran into *reality*." And he formulates one of his most famous dicta—one that has been used against him ever since: "To withdraw *myself* from *myself* (oh that cursed selfishness!) has ever been my sole, my entire, my sincere motive in scribbling at all; and publishing is also the continuance of the same object, by the action it affords to the mind, which else recoils upon itself. . . ." He thinks of "expectorating a romance, or rather a tale in prose." Even writing in his journal is a relief. Yet for all this he knows that he cannot escape, that even while trying "in rhyme" to "keep more away from facts . . . the thought

---

[50] Ltr. to Hodgson, 3 Oct. 1810, in *LJ*, I, 299; ltr. to Mrs. Byron, 14 Jan. 1811, in *LJ*, I, 309.
[51] *LJ*, I, 309.
[52] Journal of 1814, in *LJ*, II, 388.

always runs through, through . . . yes, yes, through"; and that however slapdash the original sketch or draft of his expectorated tale, he will return to it again and again, revising, adding, re-arranging, formalizing, focusing.[53]

We should not be surprised, then, to find a mass of manuscripts, insertions, deletions, additions, revisions, and corrected proof copies for the very poem Byron seemed proudest about completing in slapdash fashion. He began it late in October, 1813 (perhaps as late as November 1), and worked on it continually, even doggedly, until its final publication on November 29 or December 2, 1813.[54] Although he was not entirely happy with its final form, he was proud of the fact that it was his "first *entire* composition of any length," with the exception of *English Bards, and Scotch Reviewers*, thus evincing a rare concern for wholeness and form.[55]

In comparison with *The Giaour* that form is greatly simplified. Almost the entire poem is in dialogue, with settings and commentary by a poet-pilgrim similar to the one in the earlier tale. Gone are the mystery and complexity of *The Giaour*, in which Byron thought the diverse and fragmentary sources of the story were necessary to establish a variety of points of view. Instead, in a move toward simplification, he uses a quasi-dramatic form in which identifiable character-speakers provide the different points of view naturally, in dialogue, monologue, and soliloquy (the last being the asides in which the thoughts of Giaffir and Selim are revealed in the opening scene). Yet Byron retains the voice of the narrator, or rather of the poet, who sets the scene and comments upon its significance and universality, whose point of view is essentially *sub specie aeternitatis*, and whose manipulation of the limited points of view against the backdrop of his own constitutes the main vehicle for the themes

---

[53] All of the quotations in this paragraph are from the Journal of 1813, in *LJ*, II, 323, 351, 314, 366, 323.

[54] See Coleridge, *P*, III, 151–53, for the history of the poem's composition, revision, and publication.

[55] Ltr. to Murray, 29 Nov. 1813, in *LJ*, II, 291.

of the work. In a sense Byron has moved us closer to the action while retaining the over-all perspective he needs to make that action meaningful.

The first stanza of Canto I of *The Bride*, which is, significantly, a last-minute addition by Byron, provides a precise parallel to the opening of *The Giaour*—we are in an apparently Edenic realm, "Where the flowers ever blossom, the beams ever shine," where the nightingale and the rose live the fable of eternal love and beauty, where all is divine "save the spirit of man."[56] From this passage alone it is clear that the poet is more than a mere narrator, for his vision, as in *The Giaour*, is of a pattern of life that he has seen before and will see again. The ominous coexistence of the cypress and the myrtle, the vulture and the turtledove, innocence and fallen man is eternal, and in this world there is never a doubt as to which is the victim. If love can create, however momentarily, a fragile heaven in the midst of hell, a place of peace and beauty in a strife-torn world, it can also, with terrible irony, marry Leander to the sea as Hassan claimed his terrible bride in battle. The poet's steps have also trod "the sacred shore" of Troy, fallen because of love and "Priam's pride"; and even the very dust of buried heroes, victims of time and the world's grim ironies, is now gone (ll. 506ff.). The human condition has been the same since Biblical days, and the fall of Eve provides the poet's archetype in the description of Zuleika: "Fair, as the first that fell of womankind" (l. 158); for her, quite properly, Selim "in those bright isles [has] built a bower / Blooming as Aden in its earliest hour" (ll. 890–91).[57]

To Byron, however, the fall of man is neither orthodox nor Miltonic, as we have seen. It has little or nothing to do with God, but has, rather, to do with man's composition. Not only is he "half dust, half deity," he is also a tortured compound of mind and heart, reason and love, worldly and otherworldly

---

[56] Coleridge suggests that these opening lines were probably inspired by Goethe's "Kennst du das Land" (*P*, III, 157n).
[57] Byron in a footnote points out that "Jannat-al-Aden" is the "perpetual abode, the Musselman paradise" (*P*, III, 197n).

ambition, imagination and the senses, cruelty and compassion—
a creature upon whom the world makes impossible demands for
bare survival and who is denied the possibility of the enduring
love which will raise him above himself; a creature in whom the
heat of passion and the coldness of intellect are both creative
and destructive; a creature whose imagination pictures to him
an Edenic past that is irretrievable and a dream of a future that
is unattainable; a creature constantly and inevitably caught and
destroyed in his own selfless plans for freedom and a place in
the sun; a creature both slave and enslaver, a product of his
own will (or lack of it), a victim of both action and inaction;
a creature alone, alienated from all save his persistent dreams of
a better world, dreams that are shattered with equal persistence
by a world intolerant or indifferent to dreams; a creature who
is a poet at heart but whose poetry captures no minds, conquers
no nations, gains no riches, wins no freedom, and is trampled
beneath the boots of the onrushing hordes of the worldly.[58]

"I might attempt to found a new Utopia," Byron once
wrote to his mother,[59] but quickly recanted, recognizing his forte
to be the writing, after "so many *divine* poems," of "Human"
poems.[60] If these human poems reveal a hell on earth and a hell
in man's heart, relieved only by fleeting visions of man's momentary (and vain) triumphs in death, they also reveal a consistent
vision of man's low estate and the futility of romantic optimism.
If his early melancholy, ennui, and *Weltschmerz* represented a
fashionable pose of superiority born largely of his consciousness

---

[58] In this Byron is unlike most—if not all—of our greatest poets, who,
as M. H. Abrams has put it, pay "the human race the compliment of
assuming that it is, in its central moral consciousness, sound"—i.e.,
that villains are recognizable as villains, daughters *ought* to be loyal
to their fathers, and so on ("Belief and Suspension of Disbelief,"
Literature and Belief ["English Institute Essays, 1957"; New York,
1958], p. 20). Byron instead persistently refuses to accept this assumption completely. While assuming a certain kind of "good" and
"evil," he then dramatizes the gray middle ground between, leaving
readers unsure of their conceptions.
[59] 1 July 1810, in *LJ*, I, 284.
[60] Ltr. to Murray, 6 Apr. 1819, in *LJ*, IV, 284.

of noble lineage, his mature melancholy was that of a man with illusions, dreams, and a powerful imagination who is reacting to the human condition with a mind incapable of accepting illusions as real. Perhaps, he writes in his Ravenna journal, man who is "born *passionate* of body" has also an innate "secret tendency to the love of Good in his Main-spring of Mind. But God help us all! It is at present a sad jar of atoms."[61] It was not merely the reading of Johnson's *Vanity of Human Wishes* (a work he had just put down) that led him to see man as eternally "an unlucky rascal. The infinite variety of lives conduct but to death, and the infinity of wishes lead but to disappointment."[62] Only in his more sanguine moments could he even imagine the possibility that man might be "the relic of some higher material being, wrecked in a former world, and degenerated in the hardships and struggle through Chaos into Conformity—or something like it."[63] That idea, however, reaches its fruition only in *Cain*, with an assist from Cuvier's *Recherches sur les ossements fossiles de quadrupedes*. In *The Bride of Abydos* we have as yet only the evolving picture of a world and man which ultimately could only be expressed, with sanity, in the irreverence and forced laughter of *Don Juan*, that ultimately depressing fable for our time, or in the fairy-tale setting of *The Island*, where love and freedom and joy once again reign over the world:

> *Again their own shore rises on the view,*
> *No more polluted with a hostile hue;*
> *No sullen ship lay bristling o'er the foam,*
> *A floating dungeon:—all was Hope and Home!*
>
> .   .   .   .
>
> *A hundred fires, far flickering from the height,*
> *Blazed o'er the general revel of the night,*
> *The feast in honour of the guest, returned*[64]

---

[61] *Detached Thoughts,* in *LJ*, V, 457.
[62] 1821 Diary, in *LJ*, V, 162. See also ltr. to Murray, 20 Oct. 1821, in *LJ*, V, 393.
[63] *Detached Thoughts,* in *LJ*, V, 459.
[64] Byron, significantly, first wrote "redeemed" for "returned."

> *To Peace and Pleasure, perilously earned;*
> *A night succeeded by such happy days*
> *As only the yet infant world displays.*
> *(ll. 401–4, 415–20)*

"Neuha's Cave," that womb-like miracle where Torquil found refuge from the world's despoilers, is here turned inside out, enveloping all forever.

    The Bride of Abydos has its cave also, but unlike the one in *The Island* it remains at best a temporary refuge, at worst a tomb, for to it the world and its terrors have easy access:

> *a grotto, hewn*
> * By nature, but enlarged by art,*
> *Where oft her [Zuleika's] lute she wont to tune*
> * And oft her Koran conned apart;*
> *And oft in youthful reverie*
> *She dreamed what Paradise might be.*
> *(ll. 582–87)*

This passage is in sharp contrast to the earlier Keatsian description of Zuleika's chamber (ll. 545–65), in which all the delights of the senses, the comforts of religion, the riches of music, poetry, and art are ineffective in dispelling the gloom of the surrounding world. Here Zuleika is likened to a Peri with "fairy fingers," locked in a "cell," who flies at every opportunity the gorgeous yet treacherous world of her tower. Yet the grotto paradise, too, is fragile: Selim, preparing to avenge himself upon Giaffir, has stored it with arms, some tinged with blood; and instead of the soft light of love,

> *That brazen lamp but dimly threw*
> *A ray of no celestial hue.*
> *(ll. 600–1)*

Selim is similarly changed. As Zuleika says,

> *This morn I saw thee gentlest—dearest—*
> * But now thou'rt from thyself estranged.*
> *(ll. 385–86)*

Thus estranged, Selim relates his tale of bloodshed and treachery, the background of his presence in Giaffir's court; he is slain on the brink of victory, and Zuleika perishes in the cave of their paradise. All that remains is an ever-blooming white rose, born "from her . . . virgin earth" but "Alone and dewy—coldly pure and pale" in an eternity of death in life and unfulfillment (ll. 1197, 1213).

The path to this complete waste and desolation, more characteristically defined (as in *The Giaour*) by Selim's "ghastly turbaned head" lying at night on the beach where he was slain, is fraught with intense Byronic irony. The opening scene is punctuated with images of death and the implacability of fate, which thwarts man's most virtuous efforts and plans. Referring to the Moslem custom of veiling the faces of virgins from the eyes of all, Giaffir says,

> *"Woe to the head whose eye beheld*
> *My child Zuleika's face unveiled!"*
>
> *(ll. 38–39)*

—thus foreshadowing the killing of Selim, the only one beside the harem eunuch, Haroun, to see Zuleika's face. As to Zuleika herself "Her fate is fixed this very hour," Giaffir says (l. 41), voicing his intent of chastising her for leaving the harem. Selim, in taking the blame for this upon his own shoulders, relates how he and Zuleika, in order to enjoy to the full the dawn, "to the cypress groves had flown, / And made earth, main, and heaven our own!" (ll. 69–70). There among the age-old emblems of death they recalled the story of Mejnoun and Leila, the Persian Romeo and Juliet. The image is a striking one, a symbolic tableau of the fragility of love in a world of darkness, of youthful joy and aspirations destroyed by the realities of things.

But the contrast is not just between death and love, or, as Marshall awkwardly puts it, between the death-giver and the love-giver;[65] it is also between mind and heart, intellect and

---

[65] *The Structure of Byron's Major Poems*, p. 41.

imagination, ambition and affection, the man of the world and the poet. Giaffir berates Selim for not being a "man": "Greek in soul if not in creed," he angers Giaffir because with "listless eyes" he

> *Must pore where babbling waters flow,*
> *And watch unfolding roses blow.*
>
> *(ll. 88–89)*

To Giaffir he is not what man must be in this world—an "arm," not a soul or a heart:

> *his arm is little worth,*
> *And scarcely in the chase could cope*
> *With timid fawn or antelope,*
> *Far less would venture into strife*
> *Where man contends for fame and life.*
>
> *(ll. 135–39)*

In contrast, Giaffir's cold, dispassionate will is early related to his mind by Byron:

> *The mind within, well skilled to hide*
> *All but unconquerable pride.*
>
> *(ll. 28–29)*

And the mind is concerned with wealth, conquest, a profitable alliance, power—and, ultimately, destruction. Zuleika herself responds to Giaffir with a keen awareness of his mental nature:

> *Affection chained her to that heart;*
> *Ambition tore the links apart.*
>
> *(ll. 191–92)*

Byron completes the image of mind by having Giaffir coldly arrange the marriage of Zuleika for political ends (ll. 193–218) and then leave abruptly to "Mix in the game of mimic slaughter" (l. 251) with his best cavalry troops.

The fragile heaven that Zuleika and Selim have harbored secretly against the world is thus threatened with the same destruction Lambro wreaks upon the idyll of Juan and Haidée. Unable to continue as Giaffir's slave (like a "Christian crouching in the fight"), Selim must either escape to a "Neuha's cave" with Zuleika and thus remain human or arm his mind to fight and thus become a "man." He chooses the latter: adopting Giaffir's very language and image pattern, he rejects Zuleika's offer of flowers, "sees" now that her love has "unmanned" him (l. 816) and that he must follow "but the bent assigned / By fatal Nature to man's warring kind" (ll. 910–11). Byron shrewdly couches Selim's decisive and fatal change in the imagery of the idyllic and fabled past, when the poet reigned and love and beauty were unfading and unthreatened, where mind and heart were one. Zuleika playfully sprinkles attar of roses about her chamber, but just as her appeal cannot pierce "his glittering vest," so the drops of perfume

> *Unheeded o'er his bosom flew,*
> *As if that breast were marble too.*
>
> (ll. 275–76)

Then, with the "childish thought" of innocence, she picks roses from the garden and makes a wreath for Selim:

> *"He loved them once; may touch them yet,*
> *If offered by Zuleika's hand.*
>
>   ·   ·   ·   ·   ·
>
> *This rose to calm my brother's cares*
> *A message from the Bulbul* [nightingale] *bears;*
> *It says to-night he will prolong*
> *For Selim's ear his sweetest song."*
>
> (ll. 281–82, 287–90)

But with Giaffir's taunt—about watching "unfolding roses blow" instead of wielding a scimitar—fresh in his ears, Selim refuses the "foolish flowers" as well as Zuleika's passionate, fervent protestations of her undying love. His ear now hears only the trumpet of war. Byron accentuates his transformation into a Giaffir by the imagery of the passage as well as by the repetition of "thoughts" that take over the whole man:

His trance was gone, his keen eye shone
With thoughts that long in darkness dwelt;
With thoughts that burn—in rays that melt.

.　　　.　　　.　　　.

A war-horse at the trumpet's sound,
A lion roused by heedless hound,
A tyrant waked to sudden strife
By graze of ill-directed knife,
Starts not to more convulsive life.

(ll. 329–31, 340–44)

Byron's last-minute change of the lovers' relationship from that of half-sister and half-brother to that of cousins is considerably less important than it has been made out to be. If it is important at all, it is as an indication that Byron himself finally saw the theme of incest to be really irrelevant to the thematic development he had in mind.[66] When Selim says, "I am not, love! what I appear," his revelation to Zuleika of a father killed, a life of oppression and indignity under Giaffir, and his own "manly" career of warfare behind Giaffir's back is Byron's way of demonstrating, even through a "sympathetic" character, the true nature of man's "warring" kind, the "necessity" imposed by the world upon man to be thus, and the inevitable triumph of mind over heart. As long as Selim, like Leander, saw only "that light of love," he was not a man in the world's eyes. Byron's opening of Canto II with the panorama of Greece's buried heroes and the triumph of dust is a proper and compelling anticipation of the end of his poem, as well as an example of how he sharpened the focus from universal to particular, from the "lone and nameless barrow" of Achilles to the grotto of Selim and Zuleika.

So completely has the atmosphere changed that upon

---

[66] Stephen Spender may be right, however, in suggesting that the incest theme (he has in mind *Parisina* in particular) is the poet's way of showing that an ideal world is being created "where there is no immorality in personal relations between human beings and where the only crimes are public ones" (Preface to *A Choice of English Romantic Poetry* [New York, 1947], pp. 23–24).

Selim's revelation that he is not Zuleika's brother, she assumes immediately that he is there to plunder and despoil, even to kill her. Her plea is the world's: instead of killing her, "Oh! bid me be thy slave!" she cries (l. 665). And just as the grotto has become a haven of death, so the Koran, an integral and important part of Zuleika's paradise on earth in her chamber and the grotto, becomes an instrument of destruction (or at least a sanction for it):

> So may the Koran verse displayed
> Upon its steel direct my blade.
>
> (ll. 671–72)

The terrible irony of all of this Byron underscores by having Selim self-righteously label his vengeful resolve, as well as his earlier piratical plundering, "freedom" (l. 869). Freedom for Byron seems to be often only another form of slavery if it must be gained through slaughter. As Selim says, he is a leader of "hordes, / Whose laws and lives are on their swords"; and he enjoys freedom only as a release from "inaction's sluggish yoke" (l. 820), in so doing forgetting his essential humanity:

> E'en for thy [Zuleika's] presence [I] ceased to pine;
> The World—nay, Heaven itself was mine!
>
> (ll. 833–34)

Obedience is the sole virtue in this lawless world, where Selim has made men "fitting instruments / For more than e'en my own intents" (ll. 855–56).

But Byron's irony is not yet complete. In a late pre-publication addition, he has Selim further sanction his actions, his tyranny and slaughter, his "freedom," by asking Zuleika (and thus all she represents in opposition to the world) to "share and bless my bark; / The Dove of peace and promise to mine ark!" (ll. 878–79). The reference to Noah is strikingly apt in its inversion of the significance of the Biblical story. Selim goes on, sounding more and more like Giaffir: just as the latter would provide Zuleika a sumptuous dowry and thus gain through her marriage the power of an ally, so Selim will "bedeck" his bride with "The spoil of nations" and "repay" her love with his "toils" (ll. 895, 900). The lost Eden will be recovered through this new "love" and creativity: "Earth—sea alike—our world within our arms!" (l. 935). And in it Selim will rule as he rules his horde:

> *No deed they've done, nor deed shall do,*
> *Ere I have heard and doomed it too:*
> *I form the plan—decree the spoil.*
>
> *(ll. 956–58)*

Zuleika's reaction to all this is predictable but none-theless effective. Like "a younger Niobe," she stands stunned and motionless, as if "hardened into stone" like Selim's breast (ll. 978, 976). The battle immediately follows, and Byron doubles the irony by having Selim, in the moment before he is dealt his death blow, and with his own bloody sword in his hand, turn to direct a last look of love toward Zuleika (ll. 1039–50). In the world, if one adapts himself to its code of values, one escapes or wins by the sword; one dies with the look of love. It is not that Byron is saying that the world is made up of either tyrants or slaves so much as that tyrant and slave are the same, that all men suffer from the tyranny of their own minds or the futility of their passions. No moral judgments are made—or indeed can be made. Neither Giaffir nor Selim is right or wrong; our sympathies lie with the apparently oppressed but our minds see the fruitlessness of it all. "There is no Tyrant like a Slave," Byron wrote; "There is ice at both poles, north and south—all extremes are the same. . . ."[67]

At the same time, it is impossible for man to occupy the "still center" by rejecting the extremes; for this stillness is a living death, a surrender or traitorous denial of the main-springs of his being. For the Byronic man, all is either action—

---

[67] Prose fragment entitled "The Present State of Greece," dated 26 Feb. 1824, in *LJ*, VI, 441; Journal of 1814, in *LJ*, II, 411.

which leads only to death—or death itself.[68] "The great object of life is sensation—to feel that we exist, even though in pain. It is this 'craving void' which drives us to gaming—to battle—to travel—to intemperate, but keenly felt pursuits of any description, whose principal attraction is the agitation inseparable from their accomplishment."[69] This early statement of 1813 is echoed again as late as 1821, in Byron's Ravenna journal: "I have a notion that Gamblers are as happy as most people, being always *excited*. Women, wine, fame, the table, even Ambition, *sate* now and then; but every turn of the card, and cast of the dice, keeps the Gamester alive: besides one can Game ten times longer than one can do any thing else."[70] But at the same time that man is "*passionate* of body" he is also passionate of mind, and here too the still center is rejected by Byron. The mind "is in perpetual activity," he writes in seeking to establish man's immortality: just as "matter is eternal, always changing, but reproduced, and, as far as we can comprehend Eternity, Eternal . . . why not *Mind*? Why should not the Mind act with and upon the Universe?"[71]

Thus the slave, for Byron, is the epitome of non-man, just as the conformist—social, political, or literary—is the object of his contempt. Cant is his language, poverty of spirit and death his environment. "Inaction's sluggish yoke" spurs to a realization of his tragically doomed manhood not only Selim, but also the Giaour, Hassan, Lara, Conrad, Alp, Manfred, Cain, and Don Juan. It is less the loss of Leila than the consciousness of "withered frame" and "ruined mind" that leads the Giaour to embrace death. If it is rest that he seeks, as he says, not paradise (l. 1270), he also wishes, characteristically, "not to feel 'tis

---

[68] W. H. Auden, among others, is thus incorrect, I think, in seeing Byron's heroes as acting not "for the sake of the act, but in order to know what it feels like to act" (*The Enchafed Flood: or The Romantic Iconography of the Sea* [New York, 1950], pp. 150–51).

[69] Ltr. to Annabella Milbanke, 6 Sept. 1813, in *LJ*, III, 400.

[70] *Detached Thoughts*, in *LJ*, V, 425.

[71] *Ibid.*, pp. 457, 458.

rest" (l. 995). We should not be surprised, then, to find Byron characterizing such disparate forms of life as love, poetry, and tyranny in the same terms of violent action. The Giaour will not, like the false lover of Petrarchanism, "prate in puling strain / Of Ladye-love, and Beauty's chain" (ll. 1103–4). Such a "death" is to be eschewed in favor of the death inherent in the vitality of "the lava flood / That boils in Eetna's breast of flame" (ll. 1101–2).

So too, in one of Byron's most famous and most misunderstood passages—in which he describes poetry as "the lava of the imagination whose eruption prevents an earthquake"[72]— the poet must be active, alive, engaged with the world, not a mere observer and describer. "Damn description," he wrote as early as 1809, "it is always disgusting";[73] and *descriptive poetry [is] the lowest department of the art.*"[74] As a poet he is like the tiger: "if I miss my first Spring, I go growling back to my Jungle"; similarly, "if Tyranny misses her *first* spring, she is cowardly as the tiger, and retires to be hunted."[75] Both poet and tyrant are vibrant and alive; refurbishing the poem and lurking in the jungle are equal forms of slavery and death, of inaction, of the "rest" which all men crave yet cannot tolerate.

The Bride of Abydos is, then, hardly "an outpouring . . . insipid in its futile vehemence," as Du Bos described it;[76] it is rather Byron's *Hamlet*, reinterpreted in the light of his conceptions of life and death. G. Wilson Knight has long advocated Byron's candidacy for the title of the greatest English poet since Shakespeare. He has sought to show us, through his method of staccato parallel quotations (too often out of context), abundant Shakespeareanism in Byron's poetry, especially

---

[72] Ltr. to Annabella Milbanke, 10 Nov. 1813, in *LJ*, III, 405.

[73] Ltr. to Hodgson, 6 Aug. 1809, in *LJ*, I, 234.

[74] Reply to Blackwood's *Edinburgh Magazine* article on *Don Juan*, in *LJ*, IV, 493.

[75] Ltr. to Murray, 18 Sept. 1820, in *LJ*, V, 120; *Detached Thoughts*, in *LJ*, V, 451–52.

[76] *Byron and the Need of Fatality*, p. 144.

the plays, and has gone so far as to "prove," in a very strained essay,[77] that the circumstances of Byron's whole life add up to a real-life *Hamlet*. While Knight is always exciting to read, though frequently irritating, I cannot share his extreme views: Byron is neither Hamlet nor a latter-day Shakespeare. That he knew his Shakespeare more than moderately well is attested to by the abundant allusions and quotations—all clearly from memory—in the letters and journals; that he consciously employed *Hamlet* for his own purposes in *The Bride* (a borrowing that Knight, unaccountably, does not see) is even more important, for it underscores the seriousness of his purpose in the poem and suggests the deliberateness and subtlety of his artistry in creating a form to carry out that purpose.

The parallels between the two works are many, and once pointed to, they are so obvious that they require little commentary but considerable admiration for Byron's skill in manipulating them. The political situation in *The Bride* is roughly similar to that in *Hamlet*. Hamlet's father conquered the elder Fortinbras and wrung from him additional lands; Selim's father participated in the defeat of "Paswan's rebel hordes" (l. 702). But now the younger Fortinbras prepares to battle for the recovery of those lands, just as Giaffir, "with fearful news from Danube's banks" (l. 457), must once again put his house in order against the possibility of rebellion.

Upon this background, all of which we do not know until Selim reveals the whole story to Zuleika in Canto II, Byron, like Shakespeare, projects his first major scene and the clash between Giaffir-Claudius and Selim-Hamlet. Although he is the murderer of Selim's father (the manner of the murder is strikingly similar to Claudius' killing of the elder Hamlet), Giaffir alternately chides Selim for his lack of manliness—as Claudius tries to convince Hamlet that his "unmanly grief" is against heaven, nature, and reason—and cajolingly invites him to act as his loving son. Claudius is of course a shrewder, subtler man,

---

[77] "Byron and Hamlet," *Bulletin of the John Rylands Library*, XLV (1962–63), 115–47.

and his misgivings over Hamlet's conduct take on none of the openly insulting tone of Giaffir's "Son of a slave" (l. 81),

> *"From unbelieving mother bred,*
> *Vain were a father's hope to see*
> *Aught that beseems a man in thee."*
>
> *(ll. 82–84)*

Yet both Claudius and Giaffir suspect the thoughts of their wards. As Giaffir says of Selim,

> *"Much I misdoubt this wayward boy*
> *Will one day work me more annoy,"*
>
> *(ll. 132–33)*

so Claudius worries about the "something" in Hamlet's soul of which "the hatch and the disclose / Will be some danger" (III, i, 172, 174–75).

Selim is no Hamlet, but this is not Byron's purpose in making use of Shakespeare. Rather, it is to suggest that Hamlet's predicament is the human condition of all men "In the corrupted currents of this world," where

> *Offence's gilded hand may shove by justice,*
> *And oft 'tis seen the wicked prize itself*
> *Buys out the law.*
>
> *(III, iii, 57, 58–60)*

Like Hamlet, Selim is content to bide his time, to wear a mask, until circumstances call forth the man of decisive action and violence to avenge his father's murder, his uncle's usurpation, and his own ignominy. Yet even in this just cause Selim's efforts, unlike Hamlet's, lead but to destruction. In the world of tragedy —of Hamlets and Lears—the universal upset is readjustable through the heroic efforts of man. In Byron's world, no such readjustment seems possible.[78] Human effort, no matter how noble, in no matter how worthy a cause, is doomed. This is the

---

[78] Cf. Newman Ivey White's interesting comment on this aspect of Byron's thinking:

Seeing life almost as it was, he was able to come closer to the heart

line separating Byron's conception from tragedy, that most affirmative literary celebration of man's greatness. For Byron, man is his own worst enemy, endowed as he is with the conflicting forces and unresolved elements his maker saw fit to embody; for it is man who makes up and governs "the world." As Hamlet says,

> this goodly frame, the earth, seems to me a sterile promontory, this most excellent canopy, the air . . . this brave o'erhanging firmament, this majestical roof fretted with golden fire, why, it appears no other thing to me than a foul and pestilent congregation of vapours. What a piece of work is a man! How noble in reason! How infinite in faculty, in form and moving! How express and admirable in action! How like an angel in apprehension! How like a god! The beauty of the world! The paragon of animals! And yet, to me, what is this quintessence of dust?
>
> (II, ii, 309ff.)

To Byron man is all these things—and dust; and the world never changes.

> *Between the pass and fell incensed points*
> *Of mighty opposites*
>
> *(V, ii, 61–62)*

the Byronic man lives and fights and dies.

---

of real tragedy than any other Romanticist. With him the struggle is not between abstract good and evil, as with Shelley and Godwin, nor between mere mental projections, as with Wordsworth and Coleridge, but between characters neither wholly bad nor wholly good and experiencing within themselves the world old conflict of good and evil impulses. The protagonist falls because his view of life is onesided; but the natural order which triumphs is not [Shakespeare's]

but rather "a natural order of rebellious courts and corrupt governments . . ." ("The English Romantic Writers as Dramatists," *Sewanee Review*, XXX [1922], 214). This runs sharply counter, of course, to Northrop Frye's identification of "tragic vision" with "ironic vision" (which tends toward a stasis of action) in nineteenth-century drama ("A Conspectus of Dramatic Genres," *Kenyon Review*, XIII [1951], 550). See also Frye's "The Mythos of Autumn: Tragedy," in his *Anatomy of Criticism* (Princeton, N.J., 1957), pp. 206–23.

Byron's Ophelia is, of course, Zuleika. In order to sharply focus man's (Selim's) position between the equally attractive and "right" causes of revenge and love (both of these fused into one through the idea of freedom), he omits the Polonius-Laertes-Ophelia subplot entirely and makes his Ophelia the daughter of the king-usurper-murderer Claudius-Giaffir. Hamlet's mother is also omitted, somewhat unfortunately, I think, since the incest theme here would have strengthened Byron's case for the corruption of Giaffir's world. This is certainly one of the reasons, perhaps even the main one, for Byron's contemplating the portrayal of Selim and Zuleika as half-siblings. His decision to change this detail, as I have said earlier, in no way detracts from his purpose—and may indeed strengthen it because the idea of incest is not allowed to qualify in any way the purity of their love. The deaths of Ophelia and Zuleika are both the result of the desire to set things right, inflicted upon the innocent; but, as Byron interprets the deaths, they are also the consequences of the critical change in the central character from lack of manliness to manliness, from inaction to action, from poet to soldier. In this change Zuleika's view of Selim as "from thyself estranged" is erroneous, for he is merely revealing his essential self, hidden till then for various reasons. In the same way Ophelia sees Hamlet as a totally different person, his mind overthrown; but Byron sees in Ophelia's madness the kind of self-estrangement that Zuleika sees in Selim: "Poor Ophelia," says Claudius,

> Divided from herself and her fair judgment,
> Without the which we are pictures, or mere beasts.
> *(IV, v, 84, 85–86)*

In a further parallel, Zuleika's fear for her life after Selim reveals that he is not her brother suggests Ophelia's fear of Hamlet's changed countenance, a fear intensified to madness when he kills her father.

Byron's *Bride* ends with no Horatio or Fortinbras to put things right. Giaffir triumphs, but only in despair at Zuleika's death, her blood very much on his hands. And Byron reinterprets Fortinbras' closing speech, as he surveys the stage strewn with corpses—"Such a sight as this / Becomes the field, but here shows much amiss" (V, ii, 412–13)—to suggest that "the place of thousand tombs" (l. 1146), which for him is the world, shows indeed "much amiss," whether in the king's palace, the hovel of the poor, or on the battlefield. Only the cypress blooms amidst death, and a rose "Alone and dewy— coldly pure and pale" (l. 1213).

Chapter V

THE CORSAIR, LARA, AND
THE SIEGE OF CORINTH

If *The Giaour* and *The Bride of Abydos* were popular, *The Corsair*, like the first two cantos of *Childe Harold*, literally took the reading public by storm. With boyish excitement, Murray wrote: "I sold, on the day of publication,—a thing perfectly unprecedented—10,000 copies"; and in a little more than a month the poem's seven editions represented over 25,000 copies.[1] If, as Marchand suggests, its success "was caused partly by the fine descriptive passages [and] the swift narrative, sustained by an authentic background known to be derived from personal observation,"[2] clearly a major portion of that success was due to the universal suspicion that Conrad was a self-portrait, fully fleshed out at last. Modern criticism also has largely accepted this suspicion as fact, thus obscuring once again the place of one of Byron's major poems in his development as an artist.

I

On January 6, 1814, Byron wrote Moore that he had "a devil of a long story in the press, entitled 'The Corsair,' in the regular heroic measure. It is a pirate's isle, peopled with my own creatures, and you may easily suppose they do a world of mischief through the three cantos."[3] To Leigh Hunt he calls it his latest "bantling."[4] It is indeed long, but it is hardly an illegiti-

---

[1] *Byron: A Biography*, I, 433.
[2] *Ibid.*, 433–34.
[3] *LJ*, III, 5–6.
[4] Ltr. of 9 Feb. 1814, in *LJ*, III, 29.

mate product of Byron's talent or an inconsequential example of his experimentation with form and structure. Though not nearly so important a poem as *The Giaour* or *The Bride of Abydos*, *The Corsair* is more than "a long story" for quick and easy public consumption. (Indeed, its astonishing success overwhelmed Byron himself as much as Murray.) Structurally, as *The Giaour* was an attempt at verticality of form, coinstantaneousness of impression, and hence a planned complex of multiple points of view, and as *The Bride* secured the integrity of individual points of view by establishing quasi-dramatic characters who were both participants and commentators—almost at the expense of the controlling poet-narrator's point of view, in *The Corsair* Byron attempts to achieve still another kind of balance among narration, drama, and comment. The fisherman-narrator-persona of *The Giaour*, absent also in *The Bride*, does not reappear. Instead, the role of *The Giaour's* poet-pilgrim-commentator, which was built up to almost half of *The Bride's* total lines, plays a somewhat larger role in *The Corsair* than in *The Giaour*, but a considerably smaller one than in *The Bride*. At the same time that his commentative function is decreased, however, his narrative function is considerably expanded, to the point where *The Corsair* becomes as horizontal in form as *The Giaour* is vertical. Beginning at one extreme, then, in his "fables," Byron moves quickly, through the mean form of *The Bride*, to the other extreme. The consequences of this are immediately obvious to the careful reader: those elements of the poems which tend to universalize the specifics of the plot have been reduced to the point where the narrative occupies almost our entire attention. Byron's problem, and I think he recognized it clearly, was to construct the narrative in such a way that it itself would convey the very universality he was sacrificing in its more overt form.[5] That is, his move was further toward the dramatic, despite the smaller proportion of dialogue than in *The Bride*, but

---

[5] Perhaps this kind of narrative structure is what Sir Egerton Brydges had in mind when he described the distinguishing characteristic of *The Corsair* as "elasticity" (*Letters on the Character and Poetical Genius of Lord Byron* [London, 1824], p. 41). A more representative judgment of the poem, however, is Taine's: "The noblest passages are disfigured by pedantic apostrophes, and the pretentious poetic

not yet far enough to warrant the complete exclusion of a narrator.

In a sense, too, *The Corsair* is a kind of summing up, a simpler and more overt statement of the human predicament than any Byron had made thus far—barring a few sections of *Childe Harold*. Perhaps it was this that led him to think of *The Corsair* as his farewell to poetry, to adopt the clarity and neatness of the "good old and now neglected heroic couplet" for the first time since *English Bards*, and to censure openly the morality of the Giaour and the repulsiveness of Harold.[6] And, finally, perhaps this is the reason for the choral beginning of *The Corsair*, in which the pirates laud their life of freedom while the recorder-narrator lightly but surely condemns their morality:

> *These are our realms, no limits to their sway—*
> *Our flag the sceptre all who meet obey.*
> *Ours the wild life in tumult still to range*
> *From toil to rest, and joy in every change.*
>
> (ll. 5–8)

In this Hobbesian Eden, all "snatch the life of Life" (l. 25), careless of the blood that dims the shine of their weapons, with the "thirsting eye of Enterprise" eager to see "where they next shall seize a spoil" (ll. 56, 58). It is no land for slaves or the "vain lord of Wantonness and Ease" (l. 11), but only for the "man" of Giaffir and the "reformed" Selim, the man of "thought,"

> *Linked with success, assumed and kept with skill,*
> *That moulds another's weakness to its will.*
>
> (ll. 183–84)

As Selim sees his horde as "instruments," so too the corsair-man

> *Wields with their[7] hands, but, still to these unknown,*

---

diction sets up its threadbare frippery and conventional ornaments" (*History of English Literature*, trans. H. Van Laun [4 vols.; Edinburgh, 1874], IV, 23).
[6] See the dedicatory letter to Moore prefixing the poem, in *P*, III, 223–25.
[7] My emphasis.

BYRON AND THE RUINS OF PARADISE

Makes even their mightiest deeds appear his own.
Such hath it been—shall be—beneath the Sun
The many still must labour for the one!
'Tis Nature's doom.

(ll. 185–89)

Conrad himself, who must be seen, I think, as Byron's archetypal man ("Man as himself"), is not extraordinary in appearance: "In Conrad's form seems little to admire"; and "No giant frame sets forth his common height" (ll. 195, 198). What makes him a leader, feared, obeyed, envied, is his "power of Thought—the magic of the Mind" (l. 182), his ability to unman himself while, ironically, making himself more manly, to deny his humanity in favor of "freedom" and action, to separate himself from man in order to be more than man. E. H. Coleridge could not be more wrong in saying that he is "an assortment rather than an amalgam of incongruous characteristics."[8] For Byron he is typical man, elevated to titanic proportions, in constant conflict with himself.

Surrounded by the luxury of his plunder, like an ascetic "he shuns the grosser joys of sense," thus nourishing "His mind . . . by that abstinence" (ll. 75, 76). "He stood alike exempt / From all affection and from all contempt" (ll. 271–72); he valued "less who loved—than what obeyed" (l. 554). When he embarks on his last piratical foray, he must shake off his unmanly love and affection; with greater strength of will than Selim, he "sternly gathers all his might of mind" and "mans himself" (ll. 520, 584). What is more important symbolically, he refuses to make the mistake Selim made and does not turn his head as he leaves Medora.[9] Then, steeled against feeling and memories of Medora left behind, he "marvelled how his heart could seem so soft" and "feels of all his former self possest" (ll. 530, 532).

Yet, for all this desperate attempt to be a "man," Conrad's essential humanity, his poetic self, one might say,

---

[8] *P*, III, 219.
[9] Byron accents the symbolic gesture by repeating it; see I, 506 and 584.

cannot be buried (I, xii).[10] The only Eden is in the heart, in Zuleika's cave or Medora's tower, the home of love—and poetry, music, art, and happiness. Thus Medora, like Zuleika, tempts Conrad to plunder no longer, instead to

> *join with me the dance, or wake the song;*
> *Or my guitar, which still thou lov'st to hear,*
> *Shall soothe or lull—or, should it vex thine ear,*
> *We'll turn the tale, by Ariosto told,*
> *Of fair Olympia loved and left of old.*
> *(ll. 436–40)*

The bugle's call to arms shatters her "fairy dreams of bliss" (l. 411), as the trumpet of war in Selim's ears drowns out Zuleika's pleas. Although Byron seems to say that Conrad was not made this way "by Nature" (I, xi), what he actually says is that Conrad was not born a pirate leader. Early "Warped by the world," his wise and compassionate nature became petrified into a fierce and wrathful pride, fed by hate, controlled by mind. But no man can obliterate that "secret spirit" of humanity within himself, however blighted and scarred, that center of his being that is both his heaven and his hell. Against "that passion vainly still he strove" (l. 285), and Medora cannot understand:

> *"How strange that heart, to me so tender still,*
> *Should war with Nature and its better will,"*
> *(ll. 396–97)*

persistently flying from love.

That war is an unequal one, and man himself—and all he loves—is always its victim. Thus at the height of the battle, with victory in his hand, at the peak of his "manhood," Conrad is unmanned by the screams of the women in Seyd's harem that "like a deadly knell / Knocked at that heart unmoved

---

[10] Medora's song (ll. 347–62) is as much a reflection of Conrad's inner self as it is a confession of her love. It is also, of course, like so many of the lyrics in *Hours of Idleness*, a presageful lament for love irrevocably lost.

by Battle's yell"—and becomes human, and lost.[11] "In that pause Compassion snatched from War," Seyd rallies his forces, counter-attacks, captures Conrad, and Medora dies of a broken heart. The tower of Eden, upon Conrad's return, holds only the cold beauty of death—like the face of Greece in *The Giaour*, the cold flowers of Zuleika—the nothingness of the world's reward. At the sight, Conrad's humanity revives, but

> *So feeble now—his mother's softness crept*
> *To those wild eyes, which like an infant's wept:*
> *It was the very weakness of his brain.*
> *(ll. 1816–18)*

Aware that in his fast-paced narrative the particulars of Medora's death and Conrad's anguish constantly threaten to blot out any significance beyond themselves, at the last minute Byron judiciously inserted here an entire stanza. Like all men's hearts, Conrad's

> *was formed for softness—warped to wrong,*
> *Betrayed too early, and beguiled too long;*
> *Each feeling pure—as falls the dropping dew*
> *Within the grot—like that had hardened too;*
> *Less clear, perchance, its earthly trials passed,*
> *But sunk, and chilled, and petrified at last.*

Parabolically, for Byron, this is the nature of things:

> *tempests wear, and lightning cleaves the rock;*
> *If such his heart, so shattered it the shock.*
> *There grew one flower beneath its rugged brow,*
> *Though dark the shade—it sheltered—saved till now.*
> *The thunder came—that bolt hath blasted both,*
> *The Granite's firmness, and the Lily's growth:*
> *The gentle plant hath left no leaf to tell*
> *Its tale, but shrunk and withered where it fell;*
> *And of its cold protector, blacken round*
> *But shivered fragments on the barren ground!*
> *(III, xxiii)*

---

[11] Convinced that Byron intended Conrad to be the Zeluco that Childe Harold failed to become, Marchand completely misinterprets him as "too softly sentimental, too weakly humanitarian under the suffering, proud exterior to be the villain he admits" (*Byron's Poetry*, p. 65).

The poem closes, properly, with Conrad, now in his full manhood, wandering Cain-like over that barren ground into eternity.

If this were all, the poem would still be worth reading as a kind of summary statement of the human condition.
But there is more. Byron is also solidifying here his view of
woman's role in this world. While she is not quite Marshall's
"Love" or the "love-giver," she is certainly the heart and the
affections, the poetic and the imaginative, the opener of the gates
of paradise. Leila, Zuleika, Medora, and Gulnare form an interesting sequence in the development of this idea. Until *The
Corsair* we have seen Byron's women in one dimension, all but
allegorically. In Medora and Gulnare we have the beginnings
of a complexity and conflict similar to that seen in the characters
of the Giaour and Selim, and Byron gives a fairly clear indication
that he sees man as temperamentally hermaphroditic—femininely creative, warm, and human, masculinely destructive, cold,
and unhuman; the heart of a woman, the mind of a man; passion's slave and the victim of his own conceptions; deity and
dust.[12]

Medora's lovely song announces her own significance,
at the same time reflecting the essential humanity Conrad has
been trying to annihilate in himself:

> *"Deep in my soul that tender secret dwells,*
>   *Lonely and lost to light for evermore*
> *Save when to thine my heart responsive swells,*
>   *Then trembles into silence as before.*
>
> *"There, in its centre, a sepulchral lamp*
>   *Burns the slow flame, eternal—but unseen;*
> *Which not the darkness of Despair can damp,*
>   *Though vain its ray as it had never been."*
>   *(ll. 347–54)*

---

[12] Again one is reminded of D. H. Lawrence's *aperçu* (see p. 49
above). I cannot, then, agree with Marchand, who sees Medora as
merely "an idealized version of the Eastern woman . . . like all the
heroines of the Oriental tales. . . . Aside from this Medora has no
character of her own; her merit is in seeing Conrad's, and that makes
her a perfect prototype of all the romantic Byronic heroines" (*Byron's
Poetry*, p. 65).

In these terms Conrad's departure is his separation from his soul, his humanity, his very being. His self-delusion and rationalization of his action are made patent by his protestations of love in terms of hate for "them," for the rest of mankind:

> "My very love to thee is hate to them,
> So closely mingling here, that disentwined,
> I cease to love thee when I love Mankind."
>
> (ll. 403–5)

And he urges Medora, characteristically, to deny her essential being to allow him to depart, by "nerving" her gentler heart (l. 408)—that is, by willing a coldness foreign to love. Medora sees clearly the implications of this but with only half-knowledge interprets her strength as weakness:

> "My Love! thou mock'st my weakness; and wouldst
> steel
> My breast before the time when it must feel."
>
> (ll. 416–17)

It is at this point that she tempts him with her love, and with music, dance, art, and poetry (ll. 420ff.). Conrad, steeling himself, will not listen, and continues to rationalize his actions until the end of his farewell with the assurance that "Security shall make repose more sweet" for her while he is gone (l. 463).

Seyd, Gulnare's husband and master, is a foil to Conrad. Even "with gore bedewed," the latter is "gentler"

> than Seyd in fondest mood.
> The Pacha wooed as if he deemed the slave
> Must seem delighted with the heart he gave.
>
> (ll. 869–72)

At the same time, however, we should also see that he is an exact counterpart of Conrad, who, we recall, "cared not what he softened, but subdued" and valued "less who loved—than what obeyed" (ll. 552, 554), the "what" being a powerful and significant dehumanization. And despite Gulnare's protestations, there are a few indications of the genuineness of Seyd's love for her, however oddly demonstrated. Still, Seyd's strength is his mind, the cold and unfeeling strategy of power, victory, manliness. Unlike Conrad, he has no thought for the harem during the battle; his Homeric epithet, like Hassan's in *The Giaour*, is "stern." His doom is assured amid the spoils of victory only when his mind relaxes its grip over his heart, and

> *His thoughts on love and hate alternate dwell,*
> *Now with Gulnare, and now in Conrad's cell.*
>
> (*ll. 1301–2*)

Convinced that Gulnare's love has turned from him to the Corsair, Seyd rejects the logical and rational capstone to his victory, the capturing of Conrad's treasure horde (ll. 1321ff.); and, equally unreasonably, he decides to keep Conrad alive long enough to satisfy his hate through the imposition of exquisite torture (ll. 1329–30). Both decisions, dictated by his heart (or his glands), lead inevitably to his death and to Conrad's escape.

Gulnare is even more interesting. With her heart trampled by Seyd in a manner reminiscent of the world's treatment of the young and feeling Conrad, initially she acts out of disloyal pity, gratitude, and the dawning of real love. It is as if for the first time she is becoming a woman after her years as a chattel, and she does not quite understand the transformation: "What sudden spell hath made this man so dear?" she asks herself (l. 1030). That he saved her life is true; but, "I come through darkness—and I scarce know why" (l. 1045). Her compassion, clearly, is the same emotion that motivated Conrad's release of the harem—and at the same time caused his defeat:

> *"Yes, if unwonted fondness now I feign,*
> *Remember—Captive! 'tis to break thy chain;*
> *Repay the life that to thy hand I owe;*
> *To give thee back to all endeared below,*
> *Who share such love as I can never know."*
>
> (*ll. 1134–38*)

Motivated by her full humanity, Gulnare will calculatingly use her love to delay Conrad's execution—and Byron accents this fusion of mind and heart, power and love by having her say, " 'but I have power / To soothe the Pacha in his weakest hour' " (ll. 1066–67). But in this world of captives and tyrants, to delay

147

is not enough, to prolong captivity is not preferable to death. Even escape is the womanly way to Conrad:

> *"Unfit to vanquish—shall I meanly fly,*
> *The one of all my band that would not die?"*
>
> (ll. 1078–79)

The power of her love over Seyd apparently failing, Gulnare "mans" her breast with "That strife of thought, the source of Woman's woes!" (l. 1375). In these words Byron dramatizes more clearly than in any other poem up to this point his association of heart with woman, mind with man. Lest the reader fall easily into the trap of allegory, however, the ultimate outcome of each poem proclaims clearly the mixture of these in all men and women, their essential humanity residing in the former (their "feminine" side), their inhumanity and corruption in the latter (their "manliness").[13] The terrible irony of Gulnare's position is indicated almost immediately. In order for her growing love for Conrad to be meaningful, she must, to put it crudely, become a man; similarly, if Conrad's love for Medora is to be consummated and their lost Eden reachieved, he must deny his pride of mind and submit to a femininely engineered, unmanly escape. Thus Gulnare, usurping Seyd's or Conrad's being, breathes revenge: "That hated tyrant . . . he must bleed!" (l. 1487). Conrad shudders at the change in that "earthly form with heavenly face" and "shape of fairy lightness" (ll. 1003, 1010) which first visited him in his cell. Seeing his reaction, Gulnare proclaims her soul "changed"; and in the remainder of her speech Byron brilliantly echoes the bitter passage in *The Giaour* on the fate of fragile beauty in the world:

---

[13] In an excellent article Ward Pafford interprets this conflict, in the poems of 1816 to 1817, as "the tension created by the warring claims of imagination and reason" ("Byron and the Mind of Man: *Childe Harold* III-IV and *Manfred*," *Studies in Romanticism*, I [1962], 105). While imagination and reason are obviously a part of the central conflict in Byron's poetry, I cannot accept those terms as, by themselves, adequately descriptive of that conflict. Nevertheless, Pafford's analyses of *Childe Harold, Manfred*, "Epistle to Augusta," "The Dream," "Darkness," "Sonnet to Lake Leman," "Prometheus," the "Monody on the Death of . . . Sheridan," and *The Prisoner of Chillon* are indispensable to the serious student of Byron's poetry.

> "What, am I then a toy for dotard's play,
> To wear but till the gilding frets away?"
>
> (ll. 1510–11)

Just as Hassan, the Giaour, and Selim rationalize their "manhood" in terms of love and hate, so too does Gulnare. It is now her whole life, and Conrad's refusal to use the womanly "secret knife" to effect his own escape leads to her final initiation into the ranks of fallen humanity, the brotherhood of Cain:

> upon her brow—unknown—forgot—
> Her hurrying hand had left—'twas but a spot—
> Its hue was all he saw, and scarce withstood—
> Oh! slight but certain pledge of crime—'tis Blood!
>
> (ll. 1582–85)

To Conrad, "that light but guilty streak, / Had banished all the beauty from her cheek!" (ll. 1594–95). For Gulnare it is her badge of courage and leadership: like Seyd, Conrad, Selim, Giaffir, and the others, she gathers her rebel band of Greek and Moor to forsake "this hated strand" (l. 1605). Conrad, free but now totally unmanned, follows "at her beck" and obeys (l. 1616). Even Conrad's band, with whom they soon reunite, would have Gulnare as "their Queen—less scrupulous are they / Than haughty Conrad how they win their way" (ll. 1678–79)—though they are perplexed at her manliness girt in lovely woman's form.

Conrad's later recognition that "The worst of crimes had left her Woman still" (l. 1690) cannot undo the deed; Gulnare's reverting to the softness of love and her momentary rest in Conrad's arms cannot change the nature of things. So Byron allows her to disappear quietly from the stage and concentrates his closing passages on scenes of Medora's death, the vacancy of her tower, the nothingness of the world, and Conrad's "shivered fragments" scattered in an eternal night of wandering.

A word needs to be said here about the sense of guilt which Byron has insisted upon more and more strongly as his conception of man develops.[14] From one point of view it is spe-

---

[14] The guilt of Byron's heroes has been discussed endlessly, but a particularly interesting treatment of it may be found in Bernard

cious, for the guilt has little, if anything, to do with the motivation of the characters. That it adds an air of mystery and gloom, that it darkens the characters' brooding melancholy, that it adds a certain spice and titillation to the reader's responses are all reasonable and partially true explanations of guilt's presence in the poems. That it is more than this, more basic to Byron's conception of the human condition and integrally related to the themes I have been tracing, can be shown convincingly, I think.

As a true Romantic Byron envisions an Edenic past from which man has fallen, a past he endows with two basic sets of values and thus two basic image patterns. On the one hand, it is the heroic past of Greece and Grecian heroes, vigorous, brave, loyal, martial, and fundamentally simple—the world in which Prometheus, before his enchainment, enabled man to be strengthened "with his own mind."[15] As early as 1806 Byron translated the following from Horace:

> The man of firm and noble soul
> No factious clamours can controul;
> No threat'ning tyrant's darkling brow
>   Can swerve him from his just intent:
> Gales the warring waves which plough,
>   By Auster on the billows spent,
> To curb the Adriatic main,
> Would awe his fix'd determined mind in vain.
>
> Aye, and the red right arm of Jove,
> Hurtling his lightnings from above,
> With all his terrors there unfurl'd,
>   He would, unmov'd, unaw'd, behold;
> The flames of an expiring world,
>   Again in crashing chaos roll'd,
> In vast promiscuous ruin hurl'd,
>   Might light his glorious funeral pile:
> Still dauntless 'midst the wreck of earth he'd smile.[16]

Blackstone's essay, "Guilt and Retribution in Byron's Sea Poems," *A Review of English Literature*, II (1961), 58–69. Ward Pafford, however, is one of the few Byron critics to keep the whole matter of guilt in Byron in proper perspective (see n. 13 above).

[15] "Prometheus," l. 38.

[16] *P*, I, 81.

This past, then, is the past of unfallen mind, a world of gods, not mortals. The other past is that of love, associated in Byron's mind not only with Adam and Eve but, as we have seen, with the garden of unspoiled nature and with childhood—a past of the unfallen heart where man, if not a god, is at least innocent, where God, nature, and man coexist in a kind of Wordsworthian unity, and where love is pure, unstained, and constant. The entire vision is, of course, sentimentally primitivistic, a fond look at the days that never were as if they once were real. Yet it is nonetheless a coherent vision, a powerful controlling factor in Byron's thinking—from the recollections of the past and farewells to bliss of *Hours of Idleness* to the one long farewell and lament that is *Childe Harold's Pilgrimage.* "From Adam till now" man "has with wretchedness strove," Byron wrote in "The First Kiss of Love"; like Prometheus, he is "in part divine, / A troubled stream from a pure source,"[17] whose vision of the past of romance, no matter how sentimental and illusory, is also imaginatively real, but whose earthly nature restrains him both from belief in the vision and from its realization. Man, then, is doubly doomed: god-like, he invents a paradise in which he cannot believe, or if he believes, cannot attain; and he takes upon himself the guilt for having lost what never was.

The guilt in Byron's poetry, then, is not so much the guilt of the sinful as the guilt of the inadequate. In *The Giaour* it is Hassan who commits the horrendous crime of drowning Leila; yet he feels no guilt. The Giaour, on the other hand, takes upon himself the guilt of her death, the loss of love and beauty in the world:

> in vain
> I wish she had not loved again.
> She died—I dare not tell thee how;
> But look—'tis written on my brow!
> There read of Cain the curse and crime
> In characters unworn by Time.
>
> (ll. 1054–59)

In *The Bride of Abydos* Giaffir evinces no guilt for the murder

---

[17] "Prometheus," ll. 47–48.

of his brother, for this is done in the world's arena of bloodshed and strife; but the blood of Zuleika, hope of his old age, his "twilight's lonely beam," the star of Helle's Eden, is very much on his head. Finally, Conrad's essential feeling of guilt is for his own loss of innocence and peace, which he himself contributed to but which he hopes to regain, not by a rejuvenation of his essential humanity but rather by a willful denial of that humanity. In his more lucid moments he himself can realize this true source of his guilt: in its chaos, at war with itself (or with the heart), the mind sees only

> The hopeless past, the hasting future driven
> Too quickly on to guess if Hell or Heaven;
> Deeds—thoughts—and words, perhaps remembered
> not
> So keenly till that hour, but ne'er forgot;
> Things light or lovely in their acted time,
> But now to stern Reflection each a crime;
> The withering sense of Evil unrevealed,
> Not cankering less because the more concealed;
> All, in a word, from which all eyes must start,
> That opening sepulchre, the naked heart.
>
> (ll. 952–61)

"You can't go home again," Byron says and says again. Medora's tower will always be empty, dark, or else it will be the tomb of hopes unfulfilled, another Eden lost because of mind and will, another irredeemable fall.

Byron's idea of guilt, then, is not specious or vague or literary or stagey. It is the heartfelt lament of man for what he is not, his recognition that the world is of his making and his acknowledgment that its repair is beyond his capacity, if not beyond his ken. Man is the eternal Cain, but he is also the eternal Abel; for it is clear that Byron saw this first act of human aggression, the first staining of the earth, the first exercise of the fallen mind and heart, as the fall of paradise. This, it seems to me, is the full significance of a poem like "Darkness," in which, after all strife is over, amid universal desolation, "men were gathered round their blazing homes / To look once more into each other's face" (ll. 14–15), the same face they had refused to acknowledge and love, for whatever reason, at the dawn of the world. Now, in darkness, it is too late. To Byron's sorrow, "Love dwells not in our will";[18] therein lies man's greatness in the midst of his doom. As Manfred says to the Abbot: "Old man! 'tis not so difficult to die" (III, iv, 151). What is perhaps impossible is to live—humanly. And therein lies our guilt.

II

If Byron was sincere in his decision to give up writing after *The Corsair*, and we have no reason to believe that he was not, his "Finale," as he called it in a letter to Murray,[19] should properly form a kind of conclusion or end. I have already called it a summing up. This theory is lent strength by his creation, some six months later, of another tale, which, while carrying forward some of the themes and echoing scenes and images of the previous three, and even suggesting itself as a sequel to *The Corsair*, is almost totally different in conception and considerably weaker in form and technique. If we are to believe Byron again, however, this next work, *Lara*, "completes the series, and its very likeness renders it necessary to the others."[20] This strong statement suggests a certain folly in my contention that the poem signals a considerable change (perhaps lapse is a better term for it) in Byron's quest for a form to dramatize his vision of the world and the human condition.

The statement, however, is not as clear and straightforward as it might be. In the first place, it is to be found in a business letter to Murray suggesting the publication of *Childe Harold* I and II and "the smaller poems, *Giaour, Bride, Corsair, Lara*" together as a unit that would sell well. Just prior to this in the same letter he says that *Lara* "is of no great promise separately; but, as connected with the other tales, it will do very well for the *vols* you mean to publish."[21] Although we

---

[18] From a poem first published in *Murray's Magazine* (February, 1887), and not included in the Coleridge edition. P. E. More prints it in his edition of the *Works*, pp. 205–6.

[19] 4 Feb. 1814, in *LJ*, III, 22.

[20] Ltr. to Murray, 2 Sept. 1814, in *LJ*, III, 131.

[21] *Ibid.* This doubt about the worth and salability of *Lara* is also found in ltrs. to Murray, 21 June and 23 July 1814, in *LJ*, III, 98–99, 109, and ltr. to Moore, 14 June 1814, in *LJ*, III, 95.

should by now be accustomed to Byron's protestations about the inadequacies of his poetry, his rather more subtle disclaimer in the second clause above rings with sincerity in my ears. Begging the question, then, I read the statement about *Lara*'s being necessary to the others to mean rather, that the others are necessary to carry *Lara*, for "it is too little narrative, and too metaphysical to please the greater number of readers."[22]

The carelessness of the poem is immediately obvious in the haphazard relationship between *Lara* and *The Corsair*. That Byron originally intended the poem as a sequel is obvious from the manuscript, in which the title is written: "Lara the sequel of 'the Corsair'"; and in the "Advertisement" to the anonymous first edition Byron tells the reader that he "may probably regard it as a sequel to the *Corsair*;—the colouring is of a similar cast, and although the situations of the characters are changed, the stories are in some measure connected. The countenance is nearly the same—but with a different expression."[23] This, says E. H. Coleridge, "forestalls and renders nugatory any prolonged discussion on the subject."[24] Samuel Chew, however, points out that the "links between the two poems are . . . few and tenuous; and for an understanding of such 'plot' as *Lara* possesses knowledge of *The Corsair* is unnecessary."[25] I agree; and the elaborate paraphrase, based to some extent on connections with *The Corsair*, which William Marshall presents to prove that Kaled, not Lara, killed Ezzelin, and that this is "the one fact in the narrative which gives it some form of structural unity," is absurd.[26]

Yet for all this looseness the stories *are* "in some measure connected," not through plot, however, but through what Byron himself called "the colouring." *Lara* "completes

[22] Ltr. to Leigh Hunt, 1 June 1815, in *LJ*, III, 201. Byron's low estimate of the poem endured almost to the end of his life (see ltrs. to Moore, 8 June 1822, in *LJ*, VI 81; to Murray, 6 June 1822, in *LJ*, VI, 77; and to Rogers, 27 June 1814, in *LJ*, III, 101).
[23] *P*, III, 323n.
[24] *P*, III, 320.
[25] *Lord Byron: "Childe Harold's Pilgrimage" and Other Romantic Poems* (New York, 1936), p. 245n.
[26] *The Structure of Byron's Major Poems*, pp. 50–62. The quotation is found on p. 50.

the series" not because the others are incomplete without it but because it represents the human condition and the world from a point of view complementary to those dramatized in the other poems.[27] As such, it employs a method that borrows a little here and there from each of the preceding three poems, thus representing little or no advance in structure. It is as if Byron simply could not decide whether to make *Lara* a sequel to *The Corsair* or to the series of tales in plot, or a sequel to either in theme. I should like to suggest that in some ways the poem is more nearly a reversion to the method of *The Giaour* (and hence a "sequel" to it) than integrally related to *The Corsair*, *The Bride*, or *Childe Harold*.[28] For Lara is not so much *the* corsair, Conrad, as he is *a* corsair who has returned from the past of "manly" freedom, battle, destruction, and spoils to the present of organized society, to what Byron was later to call consistently "the World."[29]

He is careful, then, not to limit the significance of his poem to Spain: "The name only is Spanish," he writes to Murray; "the country is not Spain, but the Moon."[30] This moon,

---

[27] Graham Hough, however, takes Byron's statement about the "series" literally, in order to bolster his thesis that Byron was "only intermittently creating separate works of art, with an independent, self-subsistent life of their own. The continuous activity on which [he] is engaged is the writing of his own *Bildungsroman*—the story of his own continual search for self-realisation. Parts of this are done as direct autobiography; parts crystallise out as fables in which warring or separable elements of the personality are personified as fictional characters . . ." (*Two Exiles: Lord Byron and D. H. Lawrence* [Nottingham, 1956], p. 11). This thesis has also been ably developed by William J. Calvert, in *Byron: Romantic Paradox*; Robert Langbaum, in *The Poetry of Experience*; Robert Preyer, in "Robert Browning: A Reading of the Early Narratives," *ELH*, XXVI (1959), 531–48; and John Wain, in "Byron: The Search for Identity," *London Magazine*, V (1958), 44–57. For an early example of the same point of view, see George Ellis' review of *The Corsair* and *Lara*, in *Quarterly Review*, XI (1814), 453–54.

[28] Clement T. Goode makes an interesting case for its structural similarity to *The Bride of Abydos* ("Byron's Early Romances: A Study," pp. 175ff.).

[29] See, e.g., ltr. to Murray, 29 Mar. 1820, in *LJ*, IV, 427; *Detached Thoughts*, in *LJ*, V, 463.

[30] 24 July 1814, in *LJ*, III, 110.

nevertheless, is more familiarly Christian, closer to home, than anything in the other three poems; it is a world of knights and ladies, of banquets and balls, of chivalric honor and feudal loyalty; a world rigidly stratified, peaceful and orderly on the surface, restless, corrupt, and oppressive beneath. It is England in the same sense that Blake's *An Island in the Moon* is England. To insist on this point, however, would be foolhardy in the face of so little evidence; what is more important is the temporal scheme of *Lara*, so similar to that of *The Giaour*. The narrative of that poem, we recall, is carried almost solely by a fisherman, whose recollection of past events bears upon his present view of the Giaour on his deathbed in the monastery. Like Lara, the Giaour in his youth was a stranger in a foreign, non-Christian land; like Lara he returns, if not to his native country, at least to his native religion, the comforts of which he rejects. As the story of the Giaour is pieced together by the fisherman from various sources as well as from his own fragmentary observation, so too the narrator of *Lara* is observer of both past and present events, but does not know the whole story. The fisherman in *The Giaour* is a fierce partisan of Hassan's; the narrator of *Lara* is clearly a Christian who wishes Lara well and worries about his apparently dissolute sojourn in a foreign land. If the Giaour were to return to his ancestral home, he would be a Lara.

I do not mean by this to deny the obvious connections *Lara* has with *The Corsair*—the Gulnare-Kaled connection, the odd relationship between Conrad and Gulnare, Lara and Kaled, Conrad's disappearance at the end of the poem, the perversion of his youthful virtues by the way of the world, and so forth; but so tangential are these to the structure of the poem and Byron's thematic emphasis that they seem to me of considerably less significance than the parallels to *The Giaour*. Whatever connections Byron had in mind, however, *Lara* is clearly an exploration of another temporal dimension in the human condition. We have been shown the youthful dissolute past of man, the present of his piratical rebellion against that past (or perhaps the logical extension of the lawlessness of the past), and the end of that present in death, or disappearance. But what of that world, either well or ill lost through love? Still there, eternally, it can always be returned to, a brave old world revisited, civilization and law and rest and order—all of the opposites of piratical "freedom." In such a world, to which Lara returns,

> *His faults, whate'er they were, if scarce forgot,*
> *Might be untaught him by his varied lot;*
>
> (ll. 57–58)

and since

> *Nor good nor ill of late were known, his name*
> *Might yet uphold his patrimonial fame.*
>
> (ll. 59–60)

His sins were merely the high-spirits of youth, says the narrator, and they "Might be redeemed" (l. 64):

> *And they the wiser, friendlier few confessed*
> *They deemed him better than his air expressed.*
>
> (ll. 113–14)

Had Byron taken the pains necessary to sustain this point of view, we would have indeed had an interesting study of the present, and perhaps even an absorbing account of the growing disillusionment of the narrator with the values of his world. As it is, however, the narrator's role in the poem stumbles into confusion and inconsistency.

In the beginning of the first canto we can see the remnants of Byron's apparent plans for him, not only in the passages quoted above but in the relative clarity of his emergence as a man who knew the land's, and Lara's, youthful situation and character and who lives in that land now, seeing it less clearly. His point of view is gently tinged by Byron with an orthodox morality and common sense: Lara's problem as a youth was due not merely to his own volatile spirits but, as a man like other men, to "that heritage of woe," sovereignty over oneself,

> *That fearful empire which the human breast*
> *But holds to rob the heart within of rest!*
>
> (ll. 14, 15–16)

And

> *With none to check, and few to point in time*
> *The thousand paths that slope the way to crime;*
> *Then, when he most required commandment, then*
>
> (ll. 17–19)

Lara was catapulted, unprepared, into manhood and the world. The narrator goes on to approve of apparent signs of reform:

> He did not follow what they all pursued
> With hope still baffled still to be renewed;
> Nor shadowy Honour, nor substantial Gain,
> Nor Beauty's preference, and the rival's pain.
> (ll. 103–6)

Further, the narrator, like the fisherman in *The Giaour*, is not omniscient, but gathers the pieces of his story together from rumor and gossip, his own observations past and present, and conjecture made on the basis of all of this. The first canto abounds in such words and phrases as "they see," "they recognize," "seemed," "appeared," "as if," "his rarely called attendants said," "they heard," "some knew perchance," "some would say," and so on.[31] But Byron, less concerned apparently with structure than with the "colouring" of "darkness and dismay" and with his character, and certainly with greater haste and less care than he gave to any major poem prior to this, alters the focus almost immediately, destroys the integrity of his narrator's point of view, sloppily shifts from present to past tense for no good reason, throws in melodramatic hints that the narrator knows more than he possibly could—clearly in the interest of darkening the mystery—and finally yields to his narrator the omniscience only he himself has. From this point (stanzas x–xii) on, the structure of the poem is chaotic except for the simple and straightforward narrative. The world of the narrator, with its hopes, however small, of redemption for Lara, dissipates too quickly into the world from which Lara has retreated.

This, of course, is precisely Byron's point—and is probably what he meant when he told Moore that the poem was more metaphysical than narrative: the past ever lives in the present,[32] the world is always and everywhere the same, man

---

[31] See, e.g., Canto I, ll. 44–45, 57, 59, 65, 113–14, 129, 135, 139, 149–53, 269–84, 291, 293–300, and 369–70.

[32] This is, of course, simply another version of the memory theme I discussed earlier. Perhaps Byron's most desperate statement about it, if we can trust Lady Blessington's memory at all, is this: "I have often . . . wished for insanity—anything—to quell memory, the

is inescapably bound to his hell within, that private microcosmic wasteland and living death in which all life is writ small. For our interest we must turn to theme, to Lara's character, and to the image patterns that characterize Byron's vision of not only the present but the present-past and future-present.

Thematically, if Lara returns to "normalcy" in space and time, he does so only as half a character, Giaffir's "man," Selim's mind-steeled new role. If he could appear gay and kind, to have "a heart as not by nature hard" (l. 304), we are told very quickly that these elements of basic humanity are submerged beneath an indomitable and obdurate will, a cerebral control that keeps him aloof from man and society. For Byron, he is a man geared to fight and plunder in order to avoid idleness, who has no one to fight and nothing more to plunder, the volcano whose very rumblings are drowned in "the carousals of the great and gay" (l. 99):

> *Ambition, Glory, Love, the common aim,*
> *That some can conquer, and that all would claim,*
> *Within his breast appeared no more to strive,*
> *Yet seemed as lately they had been alive.*
>
> *(ll. 79–82)*

Whereas earlier he had sought in the intenseness of his abandon "an escape from thought" (l. 122), now his mind has swung him to the other extreme.

> *With more capacity for love than Earth*
> *Bestows on most of mortal mould and birth,*
>
> *(ll. 321–22)*

he refuses to see his own mind and will as the cause of his fall and "crimes." To protect himself from fate and Nature, then, and to steel his heart against man, who also was to blame,

> *His mind abhorring this had fixed her throne*
> *Far from the world, in regions of her own.*
>
> *(ll. 349–50)*

---

never-dying worm that feeds on the heart, and only calls up the *past* to make the *present* more insupportable" (*Conversations of Lord Byron with the Countess of Blessington*, p. 311).

Lest his heart be thought soft (and human)

> *his Spirit seemed to chide*
> *Such weakness, as unworthy of its pride,*
> *And steeled itself . . .*
>
> .   .   .   .   .
>
> *To know no brotherhood, and take from earth*
> *No gift beyond that bitter boon—our birth*
>   *(ll. 305–7, 552–53)*

(though this latter is said of Kaled, about whom I shall have more to say in a moment, obviously it describes Lara equally well). For Lara "all was stern collectedness and art" (l. 722), and with this defense he could be a god unto himself, and to his vassals "a stranger in this breathing world" (l. 315).

Byron thus creates a character trebly doomed by his return to this world: although it is "breathing," the world of Byron's imagery is dead, a wasteland, no better nor no worse than that from which Lara returns. Superficially a world of gaiety and balls, warmth and friendship, peace and order and love, it is in reality a world of mind, of disorder and violence, of hatred and destruction; Lara returns armed against the very love and compassion out of which a better world is created, or at least envisioned, thus cutting himself off from the very humanity he must love as well as from that essential spark of humanness in himself.

Byron moves us into this world of "society" and civilization gradually and with considerable skill, however careless other elements of the poem are. It is a world of serfs and lords, retainers and chieftains, and if they are "glad" at Lara's return with his presumably benevolent rule, obedience and virtue, not love, are still the chief demands. "Slavery," Byron writes, but *"half* forgets her feudal chain" (l. 2; my italics). After a by now familiar glance at man's lost Eden (here considerably less related and central a scene than in the preceding three tales), Byron begins to insert more frequently the death images of the modern wasteland. The skull that sits on Lara's table, thus characterizing his own life, leads to the scene in the gallery with its painted dead and stained-glass saints, "Like life, but not like mortal life" (l. 196), mirroring Lara's own spectral attributes. The blatant, suffocating Gothicism of the scene should not blind us to its thematic significance in the context of the whole poem, for to Byron Gothic terror and death are no fancy but reality—life.

After Lara's encounter with Ezzelin, which is a transparent device to dramatize the presentness of all the past and the inescapability of one's self, one's own inner world, Byron makes the death-in-life images explicit. Sleep, the great leveler, allows man the luxury of forgetting life, "Love's feverish hope, and Cunning's guile, / Hate's working brain, and lulled Ambition's wile" (ll. 634–35). "Quenched existence" thus "crouches in a grave" of rest, with sleep and death representing the only cessation of "Being's strife" (ll. 637, 632). It is "the universal home," where all are equal, high and low, a dimmer Eden where "Weakness—Strength—Vice—Virtue" are meaningless (ll. 639, 640). From this haven ("heaven" would be very nearly as accurate a term) of the grave, man wakes not to a surrogate death but to real death, wrestling with its dread, shunning, paradoxically, "though Day but dawn on ills increased— / That sleep,—the loveliest, since it dreams the least" (ll. 644–45). The significance of the narrator's earlier rhetorical question about Lara's change from his youthful extremes, "How woke he from the wildness of that dream" (l. 128), is now clear. For man there is no waking but to death; each morning, as "Light awakes the world," man merely "has another day to swell the past, / And lead him near to little, but his last" (ll. 647–49). This opening to Canto II, with its ironic dispelling of night and sleep and the mock glory of sunrise, lengthens into bitterness as Byron becomes more explicit in his theme:

> *But mighty Nature bounds as from her birth,*
> *The Sun is in the heavens, and Life on earth;*
> *Flowers in the valley, splendour in the beam,*[33]
> *Health on the gale, and freshness in the stream.*
> *Immortal Man! behold her glories shine,*
> *And cry, exulting inly, "They are thine!"*
> *Gaze on, while yet thy gladdened eye may see:*

---

[33] The possible echo of Wordsworth's "splendour in the grass" in this context would be a happy example of the inveterate un-Wordsworthian quality of Byron's Nature.

A morrow comes when they are not for thee:
And grieve what may above thy senseless bier,
Nor earth nor sky will yield a single tear;
Nor cloud shall gather more, nor leaf shall fall,
Nor gale breathe forth one sigh for thee, for all;
But creeping things shall revel in their spoil,
And fit thy clay to fertilise the soil.

(*ll. 650–63*)

Thus, as the second canto develops, the apparent order and peace of the feudal state collapses into a duel, rebellion, murder, slaughter, madness, and the death of love—what Byron calls "The feast of vultures, and the waste of life" (l. 910); "And Carnage smiled upon her daily dead" (l. 926), a powerfully shocking mockery of the Lord's Prayer and the peace that passeth understanding.

But the perversion of Byron's nightmare world, with its "expense of spirit in a waste of shame" and its wasteland-ish implications, is still not complete. With Ezzelin's disappearance and public sentiment turned against him, Lara "mans" himself and steels his heart to action. He woos his vassals, slaves, and all other malcontents; capitalizes on factional growth and unrest; and cynically frees the serfs, thus providing them the one word ("freedom") that is "enough to raise Mankind to kill" (l. 868). What "cared he for the freedom of the crowd? / He raised the humble but to bend the proud" (ll. 897–98). The ensuing battle seesaws until, in a desperate charge, Lara's band verges on victory—for a moment. But in that moment Byron has Lara exercise his fatal gesture, a perverse parody of the compassionate gestures of Selim and Conrad: no longer, as with the former two, is it a dramatic revelation of his residual essential humanity, but rather an affirmation of the unyielding inhuman, the sign of victory and revenge and pride, the gesture of mind and hate.[34] But "the wasting brand" is indiscriminate—and Lara's heart is pierced.

---

[34] As if to accentuate the difference between this poem and the previous two, Byron does insert the familiar tender, human moment (II, xiv, 993–1004), but makes it no turning point in the battle. Further, it should be noted that the fierce gesture of pride and hate occurs in a stanza added after the manuscript of the poem was completed.

Kaled's character is even more interesting than Lara's as an example of the perversion of humanity and of death in life. It has been tacitly assumed by all the commentators I have read that Lara knows that Kaled is Gulnare in disguise. But if he knows, why should he keep Kaled-Gulnare in a position of servitude? Why perversely insist on her being unsexed? Why lead her foolishly into battle and almost certain death? But if the assumption *is* correct, which I doubt, we have an even more powerful image of Lara's perversion of life, love, and humanity than we would otherwise. Still, I prefer to see the perversion, as Byron certainly did, as something accomplished by Kaled-Gulnare herself, through an effort of will comparable to the mental "manhood" which steels Lara's heart against himself and all men. Though she readily recalls friends, kin, and parents whenever Lara speaks to her in her native tongue, in the name of love she has "abjured" all of these for Lara (ll. 524–25), who, though he treats her kindly, still treats her as a slave. She has, in effect, condemned herself to unrequited love, to a hell on earth perhaps more exquisitely painful than Lara's own. The dominance of Kaled-Gulnare's mind is shown in other ways as well: her blush was "a hectic tint of secret care" rather than "such blush as mounts when health would show / All the heart's hue in that delighted glow" (ll. 534, 531–32). She lived apart

> *From all that lures the eye, and fills the heart;*
> *To know no brotherhood, and take from earth*
> *No gift beyond that bitter boon—our birth.*
> *(ll. 551–53)*

"A latent fierceness" characterized her eyes, and

> *Still there was haughtiness in all he did,*
> *A spirit deep that brooked not to be chid.*
> *(ll. 580, 558–59)*

Kaled-Gulnare is, then, in a sense, the very humanity—warm, loyal, loving—Lara has destroyed in himself, here externalized so that it may be dramatically warped to madness and eventually destroyed by the world. At the same time she is a fine example of mankind's being "Chained to excess, the slave of each extreme" (l. 127)—passion's slave and the mind's slave at once, two extremes which cancel each other out. "Never yet beneath / The breast of *man* such trusty love may breathe!" (ll. 1157–58)—it breathes only in woman; yet, if "human love" is not "the growth of human will" (l. 1176), the death of love is. Curiously, even after having created the several major characters of *Childe Harold* and the earlier tales, having established once and for all the full dimensions of the Byronic hero in Lara, Byron presents us his most intensely rounded human in the person of a woman who does not speak, acts little, and is accepted by most readers as a mere incidental character.

One can, of course, make too much of this point, and I do not intend to elevate Kaled-Gulnare's significance above her just deserts. She is as yet only a sketch of Byron's total man, and whether Byron himself was fully aware of what he had created is doubtful. His mind was too full of the character of Lara to concentrate on much else, and it took the late additions of stanza xviii of Canto I and stanza xv of Canto II to connect his character thematically with those he had already drawn. Even if *Lara* is "a study in personal anguish"[35] (which I doubt) or the nearest Byron approached "to the nadir of destructive nihilism"[36] (which is nearer the truth), I still find the poem as a whole singularly disappointing. There is little, if anything, new in character, structure, plot, or over-all theme—barring the few fairly isolated passages concentrated on above. Byron was right: the other tales, and even *Childe Harold*, were needed to carry its dead weight, for it is almost certainly a potboiler.

III

The Siege of Corinth is even worse; it is certainly Byron's most slipshod production, published, oddly enough, with one of his best, *Parisina* (in February, 1816). Yet it is of considerable interest in the development I have been tracing of Byron's interest in theme and form throughout the "series" that begins with *Childe Harold* I. That interest, however, resides more in the circumstances of the poem's evolution than in the

---

[35] Knight, "Byron and Hamlet," p. 125.
[36] Bostetter, *The Romantic Ventriloquists*, p. 273.

finished product. Here I must frankly speculate, since the evidence of the poem's origin and date of composition is at best uncertain and even conflicting. All of Byron's responsible editors and biographers rely upon Byron's letter to S. T. Coleridge of October 27, 1815, containing his apology for what may be pure coincidence or an example of unconscious echoing—the similarity between lines 521–32 of *The Siege* and some lines in *Christabel* —for dating the composition of the poem: ". . . this thing was begun in January [1815], and more than half written before the Summer."[37] The manuscript that E. H. Coleridge calls "the original MS." and that he used for his variant readings bears this out, for it is dated January 31, 1815. This manuscript consists of sixteen folio and nine quarto sheets, with only "occasional and disconnected pagination."[38] Judging from this and from what are apparently, according to Coleridge's notes, the relatively few changes in the manuscript, Coleridge conjectures that "this MS. consists of portions of two or more fair copies of a number of detached scraps written at different times, together with two or three of the original scraps which had not been transcribed."[39] I suggest that this manuscript is a fair copy of the University of Texas manuscript, which is heavily overwritten and revised and which consists of two folio and ten quarto sheets, numbered not disconnectedly but consecutively. The Texas manuscript, entirely in Byron's hand, is dated "Jy 30th 1815"—that is, January, not July—indicating, I believe, the day on which he began work on this manuscript. When Byron came to make the almost identically dated fair copy Coleridge used for his edition, he either made a simple error in recording the date of his fair copy (which is unlikely, since he was most precise about such matters) or intended to indicate not when Coleridge's manuscript was written but rather when the original was begun.

I rehearse these dry facts here, however, not because they are important in themselves but rather because they are the basis for the speculation I spoke of earlier. E. H. Coleridge's

---

[37] *LJ*, III, 229.
[38] *P*, III, 448.
[39] *Ibid.*

conjecture about his manuscript being a fair copy made from scraps written at various times applies, I think, though not so sweepingly, to the Texas manuscript. The first two sheets of this are folio, numbered clearly "1" and "2" on the recto; of the remaining sheets, all quarto, Byron numbered the first "4" in the center of the recto, deleted that, numbered it "4" again in the upper left corner of the recto, and then wrote a "3" over the "4." The second quarto sheet has the same kind of correction, being numbered originally "5" in the upper left corner with a "4" written over the "5." The remaining quarto sheets are numbered, without changes, from "5" through "10." While it is at least possible that other conclusions can be drawn from this evidence, not the least of which is that of a slip of the pen due to Byron's inveterate haste, I believe it logical to assume that on January 30, 1815, he was picking up with a poem already begun sometime earlier and laid aside—for reasons I see no virtue in speculating upon here. My guess is that he almost entirely scrapped his earlier beginning as a false start, wrote the 190 lines of the first two folio sheets to replace it, dovetailed this new opening with the already completed lines 191–322 (of the first two quarto sheets), and then continued the poem to the end through the spring and summer of 1815.

Precisely when Byron's abortive start was made cannot be decided with certainty, but that it was considerably earlier than the extant manuscripts I have no doubt. In a letter to Leigh Hunt of February 26, 1816, Byron says that he had requested Murray to send Hunt "a pamphlet with two things of mine in it, the most part of both of them, and of one in particular, *written* before *others* of my composing, which have preceded them in *publication*."[40] From the dates and the particulars of Murray's publication of Byron's works through early 1816, it is obvious that *The Siege* and *Parisina* are the poems referred to. The "others" of his composing, I suggest, are *The Bride*, *The Corsair*, and *Lara*. The evidence for this conjecture is in Bryon's manuscript of the introductory forty-five lines of *The Siege*, lines absent from both manuscripts described above and sent to Murray belatedly on December 25,

---

[40] *LJ*, III, 266.

1815, while *The Siege* was in press. In his covering letter of that date Byron writes: "I send some lines, written some time ago, and intended as an opening to the *Siege of Corinth*. I had forgotten them, and am not sure that they had not better be left out now:—on that, you and your Synod can determine."[41] That he had forgotten them is not difficult to understand, for the manuscript is dated October 23 (no year). That it is October 23, 1813, is suggested by the title ("The Stranger's Tale"), by the connections with the just completed *Giaour*, and by the echoes of *Childe Harold* I and II and Byron's grand tour.

Of these, the first two points are key ones. Having just experimented radically, in *The Giaour*, with a complex form to embody his conceptions and to facilitate mobile and varying points of view, it was logical for Byron to attempt the tale told by a narrator-participant again. Further, with the Giaour-infidel figure fresh in his mind, a similar figure, more dramatically and fully committed to his apostasy, would be a likely follow-up. (In passing we might note that both the Giaour and Alp are Venetians.) The scenes of his tour still vivid in his mind, partly because he had written of them so recently in *Childe Harold* and *The Giaour*, Byron began his new tale, calling it "The Stranger's Tale," on October 23, 1813. The "stranger" was most likely a fisherman type of character; the poet, who invites the stranger to sit with him "on Acro-Corinth's brow" (l. 45), is the same poet whose point of view subsumes, enlarges, and interprets all the other points of view in *The Giaour*.

It is to be regretted that Byron's unrecognized concern for form did not evince itself in a poem equal in interest to *The Giaour* and *The Bride*. Whatever led him to lay it aside in favor of *The Bride*, his disparagement of which is all the more suspect now in view of his rejection of *The Siege's* beginning, it is clear that the dissipation of his concern for form in *Lara* dictated the haphazard and careless completion of *The Siege* as we have it today. Though Byron defended, with remarkable incompetence, the versification of *The Siege*, justifying

---

[41] *LJ*, III, 250. The lines do not appear in the Huntington Library set of proof sheets, dated January 19, 1816. They were finally prefixed to the poem in 1832.

it mainly because of its difference from that of others of his works,[42] he not only thought it not "at all equal to my own notions of what [it] should be" and on a subject "I have apparently exhausted";[43] he was also, I think, genuinely ashamed of it. As he wrote to Murray in November, 1815: "And now to my last—my own, which I feel ashamed of after the others;— publish or not as you like, I don't care *one damn*. If *you* don't, no one else shall, and I never thought or dreamed of it, except as one in the collection. If it is worth being in the fourth volume, put it there and nowhere else; and if not, put it in the fire."[44] Yet, as I have said, it is not totally without value, for despite its galloping narrative, characters of little or no interest and depth, and almost a total absence of theme aside from Alp's incredible revenge, there are several sections which deserve notice as perhaps the ultimate extensions of the death-in-life, wasteland theme of *Lara*.

Byron opens the poem with a vision of Corinth as freedom's eternal citadel and monument, even in a land fallen. The fall of Corinth to him is not merely another battle won or lost, but the greatness of the past, of truth and freedom and beauty, crushed forevermore by man and the world—and perhaps most especially by a man who is a traitor to that past, Alp the renegade. Seeking love through conquest, as Byron's man inevitably and ironically does, confusing love and hate, mind and heart, war and peace, Alp courts Francesca with his siege,

---

[42] Ltr. to Murray, 20 Feb. 1816, in *LJ*, III, 263–64.

[43] Ltr. to Murray, 3 Jan. 1816, in *LJ*, III, 251; ltr. to Moore, 8 Mar. 1816, in *LJ*, III, 274.

[44] *LJ*, III, 246. The vast majority of critics from Byron's day to ours, including Murray's reader, William Gifford, share his low opinion of the work, especially of its technical aspects. It has had its few champions, however. William Dick thought it probably the best of the tales (*Byron and His Poetry* [London, 1913], p. 68); Ethel C. Mayne judged it "incomparable, among Byron's narrative poems, for music" (*Byron*, II, 50); Swinburne coupled it with *The Giaour* as the best of the narratives (*Essays and Studies*, p. 250); and A. Hamilton Thompson charitably tried to justify its flaws as follows: "it may even be argued that its shapelessness and tunelessness are appropriate to the chaos of destruction over which its renegade hero broods" (*Selections from the Poems of Lord Byron* [Cambridge, 1920], p. xxix).

polluting virginity in the same way that war's presence mocks the Eden of the Grecian night:

> *Blue roll the waters, blue the sky*
> *Spreads like an ocean hung on high,*
> *Bespangled with those isles of light,*
> *So wildly, spiritually bright;*[45]
> *Who ever gazed upon them shining*
> *And turned to earth without repining,*
> *Nor wished for wings to flee away,*
> *And mix with their eternal ray?*
>
> (ll. 244–51)

In this silence rises the Muezzin's voice, the call to prayer that, in a strange reversal, sounds to the Corinthians "prophetic of their fall" and to the besiegers "ominous and drear" like the "passing-bell" of the death knell (ll. 275, 277, 282). At dawn the cry, now perverted completely, gives way to the fierce cry of slaughter. Alp, the fiercest of all (unless that title should go to the Christian Minotti), is Byron's man of steel heart who, in a presentation more telling and brutal than Byron has attempted thus far, is seen as the lion who slays hungrily what the jackal sights as his prey (ll. 328–29).[46]

High above this scene of man's perversion towers what is perhaps Byron's loveliest symbol of the lost Eden, "High

---

[45] In this line, unrecorded in Coleridge's list of variants, Byron wrote first "blessedly" instead of "wildly." Though it was, in the context, a better if awkward word, it obviously did not scan and he crossed it out.

[46] Further evidence of the primacy of the University of Texas manuscript is Coleridge's transcription of this passage from the Lord Glenesk manuscript he used (*P*, III, 462n). The Texas manuscript reads as follows:

> *[As] So lions o'er the jackal sway*
> *[By springing dauntless on the prey]*
> *They [only] but prescribe—he fells the prey—*
> *[They who follow on and] Then [baser] on the*
> *   vulgar yelling press*
> *To gorge the [fragments] relics of success.*

Coleridge also remarks that ll. 329–31 "are inserted in the copy." There is no indication of insertion in the Texas manuscript.

and eternal," ever bright, but now a "hovering shroud"—
Parnassus:

> *It will not melt, like man, to time:*
> *Tyrant and slave are swept away,*
> *Less formed to wear before the ray;*
> *But that white veil, the lightest, frailest.*[47]

(ll. 369–72)

It is an impressive externalization and universalization of Francesca's innocence, virginity, love, perhaps even operative as a
symbol of imagination and poetry, for "that white veil,"

> *Which on the mighty mount thou hailest,*
> *While tower and tree are torn and rent,*
> *Shines o'er its craggy battlement;*
> *In form a peak, in height a cloud,*
> *In texture like a hovering shroud.*[48]

(ll. 373–77)

And the heroes of the past, who lived and fought in freedom's
name, are incarnate in the mountain's very being, and in nature:

> *The very gale their names seemed sighing;*
> *The waters murmured of their name;*
> *The woods were peopled with their fame;*
>
> .   .   .   .   .
>
> *Their spirits wrapped the dusky mountain,*
> *Their memory sparkled o'er the fountain;*
> *The meanest rill, the mightiest river*
> *Rolled mingling with their fame for ever.*[49]

(ll. 407–9, 412–15)

---

[47] Coleridge points out the similarity here to Byron's image of Parnassus rising above the battle of Hassan and the Giaour (ll. 565–66)
(*P*, III, 464n).

[48] Coleridge lists no variants in these lines, although in the Texas
manuscript there are two complete lines (376–77) crossed out and
rewritten.

[49] Here again Coleridge's variants are obviously from a later manuscript. In addition to omitting the important deletions of the originals
of ll. 410–12, he lists "Their memory hallowed every fountain" as
the first version of l. 413 instead of "Their glory hallowed every
fountain." He also records, accurately, two lines that appear in manuscript after l. 417 but lists them as "erased" (*P*, III, 466n). In the
Texas manuscript they are not erased or deleted.

But there where "Her prophet spirit spake in song" (l. 381) sings now the fallen bard of senseless slaughter and the obscene laughter of the jackal.

Into this eternal Eden, now at once indifferent to fallen man and a symbol of his lofty origin, Byron introduces two spectacularly contrasting scenes, indeed so extreme that one almost balks at their juxtaposition. The first of these (ll. 454ff.) Rutherford labels "crude sensationalism, the ghoulish delight in horrors" and "ludicrous exaggeration and a deliberate exploitation of the gruesome."[50] That it is written with a certain verve and relish cannot be denied, but it seems to me that Rutherford misses the whole point of the scene. In the first place, it is overwritten to the point of nightmare or terror-filled hallucination, an effect Byron encourages by the eeriness that precedes it: Alp walks almost beneath Corinth's walls without a shot being fired upon him (ll. 440ff.). Gifford urged Byron to omit the whole passage,[51] but he stubbornly resisted the advice, giving us thereby an unforgettable passage on the inheritors of the earth, the "lean dogs" holding "o'er the dead their Carnival" (ll. 454, 455), watched only by vultures and wolves:

> *worms of the earth, and fowls of the air,*
> *Beasts of the forest, all gathering there;*
> *All regarding man as their prey,*
> *All rejoicing in his decay.*[52]
>
> (ll. 491–94)

For that last "All" Byron originally wrote "Nature," a better choice, for his point is that the sickening scene in all its crudeness is merely a hyperbole for human life, and that the purity of Eden, the "natural order being re-established after an unnatural rebellion" that Rutherford says is missing from all the tales,[53] *is* being re-established with the end of fallen, bestial man.

---

[50] *Byron: A Critical Study*, p. 177 and n.

[51] Coleridge merely notes that Gifford "has drawn his pen through lines 456–478" (*P*, III, 467n).

[52] Still another indication of the primacy of the Texas manuscript is Coleridge's note (*P*, III, 469n) that ll. 487–88 "are inserted in the copy in Byron's handwriting." These lines do not appear at all in the Texas manuscript.

[53] *Byron: A Critical Study*, p. 44.

The second scene is straight out of *Childe Harold* (cf. II, i–x), with a significant and daring addition. Amid the rotting corpses stands a ruined temple, overgrown with grass (again Nature re-establishing herself), the remnant of man's progress, his religion, and his domination of nature:

> *Till Ruin makes the relics scarce*
> *Then Learning acts her solemn farce*
> *And scanning through the marble waste*
> *Prates of beauty art and taste.*[54]

Byron canceled these lines on second thought, for they clearly suggest an enduring humanity that his scene of utter desolation could not permit. Into the ruined temple the second hallucinatory vision descends; it is a vision of Francesca, youthful, bright, the embodiment of the very purity, love, grace, art, love, and Eden which Byron had earlier ascribed to Parnassus. As the eternal white veil of the mountain is now a shroud, so Francesca appears like the newly dead beauty of *The Giaour*, unsmiling, her eyes cold, her "glance, though clear . . . chill" (l. 553). She clearly represents the eternal bride, come to woo her lover away from mind and hate, slaughter and death, apostasy and damnation. Alp answers her, without bitterness, but with all the horror Byron can infuse into his significance:

> *"And where should our bridal couch be spread?*
> *In the midst of the dying and the dead?"*
>
> > (ll. 581–82)

The echo of the bridal gift in *The Giaour* is patent and deliberate. They will slaughter all Christians, Alp says, unswayed, but he will save her and bear her

> > to a lovely spot
> *Where our hands shall be joined, and our sorrows*
> > > forgot.
> *There thou yet shalt be my bride.*
>
> > (ll. 587–89)

---

[54] These lines, crossed out by Byron, follow l. 506 in the Texas manuscript.

But there is no lovely spot, and their joining of hands in the ruined temple amid the dead is the enactment of that truth:

> *Upon his hand she laid her own—*
> *Light was the touch, but it thrilled to the bone,*
> *And shot a chillness to his heart,*
> *Which fixed him beyond the power to start.*
> *Though slight was that grasp so mortal cold,*
> *He could not loose him from its hold;*
> *But never did clasp of one so dear*
> *Strike on the pulse with such feeling of fear,*
> *As those thin fingers, long and white,*
> *Froze through his blood by their touch that night.*
> *(ll. 595–604)*

The hope of paradise regained, love's touch, has become skeletal, and Francesca takes on completely the aspect of the beautiful dead of *The Giaour* and the pictured dead of *Lara*:

> *her motionless lips lay still as death,*
> *And her words came forth without her breath,*
> *And there rose not a heave o'er her bosom's swell,*
> *And there seemed not a pulse in her veins to dwell.*
> *Though her eye shone out, yet the lids were fixed,*[55]
> *(ll. 612–16)*

and her figure was "Lifeless, but life-like, and awful to sight" (l. 623). Francesca makes one more plea, "for the love of Heaven" (l. 629), if not for love of her, lest "Its love for ever shut from thee" (l. 642). Alp in his madness refuses—" 'tis too late" (l. 668)—and Francesca is gone. The only assertion is what Charles du Bos describes rightly as "Byron's massive sense of nothingness":[56] "Nothing is there but the column stone" (l. 675); "He saw not—he knew not—but nothing is there" (l. 677). With all light and life thus gone, the day dawns mockingly "As

---

[55] Coleridge records only an inconsequential variant in this passage (in l. 614), while the Texas manuscript is at this point heavily over-written and revised.

[56] *Byron and the Need of Fatality*, p. 72. The "burden of *nihil*" that Georg Roppen and Richard Sommer see in the Rome stanzas of *Childe Harold* IV (*Strangers and Pilgrims*, p. 267) is certainly not more powerfully expressed there than here in *The Siege*.

if that morn were a jocund one," a touch Gifford misses completely (he said to leave out the lines) just as he praises the three stanzas of Francesca's appearance as "all . . . beautiful," obviously unaware of their utter pessimism and despair.[57] Alp dies, properly, at the moment when he hears of Francesca's death, in an awkward imitation of the "fatal gestures" of Selim and Conrad (ll. 853–66).

Carried away by his irony, Byron at one point exclaims, much to Gifford's dismay, "Oh, but it made a glorious show" (l. 997),[58] as the Turks despoil the church, the altar, the sacramental vessels. As the

> *Madonna's face upon him shone,*
> *Painted in heavenly hues above,*
> *With eyes of light and looks of love,*
>
> > *(ll. 949–51)*

Minotti makes "the sign of the cross with a sigh" and fires the magazine whose storage place is, ironically, this haven of love and peace. However overdone the battle scene, it is clear that Byron is here at once perverting and annihilating the last resort of fallen man. Just as Selim first ignores Zuleika's Koran and then puts it, engraved on his sword, to the uses of war, so here the mother of God sits with "the boy-God on her knee" smiling over the slaughter, a kind of idiot sentinel, guarding Minotti's magazine. The torch from the altar ends it all:

> *Spire, vaults, the shrine, the spoil, the slain,*
> > *The turbaned victors, the Christian band,*
> *All that of living or dead remain,*
> *Hurled on high with the shivered fane,*
> *In one wild roar expired!*
>
> > *(ll. 1016–20)*

Even Nature, the earth, reacts convulsively to the total cataclysm (ll. 1022–24). The jackals inherit the earth, and

---

[57] *P*, III, 479n, 470n.

[58] Coleridge says that Gifford erased the line and added three exclamation points after it (*P*, III, 492n). In the Texas manuscript Gifford simply wrote "Out" next to the line. Since Byron obviously did not heed his advice this time, in Coleridge's fair copy manuscript Gifford simply took it upon himself to delete the line.

The eagle left his rocky nest,
And mounted nearer to the sun,
The clouds beneath him seemed so dun;
Their smoke assailed his startled beak,
And made him higher soar and shriek.

(ll. 1074–78)

"Thus was Corinth"—and the world, Eden, everything—"lost and won" (l. 1079). If it is true, as G. S. Fraser says, that "there is a certain maturity of attitude in not getting into too much of a rage with the human situation as one finds it,"[59] one must acknowledge Byron's "immaturity" here. I prefer, however, Gilbert Highet's judgment of Byron's "unrelenting pessimism" as being not that "of an isolated intellectual" but rather "the considered verdict of an educated, experienced, reflective man who has the gift of poetry"[60]—even if that gift informs only a small portion of *The Siege of Corinth.*

---

[59] "Passion's Ironist," *New Statesman*, LX (1960), 750.
[60] "The Poet and His Vulture," p. 118.

Chapter VI

PARISINA AND THE PRISONER OF CHILLON

I

Like *The Siege of Corinth*, *Parisina* was begun considerably before its publication early in 1816 but probably not before *The Siege*, as Coleridge states.[1] The letter to Leigh Hunt mentioned in the previous chapter is corroborated by Byron's note to the combined first edition of *The Siege* and *Parisina*: "the greater part of [*Parisina*] was composed prior to *Lara*, and other compositions since published."[2] As such it is a poem combining elements of Byron's earlier search for a form, and some of the earlier image patterns, with a more mature versification and a growing interest in the psychology of character rather than the narrative rendering of the consequences of character.[3] In plot it is similar to *The Bride of Abydos*, in handling of point of view similar to *Childe Harold* I and II and

---

[1] *P*, III, 499.

[2] *Ibid.*, 508n.

[3] In general *Parisina* has fared much better than its predecessors at the hands of Byron's critics. Although the contemporary critical journals were repelled by it, solely because of the incest theme, Murray thought it a "Pearl" and Isaac D'Israeli, John Ward, and Gifford (Murray's readers) were unanimously enthusiastic about it (*P*, III, 499). Most critics since Byron's time have agreed that it is the best of Byron's tales to date—except for Swinburne, who, in a rare moment of critical obtuseness, labeled the poem (along with *The Bride of Abydos*) as Byron's worst (*Essays and Studies*, p. 250). The biographical heresy still remains strong, however. Marchand, for example, can praise *Parisina* for its distinct superiority "in poetic nuances of character and situation to anything in Byron's previous narrative poems" and yet conclude that "it is not his best work for the very reason that he was not distilling the essence of his own

perhaps *The Giaour*, while in the conception of character and the development of the themes of appearance and reality, dream and awakening, it looks forward to *The Prisoner of Chillon*, *Manfred*, "Darkness," and "The Dream."

The role of the narrator of *Parisina* is of first importance. At first glance he seems to seesaw uncertainly between sympathetic omniscience and moral condemnation, a technique similar to the conflicting voices and attitudes of *Childe Harold* I and II or the distinction between the poet's overview and the fisherman's narrow partisanship in *The Giaour*. Byron attempted something in *Parisina*, however, that goes beyond the technique of either of those two poems—or, indeed, of the other tales. He sought to dramatize the ultimate impossibility of certainty of judgment by making the reader aware, simultaneously, as it were, of conflicting judgments, each of which is right, or wrong, when isolated from the others. The key to this interpretation of the apparent inconsistency of the narrator's point of view can be found, I believe, in Byron's prefatory note to the poem. It reveals not only his own uncertainty about the subject (the same uncertainty which not long before led him at the last minute to make Selim Zuleika's cousin rather than her brother in *The Bride of Abydos*) but also his tacit approval of Gibbon's implicit judgment of "the facts on which the story is founded."[4]

After sanctioning his use of the incest theme by referring to the Greek dramatists, "the best of our old English writers," Alfieri, and Schiller, Byron quotes the following from Gibbon's account of the "Antiquities of the House of Brunswick":

> Under the reign of Nicholas III. Ferrara was polluted with a domestic tragedy. By the testimony of a maid, and his own observation, the Marquis of Este discovered the incestuous loves of his wife Parisina, and Hugo his bastard son, a beautiful and valiant youth. They were beheaded in the castle by

---

experience" (*Byron's Poetry*, pp. 68–69). More acute as a critical *aperçu* is W. W. Robson's remark that the "impressiveness" of Byron's best poems "derives partly from our feeling that there is *not* [a] complete identification" of poet with emotion expressed ("Byron as Poet," p. 40).

[4] "Advertisement" to *Parisina*, in *P*, III, 503.

the sentence of a father and husband, who published his
shame, and survived their execution. He was unfortunate, if
they were guilty: if they were innocent, he was still more
unfortunate; nor is there any possible situation in which I
can sincerely approve the last act of the justice of a parent.[5]

I quote this in full to underscore Gibbon's own uncertainty: the
incest is a pollution but he cannot condone the execution of the
lovers; he is uncertain as to their guilt even while narrating the
"domestic tragedy" as fact. In addition, Byron's own view of
the pollution of the world, the irony that love leads to inevitable
disaster, is obviously reinforced by Gibbon's historical account.
And finally, Byron's many departures from this historical account (despite his oft-stated passion for fact in his poetry) are
clearly geared to the intensification of his themes of reality and
appearance, waking and dreaming.

The problem that Byron undertook, then, in *Parisina*
is a large one—and so ambiguous as almost to defy clear treatment. Having established in the previous poems the fact that
Eden is lost, that all attempts to redeem it are doomed to failure,
and that even man's most human moments lead but to destruction, he writes his first poem fully emphasizing the ineluctable
power of that fallen world. For all the admirable and largely
new attention to subtleties of characterization, the burden of
Parisina is man—the same society he will take to task in *Beppo*
and *Don Juan* but from a very different point of view. In that
society, or "world," the only gladness is guilty; justice and
morality, though "good," lead to death (or at best a living
death); people in their self-righteousness judge "sinners" hypocritically and with sobering cruelty; no illusion or dream can
remain unshattered for long, and the awakening to reality and
truth is also an awakening to death; all men are guilty, yet none
accepts that guilt fully; the future is as black as the past and
present,

> *With glimpses of a dreary track,*
> *Like lightning on the desert path,*
> *When midnight storms are mustering wrath;*
> (*ll. 365–67*)

---

[5] *Ibid.* In later editions Byron corrected "a maid" to "an attendant."

and, finally, right is wrong and wrong is right and the wasteland flourishes as the landscape of both the living and the dead.

In order to accomplish all of this Byron fused in his single narrator the very fluctuations of point of view and conflicts of judgment that characterize the ambiguity of the human condition and life. The poem begins with the narrator setting the usual Edenic scene, "the hour when lovers' vows / Seem sweet in every whispered word" (ll. 3–4). Yet it is not quite the same as the paradisaical passages in the previous poems; the "Seem" already indicates the falseness of the illusion. The second stanza expands on this point:

> But it is not to list to the waterfall
> That Parisina leaves her hall,
> And it is not to gaze on the heavenly light
> That the Lady walks in the shadow of night;
> And if she sits in Este's bower,
> 'Tis not for the sake of its full-blown flower;
> She listens—but not for the nightingale.
>
> (ll. 15–21)

She does not do any of these things because there is no Eden on earth, only its illusion; and Parisina, unlike Byron's other heroines, has no illusions. The scene is illusion made real, and thus compromised by fear and guilt, shadowed by death. In the third stanza Byron brilliantly summarizes the whole point. First the illusion:

> And what unto them is the world beside,
> With all its change of time and tide?
> Its living things—its earth and sky—
> Are nothing to their mind and eye.
>
> .   .   .   .   .
>
> They only for each other breathe;
> Their very sighs are full of joy
>   So deep, that did it not decay,
> That happy madness would destroy
>   The hearts which feel its fiery sway.[6]
>
> (ll. 29–32, 36–40)

---

[6] It is interesting and instructive to compare these last four lines with

Byron's point, of course, is that it *is* madness; it is a refuge from the destructive "sanity" of the world, but the refuge is crumbling at the very moment of its inception. Reality will not be circumvented. Thus the lovers' very ecstasy is a kind of death:

> *And heedless as the dead are they*
> *Of aught around, above, beneath;*
> *As if all else had passed away.*
>
> (*ll. 33–35*)

Such illusory moments as these are dead as soon as born, though "we must awake before / We know such vision comes no more" (ll. 47–48). In the clear light of day "that tumultuous tender dream" (l. 42) of idyllic love and Eden is a "spot of guilty gladness past" (l. 50), and though the lovers hope and vow, they know full well the perishability of their dreams: "they grieve, / As if that parting were the last" (ll. 51–52).

Byron seems to be saying that with paradise lost, all love is guilty, all dreams false and treacherous. Man swings pendulum-like from the dream to the reality, each a refuge from the other, each swing more terrifying than the last. When Parisina enters the reality of her husband's lawful bed, her dreams are both of Eden and of fear: with the power of mind that controls the heart in abeyance, her heart goes out to Hugo while her arms embrace Azo (stanza v). The latter, whose fragile paradise rests in his love for Parisina, wakes at her touch:

> *And, happy in the thought, mistakes*
> *That dreaming sigh, and warm caress,*

Shelley's "Hymn to Intellectual Beauty" (written in 1816 after the tour with Byron around Lake Geneva), especially ll. 39–48:

> *Man were immortal and omnipotent*
> *Didst thou, unknown and awful as thou art,*
> *Keep with thy glorious train firm state within his heart.*
> *Thou messenger of sympathies*
> *That wax and wane in lovers' eyes;*
> *Thou, that to human thought art nourishment,*
> *Like darkness to a dying flame!*
> *Depart not as thy shadow came:*
> *Depart not, lest the grave should be,*
> *Like life and fear, a dark reality.*

> *For such as he was wont to bless;*
> *And could in very fondness weep*
> *O'er her who loves him even in sleep.*
>
> *(ll. 76–80)*

Azo's waking dream is shattered, however, by Parisina's mumbling of Hugo's name; and Byron completes his cosmic metaphor by leaping from Eden to the Last Judgment:

> *Why doth Prince Azo start,*
> *As if the Archangel's voice he heard?*
> *And well he may—a deeper doom*
> *Could scarcely thunder o'er his tomb,*
> *When he shall wake to sleep no more,*
> *And stand the eternal throne before.*
>
> *(ll. 83–88)*

From this point on in the poem Azo sleeps no more, his life an immortality of death—

> *The massy trunk the ruin feels,*
> *And never more a leaf reveals.*
>
> *(ll. 585–86)*

Parisina's "sleeping whisper of a name"[7] neatly combines the multiple guilt of the three characters: it "Bespeaks her guilt and Azo's shame" (ll. 91, 92)—his shame at the incest but also the shame of his seduction of Bianca and the birth of the bastard Hugo. The whispered name Byron sees, then, as totally destructive both of the reality of the human relationships involved and of Azo's dream of enduring love and peace: it

> *Sounds fearful as the breaking billow,*
> *Which rolls the plank upon the shore,*
> *And dashes on the pointed rock*
> *The wretch who sinks to rise no more.*
>
> *(ll. 94–97)*

At this point in the poem an interesting shift begins to take place in the point of view. Until now the guilt has been

---

[7] Coleridge reminds us that Leigh Hunt claimed credit for suggesting to Byron Parisina's revelation in her sleep, though he also points out that the source (if one was needed) might well have been *Macbeth* or Henry Mackenzie's *Julia de Roubigné* (P, III, 510n).

solely Hugo's and Parisina's, but while the narrator has paid lip
service to the moral canons that guilt reflects, he has sympa-
thetically given more emphasis to the idyllic nature of their love.
The reasons for this seemingly "immoral" (or amoral) attitude
are revealed when the narrator informs us that Hugo is

> *The offspring of his [Azo's] wayward youth,*
> *When he betrayed Bianca's*[8] *truth,*
> *The maid whose folly could confide*
> *In him who made her not his bride.*
>
> *(ll. 103–6)*

But the point of view here is even more complex than this, for
it merges that of Azo himself with the already dual attitude of
the orthodox moral commentator. Azo's reaction to hearing
Hugo's name on Parisina's lips is revealed in these lines:

> *'Tis Hugo's,—he, the child of one*
> *He loved—his own all-evil son—*
> *The offspring of his wayward youth.*
>
> *(ll. 101–3)*

Hard upon this, with perhaps a hint of Azo's self-condemnation,
is the clear note of moral condemnation:

> *The offspring of his wayward youth,*
> *When he betrayed Bianca's truth,*
> *The maid whose folly could confide*
> *In him who made her not his bride.*
>
> *(ll. 103–6)*

It is perhaps a confused and confusing series of voices, yet heard
aright, the passage is a fine jumbling of various possible points
of view which in concert dramatize the impossibility of judgment and say, in effect, that this is what life is. Bianca's "truth"

---

[8] In the original manuscript Bianca was called Medora, a further
indication that *Parisina*, as well as *The Siege*, was originally begun
much earlier than supposed—probably in 1814. In February of that
year *The Corsair* was published with Medora as its main female character (aside from Gulnare). Having used the name in that poem,
Byron, when returning to what were probably only early scraps of
the manuscript that was ultimately to become *Parisina*, crossed out
"Medora" and substituted "Bianca."

is also her "folly"; Azo's love for her is also betrayal; the child of love is also "all-evil"; marriage for Bianca would have been "right," yet Azo's marriage to Parisina is doom; and so on.

At this point Byron's shrewd use of Gibbon should be noted. Taking his cue from the historian's suggestion that Hugo and Parisina were possibly innocent, Byron omits the detail of Nicholas' personal spying on the lovers to corroborate the servant's story,[9] and has Azo rely entirely on the frightened face-saving testimony of the "long conniving damsels" of Parisina's bedchamber (stanza viii). To save themselves they "would transfer / The guilt—the shame—the doom—to her" (ll. 125–26). Thus, though the reader knows at first hand of the incestuous relationship, Azo does not, but proceeds summarily as if he did, and the corrupt "world" of the palace testifies to the "corruption" of the lovers. This point is made dramatically clear in stanza x, in which the appearance of friendship, idolization, eagerness to serve, and love is stripped away by the hypocritical self-righteousness of the world: to the "high-born men" who "were proud to wait" on Parisina, the court beauties who "watched to imitate" her, and the "warriors" eager to leap forth with "A thousand swords" to make "her quarrel all their own,"

> Now,—what is she? and what are they?
> Can she command, or these obey?
> All silent and unheeding now,
> With downcast eyes and knitting brow,
> And folded arms, and freezing air,
> And lips that scarce their scorn forbear,
> Her knights, her dames—her court is there.
>
> (ll. 160–66)

Once again, though Hugo and Parisina are presented in this "trial" scene as "the sinful pair" (l. 137) the narrator's description of them against such a background of worldly corruption and of Azo's rage is clearly sympathetic (Byron added the

---

[9] *P*, III, 506n. This detail is from Byron's footnote quotation of the entire story as told by Antonio Frizzi in his *Memorie per la Storia di Ferrara* (1793).

beautiful lines 175–82 to Lady Byron's fair copy of the poem to accentuate this point).

When the narrator turns to Hugo and to Azo, however, his angle of moral vision shifts once more. Like all of Byron's heroes Hugo steels his heart against this ordeal: "He would not shrink before the crowd" (l. 188), and he refuses the fatal compassionate gesture of Selim and Conrad:

> *But yet he dared not look on her* [Parisina];
>
> .   .   .   .   .
>
> > *he dared not throw*
> *One look upon that death-like brow!*
> *Else had his rising heart betrayed*
> *Remorse for all the wreck it made.*
>
> > > > *(ll. 189, 194–97)*

Thus Hugo, as Byron's typical fallen man, smothers his love, compassion, and basic humanity, the very "heart" that has caused "the wreck" of the lovers' illusory paradise. Throughout the brief passage (stanza xi) Byron fills his narrator's lines with references to Hugo's guilt, "all good men's hate," and Azo's righteous wrath. Lest we take this as a legitimate cue to the moral rightness of Azo's actions, however, Azo is next heard to belie his earlier statement of hatred for his "all-evil son." "But yesterday," he says,

> *I gloried in a wife and son;*
> *That dream this morning passed away.*[10]
>
> > > *(ll. 198–99)*

With the shattering of that dream by Parisina's sleeping whisper of Hugo's name, Azo's voice quickly modulates to the reality of guilty, self-righteous rationalization, the voice of moral condemnation and of the world:

> > *there breathes not one*
> *Who would not do as I have done:*
> *Those ties are broken—not by me;*
>
> > .   .   .   .   .

---

[10] The fact that this is also Azo's public voice presenting himself in the best light before his subjects does not invalidate the point I am making, which is corroborated by Byron's sustaining here his dream-reality imagery.

> *Hugo, the priest awaits on thee.*
> *And then—thy crime's reward!*
>
> *(ll. 203–5, 207–8)*

In heaven there may be mercy, Azo says, but "here, upon the earth beneath" there is only revenge and destruction, "justice" and the law, "morality" and "truth."[11] Hugo is condemned to death, Parisina to a life of shame, and the blood rests, says Azo, not on his hands but upon hers (l. 220). Since he is God, Parisina will be Cain.

But yet again the perspective changes as Azo is visibly shaken by his own actions and Hugo adopts a stance of self-righteousness. " 'Tis true that I have done thee wrong," he says (l. 252), but then argues the justice of so doing in view of Azo's earlier wrongs—his mother's "slighted love and ruined name, / Her offspring's heritage of shame" (ll. 244–45). Even Parisina is at fault:

> *But wrong for wrong:—this—deemed thy bride,*
> *The other victim of thy pride,—*
> *Thou know'st for me was destined long;*
> *Thou saw'st, and coveted'st her charms;*
> *And with thy very crime—my birth,—*
> *Thou taunted'st me—as little worth;*
> *A match ignoble for her arms;*
> *Because, forsooth, I could not claim*
> *The lawful heirship of thy name.*
>
> *(ll. 253–61)*

Hugo goes on in this remarkable speech to point out to Azo that he is "in my spirit—all of thee" (l. 287), that Azo's guilty love has produced in turn the guilty love of the son:

> *As erred the sire, so erred the son,*
> *And thou must punish both in one.*
> *My crime seems worst to human view,*
> *But God must judge between us too!*[12]
>
> *(ll. 314–17)*

---

[11] This is again an example of the point made by Newman Ivey White, quoted earlier (see pp. 135–36n).

[12] Emphasis added. The anonymous reviewer for the *Critical Review* properly took Byron to task for the infelicity of the last line with its

The ritualistic confessions have now come full circle: Azo is innocent, yet guilty for having dishonored Bianca and "stolen" Parisina from Hugo; Hugo is guilty, yet justified in his Greco-tragic revenge upon his father; Parisina is guilty, yet somehow pure and virginal through the entire proceedings; the world and society (as Azo) are morally right in their condemnation of the guilty pair, yet guilty in their own hypocrisy. There is, then, no innocence or guilt, law or right, morality or love; there is only insanity and death in a world where the past is ever alive in the present determining the future—"and at last / The future can but be the past" (ll. 304–5).

It is right, then, that Parisina does not defend herself, for in a sense she has no defense. Like all of Byron's heroines she embodies love and the hope of paradise regained. In the world of *Parisina*, however, that hope is long gone, that paradise a jungle. Yet the "world" hypocritically expects from her a final protestation of love and loyalty: "Would she thus hear him doomed to die!" (l. 325). The world cannot see that even that human gesture is now impossible; and as the narrator's voice modulates to that of society,[13] both see her now as *the* guilty one, "The living cause of Hugo's ill" (l. 327)—

> *that living guilty thing,*
> *Whose every passion was a sting,*
> *Which urged to guilt, but could not bear*
> *That guilt's detection and despair.*
>
> *(ll. 352–55)*

---

curious homonym—an infelicity which is all the more inexplicable because Byron worked hard on Hugo's speech and was concerned enough about its effect to add 10 lines in a late revision (*P*, III, 518n). Marshall's interpretation of Hugo's speech, as well as his reading of the entire poem, is clearly on the right track but is obscured and muddied by psychoanalytical jargon ("Byron's *Parisina* and the Functions of Psychoanalytical Criticism," *The Personalist*, XLII [1961], 213–23; and *The Structure of Byron's Major Poems*, pp. 62–71). A sensible if limited analysis of the poem may also be found in Clement T. Goode's 1959 doctoral dissertation, "Byron's Early Romances: A Study."

[13] Lest the reader forget the narrator's presence and the importance of his role and point of view, Byron carefully inserted "I said" in l. 326.

Her one reaction is a tear for all of fallen humanity and the inarticulate, wordless shriek of universal misery (ll. 336–47). Murray was right to "admire the fabrication of the 'big Tear,' which is very fine,"[14] but he clearly did not understand it, as his twitting of Byron reveals—"much larger, by the way, than Shakespeare's." In a sense it *is* larger, encompassing all of human woe and the universe of death, just as Parisina's Ophelia-like madness epitomizes man's titanic struggle to awaken from the Bedlam-like nightmare of reality:

> *All was confused and undefined*
> *To her all-jarred and wandering mind;*
> *A chaos of wild hopes and fears:*
> *And now in laughter, now in tears,*
> *But madly still in each extreme,*
> *She strove with that convulsive dream.*
>
> *(ll. 378–83)*

As Parisina strives vainly to wake from the dream (l. 385), Byron properly has the convent bells toll the doom of man,

> *The song for the dead below,*
> *Or the living who shortly shall be so!*
>
> *(ll. 392–93)*

The image Byron creates for this final drama of man's life is fitting: we see Hugo "Kneeling at the Friar's knee" (l. 397)—as he had knelt at Parisina's, or Love's, earlier—both overshadowed by the eternal "headsman"; and "While the crowd in a speech-less circle gather," the archetypal fall of the "Son . . . by the doom of the Father" (ll. 405, 406) takes place in the "lovely hour . . . / Before the summer sun shall set" (ll. 407–8). The ritualism of the beheading, the deliberate confusion of points of view, the consolidating of guilt into mankind at large all empha-size the fact that Azo's murder of Hugo and sentencing of Parisina to an eternal death in life are also, and essentially, his own self-destruction. Although he marries again and raises "goodly sons" (l. 531), Azo's life is a perpetual torture in the private hell of his own being, where life goes on against his

---

[14] Ltr. to Byron, in *P*, III, 519n.

will—his death-like ahumanity reinforced by the familiar Byron images of mind.[15] "On his cold eye" the growth of his sons is "glanced unheeded by" (ll. 534, 535), and

> *never tear his cheek descended,*
> *And never smile his brow unbended;*
> *And o'er that fair broad brow were wrought*
> *The intersected lines of thought;*
>
> .   .   .   .   .
>
> *Scars of the lacerating mind*
> *Which the Soul's war doth leave behind.*
> *He was past all mirth or woe:*
> *Nothing more remained below*
> *But sleepless nights and heavy days,*
> *A mind all dead to scorn or praise,*
> *A heart which shunned itself—and yet*
> *That would not yield, nor could forget,*
> *Which, when it least appeared to melt,*
> *Intensely thought—intensely felt:*
> *The deepest ice which ever froze*
> *Can only o'er the surface close;*
> *The living stream lies quick below,*
> *And flows, and cannot cease to flow.*
>
> (ll. 537–40, 543–56)

As a god, Azo had tried to lop "The tainted branches of the tree" to give "a strength"

> *By which the rest shall bloom and live*
> *All greenly fresh and wildly free;*
>
> (ll. 581–82)

but unlike God, whose touch is sure, man's lightning blasts the entire tree—and, to mix the metaphor, there is no Noah to survive.

The final irony has yet to be commented upon. To society, to the narrator's sense of morality and right, the blasting of that tree is just: "Dark the crime, and just the law" (l. 428), the narrator pontificates, while "Even the stern" and already

---

[15] Those images, concentrated in ll. 539–44 and 551–56, were inserted by Byron in a late revision.

189

cold "stood chilled with awe" and "shuddered as they saw" (ll. 427, 429). Still, in their eyes, and in the narrator's, Hugo

> *died, as erring man should die,*
> *Without display, without parade;*
> *Meekly had he bowed and prayed,*
> *As not disdaining priestly aid,*
> *Nor desperate of all hope on high.*
>
> .   .   .   .   .
>
> *No more reproach,—no more despair,—*
> *No thought but Heaven,—no word but prayer.*
>   *(ll. 462–66, 471–72)*

Law and order are restored, and man returns to the nightmare of life, where, oddly oblivious to it, his "massy trunk the ruin feels, / And never more a leaf reveals" (ll. 585–86).

II

Although Marshall is certainly correct in seeing *Parisina* in terms of a pattern of guilt and guilt transference, I cannot agree with his attribution of a messianic role to Hugo, nor can I see those psychological patterns as the final meaning of the poem.[16] For the poem, in the end, belongs to Azo. It is he who inherits the earth he has helped to create; he is God the creator as well as destroyer; he is man sinning and sinned against; he is the ultimate cause of suffering and the sufferer; he is his own hell, eternally isolated, more dead than living in the nightmare of his own wasteland. If Parisina's mad shriek of lament mourns the lostness of man, it is, ironically, a lament for Azo; and if Azo awakens from his dreams of blissful love to the harsh reality of sin, disloyalty, hate, and destruction, his final sleep at the end of the poem is that reality of which nightmares are made, grappling with which demands a kind of insanity.

That kind of insanity, which is another word for survival in a nightmare world, is the burden of *The Prisoner of Chillon*, written in Switzerland immediately after Byron's de-

---

[16] See *The Structure of Byron's Major Poems*, pp. 62–71.

parture from England in 1816. Although it has been acclaimed more often than *Parisina* as the best of Byron's verse tales,[17] the poem has consistently been misread as a tribute to the unconquerable nature of the human mind, or (with reference to the "Sonnet on Chillon" that Byron added later) a hymn to liberty, or "the story of a martyr to political liberty," or a "grandiose expression of romantic defiance."[18] Rather, it is a chronicle of the slow decay of the human mind in the dungeon of its being. In a true sense, just as his earlier tales had better been named "fables," *The Prisoner of Chillon* is, as its generally ignored subtitle tells us, "A Fable" for Byron's own time as well as a paradigm of the eternal human condition.

Byron's apology, in a note to the poem, for his ignorance of the true facts of Bonivard's life and career should not obscure the fact that in this same apology is a fairly clear statement of his greater interest in the *idea* of imprisonment than in any celebration of "courage" and Bonivard's "virtues."[19] Indeed, Byron's letters at this time tend to suggest that his own focus was upon the prison rather than the prisoner, for he refers to the poem consistently as the "Castle of Chillon."[20] At the same time, however, he arrives at a final solution of one of his most gnawing problems in the handling of point of view—the same problem that led him in *The Giaour* to adopt both the limited point of view of the fisherman-narrator-participant and the larger, more universal point of view of the poet. In *The Prisoner of Chillon*, by using, as Marshall says, the basic struc-

---

[17] See, e.g., Andrew Rutherford's excellent chapter on the poem in his *Byron: A Critical Study*, pp. 66–75.

[18] The quotations are from Samuel C. Chew, *Lord Byron: "Childe Harold's Pilgrimage,"* p. 300n, and Willis W. Pratt, "Byron and Some Current Patterns of Thought," p. 150.

[19] Chew interprets Byron's prefixing of the "Sonnet on Chillon" and his calling the poem "A Fable" as the poet's way of apologizing for not doing justice to Bonivard's "republicanism and his struggle to free Geneva from the overlordship of the Duke of Savoy" (*Lord Byron: "Childe Harold's Pilgrimage,"* p. 300n). Perhaps. For a completely different estimate of Bonivard—as a cunning, avaricious libertine (a view Byron obviously was never aware of), see A. van Amstel [Johannes C. Neuman], "The True Story of the Prisoner of Chillon," *19th Century*, XLVII (1900), 821–29.

[20] E.g., ltr. to Murray, 28 Aug. 1816, in *LJ*, III, 345.

ture of a dramatic monologue, Byron can fuse time past, present, and future in the point of view of the prisoner, who is both an actor in and an observer of the events of the narrative. Yet, as Marshall also establishes (though I cannot agree with his interpretation of its implications), the point of view of Bonivard is necessarily limited; it is a view from within the action, as it were. His interpretation of that action, and of his own reactions, is therefore colored by *his* condition, limited by *his* perception and mind, and circumscribed by the boundaries of *his* time and space.

The brilliance of the poem, and of Byron's handling of point of view and theme in the poem, lies in the prisoner's revelation of more than he knows, or can know; that is, he exists for himself as a man, while he grows for the poet (and the reader) into a microcosm of mankind. In the same way, the prison exists as a political and religious fact in time, but its ultimate significance rests on its symbolic proportions and consequent universal implications. The poem is dramatic precisely because of this fusion of points of view. The result is a kind of tension that the earlier tales generally lack because in them Byron's dual or multiple points of view are presented through separate speakers and do not emerge, as here, from what is apparently a single-dimensional outlook. This new method is additionally dramatic in that the words themselves develop, as characters, into symbols, playing out an eternal truth, which for Byron is the archetypal drama of human existence.

With this total conception more firmly in his mind than ever before, Byron saw immediately that it was important to de-emphasize the specific background of Bonivard's imprisonment. That his punishment is for his father's beliefs reminds us of the doom of Hugo and Azo, with the son inheriting his father's world: in *The Prisoner of Chillon* that world is "darkness" (l. 16), in which "the goodly earth and air / Are banned, and barred—forbidden fare" (ll. 9–10). Quite deliberately Byron denies the reader the opportunity to judge the equity or moral rightness of the imprisonment. Obviously, to the prisoner, who speaks, all foes are persecutors; just as obviously, to the "persecutors" all who refuse to forsake their tenets and "the God their foes denied" (l. 24) are enemies to be slaughtered in war or cast in dungeons. Byron accents the universality of this condition by relying, with the same care he used for the words "Son" and "Father" in *Parisina*, upon generic nouns and discrete capitalization: it is "Persecution's rage" (l. 20), not the rage of the Christians or the Turks or the Venetians or whatever, that seals the fate of conqueror and conquered alike. At the end of the poem we are given no historical explanation for the release of Bonivard: his condition of imprisonment depends upon no political or religious dispensation, nor does it depend upon time—for to him it is eternally the same "Fettered or fetterless to be" (l. 373).

Similarly, Byron takes liberties with the size of the Bonivard family: whereas there were actually only three brothers (and the father), he makes their total seven, certainly aware of the magic of that number and its symbolism of completeness:

> *We were seven—who now are one,*
> *Six in youth, and one in age,*
> *Finished as they had begun,*
> *Proud of Persecution's rage.*[21]
>
> *(ll. 17–20)*

Thus the race of man, begun in battle and ended in death and imprisonment, is memorialized in the "seven pillars of Gothic mould," the "seven columns, massy and grey" (ll. 27, 29), the seven rings in the seven pillars, and the seven chains in the seven rings—iron clanking against stone. "Dim with a dull imprisoned ray" of sunlight "Creeping o'er the floor so damp," "Chillon's dungeons deep and old" (ll. 28, 30, 34) thus very quickly become an epitome of earthly life, of what Bonivard calls with unconscious irony "this new day" (l. 41). It is perhaps

---

[21] Karl Elze suggests that the idea of the seven brothers came from the monument of Richard Lord Byron in Hucknall-Torkard Church: "Beneath in a vault is interred the body of Richard Lord Byron, who with the rest of his family, being seven brothers . . ." (*Lord Byron: A Biography with a Critical Essay on His Place in Literature* [orig. German ed., 1870; London, 1872], p. 4n). The more obvious source, if one needs to find one, is Wordsworth's "We Are Seven." In passing it might be noted that Byron early singled out Wordsworth's "Seven Sisters" as possessing "all the beauties, and few of the defects, of the writer" (Review of Wordsworth's *Poems* [1807], in *Monthly Literary Recreations*, July 1807).

even conceivable that Byron saw the three brothers chained to their columns as a grotesque modern echo of the Crucifixion, for clearly to him modern man was Christ eternally crucified, the Son's "fall by the doom of the Father." Unable to see each other in "that pale and livid light" (l. 52), they are but shadows of themselves; even their voices sound progressively more unlike their own.

Our sense that it is mankind Byron writes of is in-increased by the next two stanzas (iv and v) in which the two younger brothers are introduced: one gentle, "beautiful," "pure and bright" (ll. 79, 86) with his "mother's brow" (l. 74) and a spirit of compassion for all the "woe / Which he abhorred to view below" (ll. 90–91); the other virile, strong, warrior-like, active. To Byron these are the feminine and masculine principles we have seen developing in the tales in terms of the metaphors of heart and mind, love and war, and Bonivard himself partakes of their essences. When they both die, he in effect dies too, for there is left nothing:

> *I had no thought, no feeling—none—*
> *Among the stones I stood a stone*
>
> *(ll. 235–36)*

—just as, we recall, at Hugo's sentence of death Parisina collapses,

> *And to the earth she fell like stone*
> *Or statue from its base o'erthrown,*
> *More like a thing that ne'er had life,—*
> *A monument of Azo's wife.*
>
> *(ll. 348–51)*

For Bonivard, then, without heart or mind to sustain him,

> *all was blank, and bleak, and grey;*
> *It was not night—it was not day;*
> *It was not even the dungeon-light,*
> *So hateful to my heavy sight,*
> *But vacancy absorbing space,*
> *And fixedness—without a place.*
>
> *(ll. 240–45)*

194

Byron foreshadows this awful nothingness with his description of the cell itself, in which again he departs from fact. In the place of the spacious and relatively airy vaulted room above the waterline of the lake that was Bonivard's actual prison and that Byron and Shelley inspected together in June, 1816, the cell of the poem is a "double dungeon" in that it is bound by walls and water; it is "like a living grave" (l. 114), a "dark vault" deep in the bowels of life, the waters of the lake spraying wantonly through the barred window to mock man's plight (ll. 116, 119–21).

Yet even this is not enough to dramatize the insistent, even fierce, negativity of Byron's vision. When the older of the two brothers dies,

> and they unlocked his chain,
> And scooped for him a shallow grave
> Even from the cold earth of our cave,
>
> *(ll. 150–52)*

even the freedom of death, which Bonivard says he "could have smiled to see" (l. 124), is circumscribed by the water, the prison walls, and finally the earth itself. Bonivard's "foolish thought" and "idle prayer" that they leave his brother's body atop the dust "whereon the day / Might shine" (ll. 153–54) is greeted with cold laughter; and his own awareness of the futility of such thoughts has already been established by his seeing even the sun as imprisoned there in the solid darkness and each "new day" the same. Still more terrible is the excruciating silence of the younger brother's death, echoing in the mind of one to whom a word, a sound, was all that was left of life and love. As the physical masculinity of the older brother decays and is assigned to a corporeal tomb within a tomb, so the femininity of the younger brother—"the flower," "The infant love of all his race" (stanza viii)—merely "faded" from view:

> so calm and meek,
> So softly worn, so sweetly weak,
> So tearless, yet so tender—kind.
>
> *(ll. 186–88)*

Bonivard, in the extremity of anguished strength, bursts his

bonds to rush to him, but "found him not" (l. 211). And this
last loss, "of all the most" (l. 201)—for to lose heart and love
and compassion is the final cessation of man's essential humanity
—is

> The last, the sole, the dearest link
> Between me and the eternal brink,
> Which bound me to my failing race.
>
> (ll. 215–17)

From this point on Bonivard is the living dead, his hand "full
as chill" as that of his brothers (l. 222), without thought or
feeling, in a world of total nothingness:

> There were no stars—no earth—no time—
> No check—no change—no good—no crime—
> But silence, and a stirless breath
> Which neither was of life nor death;
> A sea of stagnant idleness,
> Blind, boundless, mute, motionless![22]
>
> (ll. 245–50)

And yet he cannot, will not die, will not submit to the final
irony, and is tortured further by the phantasm of hope, the
illusion of freedom, and finally by freedom itself.

This last section of the poem (stanzas x and xiv) has
been read with greatest understanding by Marshall and Rutherford, yet each of their readings is only partial—and certainly
more positive than Byron intended. The suggestion, echoing an
early charge in the *Critical Review*[23] that Byron here capitulates
to the "Lakers" (especially in stanza xiii), is particularly misleading. Unlike Wordsworth, whose heart "leaps up" when he
beholds "a rainbow in the sky," recalling him to his early faith
in the trinity of Man-Nature-God, Bonivard's "brain" is momen-

---

[22] The echoes of Coleridge's *The Ancient Mariner* are clearly inten-
tional here. For a study of Coleridge's influence on Byron, though it
is limited and somewhat simplistic, see Edwin M. Everett, "Lord
Byron's Lakist Interlude." It is also useful to note here that Byron
was impressed by "Kubla Khan" mainly for its "psychological" base
as well as for its "perfect harmony of versification" (Thomas Medwin,
Journal, p. 120).

[23] 5th ser., IV (1816), 568–73.

tarily restored to sanity by the carol of a bird—but only to the point at which the blessed nothingness and vacancy of darkness yield to a renewed clarity of perception and a consequent doubled sense of imprisonment and death:

> *I saw the dungeon walls and floor*
> *Close slowly round me as before.*[24]
>
> (*ll. 261–62*)

His senses "by dull degrees came back" to "their wonted track" (ll. 259–60); the bird has "brought [him] back to feel and think" (l. 278). But just as

> *All was confused and undefined*
> *To her [Parisina's] all-jarred and wandering mind;*
> *A chaos of wild hopes and fears:*
> *And now in laughter, now in tears,*
> *But madly still in each extreme,*
> *She strove with that convulsive dream;*
> *For so it seemed on her to break:*
> *Oh! vainly must she strive to wake!*
>
> (*ll. 379–85*)

so too Bonivard, in his new-born shattered humanity, strives vainly to destroy the convulsive dream of death in life by seeing the bird as "come to love" him, "A visitant from Paradise," his "brother's soul come down to" him—only to have reality burst that illusion with the crushing awareness of the bird's mortality:

> *'twas mortal well I knew,*
> *For he would never thus have flown—*
> *And left me twice so doubly lone,—*
> *Lone—as the corse within its shroud.*
>
> (*ll. 290–93*)

All avenues, however, have not yet been closed, and Byron must close them all to seal man's fate irrevocably in dark-

---

[24] The sense of physical reality's double oppressiveness after a visionary experience or flight of fancy is a familiar theme in Romantic poetry—perhaps most movingly and intensely expressed by Keats in "Sleep and Poetry" (ll. 155ff.), "La Belle Dame Sans Merci," "Epistle to J. H. Reynolds Esq.," and "Lines Written in the Highlands after a Visit to Burns's Country."

ness. First, the remnants of man's compassion must be perverted. Bonivard's keepers do not refasten his shackles, thus allowing him his spot of earth, the

> *liberty to stride*
> *Along my cell from side to side,*
> *And up and down, and then athwart,*
> *And tread it over every part;*
> *And round the pillars one by one,*
>
> (ll. 306–10)

only to return "where my walk begun" (l. 311). With such freedom he makes "a footing in the wall," not to escape, but to enlarge his world, with full knowledge that the vision of the world available to him through the cell bars mocks his very loss of that world, and that even could he attain that ultimate freedom "the whole earth would henceforth be / A wider prison unto me" (ll. 322–23). Still he climbs up to his window to look out, almost masochistically, for the mountains, lake, river, trees, and town are all there, as they always were, oblivious to his plight. Not only is his view of this brave new world severely circumscribed by the square horizons of his window and laced with their bars, but the one island he sees turns him back upon his own condition by its parody of his death in life, of his universe of three graves:

> *A small green isle, it seemed no more,*
> *Scarce broader than my dungeon floor,*
> *But in it there were three tall trees,*
> *And o'er it blew the mountain breeze,*
> *And by it there were waters flowing,*
> *And on it there were young flowers growing,*
> *Of gentle breath and hue.*
>
> (ll. 344–50)

After such a vision—which contains nothing of what Marshall calls transcendence or rebirth, nothing of the Wordsworthian pantheistic peace and comfort, but rather the terror of Coleridge's *Christabel* and *The Ancient Mariner* or of the naturalistic novelists' indifferent nature—Bonivard's own darkness is a relief as well as "a new-dug grave" (l. 362).

198

His release from prison, then, is anticlimactic, for we have moved from stone-like immobility to the world of the cell, to the world within the window's frame, to the world of the island, and now to the universe at large—wall-less, uncircumscribed, daylit, free; that is, we have moved from microcosmic imprisonment to macrocosmic imprisonment, from the world of space and time (and thought and feeling) to the ultimate eternal darkness. Such "long communion" with darkness "tends / To make us what we are" (ll. 390–91); and there is no possibility of change. We are "all inmates of one place" (l. 385).

III

It is not a giant step from Bonivard's world to the world of Byron's poem "Darkness," whose original title was, significantly, "A Dream." First published in the same volume as *The Prisoner of Chillon*, this poem paints Bonivard's world with a cosmic brush and translates the battlefield of *The Siege of Corinth* into the universe. So totally terrifying is the vision that Byron must have felt at first that he could only couch it in terms of a dream, and yet, as the crucial first line of the poem points out, it "was not all a dream." It is again a fable for Byron's time, the logical end product of what Du Bos calls his "massive sense of nothingness"[25]—a world without light and without

---

[25] *Byron and the Need of Fatality*, p. 72. The poem was not kindly received by Byron's contemporaries (not even Walter Scott), who thought it strangely unByronic or "incomprehensible rant" imitative of "the German school" (George Clinton, *Memoirs of the Life and Writings of Lord Byron* [1st ed., 1825; London, 1827], p. 356; see also Scott's review in *Quarterly Review*, XVI [1816], 204). Modern critics have responded to the poem in almost precisely the same way. Paul West, for example, calls it "febrile," somehow totally unlike what he describes as the "intelligent despair, [the] inspired gibbering in the lazar-house of the human condition" of the more Byronic *Don Juan* (*Byron and the Spoiler's Art*, pp. 81, 127); and Leslie Marchand sees it, more or less accurately, as a product of Byron's "immitigable cynicism and despair" at "the unheroic end of the last man on a dying planet" (*Byron's Poetry*, p. 128)—but he does not consider it as having any significant relationship to the rest of Byron's poetry. Only George M. Ridenour, I think, sees that relationship. For him the poem evinces a characteristic "radical pessimism" in a characteristically "unin-

prisons, palaces, huts, or class distinction, a world with the ultimate freedom and democracy but no love, a world of canni-
balistic warfare, the death of God, the eternal void:

> The populous and the powerful was a lump,
> Seasonless, herbless, treeless, manless, lifeless—
> A lump of death—a chaos of hard clay.
> The rivers, lakes, and ocean all stood still,
> And nothing stirred within their silent depths;
> Ships sailorless lay rotting on the sea,
> And their masts fell down piecemeal: as they dropped
> They slept on the abyss without a surge—
> The waves were dead; the tides were in their grave,
> The Moon, their mistress, had expired before;
> The winds were withered in the stagnant air,
> And the clouds perished; Darkness had no need
> Of aid from them—She was the Universe.
>
> (ll. 70–82)

"The Dream," written in July, 1816, and published
first with The Prisoner of Chillon and "Darkness," also reflects
this unrelieved gloom, as well as Byron's interest in the interanimation and confusion of dream and reality[26] (whether or not
it is an autobiographical account of his love for Mary Chaworth
seems to me totally irrelevant). As in Parisina, The Prisoner,
and "Darkness," he presents the dream world of sleep as another
world, "A boundary between the things misnamed / Death and
existence" (ll. 2–3). These lines are most important, for they define the shifting, blurring line between life and death, a fusion
of supposed opposites which meet in sleep, that "wide realm
of wild reality" (l. 4), not to relieve man's cares or soothe his

---

dignant way": "this vision of human weakness in the face of unman-
ageable forces lies behind all of Byron's work. No power of imagination can change this, no vision can make much difference. It is the
outside limiting factor, like the 'fate' of the Greeks, that nothing can
be done about" ("Byron in 1816," p. 459). My own emphasis, of
course, is slightly different.

[26] See Ridenour's excellent analysis of this interanimation in the essay
cited in n. 25.

fevered brow, but rather to plague his rest and draw all into the vortex of shadow and darkness.

"The Dream" begins happily enough with Byron's favorite Edenic scene: "a most living landscape" peopled with the "Boy" and "Maid" of eternal spring and love and peace (stanza ii). Indeed, the idyllic nature of the union reminds us of Shelley's description of the Edenic isle in the latter part of *Epipsychidion*. To the Boy's eye, writes Byron,

> *There was but one belovéd face on earth,*
> *And that was shining on him: he had looked*
> *Upon it till it could not pass away;*
> *He had no breath, no being, but in hers;*
> *She was his voice; he did not speak to her,*
> *But trembled on her words; she was his sight,*
> *For his eye followed hers, and saw with hers,*
> *Which coloured all his objects:—he had ceased*
> *To live within himself; she was his life,*
> *The ocean to the river of his thoughts,*
> *Which terminated all.*
>
> *(ll. 48–57)*

But this paradisaical unity transcending time, space, and all separability is, as always in Byron, illusory. Just as Shelley's imagination can seldom sustain its image of oneness against the world's slow stain, just as his

> *one life, one death,*
> *One Heaven, one Hell, one immortality,*
> *And one annihilation*

crumbles under the chains of lead which bind all flight and imagination,[27] so the sighs of Byron's Maid, even in the midst of Eden, "were not for him" (l. 63), and "A change [comes] o'er the spirit of [his] dream" (l. 75). With each successive change eternity fades into time, vision into the light of common day, day into darkness; and melancholy, "the telescope of truth,"

> *strips the distance of its fantasies,*

---

[27] *Epipsychidion*, ll. 585–91.

And brings life near in utter nakedness,
Making the cold reality too real![28]

(ll. 180–83)

The dreamer, with a superb understatement, closes the poem
marveling

that the doom
Of these two creatures should be thus traced out
Almost like a reality—the one
To end in madness—both in misery.

(ll. 203–6)

Man's dreams are but the caverns of his despair, the world the
macrocosmic externalization of his inner hell.

But here we should take stock lest we be trapped by
Byron's wholesale plunge into darkness and nothingness. Before he completed, though almost certainly not before he began,
Parisina and *The Siege of Corinth*, and before he wrote "Darkness" and "The Dream," Byron was writing *Hebrew Melodies*
(in late 1814 and early 1815), a number of lyrics (including
"Farewell! If Ever Fondest Prayer," "When We Two Parted"),
five poems entitled "Stanzas for Music," and several poems on
Napoleon and Waterloo. And he completed Canto III of *Childe
Harold* before "Darkness" and "The Dream." It is well, then,
that we turn to some of these poems, written amid the gathering
gloom, to study what seems to be the familiar bifurcation of
Byron's poetic efforts.

---

[28] Marchand, clearly with this passage in mind, interprets the whole
poem as an example of Byron's discovering "that he could be more
truthful in verse than in prose." This is quite different, I think, from
the point I made in the earlier chapters about his private-public and
public-private voices. In any case, Marchand goes on, assuming that
the poem is totally and only biographical, to say that it is an example
of Byron's "safety-valve" theory of the imagination in operation
(*Byron's Poetry*, p. 129). Cf. in particular, Ridenour on this passage
("Byron in 1816," p. 461).

Chapter VII

HEBREW MELODIES AND OTHER LYRICS OF 1814–1816

There has probably been more disagreement over the quality of Byron's lyric poetry than over any other kind of poetry he wrote.[1] The case against it is admirably stated by Ernest de Selincourt. The best of Byron's lyrics, he writes, have, "doubtless, a vigour and a colour of their own, but how poor and obvious is their music beside that of Shelley or Keats, Tennyson or Robert Bridges! Byron sets his emotion to a familiar, almost hackneyed, tune: the true lyrist, even if he accepts a conventional framework, weaves upon it his own melody, of which every cadence seems responsive to the finer shades of his emotion." Byron has, De Selincourt concludes, "no magical power over words, no subtlety in verse-music. Hence, though no poet ever succeeded more fully in the expression of himself, he never succeeded in the lyric. . . ."[2] Northrop Frye explains the problem this way: the lyrics in general contain "nothing that 'modern' critics look for: no texture, no ambiguities, no intellectual ironies, no intensity, no vividness of phrasing, the words and images being vague to the point of abstraction."[3] And Eliot blamed all on Byron's "imperceptiveness . . . to the English word" and "a defective sensibility."[4]

Although there are no rousing defenses of Byron's lyric talent—indeed few defenses at all for his corpus of lyric

---

[1] Byron is rarely given credit for his extraordinary range of poetic and metrical experiments. As De Selincourt reminds us, few poets experimented more than he: "romance, descriptive and lyrical, drama—monologue—song: in octosyllabic and heroic couplets, Spenserian stanza, blank verse—and a great variety of lyrical measures" (*Wordsworthian and Other Studies*, p. 121).

[2] *Ibid.*, pp. 106–7.

[3] "George Gordon, Lord Byron," p. 152.

[4] "Byron," in *On Poetry and Poets*, p. 201 (reprinted from *From Anne to Victoria*).

poetry—one cannot conveniently and easily ignore L. C. Martin's careful and intelligent lecture entitled "Byron's Lyrics," in which the very shortcomings or lacks that Frye and Eliot note are seen as at least potential virtues. In the best lyrics, Martin suggests, "the style is simple without *simplesse*. . . . Byron can write with [an] avoidance of cliché and [a] reliance upon bare emotive phrasing" that produce an impressive and moving poetry in its own right—what he calls in another connection a "bare but grand sufficiency in style."[5] Herbert Read noticed the same quality, which he describes as an "explicit felicity" of expression: "no image, no word, is far-fetched," and often there is deliberately "the obvious cliché."[6]

Whether or not one agrees with these apologia; whether or not we see a fundamental lack of what Read calls "grace" in the lyrics;[7] whether or not, as Leigh Hunt says, Byron "wanted faith in the interior of poetry";[8] and whether or not he lacks that "something in the mere progress and resonance of the words" that Swinburne thought all great poetry should have, "some secret in the very motion and cadence of the lines, inexplicable by the most sympathetic acuteness of criticism,"[9] Byron's lyric poetry is an integral part of his developing vision and must be examined, to do it full justice, in the evolving context of his total canon.

I

The earliest of the *Hebrew Melodies* in date of composition is the famous and exquisite "She Walks in Beauty." As an anthologist's delight, however, it is always read in isolation, out of its proper context. Byron was certainly aware that, like "Oh! Snatched Away in Beauty's Bloom" and "I Saw Thee Weep," the song was no Hebrew melody. Their apparently dis-

---

[5] The Byron Foundation Lecture, published as *Byron's Lyrics* (Nottingham, 1948), pp. 10, 13.
[6] *Byron* (London, New York, and Toronto, 1951), p. 24; *The True Voice of Feeling* (New York, 1953), p. 307.
[7] *Byron*, p. 24.
[8] *Lord Byron and Some of His Contemporaries* (2 vols.; London, 1828), I, 78.
[9] *Miscellanies*, p. 127.

ruptive and inconsonant inclusion in the volume I take as evidence that the themes of the tales and their pessimistic view of the human condition were never far from Byron's mind no matter what the immediate occasion for poetry or the immediate stimulus to write. In the context of the whole of *Hebrew Melodies,* "She Walks in Beauty" takes on aspects of the Edenic sections of the tales: "All that's best of dark and bright" meet in the figure of woman,

> *Thus mellowed to that tender light*
> *Which Heaven to gaudy day denies.*

Though severely underplayed, the clash between "tender" and "gaudy" should not be overlooked, nor the fact that "Heaven" bestows the perfection. The by now familiar Byronic duality of mind and heart is here fused in an other-worldly light, poised supernaturally above "all below," innocence not yet seared by the world's fierce conflict. "She" is *not* merely Lady Wilmot, about whom the poem was ostensibly written, but rather Woman —or mankind; and if the inspiration was a ball at Lady Sitwell's,[10] one can marvel at Byron's superb control and craft in fashioning the occasional *vers de société* to his own ends. (The thematic picture is even more complete if, adopting the technique of the insistent biographizers, we discover that Lady Wilmot was dressed in mourning at the time of the party[11]— Byron's vision of death in life par excellence.)

This opening poem is immediately followed in the collection by an unusual hymn to the immortality of sound and poetry, "The Harp the Monarch Minstrel Swept," in which music and poetry are equated with a lost heaven: the sounds of David's harp, grown "mightier than his Throne," "aspired to Heaven and there abode!" But now on earth "its chords are riven," and man is left with only the desperate hope that that "bursting spirit" will "soar" again

---

[10] The circumstances of the poem's composition are found in a manuscript note by James Wedderburn Webster on Byron's letter to Webster of 11 June 1814, in *LJ,* III, 92n.

[11] *P,* III, 381n.

To sounds that seem as from above,
In dreams that day's broad light can not remove.[12]

But it is only in dreams, as we have seen, that music soars and valleys ring—in dreams or, at best, in a lost past recalled now through ruins or through song. In such a world death is inviting. As Keats wrote, luxuriating in the immortal song of the nightingale,

Now more than ever seems it rich to die,
To cease upon the midnight with no pain,
While thou art pouring forth thy soul abroad
In such an ecstasy—

so Byron writes in "If That High World," "How sweet this very hour to die"—but *only* if "there the cherished heart be fond, / The eye the same, except in tears." If one could only be sure of immortality, it would indeed be sweet

To soar from earth and find all fears
Lost in thy light—Eternity!

"It must be so," says man's conscious mind, for sanity demands the dream that gives us respite from our thoughts of death; let us therefore channel the mind toward that dream:

let us think
To hold each heart the heart that shares,
With them the immortal waters drink,
And soul in soul grow deathless theirs!

The syntax is crabbed and obscure, but the forcefulness of the exhortation to believe that all hearts are those that share belies the conviction that the second stanza ostensibly

---

[12] In manuscript the last six lines of the poem are even more unequivocally negative:

It there abode, and there it rings,
But ne'er on earth its sound shall be;
The prophets' race hath passed away;
And all the hallowed minstrelsy—
From earth the sound and soul are fled,
And shall we never hear again?

(P, III, 383n)

206

conveys. Like "Israel's scattered race" in the superb "The Wild Gazelle," all hearts are doomed to "wander witheringly" further and further from "scenes of lost delight," until in death they find, not peace, but eternal exile, misery, and separation:

> *And where our fathers' ashes be,*
> *Our own may never lie;*

"And Mockery sits on Salem's throne." As in all of the tales, but perhaps especially in *The Prisoner of Chillon*, nature is indifferent—and different—at once providing both a foil for man's misery and enslavement and an illusory escape from that condition. Thus while the Jews had "Inhabitants more fair" than the stately gazelle, "Judah's statelier maids are gone" and

> *The wild gazelle on Judah's hills*
> *Exulting yet may bound,*
> *And drink from all the living rills*
> *That gush on holy ground;*
> *Its airy step and glorious eye*
> *May glance in tameless transport by.*

So too, while Israel's scattered tribes "must wander witheringly," the palm tree remains

> *In solitary grace:*
> *It cannot quit its place of birth,*
> *It will not live in other earth.*

For Byron the homeless Jews wandering in strange lands, whom not even death can reunite, are symbolic of man[13]—just as the modern Greek, enslaved and cowed, is also man.

---

[13] Marchand, in one of the few intelligent commentaries on *Hebrew Melodies*, will not go quite this far, but he does isolate two main themes in the work, "the deep pathos of the loss of Eden, the wail of a wandering and homeless people, and . . . the battle cry of Jewish Nationalism. The lost Eden was easily identified in Byron's feelings with the general romantic lament for lost innocence and beauty" (*Byron's Poetry*, p. 134). At the other extreme from Marchand's sensitive reading is Sir Arthur Quiller-Couch's wholesale and imperious condemnation of the entire volume as "turgid school-exercise

Since slavery, exile, and death have become synonymous with life, man can only be mourned, as in "Oh! Weep for Those," "By the Rivers of Babylon We Sat Down and Wept," and "By the Waters of Babylon." Amid the general mourning, however, there are occasional notes of defiance and hope, perhaps even more striking because of the general gloom surrounding them and their tone of desperation rather than conviction. For example, in "Thy Days Are Done" weeping is deplored. Yet even here, while hope seems to be sustained, it depends, paradoxically, on the hero, the "chosen Son," who is now dead. To weep would do his glory wrong, and, with a curious Byronic infelicity that may be a studied ambiguity, the dead hero "shalt not be deplored." The battle songs take their cue from this note: it is the "Song of Saul before His Last Battle" that is sung, its martial positiveness severely qualified by Saul's imminent death and by the companion poem, "Saul," in which Death appears *in propria persona* to claim

> "Crownless—breathless—headless . . .
> Son and Sire—the house of Saul!"

Jerusalem is destroyed by Titus and his Roman hordes ("On the Day of the Destruction of Jerusalem by Titus"), and the fist-shaking last stanza of that poem, spoken by one whose home, temple, and God have been lost, simply cannot redeem the time nor call forth the miraculous thunderbolt to "burst on the Conqueror's head!"

Even in victory the cost of battle is immense, and, as in the bullfight and gladiator scenes of *Childe Harold*, Byron's emphasis is ever on the loss rather than the gain. Though Jephtha is victorious over the Ammonites (in "Jephtha's Daughter"), Byron shrewdly makes his daughter the speaker of the

---

work," in an essay which trails throughout the red herring of Byron's "sincerity" or "insincerity" ("Byron," in W. A. Briscoe [ed.], *Byron, the Poet* [London, 1924], p. 10; first published in *Studies in Literature*, 2d ser. [Cambridge, 1922]). What is more surprising, perhaps, is the total neglect of *Hebrew Melodies* in two of the most recent attempts to study Byron as a poet, those of Andrew Rutherford (*Byron: A Critical Study*) and M. K. Joseph (*Byron the Poet*).

poem, emphasizing thereby the essential idiocy of demanding the death of love as the price of victory. Byron's choice of language in her speech creates an undertone that condemns the God and the human condition that render such sacrifice necessary, and inculcates the sense of horror, not jubilation, with which we are to read the entire poem. Similarly, in the much-acclaimed as well as abused "The Destruction of Sennacherib,"[14] although the forces of "right" win, it is difficult to ignore Byron's emphasis on the loss, the waste, and the horror inherent in the slaughter of the Assyrians. It is as if all nature died in this landscape of death, the final victory hollow and wintry. The Assyrian horde descends on "the fold" like wolves (reminiscent of the jackals, hyenas, and wild dogs of *The Siege of Corinth*), and the Lord's triumph is seen as tantamount to the coming of winter's blasts, bringing not life but the breath of the "Angel of Death," awakening "the sleepers" from their dream of life to the "deadly and chill" reality of eternal darkness. The "glance of the Lord" surveys not a new world, or even victory, but a wasteland where steed and man lay "distorted and pale"—

> *And the tents were all silent—the banners alone—*
> *The lances unlifted—the trumpet unblown*

—all life destroyed at its moment of awakening.[15]

---

[14] E.g., G. Wilson Knight thinks that "in short space [it] condense[s] almost all the main values of Byron's weightier, tragic and religious, genius" (Review of W. W. Robson's *Byron as Poet, Essays in Criticism*, IX [1959], 88); Martin calls it "the apex, the crown of Byron's lyrical writings" (*Byron's Lyrics*, p. 15); and Marchand sees it "rightly admired as one of Byron's most musical lyrics. It is a tour de force but a brilliant one with perfect blending of mood and meter. . . . it transcends the alliterative and anapestic and sound-association devices and even the common melodramatic theme and captures the imagination and feelings of anyone sensitive to music and poetry" (*Byron's Poetry*, p. 135). On the other hand, Samuel C. Chew describes it, I think accurately, as "famous but overrated" (*Lord Byron: "Childe Harold's Pilgrimage,"* p. 488n).

[15] Despite the radically different circumstances, "Herod's Lament for Miriamne" may be seen as a variation on the same theme; indeed, with but slight change, it can be read as Jephtha's answer to his daughter's brave speech of farewell, except that in this case it is the

Apart from the awkward Elizabethanism of "I Saw Thee Weep," then, all of the *Hebrew Melodies* are hymns to loss, elegies, celebrations of victories without triumph, prophecies of doom, or landscapes of despair. Even the so-called love poems, which do not seem to fit the over-all theme of the volume, reflect similar attitudes and states of mind.[16] "Oh! Snatched Away in Beauty's Bloom," which H. W. Garrod sees as a rare "perfect lyrical whole,"[17] points out that "tears are vain," that "Death nor heeds nor hears distress," and that the dead past lives indelibly in memory as a grim force in the present. Man who is left alone, without love, wanders eternally, his soul dark, with only poetry and music for release and relief. In " 'All Is Vanity, Saith the Preacher,' " Byron reasserts the lack of peace or hope even in memory, for as the speaker of that poem tries to recall days he would wish to live over, he finds that

> *There rose no day, there rolled no hour*
> *Of pleasure unembittered;*
> *And not a trapping decked my Power*
> *That galled not while it glittered.*

In the lines Byron wrote originally to follow these, the unrelieved darkness of his vision evinced itself in a picture of the eternity of man's woe, the impossibility of change in the world and in the human condition:

> *Ah! what hath been but what shall be,*
> *The same dull scene renewing?*
> *And all our fathers were are we*
> *In erring and undoing.*[18]

---

tyrant Herod who grieves over *his* killing of love (see especially ll. 13–24). The similarity between this relationship and its destruction to the history of the lovers in the tales and "The Dream" is striking.

[16] Only Marchand has commented on this extraordinary unity of tone and theme. Although he excludes "She Walks in Beauty" (erroneously, I think), he sees in all the love songs the same "haunting sadness and the sense of desolation which inform the poems voicing a wild lament for the lost Jewish homeland" (*Byron's Poetry*, pp. 133–34).

[17] *Byron, 1824–1924* (Oxford, 1924), pp. 18–19.

[18] *P*, III, 395n.

No spell or art, neither wisdom nor music, can lure the serpent thought from round the heart. For Byron, as man in the large consistently represents Adam fallen and Christ crucified, in small, he is the heart eternally stung and galled. Here is no mere melancholy, stagey or otherwise, but rather a considered despair that is not alleviated even in his conception of immortality. In one of his rare poems on the subject, "When Coldness Wraps This Suffering Clay," the mind, as usual with Byron, is seen as immortal, leaving "its darkened dust behind." What is striking about his vision, however, is its lack of humanity, its void, even while the mind encompasses all in its passionless and pure eternity. Terrifyingly like its counterpart, the "suffering clay" that is doomed to wander the earth in a vain search for peace and paradise, the "Eternal—boundless—undecayed" but also "unembodied" mind strays amid the stars, uncircumscribed by time or space or history, yet "Fixed in its own Eternity." Soaring above all humanity and earthly things, it is also above humanity's love and hope, and exists "A nameless and eternal thing" lost in the void. Such "freedom" is only the freedom of Bonivard extended to infinity, the universe of Manfred, which gives the final lie to the aspiring hope of suffering clay—what Byron in "A Spirit Passed Before Me" calls succintly "all formless—but divine."

Byron's views of immortality remained unusually consistent throughout his life, and they constantly reflect, as in *Hebrew Melodies*, his uncomfortable relationship with God. The will to believe is always there: his heart will have it so, but his mind denies it and his experience only serves to corroborate his doubt. "It is useless," he writes in his *Detached Thoughts*, "to tell me *not* to *reason*, but to *believe*. You might as well tell a man not to wake but *sleep*."[19] In the context of Byron's deliberate fusion of the darkness of dreams and the darkness of reality in the poems of 1815 to 1816 studied in the previous chapter, his use of the same terms here is especially significant. If doubt and faith are equally real, the latter (the dream) is the less real to the extent that it is what we wish, not what is. Ultimately, of

---

[19] *LJ*, V, 457. The italics are Byron's.

course, the mind triumphs, steeling itself against the heart's desire and hope and thus destroying any sense of God as a meaningful presence in the universe. Deistically, for Byron, "a *Creator* is a more natural imagination than a fortuitous concourse of atoms."[20] Realistically, experience tells him that Christianity is absurd: "It is a little hard to send a man preaching to Judaea, and leave the rest of the world—Negers and what not— *dark* as their complexions . . . and who will believe that God will damn men for not knowing what they were never taught?"[21] Again, in his journal, his heart reaches out to accept God, but his mind cancels the gesture: ". . . let me live. . . . The rest is with God, who assuredly, had He *come* or *sent*, would have made Himself manifest to nations, and intelligible to all."[22]

Byron's incipient deism, then, is simply a convenient device for imagining creation. Unlike the deist's divine mechanism whose perpetual motion is governed by immutable laws and whose central truth is that whatever is, is right, Byron's created universe, in perpetual motion but governed by no apparent laws, is instinct with the central truth that whatever is, is painful. It is a world torn religiously by sects which in turn tear "each other to pieces for the love of the Lord and hatred of each other,"[23] torn politically by man in his lust for the power of godhood, torn socially by stratification and hypocritical self-righteousness, and torn morally by the very laws geared to maintain its peace and well-being.

Eternity or immortality for Byron is, somewhat curiously, both mental and material. The mind, an organ of "perpetual activity" which acts often "very independent of body,"[24] is man's immortality; but whereas even in the privacy of his

---

[20] *Detached Thoughts*, in *LJ*, V, 459. The frequently quoted ltr. to Ensign Long of 16 Apr. 1807 ("I have lived a *Deist*, what I shall die I know not") hardly "proves" Byron a consistent deist throughout his life, as some critics have averred. The letter is found in *LJ*, II, 19–20n.

[21] Ltr. to Hodgson, 3 Sept. 1811, in *LJ*, II, 21.

[22] *Ibid.*, pp. 22–23.

[23] *Ibid.*, p. 22.

[24] *Detached Thoughts*, in *LJ*, V, 457.

journals he will not speculate on how far that future life "will at all resemble our *present* existence,"[25] in "When Coldness Wraps This Suffering Clay" he does see it as at least analogous to worldly wandering, a parallel chaos. On the other hand, if "Matter is eternal, always changing, but reproduced, and, as far as we can comprehend Eternity, Eternal,"[26] then why not man, this suffering clay? "We are miserable enough in this life," he writes to Hodgson, "without the absurdity of speculating upon another. If men are to live, why die at all? and if they die, why disturb the sweet and sound sleep that 'knows no waking'?"[27] Thus man's immortality exists in the eternity of his mind as well as in the perpetuity of what Byron calls "the congregated dust called Mankind."[28] Yet he sees both eternal mind and mankind as doomed to sorrow, tragedy, and death, or at best to perpetual lonely wandering. "It cannot die, it cannot stay," he writes of the "immortal mind" in "When Coldness Wraps This Suffering Clay"; its existence is a continual fluctuation or dizzying pendulum swing between the extremes of mortality and immortality, or, in the language of the tales, between heart and mind, love and hate, peace and war, life and death. It is certainly because of this intense sense of life's violence and uncertainty, its irony and perverseness, that Byron can say, on occasion, and certainly with more conviction than in his other pronouncements upon life, love, God, and man, "Like Sylla, I have always believed that all things depend upon Fortune, and nothing upon ourselves"[29]—much less upon a God who may or may not have really "come" or "sent."

---

[25] *Ibid.*
[26] *Ibid.,* p. 458.
[27] Ltr. of 3 Sept. 1811, in *LJ,* II, 18–20. Byron quotes Seneca to clinch his point, emphasizing the negative in the last line:

> *Post mortem nihil est, ipsaque mors nihil*
>
> .   .   .   .   .   .
>
> *Quaeris, quo jaceas post obitum loco?*
> *Quo* non *nata jacent.*

[28] *Detached Thoughts,* in *LJ,* V, 458.
[29] *Ibid.,* p. 451.

II

The other lyric poetry written about the same time as *Hebrew Melodies* is the most autobiographical of all, and one must strongly resist the temptation to tie it to specific occasions or personal circumstances if one is to see there the substantial evidence of the controlling vision in Byron's poetry as a whole.[30] The vanity or impossibility of love in this world is one of the major themes in these lyrics, as it was in *Hours of Idleness*, and is frequently embodied in farewells. "Farewell! If Ever Fondest Prayer" is such a poem, in which "to speak—to weep—to sigh" is vain:

---

[30] Happily, the inveterate biographizing of the poems in recent years has yielded to controversy over the critical propriety and usefulness of biographical evidence in studying Byron's poetry. But even now it is rare to find analyses of the poetry and a conviction that it can be read without biographical assistance. If Patricia Ball can assert that "it is possible to get nearer to the poems by leaving aside the problems of the Byronic personality altogether" ("Byronic Reorientation," *The Twentieth Century*, CLXVIII [1960], 328), and W. W. Robson can flatly demand that "the assessment of Byron's poetry . . . must begin and end with the poetry" ("Byron as Poet," p. 30), the loudest voices are still those of such critics as Patrick Cruttwell and Paul West. The latter not only wrote a book (*Byron and the Spoiler's Art*) in which all of Byron's poetry is seen as a function of his need to "eliminate" but also wrote, in another place (Introduction to *Byron: A Collection of Critical Essays* [Englewood Cliffs, N.J., 1963], pp. 1–2, 10–11):

> To try excluding the man is eventually to discover that little of the poetry can stand alone and, if it is made to, seems like fragments from the hands of various pasticheurs. . . . He obtrudes, and he sabotages the "text-only" kind of study. . . . It is no use reorganizing and tabulating the works of this scintillating and uncomfortable man. Byron is now not the celebrity or the hot issue he used to be; so, unfortunately, the academic feels safer in trying to systematize and factorize the restless quality of the poems.

And Cruttwell says, ironically enough in reviewing West's book, that it "fails because that poetry just will not, cannot stand up by itself. It has to lean on the letters and journals, and they on the man behind them; and if interest of that sort is vulgar, is unliterary, so be it: for Byron, it is the only interest" ("Romantics and Victorians," *Hudson Review*, XIV [1961–62], 602). In a sense this study is intended to refute, at least in part, the Cruttwells and the Wests.

> *I only know we loved in vain—*
> *I only feel—Farewell!—Farewell!*

"When We Two Parted," "I Cannot Talk of Love to Thee," "I Speak Not, I Trace Not, I Breathe Not Thy Name," and "Bright Be the Place of Thy Soul" are others, relieved only momentarily by "There Be None of Beauty's Daughters." Perhaps most characteristic of the lyrical poems of this period, however, and with interesting echoes of the music, as well as the despair, of *Hebrew Melodies,* are two of those entitled simply "Stanzas for Music" (one beginning "There's not a joy the world can give," the other beginning "They say that Hope is happiness"). Of the first Byron wrote flippantly to Moore that he felt "merry enough to send . . . a sad song," but the genuineness of its sentiment is attested to by his two other letters to Moore (one written six days later than the above, one a year later[31]) and his elegy "On the Death of the Duke of Dorset." The sudden death of Dorset, a friend from Harrow days, set Byron to "pondering, and finally into the train of thought which you have in your hands."[32] It is a crucial train of thought for our purposes here, for it describes the beginnings of a turning point in Byron's poetic career.

Ever since the youthful lyrics of *Hours of Idleness* and the arrogant abusiveness of *English Bards, and Scotch Reviewers,* Byron's vision of the world and man, what I have been calling the human condition, has been growing darker and darker. We have seen how, in *The Bride of Abydos,* for example, even wrenching his thoughts away from reality by plunging into fantasy merely led him to picture a fantasy grimmer than the reality from which he sought relief. There is considerable significance, then, in the step he takes in "My Soul Is Dark" of the *Hebrew Melodies:* poetry, at least in his conscious dealings with it, has ceased to be an escape from reality's dark dream and has become instead a means for expressing his grief and despair. His earlier (1813) image of its being "the lava of the imagination

---

[31] Ltrs. to Moore, 2 and 8 Mar. 1815 and 8 Mar. 1816, in *LJ,* III, 181, 183–86, 272–75.
[32] Ltr. to Moore, 8 Mar. 1815, in *LJ,* III, 183–84.

whose eruption prevents an earthquake" has been transformed from image to reality. For the issue now, in 1815 to 1816, is no longer escape: even death and a possible immortality hold no certain rest. The issue is that of one's sanity in the face of what inevitably must be, the discovery of the means by which the heart (and hence essential humanity) can endure the constant attacks upon its very sanctuary. In "My Soul Is Dark" that heart, doomed now to know the worst, will "break at once" if it does not, or cannot, "yield to song"; now the lava must flow lest the earthquake destroy that last refuge of man, the world of his mind.

Yet the very expression of grief, personal or universal (for they are one and the same for Byron), can soon become unbearable; the bleeding heart runs dry; the elegies become increasingly powerless to preserve the mind's sanity. To harden one's heart, to become in a sense less than human (as so many of the heroes in the tales do), to gain life and sanity at the expense of feeling—or at the very least to evolve a poetic point of view and construct sufficient to support such self-discipline— is the logical step for Byron the man and poet to take. Canto III of *Childe Harold* is the first major product of this turn: Harold himself deems

> *his spirit now so firmly fixed*
> *And sheathed with an invulnerable mind,*
> *That, if no joy, no sorrow lurked behind.*
>
> *(x)*

And in the superb stanzas on the death of "young, gallant Howard" and all the myriad slain at Waterloo, we are told that

> *There is a very life in our despair,*
> *Vitality of poison,—a quick root*
> *Which feeds these deadly branches; for it were*
> *As nothing did we die; but Life will suit*
> *Itself to Sorrow's most detested fruit.*
>
> *(xxxiv)*

Without steeling the heart, it "will break, yet brokenly live on,"

> *Even as a broken Mirror, which the glass*
> *In every fragment multiplies—and makes*

> *A thousand images of one that was,*
> *The same—and still the more, the more it breaks;*
> *And thus the heart will do which not forsakes,*
> *Living in shattered guise; and still, and cold,*
> *And bloodless, with its sleepless sorrow aches,*
> *Yet withers on till all without is old,*
> *Showing no visible sign, for such things are untold.*[33]
>
> (*xxxiii*)

But such control is evinced in other ways as well, as the evolution of the creative poet in *Childe Harold* III and IV shows. The mind is more than a controller of the heart; it is also a creator of a brave new world, of life that is, paradoxically, more intense, of a new heart—but only so long as self is dissociable from creation:

> *'Tis to create, and in creating live*
> *A being more intense that we endow*
> *With form our fancy, gaining as we give*
> *The life we image, even as I do now—*
> *What am I? Nothing: but not so art thou,*
> *Soul of my thought! with whom I traverse earth,*
> *Invisible but gazing, as I glow*
> *Mixed with thy spirit, blended with thy birth,*
> *And feeling still with thee in my crushed feelings'*
> > *dearth.*
>
> (*III, vi*)

Thus the mind's creativity, as well as its vain control, re-creates life and feeling, and, perhaps most important, preserves man's sanity amid desolation.[34] But if that creativity and control can

---

[33] Cf. what Byron may have said to Lady Blessington—or what may be her plagiarism of this passage: "Memory, the mirror which affliction dashes to the earth, and, looking down upon the fragments, only beholds the reflection multiplied" (*Conversations of Lord Byron*, p. 177).

[34] For excellent but differing interpretations of this crucial stanza in Byron's development as a poet, see, e.g., Ridenour's dissertation, "Byron and the Romantic Pilgrimage," *passim.*; Pafford's "Byron and the Mind of Man"; and Wasserman's *The Subtler Language*, pp. 6ff. (a very brief but acute analysis). Harold Bloom's interpretation of the stanza as Byron's affirmation of "a therapeutic aesthetic idealism" is, I think, very misleading (*The Visionary Company*, p. 234).

sustain, through a philosophy of art, the essential lyricism of *Childe Harold* even through the fading of those visions and the sinking of that spirit in Canto IV, it can also, with what Byron learned in his struggle for a structure and mobile point of view in the tales, produce beings more intense, more dramatic in conception, who live and love and fight and die in a world whose limits are history and whose integrity as inviolable, independent creatures, divorced yet not divorced from their creator, is assured by their historical truth or their mythological reality. Or that mind can inure itself against its own agony by laughing so that it may not weep, by seeing the horror of the human condition as comically absurd. Thus Beppo lands at Venice and, as in all fairy tales, reclaims "His wife, religion, house, and Christian name" (*Beppo*, xcvii); there is no final cataclysm as in *The Siege of Corinth*, where Alp remains a renegade to the end and the top blows off the universe in a climax reminiscent of MacLeish's "The End of the World." King George III slips into heaven unnoticed at the conclusion of what must be called, for sanity's sake, "this true dream" (stanza cvi), the farcical and brilliant *The Vision of Judgment*. And in *Don Juan* Byron makes the point explicit a number of times:

> *No more—no more—Oh! never more, my heart,*
> * Canst thou be my sole world, my universe!*
> *Once all in all, but now a thing apart,*
> * Thou canst not be my blessing or my curse:*
> *The illusion's gone for ever, and thou art*
> * Insensible, I trust, but none the worse,*
> *And in thy stead I've got a deal of judgment,*
> *Though heaven knows how it ever found a*
> *   lodgement;*
> *   (I, ccxv)*

and, with direct reference to the somberness of *Hebrew Melodies*,

> *So Juan wept, as wept the captive Jews*
> * By Babel's waters, still remembering Sion:*
> *I'd weep,—but mine is not a weeping Muse;*
> *   (II, xvi)*

and, most revealing of all,

> *if I laugh at any mortal thing,*
> *'Tis that I may not weep; and if I weep,*
> *'Tis that our nature cannot always bring*
> *Itself to apathy, for we must steep*
> *Our hearts first in the depths of Lethe's spring,*
> *Ere what we least wish to behold will sleep:*
> *Thetis baptized her mortal son in Styx;*
> *A mortal mother would on Lethe fix.*
>
> (IV, iv)

In such a world, when laughter is not possible (for example, at the madness and death of Haidée), the poet can always force himself into flippancy:

> *But let me change this theme, which grows too sad,*
> *And lay this sheet of sorrows on the shelf;*
> *I don't much like describing people mad,*
> *For fear of seeming rather touch'd myself—*
> *Besides, I've no more on this head to add.*
>
> (IV, lxxiv)

A "capricious" muse is all he'll have, a main character from legend, and "The monde" (XIV, xix), whose "grand arcanum" is "not for men to see at all" (xxii). "And therefore what I throw off is ideal" (xxii); the facts that the same mind cannot afford to admit are facts, the secret horrors of life that, once revealed, must not be acknowledged as such.

The "train of thought" that Byron mentions to Moore as having been aroused by his contemplation of the death of Dorset is this very steeling and hardening that the creation of poetry makes possible—the defensive posture of the psyche that finally calls an urgent halt to the perpetual fragmentation of the heart. On hearing of Dorset's death Byron can say "I heard thy fate without a tear," even though his friend was "surpassing dear, / Too loved of all to die." Instead, dry tears fall "dreary" on his heart,

> *dull and heavy, one by one,*
> *They sink and turn to care,*
> *As caverned waters wear the stone,*
> *Yet dropping harden there:*
> *They cannot petrify more fast.*

Than feelings sunk remain,
Which coldly fixed regard the past,
But never melt again.

Byron brilliantly universalizes this particular loss in the first
"Stanzas for Music" mentioned above, a poem which by its very
title and nature describes the turning point I spoke of earlier. It is
simultaneously the poet's cry for music and song to prevent the
earthquake of mind and his recognition that such a public vent
of emotion is no longer sufficient to guarantee the mind's
equipoise:

> *There's not a joy the world can give like that it*
> > *takes away,*
> *When the glow of early thought declines in Feeling's*
> > *dull decay.*

The visions of Eden that inform and characterize the
boy too young to know the irrevocability of its loss and therefore blindly persistent in his attempts to recover it reveal themselves here with double force as a panorama of ruin:

> *the few whose spirits float above the wreck*
> > *of happiness*
> *Are driven o'er the shoals of guilt or ocean of excess:*
> > *The magnet of their course is gone, or only points*
> > > *in vain*
> *The shore to which their shivered sail shall never*
> > *stretch again.*

> *Then the mortal coldness of the soul like Death itself*
> > *comes down;*
> *It cannot feel for others' woes, it dare not dream*
> > *its own;*
> *That heavy chill has frozen o'er the fountain of*
> > *our tears,*
> *And though the eye may sparkle still, 'tis where the*
> > *ice appears.*

> *Though wit may flash from fluent lips, and mirth*
> > *distract the breast,*
> *Through midnight hours that yield no more their*
> > *former hope of rest;*

> 'Tis but as ivy-leaves around the ruined turret wreath,
> All green and wildly fresh without, but worn and
> grey beneath.

If "midst the withered waste of life" tears *could* fall, they would be sweet; but the poet knows too that even that sweetness is illusion, the sweetness of residual pain after torture ceases, for the springs found in deserts only *seem* sweet because of their real brackishness (stanza v).

In the second "Stanzas for Music" ("They say that Hope is happiness"), the vision is even darker; both hope and memory are lost,

> And all that Memory loves the most
> Was once our only Hope to be,
> And all that Hope adored and lost
> Hath melted into Memory.

Time future and time past fuse in the desert of present ruins:

> Alas! it is delusion all:
> The future cheats us from afar,
> Nor can we be what we recall,
> Nor dare we think on what we are.

When Byron writes to Moore in early 1816 that "There's Not a Joy" is "the truest, though the most melancholy, [poem] I ever wrote,"[35] it is impossible to dismiss this judgment as another of his offhand indiscriminate remarks. Melancholy's shadow has lengthened into despair; the "wandering outlaw of his own dark mind" has become the fully mature poet, aware now of his own vision, and urgently needing a control, a form, a technique by which to cope with that vision (Byron calls it in one of his poems to Augusta "that deep midnight of the mind"[36]).

The other alternative for the aware man is, of course, death, and it must be admitted that to Byron that possibility of eternal rest and peace is powerfully seductive.

---

[35] Ltr. of 8 Mar. 1816, in *LJ*, III, 274.
[36] "Stanzas to Augusta," beginning "When all around grew drear and dark."

Count o'er the joys thine hours have seen,
  Count o'er thy days from anguish free,
And know, whatever thou hast been,
  'Tis something better not to be,

he wrote as early as 1812 in "Euthanasia." Still, like Shelley
and Keats, Byron saw the prospect of death as not without its
risks and uncertainties. All three could only be "half in love with
easeful death," for the possibility of utter extinction to Shelley
and Keats weighed equally in the scales with their visions of
eternal peace, love, and beauty. For Byron, as we have seen in
Hebrew Melodies, death might also be an eternal lonely vigil
in the exile of spacelessness and timelessness. Further, to yield
weakly to the archetypal tyrant was for him the final slavery,
the surrender of the will and dominion of the mind. The hymn
to Prometheus is thus both a lament for archetypal man's sentence of eternal life—

> *Titan! to thee the strife was given*
>   *Between the suffering and the will,*
>   *Which torture where they cannot kill;*
> *And the inexorable Heaven,*
> *And the deaf tyranny of Fate,*
> *The ruling principle of Hate,*
> *Which for its pleasure doth create*
> *The things it may annihilate,*
> *Refused thee even the boon to die*
>
> *(ii)*

—and a paean of praise for his "impenetrable Spirit, / Which
Earth and Heaven could not convulse." Prometheus is the epitome of man's

> *firm will, and a deep sense,*
> *Which even in torture can descry*
>   *Its own concentered recompense,*
> *Triumphant where it dares defy,*
> *And making Death a Victory.*[37]

---

[37] For somewhat different interpretations of this poem (which Arnold
and many of his followers saw, and is still seen by some, as Byron's
"typical" poem, an example of his "titanism"), see especially Ridenour's *The Style of "Don Juan"* and Bloom's *The Visionary Company*

Man's eternal conflict is not merely between his dust and deity, but also between his will and suffering, between his mind and fate. If defeat, man's "funereal destiny," as Byron called it in "Prometheus," is inevitable, the quality of his resistance is the measure of his stature and the exercise of his godhood. That resistance is his ultimate and only freedom, whereas suicide or the life of a captive is his final surrender. Even so, the choice is not so simple. Bonivard's indomitable will only leads him to love his prison and to give thanks for a world of mice and spiders over which he may rule as monarch. Thus his final "freedom" is the universal prison and slavery of the "free" world.

The poems to Napoleon of 1814 to 1816, the most outspoken of which is the *Ode to Napoleon Buonaparte,* reflect the same dilemma. After completing *The Corsair* Byron had promised Murray no more poetry, but Napoleon's abdication of the "throne of the world" made it "physically impossible to pass over this damnable epoch of triumphant tameness."[38] What is important about the poem is that it is not political. Byron had always been stirred by Napoleon's greatness, as well as aware of his tyranny:

> *The sword, the sceptre, and that sway*
> *Which man seemed made but to obey.*
>
> (iv)

The epithets liberally sprinkled through the *Ode* reveal his continued ambiguity of attitude: he is the tyrant "who strewed our earth with hostile bones" (i), one of "Those Pagod things" (iii), a "Desolator," "Victor," and "Arbiter of others' fate" (v), an "All Evil Spirit" and "a thing so mean" (ix), a madman who arose "To shame the world" (xi), "a throneless Homicide" (xiii),

---

(the latter's promisingly titled essay, "Napoleon and Prometheus: The Romantic Myth of Organic Energy," in *Yale French Studies*, XXVI [1960–61], 79–82, is notably unhelpful). H. J. C. Grierson sees "Prometheus," curiously, as Byron's " 'Everlasting No' " ("Lord Byron: Arnold and Swinburne," *Proceedings of the British Academy*, IX [1920], 16).
[38] Ltr. to Moore, 20 Apr. 1814, in *LJ*, III, 70.

a "Timour" (xv), a Prometheus (xvi).[39] Byron's anger is not for any of these, nor for Napoleon's "surrender," nor is the poem a call for the renewal of tyranny and slaughter. Rather, it is an attack upon Promethean man for yielding meekly to the world and its prison. He is now "a nameless thing" (i), an "Ill-minded man" (ii) whose self-destruction is a scourge to man's potential greatness, whose "dread of death alone" led him to the "ignobly brave" choice of living a slave rather than dying a prince (v):

> It is enough to grieve the heart
>   To see thine own unstrung;
> To think that God's fair world hath been
> The footstool of a thing so mean.
>
>   (ix)

The lesson of the poem is at least twofold: with Napoleon's fall "mortals" can finally see "Ambition's less than littleness" (ii):

> Thanks for that lesson—it will teach
>   To after-warriors more
> Than high Philosophy can preach,
>   And vainly preached before.
> That spell upon the minds of men
> Breaks never to unite again,
>   That led them to adore
> Those Pagod things of sabre-sway,
> With fronts of brass, and feet of clay,
>
>   (iii)

but they can also see, alas, that even history's most Promethean spirits, however warped and contemptuous of mankind, however perverted by lust for power, settle sadly for a breathing ignominy rather than a defiant death. Out of such an attitude comes, two years later, the triumphant heroism of *Manfred*, as well as the surrender of Cain.

---

[39] The ambiguity can further be seen in the University of Texas manuscript of the poem, to which Coleridge did not have access. For example, in stanza ix, for "Evil Spirit" Byron originally wrote "Evil greatness," and in stanza xi, for "Some new Napoleon" he wrote first "Some other madman."

Chapter VIII

CHILDE HAROLD'S PILGRIMAGE, CANTO III, AND *MANFRED*

Commentary on Canto III of *Childe Harold* is abundant, much of it very good indeed, although most of it suffers to a degree by assuming the independence of the canto from Cantos I and II, or even IV. Partly for this reason, attempts to describe Canto III thematically, to find in it coherence and structure, have either failed or, while embodying valuable insights into the nature of this one canto, finally emerge as only partial views.[1] Rather than quarrel with individual interpretations of the canto, I propose to assimilate the best of them into a larger perspective, to see the canto against the background of thematic emphasis that has emerged from my analysis of the two that preceded it. Further, since Canto III shows a considerably greater artistic self-consciousness than the first two,[2] I shall also discuss that thematic emphasis in relation to the notable technical changes Byron effects.

Perhaps the first major obstacle to a clear understanding of *Childe Harold* III is the date of its composition, 1816, that most momentous and turbulent year of Byron's separation from Lady Byron, of bitter charge and countercharge, of national ignominy, isolation from Augusta, and final exile from England.

---

[1] The most helpful commentaries are George M. Ridenour's "Byron and the Romantic Pilgrimage," Andrew Rutherford's *Byron: A Critical Study*, Georg Roppen and Richard Sommer's *Strangers and Pilgrims*, Ward Pafford's "Byron and the Mind of Man," Ernest J. Lovell's *Byron: The Record of a Quest*, and E. E. Bostetter's *The Romantic Ventriloquists*. See also the very interesting recent essay by Kenneth A. Bruffee, "The Synthetic Hero and the Narrative Structure of *Childe Harold* III," *SEL*, VI (1966), 669–78.

[2] To my knowledge, only Ridenour and Bruffee have given Byron full credit for this self-consciousness (see n. 1 above). See also Ridenour's essay, "Byron in 1816," pp. 454–55.

If it is difficult to avoid biographizing Byron's poems of other years, it is well-nigh impossible to resist it here. Indeed, several elements of the canto openly encourage this sort of reading: the opening stanza with its reference to his wife and child as well as to his departure from England; the reference in stanzas iii–iv to his having written the earlier cantos of *Childe Harold*; the personal nature of stanza xxix on the "young, gallant Howard"; the concluding stanzas (xcv–xcviii) addressed to his daughter; and, of course, the close relationship between the scenes and places in the poem and Byron's own travels in Switzerland. Although one cannot ignore these facts, too much is usually made of them. On the face of it, it seems indeed an easy transition from the Childe Harold of Canto I to the Byron of Canto III, from fiction to reality, from affected pose to the "truth"—an apparent justification for considering the first two cantos as trumpery and the third as somehow sincere because there we finally hear Byron speaking of himself "as he really was."[3] Yet for Byron to be himself now, and also to be the Childe Harold that he was in the earlier cantos, either demands a monumental exercise of illogic or is a tellingly cogent argument in favor of Byron's remarkable prophetic vision of his future in Canto I. Finally, if Byron has now become Childe Harold (and his dropping of Harold from the poem in Canto III seems to prove this), there has been little speculation about the reasons why Cantos III and IV are not simply a rehash of I and II—or, indeed, why the last two were written at all by a man who was obviously satisfied with his own earlier prophecy.

  The problem of Harold's presence in Canto III, however, cannot be so easily dismissed, nor can his abrupt fadeout after singing "The Castled Crag of Drachenfels." Related to this, of course, is Byron's apparent presence in the poem, finally, *in propria persona*. If Canto III is viewed as a separate poem, there is no solution to these problems other than that of assuming that Byron has become Harold, or Harold Byron (Byron using some 55 stanzas to establish that fact and then dispensing

---

[3] Quiller-Couch was probably most responsible for raising this false issue of "sincerity" or "insincerity." See his essay, "Byron," in which, among other assertions, he flatly declares that Byron's sincerity begins with Canto III of *Childe Harold* and not before.

with Harold's persona as soon as the identification is complete). The basic illogic of this assumption does not seem to have occured to anyone: by becoming in Canto III what Harold *was* in Cantos I and II, Byron is justified in dismissing what Harold *is* in Canto III; and yet somehow Canto III can still be seen as an independent poem totally separate from the first two cantos. The folly of the facile identification of author and persona cannot be better demonstrated.

Yet even if we accept the idea of a persona or personae (or voices), as I have in my discussion of Cantos I and II, a problem remains: is it quite correct to say that since Byron indeed "may in some sense have become his hero after the fact,"[4] we must deal with the "I" of Canto III (and IV) as though it were Byron himself? I think not, unless we are willing to agree that what I have been calling the poet's point of view and voice in the earlier cantos are, simply, Byron's. To this I do not object, except to point out, as I have tried to do in earlier chapters, that Byron the poet and Byron the man of the world, the husband of Lady Byron, etc., while obviously related, are not the same person. Again and again Byron reiterated this truism, which almost all his critics have denied: "A man's poetry," he wrote to Moore in 1821, "is a distinct faculty, or soul, and has no more to do with the every-day individual than the Inspiration with the Pythoness when removed from her tripod."[5] "My *figures* are not portraits," he said,[6] and insisted to Trelawny, with some petulance, that it was not "as easy to write poetry as smoke a cigar. . . . Extemporizing verses is nonsense; poetry is a distinct faculty,—it won't come when called,—you may as well whistle for a wind."[7] And again, even more revealingly: "I can only write when the *estro* is upon me; at all other times I am myself."[8]

---

[4] Peter Thorslev, *The Byronic Hero*, p. 12.

[5] 16 Nov. 1821, in *LJ*, V, 479.

[6] Reply to Blackwood's *Edinburgh Magazine* article, in *LJ*, IV, 477.

[7] E. J. Trelawny, *Recollections of the Last Days of Shelley and Byron* (Boston, 1858), pp. 184–85. See also p. 197 for Byron's flat denial that he "told [his] own story in [his] writings."

[8] Trelawny, *Records of Shelley, Byron, and the Author* (New York, 1867), p. 22. Cf. Lady Blessington's *Conversations of Lord Byron*, pp. 333, 389.

But what of Childe Harold, who, after all, is present for about half of Canto III? And is it not true that the "I" of Canto III *is* very much like the Harold of Cantos I and II? And where is the narrator? All of these questions are related to each other, as I pointed out in my concluding paragraphs on Canto II: all three of the voices, or personae, were aspects of Byron's vision from the beginning, points of contact, as it were, on the circumference of a circle of vision whose center is the mind of the poet controlling all by the radii of thought and imagination. At the same time they were aspects of man's attitude toward and response to his world, seen through the eyes of three pilgrims wandering along the endless track of human existence.

By the end of Canto II, however, Byron came to see that the specifics of fallen man's perception tended to narrow rather than universalize the vision of the poem. While their very down-to-earth quality (both in Harold's lack of response and in the narrator's energetic reactions) tended to solidify perception in reality and to create a common ground for the reader to tread upon, that same communal tie tended to preclude the establishment of, or to fragment, a vision of the whole. The poet's voice was simply not strong enough. At the same time, as the poet struggled to organize the voices, perceptions, attitudes, and characters of Harold and the narrator into a larger scheme of things, that very scheme, emerging with a clarity that was more and more frightening, tended to throw the poet back upon his private and individual resources for sane survival in such a world. A sense of his own two-fold nature began to weigh more and more heavily upon him, so that, as man himself as well as detached poet, he could no longer simply be the one without being the other. To be merely man was to be Childe Harold—alone and resourceless, a ruin amid ruins, not altogether erect, as Byron's broken columns habitually are—or the narrator, with his inherent narrowness, his rational disgust and caution and hope, his mind controlled by the sequential environs of spatial and temporal history. To be merely poet was to presuppose his ability to remain disengaged from a world to which he was wedded by his very mortality, to pretend to the wisdom bought only by suffering in that world.

In the context of the developing poem, then, the poet grows through the hard-won experience of Cantos I and II and sees himself thereby as both poet and participant, visionary and sufferer,[9] deity and dust, if you will. He will not resign the vigorous and practical rationality of the narrator, but he can now reject as insignificant the merely local bickerings of an angry but insular mind. To put it another way, by virtue of his poet-persona, Byron can be his own subject as well as his own object; the imaginative achievement of a fiction can objectify personality into myth as well as mythmaker. As for Harold, I think it possible to see the transition of Canto III in two ways: first, as the poet absorbing into himself his own metaphor of fallen man, for properly such a metaphor remains a mere counter, a figure in a tableau, unless it is made articulate through the imagination of his creator; and second, as Harold, finally become articulate, not merely in lamentations of his own personal plight but as the visionary historian of man's eternal lot amid the ruins of a universe not well lost and a nature glorious and beautiful but flatly indifferent. The second is, of course, the less satisfactory of the two possibilities, for there is little reason, given Harold's beginnings and fate, for him to suddenly become the fully aware spokesman for his race. Yet along with the first it does provide us a means of fully understanding the apparent merger of Byron and his character.

In one sense it is right to say that Cantos III and IV are a repeat of Cantos I and II, for the theme does not change. It only deepens. But now, with the poet his own metaphor—at once the symbol of lost, fallen man in a lost, fallen world and

---

[9] Cf. Frank Kermode's idea that "the power of joy [inherent in the poet's "vision"] being possible only to a profound 'organic sensibility,' a man who experiences it will also suffer exceptionally. He must be lonely, haunted, victimised, devoted to suffering rather than action" (*Romantic Image* [New York, 1957], p. 6). My own argument about the relationship in Canto III of poet, narrator, and Harold was developed before I read Kenneth Bruffee's study (see n. 1 above), but I am pleased to acknowledge his very able analysis of the same problem as complementary to my own—although he does insist on Canto III as "a distinct work in its own right" ("The Synthetic Hero," p. 672).

of the articulated agony of that man and world—the apparently personal utterance becomes a universal cry,[10] and that very cry, however despairing, becomes the imaginative device by which its author remains sane and strong. Matthew Arnold said that Byron "has no *light*, cannot lead us from the past to the future. . . . The way out of the false state of things which enraged him he did not see,—the slow and laborious way upward; he had not the patience, knowledge, self-discipline, virtue, requisite for seeing it."[11] Perhaps. Yet the extraordinary vitality of his vision of doom and his unconquerable persistence in remaining sane while expressing that vision in its infinite variety seem to me to provide a kind of light of their own. The Arnoldian poetic vision, after all, was no different from Byron's, but the latter's was, over all, manifestly more powerful and moving. The typical romantic reaction to an anarchic universe, in which the poet "can connect nothing with nothing," is to seek a principle of order in the self, or impose an imaginatively conceived order on the chaos of existence; Byron finds that principle of order in the journey that ordinarily leads to order and meaning. In the place of "a spiritual journey through 'The Heart of Darkness' to a personal salvation,"[12] however, Byron makes a real journey into the bowels of nothingness and despair, a pilgrimage without faith or shrine, Cain's journey further and further east of Eden.

I

To see the frame within which Canto III is painted as merely further evidence of Byron's autobiographical intent in the poem is to miss completely its contribution to the evolution

---

[10] Although he was not the first, of course, to advance the idea, Ernest de Selincourt's phrase, "a sense of tears for human things," is in its stark simplicity a most eloquent summary of my point (*Wordsworthian and Other Studies*, p. 126).

[11] Preface to *Poetry of Byron*, pp. xxvii–xxviii. Cf. Roden Noel, "Lord Byron and His Times," *Essays on Poetry and Poets* (London, 1886): Byron did not have, says Noel, "the power of thought necessary for shaping for himself our eternal Christianity anew. . . . Byron's is the wail of baffled human understanding, without faith, hope, resignation, self-control, inward harmony" (pp. 63, 99).

[12] The distinction is made also by Karl Kroeber in his *Romantic Narrative Art*, p. 103, from which the quotation comes.

of the poem and its clear indication of Byron's growing consciousness of what he is about. If the voice that speaks across the waters to Ada in the first stanza is Byron's, we must also hear in its accents the voice of *To Ianthe*, as well as that of the invocation to Canto II—the voice of the poet. It is the public-private voice of the juvenile poems, the voice that tolled the death of love at the end of Canto II of *Childe Harold*. In the last line of stanza xcv, we recall, Byron, groping for a clear view of his own conception, originally wrote, "Would *I* had ne'er returned to find fresh cause to roam": that first person singular was a step toward the structure of Canto III, and needed only the experiments with point of view in the tales to develop into a giant step. Nevertheless, this stanza of Canto II, with its corrected pronoun, prepared adequately for the all-inclusive despair, concentered in the self of the poet, of the last stanza:

> *What is the worst of woes that wait on Age?*
> *What stamps the wrinkle deeper on the brow?*
> *To view each loved one blotted from Life's page,*
> *And be alone on earth, as I am now.*

With "Hearts divided" and "Hopes destroyed" the poet can but endure the "vain days" which "Roll on . . . full reckless."

The address to Ada opening Canto III quite deliberately picks up this note. The poet's return at the end of Canto II (*with* his created character, Harold, not *in* him) is but a preparation for this further parting, the last parting—without hope or goal. Here Ada plays the role Ianthe did in presiding over Cantos I and II, with one major exception. If Ianthe embodied all of youth, love, innocence, and hope, her aspect has now darkened into Ada's face, which the poet, significantly, can no longer remember: "Is thy face like thy mother's, my fair child!" Whether her eyes now smile, as they did when he saw them last, he will not know, for all joy has faded into disillusion, leaving only

> *a sterile track behind,*
> *O'er which all heavily the journeying years*
> *Plod the last sands of life,—where not a flower appears.*
> (*iii*)

These lines, of course, refer not to the poet's relationship to his child but to the poet's reaction to his own creation, the Harold of Cantos I and II, and this is precisely Byron's point. His poet-speaker has come to see that his own "Tale," in which he finds only "The furrows of long thought, and dried-up tears," is the tale of all human relationships, including that with Ada. Thus, as the "I" of Canto II sees time rolling on in an eternity of vain and reckless days, so Harold in Canto III

> *once more within the vortex, rolled*
> *On with the giddy circle, chasing Time,*
>
> *(xi)*

and the poet gives himself up to the guidance of the heaving waters "wheresoe'er it lead":

> *Still must I on; for I am as a weed,*
> *Flung from the rock, on Ocean's foam, to sail*
> *Where'er the surge may sweep.*
>
> *(ii)*

This rather extraordinary collocation of images is not only important in itself, but it also prepares for the famous passage on the ocean in Canto IV. Essentially, what Byron has done is to equate the sterility of a wasteland, streaked with the traces of dried-up tears, with the ocean upon which his poet is tossed crazily, like a drifting weed torn from its rocky home.[13] Added to this is the cosmic image of Harold giddily chasing time in an endless circle. Thus the conventional image of ocean as the source of life is transformed into ocean as an endless sterile desert, the symbol of eternity a series of man's footprints circling dully round his own past and present.

In such a pattern of images one is tempted to find once again easy justification for seeing Harold as Byron, or vice versa; but also once again it needs to be said that it is the poet's voice we hear at the close of Canto II and at the beginning of Canto III. What is to the point is Byron's emphasis upon the

---

[13] Only Bostetter, so far as I know, sees the equatability of the images of ocean and desert.

poet's deliberate creation of Harold to gain the life and love and warmth now denied him by the world. The irony is obvious: in Harold the poet hopes to feel once again, perhaps to love, to gain all that he has lost, only to find that his own creation is a mirror of his despair and the manifold causes of that despair:

> But where is he, the Pilgrim of my Song,
>   The Being who upheld it through the past?
>   Methinks he cometh late and tarries long.
>   He is no more—these breathings are his last—
>   His wanderings done—his visions ebbing fast,
>   And he himself as nothing:—if he was
>   Aught but a phantasy, and could be classed
>   With forms which live and suffer—let that pass—
> His shadow fades away into Destruction's mass,
>
> Which gathers shadow—substance—life, and all
>   That we inherit in its mortal shroud—
>   And spreads the dim and universal pall
>   Through which all things grow phantoms.
>   (IV, clxiv–clxv)

But this total gloom is not yet upon the Byron of 1816. Then, "half mad . . . between metaphysics, mountains, lakes, love unextinguishable, thoughts unutterable,"[14] if there seemed no hope to cling to, he maintained at least the illusion of willing its possibility, and if peace seemed unattainable, he saw at least a possible means to sanity amidst the insane self-desolation of mankind.

Thus Byron properly completes the frame for his third canto by having his poet, sustained at some moments by the act of creation and at others by an illusory but momentarily satisfying immersion in nature, address Ada once again (in stanzas cxv–cxviii) in those peculiarly contradictory terms we have seen often in the tales. On the one hand, through his "theme" the poet has learned to steel his heart ("the tyrant Spirit of our thought") against itself so that he will no longer be betrayed into that love which seems to promise paradise but leads only to dust and despair (cxi). So girded in the armor of thought

---

[14] Ltr. to Moore, 28 Jan. 1817, in *LJ*, IV, 49.

he can still "stand alone,—remembered or forgot" (cxii); if not triumphant over the world, he is at least alive. On the other hand, his love for Ada (daughter, wife, mistress—it does not matter), his love for another human being, represents his indestructible humanity as well as the fragility of his armor. He can neither see her nor hear her (cxv); but just as her smiling eyes appear as a dream perhaps attainable in the opening stanza, so at the end of the canto the creative force of love wills his voice to "reach into thy heart" (cxv). "I know that thou wilt love me," he desperately cries in a significant repetition; "Still thou would'st love me" (cxvii). And the canto closes with that by now familiar universalizing of the personal by Byron: perhaps in the "child of Love," the artist's human creation, the elements of humanity will be "more tempered," more harmoniously mixed.[15]

Canto IV will deny this implicitly (it is the only canto, as Georg Roppen and Richard Sommer shrewdly point out,[16] that contains no living beings), but for the moment we need to explore further the structure of the present canto and its presentation of the ground for hope and the possibility of love.

Precisely how to "absorb" Harold without becoming him was the crux of Byron's problem, and he handles it, brilliantly I think, in two complementary ways. Interestingly, both are the result of growing self-awareness—the poet's stronger sense of the viability of his own vision and hence an increase in his power to assimilate all partial views into that total vision, and Harold's increased sense of his own typicality and universality. With the poet's awareness that the product of his creative mind is less important than the act of creating him, and with Harold's move from provinciality and the abyss of his own

---

[15] One is reminded, of course, of the Abbot's speech in *Manfred*, III, ii, 160ff.

[16] *Strangers and Pilgrims*, p. 281. On the other hand, Roppen and Sommer seem to me quite wrong in saying that from his journey Byron gains "a regeneration of emotional vitality which enabled him to rediscover, if only in glimpses, the essential values in human existence" (p. 251). The source of this "life-value," as they call it, they see in "caves of imagination" and nature (p. 237).

personal sins to a sense of his fundamental humanity, Byron finds that it is all but impossible to keep the two figures distinct. It is not, then, simply that Harold has become the poet or the poet Harold, but rather that the poet has come to see that an aspect of his own vision, to which he has reacted in two cantos, is no longer separable from the total vision. Harold's being, as a separate, definable character, has become to the poet so fully identified with the universal desolation that he no longer has a function as one who responds to that desolation. To put it another way, Harold's response to his world, narrow and confining as it has been, can now only tend to fragment the totality of vision which Byron more and more insists upon for his poet. The fiction of Harold has become the reality of mankind; and that reality the poet comes to see more and more in himself rather than merely outside himself in the world or in another character. As god-like creator, the poet has tended to see himself apart from the world, "Invisible but gazing" (III, vi); it is true that he is more and more despairing at what he sees, but he is somehow not *of* the desolation—deity but somehow not dust. Thus the personal close of Canto II and the similar opening of Canto III announce the poet's own suffering as the world's.[17]

The evolution here is not merely of what Willis Pratt calls "that poise of spirit which every thoughtful man must struggle after";[18] it is rather the development, through the tales and lyrics already studied, not only of a point of view and struc-

---

[17] Cf. Ridenour's "Byron and the Romantic Pilgrimage," p. 41. T. G. Steffan's view of this development is a typical distortion due to biographizing ("The Token-Web, the Sea-Sodom, and Canto I of *Don Juan,*" *University of Texas Studies in English,* XXVI [1947], 124):

> The anger with Lady Byron, her family, and the lawyers, the humiliation and social opprobrium of the separation, and the grief and resentment over being forced away from his half-sister Augusta and his daughter Ada soon produced in Byron's mind the gigantic distortion of himself—of his own position in the pageant of the world's tragic and pathetic figures—that he publicized with somber and painful grandiloquence in the poems of 1816–17—in *Manfred,* the third and fourth cantos of *Childe Harold,* the "Epistle to Augusta," the "Stanzas to Augusta," "The Dream," as well as in the personally symbolic "Darkness" and "Prometheus." . . .

[18] "Byron and Some Current Patterns of Thought," p. 151.

ture to encompass a cosmic vision, but also of a *voir divinement*, what A. G. Lehmann calls "a more acute consciousness" which cannot be "brought about prior to the activity of producing art to communicate it, but by the very act and at the very instant of clothing one's inchoate attitude in the shapes of language":[19]

> *'Tis to create, and in creating live*
> *A being more intense that we endow*
> *With form our fancy, gaining as we give*
> *The life we image, even as I do now.*
>
> (*III, vi*)

The third person plural is important, for it is the poet, Harold, the narrator, *all* mankind who do this, whether in dream or fantasy, in poetry or sculpture, in architecture or painting. To make the point doubly clear, Byron has Harold, "Like the Chaldean," peopling the stars "with beings bright / As their own beams" (xiv); and man's "Thought" seeking

> *refuge in lone caves, yet rife*
> *With airy images, and shapes which dwell*
> *Still unimpaired, though old, in the Soul's haunted*
> *cell;*
> (*v*)

and, finally and all-inclusively, "true Wisdom's world" existing "Within its own creation" (xlvi).

But lest we think such a process Shelleyan (or Rousseauvian[20]), and hence evidence of Byron's complete absorption, during their sojourn in Switzerland, of the younger poet's creation of ideal beings toward whom all men ought to aspire, we should recall that Byron's poet creates no epipsyche, no union of Asia and Prometheus, but a more intense reality than even history yields, the reality of man's hell within himself, which belies the escape in Canto III into "therapeutic aesthetic idealism" with which Harold Bloom, for one, has charged him.[21]

---

[19] *The Symbolist Aesthetic in France 1885–1895* (Oxford, 1950), p. 177.
[20] See Ridenour, "Byron in 1816," pp. 463–64.
[21] *The Visionary Company*, p. 234.

Arthur Symons long ago described Byron's reality, quite properly, as "a cracked mirror, in which everything reflected itself directly, but as if scarred."[22] Not merely "as if," however, for the burden of *Childe Harold's Pilgrimage* finally is what Roppen and Sommer call the "burden of nihil,"[23] the poet's lonely struggle with his own despair at the pattern of universal waste and ruin to which he himself, as a man, also contributes. "These fragments I have shored against my ruins," Eliot wrote in *The Waste Land*; in *Childe Harold* whatever shoring is possible is the mind's self-discipline against madness, against the brain "boiling"

> *In its own eddy . . . and o'erwrought,*
> *A whirling gulf of phantasy and flame,*
>
> (*vii*)

as Byron terrifyingly put it.

But what of the narrator of Cantos I and II, whose Hobhouse-like accents gave us the rational man's view of history? In Canto III he too, like Harold, is less easily differentiated from the poet. In effect, with Harold's absorption into the poet's overview, one of the basic functions of the narrator is obviated; no longer must he urge the Childe on his way, maintaining the continuity of horizontal narrative structure, for that structure is rapidly giving way to one in which landscape and historical event become the state of soul of the observer, the poet.[24] In such a structure, the exigencies and claims of time are obliterated in favor of an evolving pattern of human actions and reactions which approach, at least, the mythic.

This transformation can be seen in several sections of the canto if they are compared to similar sections of Canto I. In the latter, it will be recalled, the narrator's conventional bias

---

[22] *The Romantic Movement in English Poetry* (London, 1909), p. 248. He may, of course, have been merely echoing Lady Blessington (see n. 26 below).
[23] *Strangers and Pilgrims,* p. 267.
[24] Cf. R. A. Foakes, *The Romantic Assertion,* p. 35. See also Josephine Miles's discussion of Wordsworth's idea of "bestowal" in her "Pathetic Fallacy in the Nineteenth Century" ("University of California Publications in English," XII [1942], 188f.).

consistently colored his description of Harold. In Canto III, the narrator describes but does not judge, as if Byron has set as a parallel to the "education" of Harold the narrator's growth of insight, compassion, and understanding. Instead of condemning Harold with faint sympathy, in Canto III the narrator begins to see the essential condition of mankind exemplified in him:

> Yet Time, who changes all, had altered him
> In soul and aspect as in age: years steal
> Fire from the mind as vigour from the limb;
> And Life's enchanted cup but sparkles near the brim.

> His had been quaffed too quickly, and he found
> The dregs were wormwood; but he filled again,
> And from a purer fount, on holier ground,
> And deemed its spring perpetual—but in vain!
> Still round him clung invisibly a chain
> Which galled for ever, fettering though unseen,
> And heavy though it clanked not; worn with pain,
> Which pined although it spoke not, and grew keen
> Entering with every step he took through many a
> scene.
> (viii–ix)

It is difficult here to separate this voice from the poet's, and properly so, for Harold's growing self-knowledge not only vitiates the validity of his separability from the figure of the poet-creator-speaker, but also the narrator's function of sitting in judgment on him (and history) from the point of view of good English conscience and patriotism.

But Byron moves with habitual slowness in such transformations, and we should not be surprised to hear at times the familiar ring of the narrator's moral condemnation, confused, rather than blended, with the poet's. For example, at bloody Waterloo, the narrator is compelled to describe the slaughter as "Fit retribution!" for Napoleon's and man's ambition (xix); and then, more angrily:

> What! shall reviving Thraldom again be
> The patched-up Idol of enlightened days?
> Shall we, who struck the Lion down, shall we

Childe Harold, Canto III, *Manfred*

> *Pay the Wolf homage? proffering lowly gaze*
> *And servile knees to Thrones? No! prove before ye*
> > *praise!*
> > *(xix)*

The fierce patriotism, the urgent advice, the championing of liberty are straight out of Canto I.[25] But these passages are few, as are the occurrences of those typical narrator-storyteller devices which so frequently announced his presence earlier (they are almost all concentrated in two stanzas of Canto III). And even in those scenes which the narrator does describe, the voice of the poet is becoming more and more insistent and powerful, overriding and thus accenting the other's limitations. For example, the narrator, time-bound, can see that "Time, who changes all, had altered" Harold "In soul and aspect as in age" (viii), but it is only the poet who can conclude, in sharply distinguishable accents and diction, that "Life's enchanted cup but sparkles near the brim" (viii). Again, while the narrator can describe Harold's continuing journey only in terms of time and space ("with every step he took through many a scene"), the poet sees Harold as a cosmic figure, rolling "On with the giddy circle, chasing Time" (xi). And, finally, while the narrator can only see the carnage of Waterloo as fitting punishment for Napoleon, the poet can easily relate the chains that bind Harold to his humanity (ix) and the chains that bind both Napoleon and all of France (xviii–xix). The thralldom which the narrator abhors politically and valiantly tries to wish away, the poet sees as the natural thralldom of man to his own humanness.

One more example of Byron's gradual elimination of the narrator is necessary, for it performs several functions in the total poem. This is the section on the "revelry by night" in Belgium's capital, the Duchess of Richmond's ball on the eve of Waterloo (xxiff.). The narration is simple, detailed, and basically unmetaphorical, just as it was in the narrator's earlier descriptions of the ball at Seville and the merriment of Stamboul (though those two were more insistently punctuated with moralistic comment). With this third occurrence of the scene, how-

---

[25] For similar revivals of the narrator's views, see stanzas xx, xxvi, lvi–lvii, and lxiii–lxiv.

ever, the narrator's very particularity of detail, truth of happening, and local color contribute toward its becoming an image of love, joy, and merriment amid the ruins of love, joy, and merriment. It is as if Byron is asking us to see in these celebrations man madly dancing on his own grave: the eyes of love look into the hollow sockets of the dead lover; young hearts madly, even desperately, chase "the glowing Hours with flying feet" (just as Harold giddily chases time), only to have those hours "press / The life from out young hearts" and choke the sighs "Which ne'er might be repeated" (xxii–xxiv); as it rings the "marriage-bell" deepens into the knell of doom (xxi). It is a powerful image, and Byron's conscious, repeated use of it bespeaks his growing awareness of his own ability and sureness of his imagination and hand. More important, perhaps, is the fact that when narration becomes an image, the narrator's function as such ceases, and he becomes merely a part of the poet's total vision.

The conclusion of the scene corroborates the process I have suggested. It is the implicit horror of the ball translated into commentary:

> And Ardennes waves above them her green leaves,
>   Dewy with Nature's tear-drops, as they pass—
> Grieving, if aught inanimate e'er grieves,
>   Over the unreturning brave,—alas!
>   Ere evening to be trodden like the grass
> Which now beneath them, but above shall grow
>   In its next verdure, when this fiery mass
> Of living Valour, rolling on the foe
> And burning with high Hope, shall moulder cold
>   and low.
>
> Last noon beheld them full of lusty life;—
>   Last eve in Beauty's circle proudly gay;
> The Midnight brought the signal-sound of strife,
>   The Morn the marshalling in arms,—the Day
>   Battle's magnificently-stern array!
> The thunder-clouds close o'er it, which when rent
>   The earth is covered thick with other clay
> Which her own clay shall cover, heaped and pent,
> Rider and horse,—friend,—foe,—in one red burial
>   blent!
>   (xxvii–xxviii)

Immediately after this summing up of the previous seven stanzas, having now expanded his vision of Waterloo to encompass all mankind in its giddy and fatal circle of time, and realizing that to continue the development of his poet as Everyman, incorporating within himself the universe, he must move as far inward as he had outward, Byron personalizes and particularizes his theme of desolation in the figure of "young, gallant Howard" (xxix). Not only does the speaker see himself as personally involved in this personal loss, not only is Howard by implication one of the merry lovers of the ball (although in fact he was not there); he is also the symbol of all the slain who made "a ghastly gap"

> *In his own kind and kindred, whom to teach*
> *Forgetfulness were mercy for their sake.*
>
> (*xxxi*)

Thus the poet's search for forgetfulness (stanza iv) and Harold's (stanzas xxf.) have been joined to the search of the "kind and kindred" of the fallen at Waterloo; and all of these searchers become man mourning, the shattered heart of humanity, who brokenly lives on, clinging, like the eternal prisoner of Chillon, without even the illusion of hope, to a life he hates:

> *They mourn, but smile at length—and, smiling, mourn:*
> *The tree will wither long before it fall;*
> *The hull drives on, though mast and sail be torn;*
> *The roof-tree sinks, but moulders on the hall*
> *In massy hoariness; the ruined wall*
> *Stands when its wind-torn battlements are gone;*
> *The bars survive the captive they enthral;*
> *The day drags through though storms keep out the*
> *sun;*
> *And thus the heart will break, yet brokenly live on:*
>
> *Even as a broken Mirror, which the glass*
> *In every fragment multiplies—and makes*
> *A thousand images of one that was,*
> *The same—and still the more, the more it breaks;*
> *And thus the heart will do which not forsakes,*
> *Living in shattered guise; and still, and cold,*
> *And bloodless, with its sleepless sorrow aches,*

Yet withers on till all without is old,
Showing no visible sign, for such things are untold.[26]
(*xxxii–xxxiii*)

George Ridenour sees the passage on St. Peter's in Canto IV as the key to the method of *Childe Harold's Pilgrimage*:[27]

Thou seest not all—but piecemeal thou must break,
  To separate contemplation, the great whole;
  And as the Ocean many bays will make
  That ask the eye—so here condense thy soul
  To more immediate objects, and control
  Thy thoughts until thy mind hath got by heart
  Its eloquent proportions, and unroll
  In mighty graduations, part by part,
The Glory which at once upon thee did not dart.
(*clvii*)

I see this description as applicable more to Cantos I and II, in which the discrete elements have not as yet formulated themselves, or been formulated by Byron, into a clear and distinct pattern. In Canto III that pattern has emerged, and with it the particular perceptions of the narrator no longer seem to stand aloof from Harold's and no longer need to be forcibly given

---

[26] Lady Blessington, certainly with this passage in mind, has Byron define memory as "the mirror which affliction dashes to the earth, and, looking down upon the fragments, only beholds the reflection multiplied" (*Conversations of Lord Byron*, p. 177). In the passage from *Childe Harold* quoted there is also a small but significant indication that Byron's imagination more and more habitually transmuted the personal into the universal. After completing Canto II of *Childe Harold*, Byron wrote to Dallas in deep despair over Edleston's sudden death: "My friends fall around me, and I shall be left a lonely tree before I am withered" (ltr. of 11 Oct. 1811, in *LJ*, II, 52). The withered tree of stanza xxxii is the literary version of the letter image, as is the passage in his 1816 journal of his excursion into the Swiss Alps: "Passed *whole woods of withered pines, all withered*; trunks stripped and barkless, branches lifeless; done by a single winter,— their appearance reminded me of me and my family" (*LJ*, III, 360; Byron's emphasis).
[27] "Byron and the Romantic Pilgrimage," pp. 14–16.

relationships to other discrete particulars by the poet. For Byron now the narrator and Harold are no longer necessary to his poem; so too Canto III's thematic relationships dominate the particulars to the point where "Our outward sense" (IV, clviii) is completely overwhelmed by our imaginative grasp of the whole: "growing with its growth, we thus dilate / Our Spirits to the size of that they contemplate" (clviii). Byron's image of the broken heart and broken mirror, then, is all the more appropriate if we can see anywhere in the poem a key to the way it is constructed (it is perhaps significant that the image is a late addition to the manuscript). It is remarkably multivalent: it signalizes the perpetuation of loss, sorrow, and despair by man's ineradicable memory, so that both the present and future are but repetitions of the past; it pictures the painful and continuous dying of the heart as each memory and new loss intensifies that death and assures not only its "shattered guise" (III, xxxiii) but its stillness, coldness, and bloodlessness; it is man's heart mirroring his broken world, suffering in it, condemning it, yet powerless to change it, clinging only to the heart's own finiteness and mortality; it is symbolic of the poet's total vision, dilated to the size of what it contemplates, yet reflecting in his own shattered individual heart the fragments of a lost Eden, a broken present, and a still more fragmented future; and, ultimately, it stands for the poem *Childe Harold*, in its unity as a journey and a pilgrimage and in its fragmented vision of doom, each shard of which is one of the "thousand images of one that was, / The same—and still the more, the more it breaks."

The poem is thus created from the intensity and vitality gained in the act of creation itself, by which the slain heart can feel again even in its "crushed feelings' dearth" (III, vi), on the one hand, and from the "Vitality of poison" that is the "life in our despair," "a quick root / Which feeds these deadly branches" (xxxiv), on the other. Creation, then, is no mere escape into illusion, for the "illusion," after all, is composed of additional fragments of the mirror of life—Harold, Waterloo, Rousseau, Napoleon, and so on. It is rather the means to maintain one's sanity in an insane world, to see coherence even if it is nihilistic, to suit one's life

Itself to Sorrow's most detested fruit,
Like to the apples on the Dead Sea's shore,
All ashes to the tasre.

(*xxxiv*)

The irony of this creation must not be missed, for it is at the core of Byron's aesthetic. To create for him was not, as for Harold (who is more nearly the true Shelleyan Romantic), to people the stars "with beings bright / As their own beams" and thus forget all "earth-born jars, / And human frailties" (III, xiv); it was to create out of despair a coherent vision of the causes of that despair in history and in himself, and thus to explore and cast light upon the human condition. That the coherence is often obscured by the claims made upon us by its apparently discrete fragments is often Byron's fault: but for it to be still obscured is our fault, for being Harolds or narrators instead of poets.

II

Within and contributing to the poem's total coherence, the themes of Canto III are relatively simple and clear: they are, first, the act of creation in its several aspects, as we have seen; second, nature, and the apparent attempt by the poet to lose his identity in this greater whole; and third, as Ward Pafford has superbly shown, the "tension created by the warring claims of imagination and reason"[28]—or, as I should prefer to call it, the warring claims of the heart and the mind.

Of the first of these I have already said a good deal, though I have largely ignored the overriding irony inherent in Byron's conception, an irony that brings together the first and third themes above. If the poet's becoming through creation "A being more intense" leads to a momentary, albeit vicarious, revivifying of his heart (thus producing, for example, the abundant compassion and sympathy for all mankind that informs Cantos III and IV), paradoxically, it also involves a further death of the heart, a "manning" of oneself against feeling and love (as

---

[28] "Byron and the Mind of Man," pp. 105–27.

we have seen often in the tales) as the only way to survive in this world. Such a steeling of the heart against itself is also, of course, an act of will, by which, ironically, man becomes the very thing he hates. This is indeed Harold's history up to this point, and Byron now merely uses Harold's particular circumstances and condition to universalize the theme:

> *He, who grown agèd in this world of woe,*
> *In deeds, not years, piercing the depths of life,*
> *So that no wonder waits him—nor below*
> *Can Love, or Sorrow, Fame, Ambition, Strife,*
> *Cut to his heart again with the keen knife*
> *Of silent, sharp endurance.*
>
> (III, v)

Having created, the poet asks, "What am I? Nothing: but not so art thou, / Soul of my thought!" (vi). The final humanity exists, then, in the creation, a fiction, which is a product of the act that dehumanizes the creator.

Similarly, Harold now feels "Secure" (a crucial word, invested of course with the values of the world) "in guarded coldness," his spirit "so firmly fixed / And sheathed with an invulnerable mind" that it is, he hopes, immune to further attack, loss, grief, despair (x). But just as the creator of ideal visions cannot be satisfied with them but must possess them physically (Shelley again comes to mind), so the "invulnerable mind" cannot "view the ripened rose, nor seek / To wear it," cannot completely eradicate that inborn human hope that the heart will "never all grow old," will never be completely dead (xi). And so the vicious circle goes on: man giddily chases time and encounters in space only fragments to mirror his own brokenness and mortality. As the poet seeks a life in nature, with which he could blend and "breathe without mankind" (xii), so Harold, unwilling to yield dominion over his mind, tries desperately to separate himself from man—to live on inhumanly without warmth or love or touch of human hand: "in Man's dwellings he became a *thing* / Restless and worn, and stern and wearisome" (xv; my italics).

For the poet and Harold the efforts are failures, and they are thrown once again back upon their own human resources and the heroic refusal to yield to inevitable death. As Byron writes,

> the heart must
> Leap kindly back to kindness, though Disgust
> Hath weaned it from all worldlings.
>
> (*liii*)

That leap back produces Harold's last words in the poem, his song "The Castled Crag of Drachenfels." In it, the heart once again, as if unbruised, creates its own paradise on the banks of the Rhine, a paradise that lacks only his love. But it is significant that the poet, who controls the set piece, places as much emphasis on the absence of the lover and the ruins of noble arches in "proud decay" as he does upon the note of smiling paradise. And the lilies Harold sends to his love, symbols of purity, will wither before she sees them.

Similarly, the poet finds, in the famous nature passages of the canto, that he can "live" as a "Portion of that around me" (lxxii): "thus . . . absorbed," he is momentarily convinced that "this is life" (lxxiii). Yet at the same time he loathes the natural fact of his own mortality and "the peopled desert past" where in "agony and strife" he had to act and suffer—that is, to be human (lxxiii). His momentary vision of the ideal, in which he clearly becomes a "being more intense," is properly in terms of a disembodied "mind . . . all free" (i.e., *sans* heart) which will, paradoxically, "Feel all I see less dazzling but more warm" (lxxiv). Yet Byron, with a sure hand, casts the whole section (stanzas lxxiv–lxxv) in the form of questions whose force is clearly not rhetorical but to which he has no answers. He then concludes flatly, "But this is not my theme; and I return / To that which is immediate" (lxxvi), that is, to the world and man as they were, and are, and always will be, "The march of our existence" (xciii).

The canto concludes with the irony of creation instinct in its lines, the poet steeling "The heart against itself" and concealing

> With a proud caution, love, or hate, or aught,—
> Passion or feeling, purpose, grief, or zeal,—
> Which is the tyrant Spirit of our thought.
>
> (*cxi*)

It is "a stern task of soul," he admits; but "No matter,—it is taught" (cxi). The tragedy is, of course, that it can never be fully taught as long as man remains alive. He will continue to wish for the return of love lost, will try to convince himself that love will live in the future (e.g., through an Ada), and will perpetually create both ideals to be shattered (as in the Haidée episode of *Don Juan*) and the endlessly proliferating mirrors of that shattering in order to *live* a being more intense. "The child of Love" must at least *seem* always possible, even though the poet knows that it will be "born in bitterness, / And nurtured in Convulsion" (cxviii)—and live a ruin amidst ruins.

The great passages of Canto III on Napoleon, the Alps, Julia Alpinula, Lake Leman, Rousseau, Clarens, Gibbon, and Voltaire all support this basic overarching theme. For example, Napoleon fallen is merely Harold, the poet, or man in another guise, "Conqueror *and* Captive of the Earth" (xxxvii), flailing futilely around in what is after all "a worthless world to win or lose" (xl). By manning himself to be a god unto himself, separate from and above all men, Napoleon became less than man, "like a tower upon a headlong rock" (xli):

> Round *him are icy rocks, and loudly blow*
> *Contending tempests on his naked head,*
> *And thus reward the toils which to those summits led.*
> *(xlv)*

The same point is made again immediately following this section. "Away with these," the poet cries in a burst of petulance and disgust—"madmen who have made men mad / By their contagion" (xlvi, xliii), and he turns to nature and "a work divine, / A blending of all beauties," the "majestic Rhine" (xlvi). But even here, amid the splendors of a natural paradise (already severely qualified by man's absence), it is "Ruin" that "greenly dwells"; and a castle stands as

> *a lofty mind,*
> *Worn, but unstooping to the baser crowd,*
> *All tenantless, save to the crannying Wind,*
> *Or holding dark communion with the Cloud.*
> *(xlvii)*

The image is a strikingly apt echo of the skull-temple section of Canto II (stanzas v–vi), thus uniting ambitious man's murder of his heart in the name of mind with the death of men and civilizations.

Indeed, even the mind seems to be vulnerable. Not only does the heart persist in "leaping back" despite the mind's severe control, but the mind itself can

> *overboil*
> *In the hot throng, where we become the spoil*
> *Of our infection, till too late and long*
> *We may deplore and struggle with the coil,*
> *In wretched interchange of wrong for wrong*
> *'Midst a contentious world, striving where none are*
> *strong.*
> *(lxix)*

An early manuscript version of that last line began with "One of a worthless [word heavily crossed out] who strive."[29] Worthless and without strength, man plunges his years "in a moment"

> *and in the blight*
> *Of our own Soul turn all our blood to tears,*
> *And colour things to come with hues of Night,*
> *The race of life becomes a hopeless flight*
> *To those that walk in darkness: on the sea*
> *The boldest steer but where their ports invite—*
> *But there are wanderers o'er Eternity*
> *Whose bark drives on and on, and anchored ne'er*
> *shall be.*
> *(lxx)*

The poet himself has become his wanderer—a man who, like all men, walks in darkness across arid wastes, chasing time, or who is flung crazily on ocean's tide. If it is better to "love Earth only for its earthly sake" (lxxi), as the poet is tempted to believe, than to doom ourselves "to inflict or bear" (lxxi), we do so only at the risk of becoming less than human—mad, as an

---

[29] Coleridge's transcription of the manuscript version is inaccurate according to Robert Zimmerman (see his "Manuscript Revision in Byron's *Childe Harold's Pilgrimage*," p. 341).

illusory escape from the world's madness. Rousseau, Voltaire, and Gibbon were all creators in the same sense that Byron's poet is, but, like Napoleon, their extremes destroyed them.

Finally, all of the nature passages reiterate nature's fundamental indifference to man's plight.[30] It is continually contrasted to "Earth's troubled waters" or "the wild world I dwelt in" (lxxxv). It is seductive, appealing, calm and beautiful, sublime, the embodiment of "life intense"—and yet it is unhuman. Tempted, the poet climbs the Alps, wishes to concenter all his "Soul—heart—mind—passions—feelings" in the crashing word of nature, "Lightning" (xcvii); he wants desperately to be "absorbed" (lxxiii); and he sees in Clarens the "birthplace of deep Love" (xcix), an eternal Eden "hallowed . . . with loveliness" (civ), but also eternally empty and lonely. In it the poet sees the same sort of last desperate hope with which he concludes the canto in his address to Ada:

> *For this is Love's recess, where vain men's woes,*
> *And the world's waste, have driven him far from*
> > *those,*
> *For 'tis his nature to advance or die;*
> *He stands not still, but or decays, or grows*
> *Into a boundless blessing, which may vie*
> *With the immortal lights, in its eternity!*
>
> > > *(ciii)*

But the poet also knows that the love which existed there was

---

[30] For other discussions of this point, see especially Lovell, *Byron: The Record of a Quest*, pp. 117ff., and Pafford, "Byron and the Mind of Man," pp. 111ff. Pafford, who says that nature for Byron is an "implacable and indifferent conqueror of all man's works and dreams," is more nearly correct than is Lovell, who sees Byron's nature as "hostile." See also Ridenour's discussion in "Byron and the Romantic Pilgrimage," pp. 29ff. In this connection it is interesting to note what Byron has to say of buildings and sculpture: they "are as *poetical* as Mont Blanc or Mount Ætna, perhaps still more so, as they are direct manifestations of mind, and *presuppose* poetry in their very conception; and have, moreover, as being such, a something of actual life, which cannot belong to any part of inanimate nature, unless we adopt the System of Spinosa [sic], that the World is the deity" (*Letter to [John Murray], Esqre, on the Rev. W. L. Bowles's Strictures on the Life and Writings of Pope,* 1821, in *LJ,* V, 548).

gone as soon as it came, for it was merely a scene allotted "To the Mind's purified beings" in Rousseau's fiction (civ). It remains for Canto IV, *Manfred, Cain,* and *Don Juan* to drive love even further afield, into oblivion, for vain man and the world's waste yield no garden within which it may grow into that "boundless blessing."

III

Manfred was created, as many critics have observed, out of the darkness that had invaded his mind and feelings, the same darkness that is inherent in the gathering gloom of *Childe Harold* III and is explicit in "The Dream," "Darkness," "Prometheus," and other poems written in mid-1816. Reinforcing these connections is Byron's insistence that neither Goethe's *Faust* nor any literary work but "the *Staubach* and the *Jungfrau*, and something else" led him to write it[31]—those same coldly sublime "Palaces of Nature" "pinnacled in clouds," enthroning "Eternity in icy halls," we have seen in Canto III of *Childe Harold* (lxii) as symbols of the unhuman self-steeled mind, tempting but indifferent. Although they offer momentary escape, they are eternal ice instead of the warmth of love and humanity.

More important than this biographical background, however, is the structure of *Manfred*. With astonishing agility, after clearly establishing the difficult amalgamation of voices and personae, of the personal, historical, and mythical, in his figure of the poet in Canto III of *Childe Harold*, he now creates, and in creating becomes, "A being more intense." Mixed with the spirit of Manfred, blended with his birth, the poet now is his own subject, the reality that infuses the myth of his creation and gives it life and meaning as well as coherence. Just as the tales represented, with uneven success, Byron's persistent, and even daring, experiments with the handling of point of view, speaker, and contrasting attitudes, *Manfred* logically solidifies those experiments in quasi-dramatic form, separating distinctly for the first time the conflicting forces of the poet's own being

---

[31] Ltr. to Murray, 7 June 1820, in *LJ*, V, 37.

and dramatizing what for Byron always was the essential war, the one within man himself.

Yet the problem, as we have seen, was not merely one of separating the elements of himself, but of striking a happy balance between separation and unification, between particularity and universality, between men and man. Throughout the tales, as well as in *Childe Harold,* the search, while I have treated it as a striving for form, was also a search for a personal mythical identity in whom the variousness of experience and the manifold layers of individual vision could be concentrated. While, on the one hand, the poet-figure usurps the stage more and more, and his larger vision makes increasingly unnecessary the fragmentation of that vision into separate created characters, on the other, his emergence necessitates a means of externalizing his character so that it can be observed and reacted to by the very limited perceptions it has absorbed into itself. Foils must be created so that the self is dramatizable by the self, so that it may be both subject and object, so that its particularity will not obscure the universality it is intended to demonstrate.

The so-called minor poems of 1816 are of especial importance to us here, as they were to Byron, for their thrust (particularly in "A Dream," "Darkness," and "Prometheus") is toward myth, not mere self-revelation or the display of a bleeding heart. In them "beings more intense" act out more intensely than in "real life" the misery and lostness of man, the eternal death of love, and the repetitive ruination of paradise. The poet has become the seer, not merely the singer, the creator, not merely the observer, and his melancholy vision is "a fearful gift":

> *What is it but the telescope of truth?*
> *Which strips the distance of its fantasies,*
> *And brings life near in utter nakedness,*
> *Making the cold reality too real!*
> ("The Dream," ll. 180–83)

But to create is to make reality even more real and terrifying, thus making it necessary to create anew in order to remain sane and human in the face of the starkness and horror of the world's insanity and inhumanity.

251

BYRON AND THE RUINS OF PARADISE

As Earl Wasserman has written, "the poem is one of the symbolic forms that permit the mind to pass from the procession of events and things to the momentary grasp of them as *real*—that is, self-enclosing, self-sustaining, self-animating, and at every point relevant."[32] For Byron, however, unlike the other Romantics, this symbolic form is only a meaningful whole in the sense that its vision grasps coherently the atomistic incoherence of reality; it is not one of a brave new world toward which man might strive. Therefore, the act of creation, rather than the created artifact itself, or its meaning, is what sustains the artist, an act which must be, as Wasserman says, "forever . . . renewed."[33]

We may ask, however, what happens if that disordered, multitudinous world of objects and human history is absorbed into the self, so that the poet is not merely conscious of chaos around him but also within him? For Byron the answer was that the act of creation was a continual and necessary reorganization of self, an urgent rejuvenation (or at least reminder) of one's own essential humanity. In this sense we must see Byron as poet eternally in agony over his own fall, fragmentation, and disunity, creating out of his despair his own being, which in turn mirrors ever more faithfully and terrifyingly his own shattered heart and soul. The poem "Prometheus" is most instructive here, for apart from the concerted, major, but painfully gradual efforts in *Childe Harold* to give full body and voice to the poet, "Prometheus" is the first poem to emancipate him completely as both creator and creature, world and man, observer and participant, seer and seen. For Byron Prometheus is not merely a conventional mythological symbol: he is that, but he is also, I believe, the poet, who "speaks but in [his] loneliness" of the agony he does not show, of his "suffocating sense of woe." His

> *Godlike crime was to be kind,*
> *To render with thy precepts less*
> *The sum of human wretchedness,*
> *And strengthen Man with his own mind.*
>
> (ll. 35–38)

---

[32] *The Subtler Language*, p. 6.
[33] *Ibid.*, p. 186.

And for this "crime"

> *inexorable Heaven,*
> *And the deaf tyranny of Fate,*
> *The ruling principle of Hate,*
> *Which for its pleasure doth create*
> *The things it may annihilate,*
>
> (ll. 19–23)

have awarded him the "gift Eternity," refused him "even the boon to die." Thus the endlessly punished god, whose immortality lies only in his deathless suffering, becomes for Byron man, the "symbol" and "sign"

> *To Mortals of their fate and force;*
> *Like thee, Man is in part divine,*
> *A troubled stream from a pure source;*
> *And Man in portions can foresee*
> *His own funereal destiny;*
> *His wretchedness, and his resistance,*
> *And his sad unallied existence.*
>
> (ll. 46–52)

Those "portions" are, of course, his creative moments, moments of vision into the nature of things, into the human condition and the heart of man. Against this vision the poet shores up his spirit with each renewed creative act, gaining as he gives the life he images and, losing that life, creating another.

⌈After all this has been said, however, it is still inadequate simply to state that Byron is Manfred. It is more nearly true to say that Manfred is the Giaour plus the poet of *Childe Harold*, Prometheus, and (as has been pointed out almost *ad nauseam*) a Gothic villain and Faust. All of these, rolled into the single figure of Manfred, represent the voice of the poet, who is man.⌋ What unites all of the figures is not that familiar common denominator, the Byronic hero, but rather the fundamental humanness, *in extremis*, which each of these disparate figures exemplifies to Byron. Each in his own way heroically and unyieldingly battles against his destiny—through defiance, Herculean efforts of the will, and deliberate flaunting of self-manacled man's less than human codes of conduct. Further, each of them is crippled by a single love and a vision of paradise that are destroyed in his very act of loving and seeing.

The similarities between *The Giaour* and *Manfred* are so striking that, did we not feel certain that Byron began the latter in Switzerland in 1816, we should be sorely tempted to credit his own description of the "Incantation" (*Manfred*, I, i, 192–261), published in *The Prisoner of Chillon and Other Poems* earlier in 1816, as "a Chorus in an unpublished Witch Drama, which was begun some years ago."[34] Whether or not *Manfred*, or some sort of "Witch Drama," was begun as early as 1813, however, is not to the point here; what is important is the fact that Byron virtually took over the basic elements of *The Giaour* to create his new "dramatic poem"—further evidence that, however sporadic or uneven the process may have been, he was quite consciously evolving in the poems a coherent view of man and the world and at the same time struggling to develop the most effective form to embody that vision. In outline, the plot of *The Giaour*, we recall, concerns his love for Leila, the slave of Hassan, Hassan's drowning of her for her infidelity, the Giaour's revenge upon Hassan in battle, and his final remorse and death in an abbey. In the same way Manfred's love for Astarte is ended by her death at the hands of another and Manfred's remorse and final death. If *The Giaour* lacks the spirit-characters of *Manfred*, it does have its chamois hunter (the fisherman) and its abbot. More important, Leila, like Astarte, is love personified, pure, holy, and innocent, and that love becomes the cause of the protagonists' deaths and the source of their lovers' eternal suffering. Just as the Giaour is tempted to suicide (ll. 822–31), so Manfred for the same reasons is tempted to shatter his body in a leap from the precipice. Both are seen to have

> *A spirit yet unquelled and high,*
> *That claims and keeps ascendancy.*
> *(The Giaour, ll. 840–41)*

In the Giaour's despair-darkened face the poet can trace "What once were feelings":

---

[34] *P*, IV, 92n.

Childe Harold, Canto III, *Manfred*

> *Time hath not yet the features fixed,*
> *But brighter traits with evil mixed;*
> *And there are hues not always faded,*
> *Which speak a mind not all degraded*
> *Even by the crimes through which it waded:*
> *The common crowd but see the gloom*
> *Of wayward deeds, and fitting doom;*
> *The close observer can espy*
> *A noble soul, and lineage high:*
> *Alas! though both bestowed in vain.*
>
> (ll. 860–70)

Of Manfred, the chamois hunter says, "Thy garb and gait bespeak thee of high lineage" (II, i, 7), and the Abbot sees him as

> *a noble creature: he*
> *Hath all the energy which would have made*
> *A goodly frame of glorious elements.*
>
> (III, i, 160–62)

Just as the Giaour has visions as of

> *some bloody hand*
> *Fresh severed from its parent limb,*
> *Invisible to all but him,*
>
> (ll. 827–29)

so Manfred frightens the chamois hunter by "peop[ling] vacancy" and seeing blood on the brim of the wine glass (II, i, 21–32). The Giaour refuses to kneel with the monks in the chapel (ll. 887–88), defying all higher powers, Manfred-like, and yet gives money to the convent, just as in the first version of Act III of *Manfred* the Abbot extorts money from Manfred in payment for his efforts to save him. Manfred is a peer among the spirits of evil, and the Abbot faces him with the complaints of his "pious brethren—the scaréd peasantry" (III, i, 44), who say

> *That with the dwellers of the dark abodes,*
> *The many evil and unheavenly spirits*
> *Which walk the valley of the Shade of Death,*
> *Thou communest.*
>
> (36–39)

Similarly, the monk in *The Giaour*, frightened by his "stony air / Of mixed defiance and despair" (ll. 907–8), desperately prays:

> *"Saint Francis, keep him from the shrine!*
> *Else may we dread the wrath divine*
> *Made manifest by awful sign.*
> *If ever evil angel bore*
> *The form of mortal, such he wore;*
> *By all my hope of sins forgiven,*
> *Such looks are not of earth nor heaven!"*
>
> *(ll. 909–15)*

And there are many more such details, speeches, attitudes, and images, too numerous to list.

To point to these similarities, however, is not intended to suggest that Byron in *Manfred* simply wished to redo *The Giaour*. Aside from more obvious surface differences, in *Manfred* Byron eliminated the earlier poem's emphasis on revenge and the Giaour's relish of its memory throughout his long final monologue. In its place is the Faustian quest and the consequent elevation of man to the god-like position of a Prometheus—or, as Rutherford rightly says, a "Prometheus manqué."[35] The two-pronged focus of the drama is thus upon Manfred as both the embodiment of the most that man can be and the emblem of his essential littleness, rather than upon the varieties of human response to a central incident and situation, as in *The Giaour*. In the latter, the poet's voice is heard only sporadically, *in propria persona* as well as being infiltrated into the speeches of the other characters by way of imagery; in *Manfred* the poet-lover-man dominates the entire poem, and the few other characters react not to what he has done but rather to what he is. In *The Giaour* the total picture of the human condition can be seen only by an imaginative effort by the reader comparable to that of the poet. He must marshal in his mind all of the particulars of the scene, the partisan and circumscribed views of a number of characters, and the too-subtle manipulation of related images. In *Manfred* the character himself is the human condition, aware of his own nature and his world, and

---

[35] *Byron: A Critical Study*, p. 89.

creating out of his despair a meaningful framework within which to die. The Giaour merely "passes," and we are simply *told* about it; Manfred dies, and can heroically say, in facing the total darkness of that last unknown, "Old man! 'tis not so difficult to die" (III, iv, 151). But we also know that his death is the final surrender to his own mortality; he is Prometheus dead upon the Caucasus, Christ eternally crucified, the creative artist's imaged life dying even as it is born: "Darkness . . . was the universe."

There has been a good deal of scholarly exploration of the drama inherent in the fundamental lyricism of the Romantic poets.[36] What Byron demands of us is an equal appreciation of the lyricism inherent in his drama. The public-private voice of the *Hours of Idleness* now bears full fruit in the self-revelations of *Manfred*; there is no longer any necessity for it to huddle beneath the more conventional tones of the private-public voice of poetic conventions. Once the poetic "I" can stand off from itself to the point of creating a form within which it can have artistic and viable being,[37] manipulations of various points of view are no longer necessary to achieve what often was an obscure or forced synthesis. If Gothicism, Prometheanism, Faustianism, and other popular issues or figures are apparent in *Manfred*, perhaps they are there because of Byron's awareness of the boldness of his step, despite his long and arduous preparation for it. It is simply easier, and safer, to speak through the mouth of tradition and accepted forms than it is to proclaim one's self as *the* poet, archetypal man, the microcosmic human condition. It is unfortunate that his public saw, and sees even to this day, his life as the epitome of his age or the Byronic hero as the man of his age, and neglected the poetry in which the Byron of dust and deity actually played out the drama of man's inevitable fall and destruction.

Thematically *Manfred* owes much to *Childe Harold*

---

[36] One of the best of these is Stephen M. Parrish's "Dramatic Technique in the *Lyrical Ballads*," *PMLA*, LXXIV (1959), 85–97.

[37] The medieval distinction (as, for example, in Dante) between the "poetic I" (which is mankind) and the pragmatic or empirical "I" of the actual poet again comes to mind. See Leo Spitzer, "Note on the Poetic and the Empirical 'I' in Medieval Authors."

III, as well as to *The Giaour* and almost every other preceding poem. Pafford is quite right in seeing the incest motif as peripheral to the basic themes;[38] it is a kind of sensationalism that readers and critics still insist is central to the poem's meaning. The tragedy, if it should be called that (and I believe it approaches tragedy more closely than any of Byron's other works), is the tragedy of the infinite human mind and the finite human heart, eternally in unresolved conflict, the one destructive of the other, each destructive of itself. The guilt involved in such destruction is not the moral guilt of committed sin, but rather, as M. K. Joseph so aptly put it, the guilt of being "a member of the human race."[39] As such, Manfred is gifted with both the capacity for knowledge and the capacity for love. His signal success in the achieving of both should have made him a god; as it is, he can only die as a man.

We see in the opening of the poem that Manfred's world is initially a world of darkness (the same darkness that pervades the poem "Darkness"). The lamp, even when replenished, will not illuminate his midnight and his sleep is "But a continuance of enduring thought, / Which then I can resist not" (I, i, 1–5). That thought, of course, is of the past, and hence of the fall from the world of light and love to the world of knowledge, ruin, despair, and darkness. Time and memory only renew the vision of ruin and, at rare moments, the vision of the irretrievable Eden. Thus when the spirits appear in Act I, Manfred sees "The steady aspect of a clear large Star" (I, i, 178), the star of man's destiny which was once

> *a World as fresh and fair*
> *As e'er revolved round Sun in air;*
> *Its course was free and regular,*
> *Space bosomed not a lovelier star.*
>
> (I, i, 112–15)

More often he sees what the star—his world and himself—has become:

---

[38] "Byron and the Mind of Man," p. 109.
[39] *Byron the Poet*, p. 106.

Childe Harold, Canto III, *Manfred*

> *A wandering mass of shapeless flame,*
> *A pathless Comet, and a curse,*
> *The menace of the Universe;*
> *Still rolling on with innate force,*
> *Without a sphere, without a course,*
> *A bright deformity on high,*
> *The monster of the upper sky!*
>
> (117–23)

The curse of man, then, is both his knowledge of the world and his knowledge of himself, knowledge gained through a vision of past, present, and future and through experience:

> *they who know the most*
> *Must mourn the deepest o'er the fatal truth,*
> *The Tree of Knowledge is not that of Life.*
>
> (10–12)

As knowledge comes with sorrow, so sorrow, despair, come with knowledge, the possession of which is but a vision "Of that which is within me" (I, i, 137). The "Incantation" pictures it as a venom stronger and deadlier than any snake's, and concludes with what amounts to a knowledgeable man's assessment of and curse upon himself:

> *By thy cold breast and serpent smile,*
> *By thy unfathomed gulfs of guile,*
> *By that most seeming virtuous eye,*
> *By thy shut soul's hypocrisy;*
> *By the perfection of thine art*
> *Which passed for human thine own heart;*
> *By thy delight in others' pain,*
> *And by thy brotherhood of Cain,*
> *I call upon thee! and compel*
> *Thyself to be thy proper Hell!*
>
> .   .   .   .   .
>
> *Though thy death shall still seem near*
> *To thy wish, but as a fear;*
> *Lo! the spell now works around thee,*
> *And the clankless chain hath bound thee;*
> *O'er thy heart and brain together*
> *Hath the word been passed—now wither!*
>
> (242–51, 256–61)

259

The chain is, of course, the "fleshly chain" of his own suffering mortality, doomed eternally to wish for and to fear death. It is the same invisible chain we have seen binding Childe Harold, galling "for ever, fettering though unseen, / And heavy though it clanked not; worn with pain" (III, ix); but in his inarticulateness "it spoke not." It is the linked chain "That keeps us from yon heaven which woos us to its brink" (xiv), the cage in which man, "a thing / Restless and worn," beats "His breast and beak against his wiry dome / Till the blood tinge his plumage" (xv); it is the vortex in which Harold eternally chases time, if with "a nobler aim," then with renewed failure and intensified despair as well.

But knowledge, memory, and vision have another aspect: along with the awareness of loss they also provide a progressively more intense vision of what was lost: the unspeakable beauty of "all this visible world . . . glorious in its action and itself" (*Manfred*, I, ii, 37–38); the days of youth and love when all "had one heart, / And loved each other as we should not love" (II, i, 27)—that is, the love that fallen man's society brands as "evil";[40] the simple, primitivistic past that Manfred sees as embodied in the chamois hunter, a peasant of the Alps—

> *Thy humble virtues, hospitable home,*
> *And spirit patient, pious, proud, and free;*
> *Thy self-respect, grafted on innocent thoughts;*

---

[40] This passage, of course, has been the crux of the argument, which flourished in Byron's day but continues into ours, that the whole poem and Manfred's character revolves around his having committed incest. Shelley vigorously and intelligently championed the literary use of incest (ltr. to Maria Gisborne, 16 Nov. 1819, in *The Letters of Percy Bysshe Shelley*, ed. F. L. Jones [Oxford, 1964], II, 531), and most critics since 1819 who were disposed to see the theme as poetically tolerable have sanctioned Byron's employment of it, as it were, by pointing away from his relationship with Augusta and toward the works of Euripides, Calderón, Lope de Vega, Racine, Schiller, Alfieri, and others (see, e.g., Samuel C. Chew, *The Dramas of Lord Byron* [Göttingen and Baltimore, 1915], pp. 36ff.). In the developing context of all of Byron's poetry, however, the fact of incest (whether autobiographical or literary) is clearly less important than the intensity and completeness of a love inimical to the values of a fallen society. The lines quoted are part of Manfred's opening dialogue with the chamois hunter (II, i, 26–27).

Childe Harold, Canto III, *Manfred*

> *Thy days of health, and nights of sleep; thy toils,*
> *By danger dignified, yet guiltless; hopes*
> *Of cheerful old age and a quiet grave,*
> *With cross and garland over its green turf,*
> *And thy grandchildren's love for epitaph;*
>
> (63–71)

and, overriding all, the primeval Edenic past when men were gods and gods men, when thoughts were things, and love and knowledge were one. Typically, Byron images this age as a woman—and/or a child (like Ianthe, Ada, Francesca, Augusta, the "Witch of the Alps"):

> *Beautiful Spirit! with thy hair of light,*
> *And dazzling eyes of glory, in whose form*
> *The charms of Earth's least mortal daughters grow*
> *To an unearthly stature, in an essence*
> *Of purer elements; while the hues of youth,—*
> *Carnationed like a sleeping Infant's cheek,*
> *Rocked by the beating of her mother's heart,*
> *Or the rose tints, which Summer's twilight leaves*
> *Upon the lofty Glacier's virgin snow,*
> *The blush of earth embracing with her Heaven,—*
> *Tinge thy celestial aspect.*
>
> (ii, 13–23)

Precisely the same image occurs in Manfred's hymn to the sun,

> the idol
> *Of early nature, and the vigorous race*
> *Of undiseased mankind, the giant sons*
> *Of the embrace of Angels.*
>
> (III, ii, 3–6)

To man, however, the sun's "gifts of life and warmth have been / Of a more fatal nature" (28–29). The mind can make a god out of clay, can probe the secrets of eternity and know past, present, and future, can, as S. T. Coleridge put it, repeat "in the finite mind . . . the eternal act of creation in the infinite I AM";[41] but in so doing man and self become con-

---

[41] *Biographia Literaria*, Chap. XIII.

temptible, the body becomes a galling chain, and death is a desired release. "Mortality predominates" (I, ii, 45):

> *this clay will sink*
> *Its spark immortal, envying it the light*
> *To which it mounts*
>
> *(Childe Harold, III, xiv)*

and the mind merely feeds itself with further evidence of its own inability to sustain its flight. The heart, on the other hand, is the agent of man's happiness, the key to the gates of paradise, the creator of new worlds to inherit:

> *Love indeed is light from heaven;*
> *A spark of that immortal fire*
> *With angels shared, by Alla given,*
> *To lift from earth our low desire.*
> *Devotion wafts the mind above,*
> *But Heaven itself descends in Love;*
> *A feeling from the Godhead caught,*
> *To wean from self each sordid thought;*
> *A ray of Him who formed the whole;*
> *A Glory circling round the soul!*
>
> *(The Giaour, ll. 1131–40)*

That promise is illusory, however, just as the mind's aspirations are vain; for man is man, not God, and his love, therefore, however full and complete, is imperfect. Its momentary glimpse of Eden also precipitates its loss. Although Manfred, unlike the Giaour, wreaked no revenge upon his foes (indeed he seems to have had no foes), his "injuries" descended "on those who loved me— / On those whom [he] best loved" (II, i, 85–86). His "embrace was fatal" (88): "I loved her, and destroyed her," Manfred cries (ii, 117); his "heart . . . broke her heart; / It gazed on mine, and withered" (118–19):

> *If I had never lived, that which I love*
> *Had still been living; had I never loved,*
> *That which I love would still be beautiful,*
> *Happy and giving happiness. What is she?*
> *What is she now?—a sufferer for my sins—*
> *A thing I dare not think upon—or nothing.*
>
> *(192–97)*

The whole movement of this theme culminates in the Phantom of Astarte's refusal either to forgive him (for what, after all, was not his doing) or to say that she loves him still (iv, 149ff.).

Thus it can be seen that man's aspirations to god-hood take two forms, and both are doomed to failure. Knowledge, he finds,

> *is not happiness, and science*
> *But an exchange of ignorance for that*
> *Which is another kind of ignorance.*
>
> *(61–63)*

His

> *passions, attributes*
> *Of Earth and Heaven, from which no power, nor being,*
> *Nor breath from the worm upwards is exempt,*
> *Have pierced his heart; and in their consequence*
> *Made him a thing—which—I* [Manfred's "Destiny"]
> *who pity not,*
> *Yet pardon those who pity.*
>
> *(64–69)*

Man's doom is thus sealed. Aspiring to be more than he is, he becomes less,

> *Loathing our life, and dreading still to die.*
> *In all the days of this detested yoke—*
> *This vital weight upon the struggling heart,*
> *Which sinks with sorrow, or beats quick with pain,*
> *Or joy that ends in agony or faintness—*
> *In all the days of past and future—for*
> *In life there is no present.*
>
> *(ii, 166–72)*

And all those days, seen spatially, are

> *as sands on the shore,*
> *Innumerable atoms; and one desert,*
> *Barren and cold, on which the wild waves break,*
> *But nothing rests, save carcasses and wrecks,*
> *Rocks, and the salt-surf weeds of bitterness.*
>
> *(i, 54–58)*

There is an alternative, however: man may indeed surrender that cherished illusion of the dominion of his mind and the divinity of his heart, accept his mortality, and meet the world on its own terms,

> breathe
> *The breath of degradation and of pride,*
> *Contending with low wants and lofty will,*
> *Till our Mortality predominates,*
> *And men are—what they name not to themselves,*
> *And trust not to each other.*
>
> *(I, ii, 42–47)*

He may shrink "back / To recreant mortality" (II, ii, 125–26)

> *and soothe, and sue,*
> *And watch all time, and pry into all place,*
> *And be a living Lie.*
>
> *(III, i, 117–19)*

Blake put it this way in "A Divine Image," that image which so many of Byron's "heroes" assume as they steel their minds against their hearts:

> *Cruelty has a Human Heart*
> *And Jealousy a Human Face,*
> *Terror, the Human Form Divine*
> *And Secrecy, the Human Dress.*
>
> *The Human Dress is forged Iron,*
> *The Human Form, a fiery Forge,*
> *The Human Face, a Furnace seal'd*
> *The Human Heart, its hungry Gorge.*

The Abbot is quite right, then, in his final audience with Manfred, to seek to touch his heart (III, iv, 45–53), for therein lie the ruins as well as the seeds of "a noble spirit." But Manfred's world is the same world of which Yeats wrote in "The Second Coming":

> *Things fall apart; the centre cannot hold;*
> *Mere anarchy is loosed upon the world,*
> *The blood-dimmed tide is loosed, and everywhere*
> *The ceremony of innocence is drowned.*

In such a world there will be no "revelation . . . at hand," no Second Coming, and man cannot tolerate, without madness, another fall. All that is left for him is to pronounce upon himself a last judgment, in the place and time of his own mind, which, after all, was "Born from the knowledge of its own desert" (III, iv, 136). The Manichaean spirits of both light and darkness will be rejected as heroically as was surrender to the life of a groveling slave: death, the final claim of mortality, will be met not on *its* terms but on Manfred's, his mind intact and unconquerable, heart still warm, and reaching out the hand of humanity to the Abbot (149). In the final analysis, the quality of Manfred's dying is thus the measure of the life intense the poet has created in him and, through him, in himself; it is further evidence that only the poet can sustain himself in such a world, the poet of *Childe Harold* IV, of *The Lament of Tasso* and *The Prophecy of Dante*, and, finally, of *Don Juan*.

Chapter IX

CHILDE HAROLD'S PILGRIMAGE, CANTO IV

Although Byron to all intents and purposes dismissed Childe Harold in Canto III, his formal farewell to his created character he reserved for the "Dedication" (to Hobhouse) which prefaces Canto IV. In this last canto, completed some eight years after he began the poem, Byron admits that

> there will be found less of the pilgrim than in any of the preceding, and that little slightly, if at all, separated from the author speaking in his own person. The fact is, that I had become weary of drawing a line which every one seemed determined not to perceive: like the Chinese in Goldsmith's *Citizen of the World*, whom nobody would believe to be a Chinese, it was in vain that I asserted, and imagined that I had drawn, a distinction between the author and the pilgrim; and the very anxiety to preserve this difference, and disappointment at finding it unavailing, so far crushed my efforts in the composition, that I determined to abandon it altogether—and have done so (*P*, II, 323).

There is a certain petulance in all of this, something of the flavor of "If you won't play the game my way, I won't play," but I am convinced that Byron had already learned (in Canto III and in *Manfred*) that he no longer needed Harold either to give "some connection to the piece" or to voice, however inarticulately, the numbing despair of the visionless lost. The poetic "I" has now taken over completely, and if it is, as Byron says, his own voice that we hear, we must listen to it as the voice of Byron the poet, not that of Byron the man or legend.

The distinction is a crucial one, even more so than in *Hours of Idleness*. Both Byron the creator and Byron the darling of biographers and gossips speak in the "Dedication," and however formal and self-conscious the language, it behooves us to hear in it their respective accents. To the man, Hobhouse is a friend, who, if not quite so glittering as Byron paints him, is certainly true and loyal: the compliments are both appropriate and graceful. To the poet, the friend has been *Childe Harold's Pilgrimage* as well, whose birth and now death were presided over, as it were, by Hobhouse; and, more important perhaps, it is *a* poem that Byron speaks of, not two or three poems, "a poetical work which is the longest, the most thoughtful and comprehensive of my compositions," a work which, now that it is complete, must "depend on itself, and not on the writer."[1] Beyond this, the canto is an augury or prophecy for England to heed, or else, like Greece and Italy, it too *"will have"* (Byron's italics) its "reward, and at no very distant period."[2]

I see no reason to doubt Byron's concern for his work as a created artifact, with a life and integrity of its own, nor do I see any confusion in the poet's voice, which now supersedes Harold's (and the narrator's) completely, but rather the fruition of often muddled but always present planning. M. Escarpit laments the fact that the distinction between Byron's "le temps 'fictionnel' du récit" and "le temps réel (le temps psychologique de l'auteur)," evidence of which distinction exists as early as Canto I, "tend à diminuer" in the later cantos;[3] and at least one recent critic, M. K. Joseph, agrees: "Byron is unable or unwilling to exploit the difference between them; and once Harold ceases to be effectively either a Zeluco or a burlesque Spenserian paladin, the attempt to differentiate between them is abandoned as purposeless. By losing sight of the distinction between narrator and titular hero, Byron sacrificed what might have been a major advantage."[4] Perhaps; but then the poem would have been a different poem, would perhaps have moved toward Don Juanism, perhaps would even have precluded the necessity of writing that vast exercise in contrapuntal points of view. Further, if indeed he did sacrifice one "major advantage," Byron also gained immensely in *Childe Harold* IV: "le temps fictionnel" and "le

---

[1] "To John Hobhouse, Esq., A.M., F.R.S. . . . ," in *P*, II, 321, 323.
[2] *Ibid.*, pp. 325–26.
[3] Robert Escarpit, *Lord Byron: Un tempérament littéraire* (2 vols.; Paris, 1955), II, 74–75.
[4] *Byron the Poet*, p. 25.

temps réel" become the same time, the poet becomes both seer and seen, and the particulars of his little span on earth become human history and *la condition humaine.*

Of all who have written on Byron, only Joyce, who did not write *on* him but absorbed him, as it were, into his own fictional universe, saw that this was so. His insertion of Childe Harold, the Giaour, Lara, and others of Byron's characters into the vast network of interlocking and overlapping characters of *Finnegans Wake* makes it clear that he saw Childe Harold as "HCE," Humphrey Chimpden Earwicker, Here Comes Everybody, mankind.[5] It is a criticism only slightly in error, for, as we have seen, Harold is ultimately only an aspect of his creator, the poet, who is the true HCE; and yet in Canto IV Byron too sees him as man, one of the "forms which live and suffer" now faded "away into Destruction's mass" (clxiv),

> *Which gathers shadow—substance—life, and all*
> *That we* [Harold, the poet, the reader, all men]
> *inherit in its mortal shroud—*
> *And spreads the dim and universal pall*
> *Through which all things grow phantoms.*
>
> *(clxv)*

It is certainly with this in mind that Byron writes in the Dedication, "I recur from fiction to truth";[6] it is his announcement of his own final clear awareness that a narrative of the invented circumstances of fictional man, however punctuated and controlled by the poet's voice, in the long run would serve him less well than the situation of man himself in and of this world and speaking in his own accents—whether he be the speaker of *Childe Harold* IV or the narrator of *Don Juan.*

Although Cantos I, II, and III of *Childe Harold* provide ample evidence of Byron's knowledge of the long tradition of topographical poetry—from Virgil, Horace, and Ovid through Denham, Pope, Thomson, Dyer, and Wordsworth—and also of the several offshoots of this main line of development (e.g., the

---

[5] See my "Byron in *Finnegans Wake*," in J. P. Dalton and Clive Hart (eds.), *Twelve and a Tilly: Essays on the Occasion of the 25th Anniversary of "Finnegans Wake"* (London, 1966), pp. 40–51.
[6] *P*, II, 321.

ruin poem, the regional poem, the travel poem), it is not until Canto IV that Byron settles his poem squarely in that tradition. As Robert Aubin indicates, *Childe Harold* is full of familiar *voyage pittoresque* motifs: "invocation, address, order in variety, praise of the women of a district, genre scenes, water-mirror, storm and calm, and graveyard and ruin sentiment thoroughly digested by the poet, 'a ruin amidst ruins.' "[7] Also inherent in this form is the practice of meditating upon the various scenes, of moralizing the song, and in Byron's "more varied, more flexible and more personal use" of this aspect of the tradition[8] lies the particular distinction of *Childe Harold*.

Yet over all there is a crucial distinction to be made between Byron's poem and, say, Spenser's *Ruines of Rome* or Dyer's "Grongar Hill" or Thomson's *The Seasons*, a distinction that is a direct result of his earlier experimentation with multiple points of view and his final absorption of these into the vision of the poet in Canto IV. There is nothing in Spenser or the other poets quite comparable to Byron's idea of the "ruin amidst ruins," of the speaker incorporating into himself the ruins of the past, the desolation of the present, and the looming darkness of the future. None of the other poets employs the particulars of one man's life as symbolic of all men's lives; and all of the others arrive at some firm consolation for the ravages of time, man's fierce but misguided ambition, and the fall of empire. "Behold," writes Spenser, for example, in *The Ruines of Time*,

> *and by ensample see,*
> *That all is vanitie and griefe of minde,*
> *Ne other comfort in this world can be,*
> *But hope of heauen, and heart to God inclinde;*
> *For all the rest must needs be left behinde.*
>
> (*ll. 582–86*)

Byron recognizes the consolations and they appear in his poem; but all are finally momentary or illusory—nature, the world of the mind, art, and in *Don Juan* even laughter. He does not so

---

[7] *Topographical Poetry*, p. 256.
[8] Joseph, *Byron the Poet*, p. 29. Cf. Kenneth Bruffee's argument that the "historico-literary travel poem" is only *Childe Harold*'s "disguise, its pretended genre" ("The Synthetic Hero," p. 672).

much reject the consolations as they reject him. What remains is the vitality of despair, nurtured continually by the dream of love and the nightmare of love lost; by the renewed sense of the heart's life and the knowledge that only once must man bear the "fardels" of that heart (clxvi); by the eternal curse of man's mortality that is also, in the end, his release from pain; by the curious strength which comes from a certain knowledge of one's own weakness and finitude.

If, then, the "central theme" of *Childe Harold*, "as it finally discloses itself, is the traditional one of lament for lost empire and for the decay of love, and of the triumph of time over human mortality," it is not, as Joseph claims, "redeemed only by that quasi-immortality which the human spirit achieves when it 'bodies forth' the forms of art and literature,"[9] but rather by man's indomitable spirit and mind, which can not only endure its desolation but can create out of universal death and chaos a coherent vision of fragments sufficient to sustain man in his dying. Byron's technique, then, is not so much that of Spenser and Du Bellay as it is that of Eliot and Yeats, Joyce and Faulkner, the human voice, at the last "ding dong of doom," still talking—and saying heroically, with Manfred, "Old man, 'tis not so difficult to die."[10]

I

The theme (to be more accurate, the interlocking themes) of Canto IV is simple: it represents the culmination of the various developments we have seen in the first three cantos, the tales, and in *Manfred*; and it is voiced, as usual, in a variety of ways that connect this last canto, and all of *Childe Harold*, with the other poems.

---

[9] *Ibid.*, p. 27.

[10] Although I cannot agree with the limited biographical implications of the last part of it, E. E. Bostetter's comment on Manfred's death speech is pertinent here: "Within the context of the drama . . . the line means 'It is not so difficult to die—alone—without comfort.' But, within the context of Byron's own dramatic struggle, it means, 'It is not so difficult to live—alone—without comfort'" (*The Romantic Ventriloquists*, p. 280).

After the initial vision of the "dying Glory" of Venice, which smiles sadly "O'er the far times" (i), the theme of creation is immediately introduced to bind together Cantos III and IV and to announce clearly and strongly the emphasis on the poet initiated in Canto III and now capitalized upon:

> The Beings of the Mind are not of clay:
>   Essentially immortal, they create
> And multiply in us a brighter ray
>   And more beloved existence: that which Fate
>   Prohibits to dull life in this our state
> Of mortal bondage, by these Spirits supplied,
>   First exiles, then replaces what we hate;
>   Watering the heart whose early flowers have died,
> And with a fresher growth replenishing the void.
>
> (v)

It is a brave statement by the poet, too brave for his incisive mind to accept as final; but it is also an extraordinarily poetic and allusive stanza. Not only does it recall the " 'Tis to create" stanza of Canto III, but the distinction between man and the unclay-like beings of his imagination, the contrast between dream and reality, the power of "Fate" that decrees and manages this dull life; and, finally, it neatly reverses the theme of exile, initially voiced by Harold and, after Canto II, by the poet, by seeing the imagination as exiling mortality and replacing it with immortality. The allusion in the last two lines is a key one, for it contains the seeds of the transition from the hope of a "brighter ray" and "more beloved existence" to a renewed realization of the futility of even that hope. If the imaginative "Beings of the Mind" here seem to have power to water "the heart whose early flowers have died, / And with a fresher growth [replenish] the void" (IV, v), we should recall that the poet's own memory of his creation of Childe Harold bears only

> The furrows of long thought, and dried-up tears,
> Which, ebbing, leave a sterile track behind,
> O'er which all heavily the journeying years
> Plod the last sands of life,—where not a flower
> appears.
> (III, iii)

Thus in Canto IV we are immediately shown that the creation of such beings "Essentially immortal" is merely a "refuge of our youth and age— / The first from Hope, the last from Vacancy" (vi). It is a "wan feeling" that haply fills the poet's page in *Childe Harold*, not a dramatic triumph; for, finally, "there are things whose strong reality / Outshines our fairy-land" (vi). Yet even these, created not out of fantasy and the teeming brain but rather out of flesh and blood, appearing "like Truth," "disappeared like dreams; / And whatsoe'er they were—are now but so" (vii). As a true Romantic, Byron asserts that he could replace them if he would, for his mind "still teems" with "many a form which aptly seems / Such as I sought for, and at moments found" (vii), but these too must be let go. They are "overweening phantasies unsound," and the poet's ear is tuned to "other voices," his eye to "other sights" (vii). This is the same thematic (or choreographic) movement we have seen earlier in *Childe Harold*. In Canto III the poet interrupts his apparent absorption in the life intense of nature with "But this is not my theme; and I return / To that which is immediate" (lxxvi). In Canto II, amid the glorious visions of Turkey and Greece the poet cannot restrain the note of present woe that asserts itself despite himself: "Alas! her [Greece's] woes will still pervade my strain" (lxxix), and in his attempt to rebuild Greece in his mind's eye, he must confess, "nor ev'n can Fancy's eye / Restore what Time hath laboured to deface" (x). With this in mind he chastises man, the "Poor child of Doubt and Death" (iii), for lifting his eye to heaven, dreaming "on future Joy and Woe" (iv):

> *Regard and weigh yon dust before it flies:*
> *That little urn saith more than thousand Homilies.*
>
> *(iv)*

Even in Canto I the same rejection of dream is apparent, though it is less clear because of Byron's imperfect separation of narrator, Harold, and poet.

The movement from fiction to truth that Byron announces to Hobhouse in the dedication to Canto IV, then, is a continual impulse of the poet, though nowhere perhaps as forceful as in this final canto. Harold disappears as if he were a dream (clxiv, clxxxv); and if perchance there were something about him

273

that "could be classed / With forms which live and suffer," that
too "fades away into Destruction's mass" (clxiv), that "dim and
universal pall / Through which all things grow phantoms" (clxv).
We must be clear on one point, however—the intensity of
Byron's hope for fame as a poet. The letters show it abundantly,
mostly by way of the vehemence with which he condemns
"scribbling";[11] and even in Canto IV of *Childe Harold* he can
write,

> I twine
> My hopes of being remembered in my line
> With my land's language.
>
> (ix)

However, he comes to see those hopes as slimmer than slim,
perhaps indeed no hopes at all, because

> Of its own beauty is the mind diseased,
> And fevers into false creation—where,
> Where are the forms the sculptor's soul hath
> seized?
> In him alone.
>
> (cxxii)

And even those forms are, in his superb phrase, "The unreached
Paradise of our despair" (cxxii). As with creation, so it is with
love; into the maw of destruction and desolation all is swept:

> Who loves, raves—'tis youth's frenzy—but the cure
> Is bitterer still, as charm by charm unwinds
> Which robed our idols, and we see too sure
> Nor Worth nor Beauty dwells from out the mind's
> Ideal shape of such; yet still it binds
> The fatal spell, and still it draws us on,

---

[11] For an excellent analysis of Byron's ambition for fame as a drama-
tist, see David V. Erdman's "Byron's Stage Fright: The History of
His Ambition and Fear of Writing for the Stage," *ELH*, VI (1939),
219–43. An earlier but less detailed discussion of this point is found
in T. H. Vail Motter, "Byron's *Werner* Re-estimated: A Neglected
Chapter in Nineteenth Century Stage History," in Hardin Craig (ed.),
Essays in Dramatic Literature: The Parrott Presentation Volume
(Princeton, N.J., 1935).

Childe Harold, Canto IV

> *Reaping the whirlwind from the oft-sown winds;*
> *The stubborn heart, its alchemy begun,*
> *Seems ever near the prize—wealthiest when most*
> > *undone.*
> > *(cxxiii)*

Love is what the sane world judges to be the madness of youth
(of Harold, Rousseau, the poet), the aura of paradise which is
dispelled by the light of common day and, to paraphrase Keats,
by the knowledge the mind sucks from the teat of experience.
The heart yearns for an ideal which the mind persistently
imagines in its quest for the new dawn of Eden, and then refuses stubbornly and humanly to acquiesce in the mind's disillusionment:

> *We wither from our youth, we gasp away—*
> *Sick—sick; unfound the boon—unslaked the thirst,*
> *Though to the last, in verge of our decay,*
> *Some phantom lures, such as we sought at first—*
> *But all too late,—so are we doubly curst.*
> > *(cxxiv)*

And, after all, love and dreams of paradise regained are no
different from "Fame, Ambition, Avarice,"

> *Each idle—and all ill—and none the worst—*
> *For all are meteors with a different name,*
> *And Death the sable smoke where vanishes the flame.*
> > *(cxxiv)*

The double curse, then, is man's birth—not the curse
of original sin but the curse of possessing a heart and mind that
aspire beyond themselves—and man's persistence, though he
is a fallen ruin, in being human. Even if, in our flawed makeup,
love does appear upon the scene, "accident, blind contact, and
the strong / Necessity of loving" having "removed / Antipathies"
(cxxv)—even if man's motives are pure,

> *Circumstance, that unspiritual God*
> *And Miscreator, makes and helps along*
> *Our coming evils with a crutch-like rod,*
> *Whose touch turns Hope to dust,—the dust we all*
> > *have trod.*
> > *(cxxv)*

Byron draws the logical conclusion, which is overwrought indeed in its total pessimism:

> *Our life is a false nature—'tis not in*
> *The harmony of things,—this hard decree,*
> *This uneradicable taint of Sin,*
> *This boundless Upas, this all-blasting tree,*
> *Whose root is Earth—whose leaves and branches*
> *be*
> *The skies which rain their plagues on men like*
> *dew—*
> *Disease, death, bondage—all the woes we see,*
> *And worse, the woes we see not—which throb*
> *through*
> *The immedicable soul, with heart-aches ever new.*
>
> *(cxxvi)*

The theological overtones of the third line seem to me drowned here in the universal cry of a humanity doomed not by its sin but by its very humanness. In such a world the ruins of paradise can never be rebuilt, love never revives, and even the bright beings of the mind slide into the morass. Shelley's wreck of hope remains a wreck eternally. Only in the mind is there refuge; there, at least in moments,

> *Though from our birth the Faculty divine*
> *Is chained and tortured—cabined, cribbed, confined,*
> *And bred in darkness, lest the Truth should shine*
> *Too brightly on the unpreparéd mind,*
> *The beam pours in.*
>
> *(cxxvii)*

That beam, however bright, carries only the burden of further darkness as we have seen, and it is only in the coherent vision of the chaos that the mind, secure in that knowledge but constantly shattered by the truth of darkness, remains whole—just as the heart, like a shattered mirror, progressively disintegrates, yet brokenly lives on. It is that strength that the poet learns; in that he will survive and go on creating those beings of the mind who are of clay after all, who will rise and fall, be celebrated and mourned, and who will continue to feed the agony of despair out of which, for Byron, the only creation can come.

276

II

Supporting these basic themes is the skeletal structure of the canto, which may best be examined in its initial form (Byron's first manuscript version) before his addition of later stanzas and sections. We know a good deal about the progress of the poem from his letters. On June 26, 1817, he wrote at least a few stanzas; by July 1 he had "roughened off about rather better than thirty"; 56 were completed by July 9; "ninety and eight" by July 15; 104 by July 19; and on July 20 he announced to Murray that he had "completed the 4th and *ultimate* Canto of *Childe Harold*. It consists of 126 stanzas. . . ."[12]

Although it is impossible to reconstruct the precise order in which Byron composed because of revisions in stanza numbers and his habit throughout *Childe Harold* of writing in blocks of stanzas (in Canto IV this is even clearer because of his further experiments with run-on stanzas[13]), it is possible to make some fairly good guesses about how the 126-stanza version of the canto originally evolved. After the opening stanza on Venice, which places the poet directly in the scene, Byron moved quickly (stanzas iii–x) to the poetry of Venice (Tasso), thence to poetry generally (Shakespeare and Otway), and thence to himself as poet, his hope for fame, and his sense of his own certain ruin:

---

[12] Ltrs. to Murray, 1, 9, 15, and 20 July 1817, in *LJ*, IV, 141, 147, 150, 153. See also Coleridge's introduction to the canto, in *P*, II, 311–19, for a list of those stanzas appearing in the original manuscript, those added later to that manuscript, and those that appear for the first time in Byron's final fair copy.

[13] Harold Stein has calculated that 1 in every 5 stanzas of Canto IV is run on—as opposed to 1 in 39 for Canto III, 1 in 38 for Canto II, and 1 in 41 for Canto I ("A Note on the Versification of *Childe Harold*," *MLN*, XLII [1927], 34–35). This indication of the much greater coherence of the inner structure of the canto is clearly a reflection of the over-all coherence and sureness of Byron's vision, as well as of his strategy of totally absorbing all voices into his own. It is interesting that Hazlitt, who greatly disliked the canto (he called it "an indigestion of the mind"), objected to the perversity of Byron's style, especially the run-on stanzas (*The Complete Works of William Hazlitt*, ed. P. P. Howe [21 vols.; London and Toronto, 1932], XIX, 36–37).

> *The thorns which I have reaped are of the tree*
> *I planted,—they have torn me,—and I bleed:*
> *I should have known what fruit would spring from*
> *   such a seed.*
>
> *   (x)*

With this description the transition back to Venice—her "withered power" and the "spouseless Adriatic" (xi)—is made easily, and the now intertwined speaker and city are brought together logically in the mind of the poet through the agency of memory and the heart:

> *I loved her from my boyhood—she to me*
> *Was a fairy city of the heart,*
> *Rising like water-columns from the sea—*
> *Of Joy the sojourn, and of Wealth the mart.*
>
> *   (xviii)*

The opening stanza of the canto is now invested with its full sense: the fairy city that rises magically in the unsullied imagination of the boy is the same city conjured up by the poet "As from the stroke of the Enchanter's wand" (i), with one difference: in the context of Venice's withered life the poet's superimposition of his renewed boyhood vision is now doomed to failure by its very nature. Only momentarily can Venice evoke in him the memory of some happy moments (xix), all too few and fleeting to blot out the rush of a dimmer past. The coda of this block of stanzas, which all deal with memory and the mind's defiant persistence in functioning despite all adversity, is a properly stark, almost foolishly heroic, image:

> *But from their nature will the Tannen grow*
> *Loftiest on loftiest and least sheltered rocks,*
> *Rooted in barrenness.*
>
> *   (xx)*

Translating for us, the poet bravely asserts, out of his own still feeling heart and indomitable mind, what we have been hearing in other forms with increasing frequency throughout *Childe Harold*:

> *Existence may be borne, and the deep root*
> *Of life and sufferance make its firm abode*

Childe Harold, Canto IV

> *In bare and desolated bosoms: mute*
> *The camel labours with the heaviest load,*
> *And the wolf dies in silence—not bestowed*
> *In vain should such example be; if they,*
> *Things of ignoble or of savage mood,*
> *Endure and shrink not, we of nobler clay*
> *May temper it to bear,—it is but for a day.*
>
> *(xxi)*

Not only is it "existence" that may be borne, but also the memories of that existence prompted by the active mind and earnest heart of man. The shift from the personal "I" of stanzas xviii–xix to the "we" of this stanza is unobtrusive but critical, for the poet speaks now not merely in his own person about himself but as man about mankind, past and present. Time thus converges, by means of what Byron calls "the electric chain wherewith we are darkly bound" (xxiii) to each other, to the past, and to mortality:

> *And slight withal may be the things which bring*
> *Back on the heart the weight which it would fling*
> *Aside for ever.*
>
> *(xxiii)*

This is the same burden Byron speaks of later in the canto as the "fardels of the heart," relief from which is gained only by the knowledge (or is it only a hope?) that we can never "be made the same" again (clxvi).

As it was originally written, the section (stanzas i, iii–xi, xv, xviii–xxv) concludes with an abrupt movement similar to what Byron has been using in the earlier cantos to revive our sense of Harold's presence. Here, however, the sudden wrenching of the mind back to the ostensible theme of his song is translated into a pulling back from the risk of too personal memory ("The mourned—the loved—the lost—too many! yet how few!" [xxiv]) to the poet's larger vision of his own essentially symbolic role:

> *But my Soul wanders; I demand it back*
> *To meditate amongst decay, and stand*
> *A ruin amidst ruins.*
>
> *(xxv)*

The road is now open to explore all of Italy, and, in particular, Rome, as the landscape of his own mind and, conversely, to explore the essential being of man as a microcosmic Rome. The dynamic interplay and counterpoint of these two movements are at the base of what sharply distinguishes the canto from other similar genre pieces, gives it its peculiarly moving quality, and provides it the coherence that it is so often denied.

Byron could never recognize quickly such clarity of conception and aim, however, and thus he must tinker and change and, especially, add. The saddest aspect of *Childe Harold's Pilgrimage* as a poem is that Byron never came to see that his "impressions," as he inveterately called them, did have initial coherence, and that his efforts to fill them in, to load every rift with what he thought was ore, were often out of tune or useless. His mind conceptualized only slowly or gradually, and his pen usually went winging on its way before the shaper in him was fully aware of where it was going. By then often it was too late. To be sure, he was not entirely to blame: if Gifford on occasion was astute enough to see that the poem was askew, all too frequently his protests were mild or unspoken (and not always articulate) and Hobhouse was simply too much there, as a busy-body midwife, throughout the entire poem. Thus, almost despite himself, as if unaware of his own absorption of the Hobhouse-narrator's function into his own persona,[14] Byron allows his ghost to parade through Canto IV, sometimes powerfully, but almost always awkwardly.

For example, to the original first twenty stanzas evoking the magic spell of Venice's fairyland of yore and her present melancholy beauty even in ruins, Byron somehow felt compelled to add stanzas xii–xiv, with their bald emphasis upon vanished power and might, excusing of enslavement in the name of glory, and matter-of-fact account of bloodshed in the name of victory. Similarly, in the added stanzas xvi and xvii the clear voice of the now-obsolete narrator is heard, with all its insular realism and devotion to fact and the particulars of history. These

---

[14] I cannot, however, agree with Lovell and others who see Canto IV as totally reflecting the attitudes of Hobhouse; for this point of view, see, e.g., *Byron: The Record of a Quest*, pp. 176–78.

lines, flawing as I believe they do Byron's total design, will not be the last we hear from him, but there are other moments when his absorption into the mind and voice of the poet are accomplished with superb skill—in the frequent paeans to liberty and its association with the idyllic past; in the less parochial visions, however fleeting and illusory, of hope (e.g., stanza xlvii); in the historical particulars of the relationship between Italy's greatest men, their art, and their homeland; and in the poet's adoption of the erstwhile narrator's storyteller mannerisms and devices (the question and answer, the confession of ignorance, the use of "perchance," "it may be," "it seems," and the like). In the hands of the poet all of these devices, which in the earlier cantos signaled the limited view of the narrator and necessitated comment, implicit or explicit, by the poet, have become auxiliaries to the central theme. That auxiliary function of the minute particulars is evident both in the passages themselves and in the kind of summary statements Byron makes, which are similar to those of the poet in earlier cantos. For example, the references to Michelangelo, Alfieri, Galileo, and Machiavelli (liv), which would have been properly made by the narrator earlier (with perhaps a simple comment on their loss and a lament that no one replaces them to make Italy great once more), are now made by the poet: their "dust," like Italy's and that of paradise, is "Even in itself an immortality" (liv); their minds, like the poet's, "Might furnish forth creation" (lv); and Time, the destroyer, will perhaps not deny them (and the poet-creator) the spirit to "soar from ruin" (lv), for their decay

> *Is still impregnate with divinity,*
> *Which gilds it with revivifying ray.*
>
> > *(lv)*

Prophetically, Byron can roll all into one ball—man, city, country, world—and thrust it before us boldly:

> *There is the moral of all human tales;*
> > *'Tis but the same rehearsal of the past,*
> > *First Freedom, and then Glory—when that fails,*
> > *Wealth—Vice—Corruption,—Barbarism at last.*
> > *And History, with all her volumes vast,*
> > *Hath but* one *page.*
>
> > *(cviii)*

And that page is man, in whom all ages and realms are crowded in one span, and in whom there is "matter for all feeling" (cix) —admiration and exultation, contempt and compassion, weeping and laughter.

But to return to the structure of the canto as it appears before the many later accretions, after the initial twenty stanzas were completed Byron probably moved directly into the subject pointed to in his introduction—Italy as a whole (stanzas xliiff.):

> *Italia! oh, Italia! thou who hast*
> *The fatal gift of Beauty, which became*
> *A funeral dower of present woes and past—*
> *(xlii)*

a passage that patently echoes the canto's opening dirge for Venice and the "spouseless Adriatic." As if to point up the organization of his whole poem, Byron envisions all of Italy united "In ruin" (xliv), even as Servius Sulpicius described it to Cicero in the famous letter on the death of his daughter.[15] Once again Byron is deliberately concentrating all time into an intense present by blending views of Italy's desolation written at the time of Cicero and at the time of his own earlier trip with the present; he then goes on to incorporate them all into his poet-persona and his poem:

> *That page* [the letter] *is now before me, and on mine*
> *His Country's ruin added to the mass*
> *Of perished states he mourned in their decline,*
> *And I in desolation.*
> *(xlvi)*

The mourning thus is for "perished states," for Italy, and for man, for the self—all "added to the mass," to which Byron later, we recall, consigns even Harold and the other beings of the mind (clxiv).

To expand the significance of Italian desolation further, and to join this last canto even more firmly to the earlier three, Byron next moves to Florence, which he calls "the Etrurian

---

[15] See Byron's note to stanza xliv of Canto IV, in *P*, II, 362n.

Athens" (xlviii). In its "fairy halls" (an echo of the description of Venice as "a fairy city") not only learning but the image of love rose and stands eternal in the Venus de Medici. In that sculpture

> *the veil*
> *Of heaven is half undrawn—within the pale*
> *We stand, and in that form and face behold*
> *What Mind can make, when Nature's self would fail.*
> *(xlix)*

It is

> *The unruffled mirror of the loveliest dream*
> *That ever left the sky on the deep soul to beam.*
> *(liii)*

Significantly, Byron's poet responds to the statue with his heart (which "Reels with its fulness"), and condemns those who with pedantry and learning would unravel the mysteries of the form (l).[16] Thus Greece and Italy are united, as it were, in an image of love frozen into stone (foreshadowing the Niobe image to appear later, in stanza lxxix), whose very beauty and significance are belied by its being

> *All breathing human passion far above,*
> *That leaves a heart high-sorrowful and cloy'd,*
> *A burning forehead, and a parching tongue.*[17]

"The weight / Of earth recoils upon us" (lii) and we must let the vision go. To Byron art is, in the long run, an unsatisfactory substitute for reality, despite its purity. His mind and heart yearn for that paradise, as did the hearts of Keats, Shelley, and others, but in the end the world of art is dead and cold, calling

---

[16] As is well known, Byron was unusually insensitive to sculpture and architecture for most of his life, and Hazlitt took him to task for displaying the very pedantry and "common cant of connoisseurship" Byron inveighs against in stanza l (Howe [ed.], *Complete Works of Hazlitt,* X, 165n). I see no reason, however, to doubt that he was genuinely moved by the Venus: the lines are instinct with feeling. Byron is also on record as saying that buildings and sculptures are more impressive and "poetical" than "any part of inanimate nature" (see p. 249n, above).

[17] Keats, "Ode on a Grecian Urn."

forth the "Spirit's homage" but yielding "Less than it feels" (lxi), and does not minister to the shattered heart.

As in Canto III, the poet turns to nature, seeking there for that which art will not or cannot yield to him. This section (stanzas lxii–lxxvii) seems to me to contain some of the weakest portions of the canto. The scenes described are neither fully digested by Byron nor incorporated within the scheme so artfully begun and by now well established. First, there is a view of Thrasimene past, when Hannibal conquered the Romans, and Thrasimene present (lxii–lxv). The stanzas have none of the power of the Waterloo scenes, nor do they go beyond the simple contrast of bloody past and peaceful present—unless the stream called Sanguinetto running through the landscape of Thrasimene present is intended, ironically, as a curse of blood on the earth. By contrast, the stream Clitumnus is described as "the purest God of gentle waters," which must "surely" be "unprofaned by slaughters— / A mirror and a bath for Beauty's youngest daughters!" (lxvi). A temple nearby gives rise to thoughts of "the Genius of the place," whose influence can sprinkle coolness on the heart

> *and from the dry dust*
> *Of weary life a moment lave it clean*
> *With Nature's biptism,—'tis to him ye must*
> *Pay orisons for this suspension of disgust.*
> *(lxviii)*

If there are only occasional and meager indications in these passages of their unity with the rest of the poem, the stanzas on the Falls of Terni almost redeem the whole. Hazlitt completely missed the point when he attacked Byron vehemently for making it,

> without any reason that I can find, tortuous, dark, and boiling like a witch's cauldron. On the contrary, it is simple and majestic in its character, a clear mountain-stream that pours an uninterrupted, lengthened sheet of water over a precipice of eight hundred feet, in perpendicular descent, and gracefully winding its way to the channel beyond, while on one side the stained rock rises bare and stately the whole height, and on the other, the gradual green woods ascend, moistened

by the ceaseless spray, and lulled by the roar of the waterfall, as the ear enjoys the sound of famous poet's verse. . . . It has nothing of the texture of Lord Byron's terzains, twisted, zigzag, pent up and struggling for a vent, broken off at the end of a line, or point of a rock, diving under ground, or out of the reader's comprehension, and pieced on to another stanza or shelving rock.[18]

I quote this passage at length for several reasons: to show Hazlitt's general lack of sympathy with Byron's verse; to illustrate the general critical misunderstanding of many of Byron's descriptive passages; and, most important, to demonstrate the difference between mere description and the kind of symbolic significance with which Byron endows his picture of the Falls. Very likely the Falls of Terni were as Hazlitt describes them, but, as Byron consistently maintained, mere *"descriptive* poetry" was "the *lowest* department of the art."[19] Like Wordsworth, and perhaps all great poets, he knew that he must wait to allow his memory to select from his initial "strong and confused" impressions and reduce "them to order."[20] If, then, the Falls of Terni stanzas are an example of the conventionally sublime (and they certainly partake of that tradition), they also constitute an evolving image of the central theme of *Childe Harold.* "The Hell of Waters" "howl," "hiss," and "boil in endless torture" and "great agony," pounding the surrounding cliffs, yet rising in mist that in turn settles to the ground to make the earth green (lxix). Destroyer as well as creator and nourisher, it is not merely "nature" here that is "Horribly beautiful" (lxxii), but life itself. And amid the torture and the agony of that "infernal surge" is the "Iris" of the sun, sitting "Like Hope upon a death-bed" or "Love watching Madness with unalterable mien" (lxxii). Thus Byron unites, with great power, the earlier image of the tannen mind wresting life from the "bleak, gray granite" of the barren

---

[18] Howe (ed.), *Complete Works of Hazlitt,* X, 258.
[19] "Reply to Blackwood's *Edinburgh Magazine,*" in *LJ,* IV, 493.
[20] Ltr. to Murray, 9 May 1817, in *LJ,* IV, 119. This does not, I think, invalidate my earlier claim that Byron's initial "impressions" were very often more coherent than he knew. It was after reducing these to "order" for the purpose of writing them down that he frequently saw less order than he thought he had achieved and then began to tinker and expand.

reaches of the Alps with this image of the heart persisting in its life "while all around is torn / By the distracted waters" (lxxii).

This is the point that Byron reached, I believe, in those "rather better than thirty stanzas" he roughened off by the first of July.[21] The insertion into the skeletal framework I have outlined of stanzas xxx to xxxix on Petrarch and Tasso was a logical move by Byron to link his own poet, standing "A ruin amidst ruins," with the tombs of two poets whom he associated with love and greatness of mind, and who also were victims of the world.[22] With *Manfred* still fresh in his mind (he had just

---

[21] The fact that the stanza on Horace (lxxvii) was originally numbered lii by Byron, and the present stanzas ii, xii–xiv, xvi–xvii, xxvii–xxix, xl–xli, xlvii, li–lii, and liv–lx do not appear in the original draft (see *P*, II, 316), lend strength to this conjecture.

[22] Byron had only recently completed *The Lament of Tasso*, the manuscript of which is dated April 20, 1817. Although ordinary in most respects, this poem, somewhat reminiscent of *The Prisoner of Chillon*, reiterates several of the themes of *Childe Harold*, *Manfred*, and many of the other poems that have been examined here. Byron imagines Tasso confined in the Hospital of Sant' Anna, battling with his agony and sustained by his undying love for Leonora d'Este. His vision of life in this madhouse is perhaps his most grimly effective description of the human condition:

> this vast Lazar-house of many woes[,]
> *Where laughter is not mirth, nor thought the mind,*
> *Nor words a language, nor e'en men mankind;*
> *Where cries reply to curses, shrieks to blows,*
> *And each is tortured in his separate hell—*
> *For we are crowded in our solitudes—*
> *Many, but each divided by the wall,*
> *Which echoes Madness in her babbling moods.*
>
> (*ll. 83–90*)

Tasso's initial strength to battle despair rises from the creation of his beings of the mind, the *Gerusalemme Liberata*. After its completion, without this "Friend" (l. 34) to lean on, he must rely on the "innate force / Of my own spirit" (ll. 45–46) and more particularly on his love for Leonora. This latter theme, in effect, becomes the main focus of the poem, which Byron manipulates into a fairly simple but effective, if too long, exploration of the irony inherent in all men's love. For Tasso, it is love that transforms mortality into godhood and nature into paradise, but it is also love that leads him to imprisonment and a living death. Love is thus his curse as well as his salvation, his gift of life as well as his sentence of death, his divinity as well as his withering mortality.

rewritten the third act in late April and early May of 1817), it is perhaps not surprising to find Byron universalizing the death of poets and the circumstances of his own life to date in terms reminiscent of the "triumph" of Manfred:

> *If from society we learn to live,*
> *'Tis Solitude should teach us how to die;*
> *It hath no flatterers—Vanity can give*
> *No hollow aid; alone—man with his God must strive:*

> *Or, it may be, with Demons, who impair*
> *The strength of better thoughts, and seek their prey*
> *In melancholy bosoms—such as were*
> *Of moody texture from their earliest day,*
> *And loved to dwell in darkness and dismay*
> *Deeming themselves predestined to a doom*
> *Which is not of the pangs that pass away;*
> *Making the Sun like blood, the Earth a tomb,*
> *The tomb a hell—and Hell itself a murkier gloom.*
>
> (xxxiii–xxxiv)

For the last phrase Byron originally wrote, "and life one universal gloom"; the flat statement was perhaps so sweepingly absolute that his own sensibilities forced him to withdraw from it in favor of the indirection of a controlling symbol.

That symbol is Rome, and most of the original manuscript of Canto IV is built around it. In Rome's collocation of ruins are absorbed Harold and the poet, the narrator and all mankind, the past and present, into a kind of eternal present mirroring life. All of the individual "agonies . . . of a day" are swept into this "world . . . at our feet as fragile as our clay" (lxxviii). The image of Niobe that introduces the Rome theme is precisely right: children dead, heart, mind, and body turned to stone, voiceless in her eternal agony, and (in Byron's addition to the traditional image) holding in her withered hands an empty burial urn (lxxix). In Rome "The very sepulchres lie tenantless" (lxxix)—a brilliant echo of the tenantless skull and ruined shrines of Greece in Canto II—and Niobe's tears look back to Canto III—

> *The furrows of long thought, and dried-up tears,*
> *Which, ebbing, leave a sterile track behind,*
>
> (iii)

—and forward to a later passage in Canto IV:

> *the tears*
> *And blood of earth flow on as they have flowed,*
> *An universal Deluge, which appears*
> *Without an Ark for wretched Man's abode,*
> *And ebbs but to reflow!*
>
> *(xcii)*

The entire canto is in many respects built around such central images, or, rather, scenes and lines that Byron builds into images. As a result the net effect of the canto, and in large measure of the whole poem, depends upon the reader's connecting image with image in one sprawling yet interlocking network.[23] Thus, in this canto, to the image of Venice dead, of Tasso and Petrarch dead, of Rome's ruin and decay, Byron adds that of the tomb of Cecilia Metella (stanzas xcix–ciii). This image conveys not the impartiality of death (she may or may not have lived a good woman, may have died young or old, the poet does not know) so much as the indifference of life, which neither rewards the virtuous nor punishes the evil, which withholds the bay from the brow of love and crowns the tyrant of hate, which ignores all woes and cuts short joy and beauty. The effect of Cecilia's tomb upon the poet dramatizes as explicitly as Byron will ever do the paradox of the creative and revivifying nature of the poet's despair and of his desperate clinging to sanity amid the indiscriminate waste. The circular chain of association goes something like this: the tomb and death → conjectures about Cecilia's past → memory → personal recollections → bright images from the past to shore against his despair → present desolation → loss of hope → thoughts of death. The whole passage is, I think, an extraordinary one:

> *I know not why—but standing thus by thee*
> *It seems as if I had thine inmate known,*
> *Thou Tomb! and other days come back on me*
> *With recollected music, though the tone*
> *Is changed and solemn, like the cloudy groan*
> *Of dying thunder on the distant wind;*

---

[23] Cf. Ridenour, "Byron and the Romantic Pilgrimage," p. 81.

Childe Harold, Canto IV

> Yet could I seat me by this ivied stone
> Till I had bodied forth the heated mind
> Forms from the floating wreck which Ruin leaves
>   behind:
>
> And from the planks, far shattered o'er the rocks,
>   Built me a little bark of hope, once more
>   To battle with the Ocean and the shocks
>   Of the loud breakers, and the ceaseless roar
>   Which rushes on the solitary shore
>   Where all lies foundered that was ever dear:
>   But could I gather from the wave-worn store
>   Enough for my rude boat, where should I steer?
> There woos no home, nor hope, nor life, save what
>   is here.
>   (civ–cv)

Byron immediately builds on these stanzas, as well as on man's inability to penetrate the mysteries of life and death while recognizing their universal power and victory, by presenting the Palatine as strewn in chaotic fragments over the landscape, unrecognizable, irredeemable even to the creative imagination of the poet:

> Cypress and ivy, weed and wallflower grown
>   Matted and massed together—hillocks heaped
> On what were chambers—arch crushed, column
>   strown
> In fragments—choked up vaults, and frescos steeped
> In subterranean damps, where the owl peeped,
> Deeming it midnight—Temples—Baths—or Halls?
> Pronounce who can: for all that Learning reaped
> From her research hath been, that these are walls.
>   (cvii)

It is in such striking image clusters or, to use Ezra Pound's term, "radiant nodes"[24] that Byron finds "the moral of all human tales," the "same rehearsal of the past," first life and freedom, then vice and corruption, at last barbarism and desolation (cviii). And if the rude boat the poet fashions out of these images is far too frail to carry hope, it is sufficient for sanity.

---

[24] *Gaudier-Brzeska: A Memoir* (1st ed., 1916; London, 1960), p. 92.

Certainly none of these clusters is more effective and compelling than that of the Colosseum and the dying gladiator, the former a scene he had already found useful in the revised third act of *Manfred* (III, iv, 8–41). In *Childe Harold*, however, Byron goes beyond the *Manfred* lines and has his poet make an offering unto Time, which out of the wreck of the Colosseum "made a shrine / And temple more divinely desolate" (cxxxi). The offering is properly the "Ruins of years." To Nemesis, Manfred-like, he leaves his vengeance (cxxxii–cxxxiii), and reserves unto himself the final curse upon mankind:

> *Though I be ashes; a far hour shall wreak*
> *The deep prophetic fulness of this verse,*
> *And pile on human heads the mountain of my curse!*
> *(cxxxiv)*

Thus, titanic and undefeated, the poet assumes for the first time the prophetic role latent in almost all of Byron's poetry, voicing Cassandra's unheeded cry of doom (and perhaps indeed assuming her madness as well) and the Christ-like role of forgiver (cxxxv). This latter role, it must be admitted, is new and somewhat startling for Byron, but that it is a deliberately considered attitude is suggested by the fact that in the original skeletal manuscript with which I have been dealing, the curse remained but a curse (cxxxiv). It is only in the stanzas added later (cxxxv–cxxxvii) that Byron as poet takes on, in a sense, the burden of prophecy that all the Romantic poets assume in one form or another: "That curse shall be Forgiveness," forgiveness not merely for the petty wrongs to self but for the "mighty wrongs to petty perfidy" that all "human things" can do. This, then, is the sum of wisdom; and emanating from it is that something within the poet

> *which shall tire*
> *Torture and Time, and breathe when I expire;*
> *Something unearthly, which they deem not of,*
> *Like the remembered tone of a mute lyre,*
> *Shall on their softened spirits sink, and move*
> *In hearts all rocky now the late remorse of Love.*
> *(cxxxvii)*

It is in this context that the poet becomes "a part of

what has been" and grows "upon the spot—all-seeing but unseen" (cxxxviii),[25] participating in the agony of the gladiator
because it is his own and all men's agony:

> *What matters where we fall to fill the maws*
> *Of worms—on battle-plains or listed spot?*
> *Both are but theatres—where the chief actors rot.*
> > *(cxxxix)*

Conversely, like the poet, the Manfreds, and absurdly heroic
men of all molds, the gladiator's "manly brow / Consents to
death, but conquers agony" (cxl), for "his eyes / Were with his
heart—and that was far away" (cxli). If the millions cry,

> *"While stands the Coliseum, Rome shall stand:*
> *When falls the Coliseum, Rome shall fall;*
> *And when Rome falls—the World,"*
> > *(cxlv)*

the poet knows that it is the gladiator's death, not the Colosseum's victory or fall, that preserves unaltered "Ruin past Redemption's skill" and "The World—the same wide den—of
thieves, or what ye will," and that seals the fate of all.

Other contributory images crowd the canto's last
stanzas, but none, I think, is so powerful as these. The dungeon
in whose dark depths time and space both recede to enable the
visionary poet to see a young woman sustaining the life of her
dying father with milk from her own breast first suggests
Caritas Romana but then, even more strongly, the prophetic
doom of what Blake called the "infant sorrow":

> *Full swells the deep pure fountain of young life,*
> > *Where on the heart and from the heart we took*
> > *Our first and sweetest nurture—when the wife,*
> > *Blest into mother, in the innocent look,*
> > *Or even the piping cry of lips that brook*
> *No pain and small suspense, a joy perceives*
> *Man knows not—when from out its cradled nook*

---

[25] Compare this passage with the somewhat more limited version of
the same idea in Canto III, vi, where the poet, "Invisible but gazing,"
blends only with Harold and his poem.

BYRON AND THE RUINS OF PARADISE

She sees her little bud put forth its leaves—
What may the fruit be yet?—I know not—Cain was
Eve's.
(cxlix)

There are also such images as the Pantheon standing "Simple, erect, severe, austere, sublime" while man continues to plod "His way through thorns to ashes" (cxlvi–cxlvii); the temple of Artemis with its columns strewing "the wilderness" and the hyena and jackal basking in its shade (cliii); St. Peter's (cliii–clix); and the Laocoön's vain struggle and "torture dignifying pain— / A Father's love and Mortal's agony" (clx). All enlarge upon the themes already established, substantially enriching with new images the impressive nodal clusters Byron created in the original manuscript version of the canto. Rather than analyze these at length, however, it would be more valuable to turn to a section of the poem I have ignored thus far. A fine example of Byron's ability to modulate his song, it stands in perfect counterpoint to the main lines of thematic development as I have been tracing them, for it embodies, perhaps more poignantly than anywhere else in Byron's poetry (with the possible exception of the Haidée section of *Don Juan*), again in image rather than narrative or mere description, the death of love. It begins with a lovely description of the grotto of Egeria:

> *Egeria! sweet creation of some heart*
> *Which found no mortal resting-place so fair*
> *As thine ideal breast; whate'er thou art*
> *Or wert,—a young Aurora of the air,*
> *The nympholepsy of some fond despair—*
> *Or—it might be—a Beauty of the earth,*
> *Who found a more than common Votary there*
> *Too much adoring—whatsoe'er thy birth,*
> *Thou wert a beautiful Thought, and softly bodied*
> *forth.*
> *(cxv)*

In it was blended "a celestial with a human heart" (cxix). From this legend, strikingly parallel to that in Keats' "Ode to Psyche" or *Endymion*, Byron expatiates on the idea of love, and for a moment shares with Keats, and others, the fond hope that

> *this earthly love has power to make*
> *Men's being mortal, immortal; to shake*
> *Ambition from their memories, and brim*
> *Their measure of content.*[26]

Upon that hope, voiced by Byron, significantly, only in the form of a question (cxix), the section stood in the first manuscript draft. But to his final fair copy of the entire canto Byron added this further revelation of his total intent in the poem:

> *Alas! our young affections run to waste,*
>> *Or water but the desert! whence arise*
>> *But weeds of dark luxuriance, tares of haste,*
>> *Rank at the core, though tempting to the eyes*
>> *Flowers whose, wild odours breathe but agonies,*
>> *And trees whose gums are poison; such the plants*
>> *Which spring beneath her steps as Passion flies*
> *O'er the World's wilderness, and vainly pants*
> *For some celestial fruit forbidden to our wants.*

> *Oh Love! no habitant of earth thou art—*
>> *An unseen Seraph, we believe in thee,—*
>> *A faith whose martyrs are the broken heart,—*
>> *But never yet hath seen, nor e'er shall see*
>> *The naked eye, thy form, as it should be;*
>> *The mind hath made thee, as it peopled Heaven,*
>> *Even with its own desiring phantasy,*
>> *And to a thought such shape and image given,*
> *As haunts the unquenched soul—parched—wearied—*
>>> *wrung—and riven.*[27]
>>> *(cxx–cxxi)*

Such creation is both the "unreached Paradise of our despair" (cxxii) and the birth of beings more intense who, after their momentary day, fade like phantoms into the universal desolation, whose heritage is only a reaffirmation of the bases for despair.

The poet as prophet, then, is at least a two-fold con-

---

[26] Keats, *Endymion,* I, 843–45.

[27] Note the difference between the intensity of theme and coherence of poetry in this passage and the similar passage on love in *The Giaour,* ll. 1131–40. Compare *Childe Harold,* III, xxxiv, the first stanza of *The Giaour,* and Shelley's *The Sensitive Plant.*

ception for Byron. If his verse shall stand, amidst other woe than ours, as the undying curse of forgiveness for the very doom it magnifies, it carries no hope of paradise regained or even of man's gradual climb upward out of the morass. Standing on Metella's grave, which for the moment concentrates in itself all of the tombs and battlefields and ruins of the poem, the poet, as we have seen (stanzas civ–cv), muses on the lack of home or hope or life "save what is here." "What is here" (cv), the poet sees, is the total burden of Byron's prophecy, as it is the burden of *Don Juan*, to which he devoted most of the rest of his life. The voice of Wordsworth's sacramental spirit and the ennobling interchange of man and nature were not his, nor was the voice of Blake's prophecies, of Shelley's mythical visions, or of Keats's anguished struggle to unite reality and the dream. In Canto III Byron recognized what his own voice was not:

> *Could I embody and unbosom now*
> *That which is most within me,—could I wreak*
> *My thoughts upon expression, and thus throw*
> *Soul—heart—mind—passions—feelings—strong*
> *   or weak—*
> *All that I would have sought, and all I seek,*
> *Bear, know, feel—and yet breathe—into one word,*
> *And that one word were Lightning, I would speak;*
> *But as it is, I live and die unheard,*
> *With a most voiceless thought, sheathing it as a sword.*
> *   (xcvii)*

In Canto IV he came to see what that voice had been all along— the sheathed lightning of the real.

III

As I indicated earlier, the later additions to the original 126-stanza manuscript and the poem's accretions even after its "completion" tend to obscure as well as to develop the themes I have been tracing. Many certainly owe their existence to Hobhouse's urging (e.g., stanzas xii–xiv, xvi–xvii, and lxxxv–lxxxvi), some represent Byron's own fiery championing of liberty and rage at the unresisting oppressed (e.g., xcvi–xcviii and cxii–cxiv), and some show his intention of commenting in verse upon the art and literature of Italy (e.g., xl–xli and liv–lx), but most, I think (such as the additions to the Egeria section already commented upon), must be laid to Byron's somewhat belated sense of the wholeness of what he had created (e.g., li–lii, lxxx–lxxxi, the superb xciii–xcv with their anticipation of the gladiator passage and their emphasis on "things allowed, / Averred, and known, and daily, hourly seen" [xcv], the already noted cxx–cxxvii and cxxxv–cxxxvii, and even the seemingly obtrusive and interruptive clxvii–clxxii, on the death of Princess Charlotte).

Perhaps the most interesting of these late additions are the two stanzas (clxxxi–clxxxii) filling out the famous apostrophe to the ocean and two stanzas (clxxvii–clxxviii) on the desert and the "pathless woods." No one has been disturbed or curious about this odd collocation of images, apparently, and almost all commentary on the ocean passage has ignored its general context and its particular position here at the end of the poem. On one level, the three images together (ocean, desert, woods) represent the last, somewhat desperate and confused groping of the poet for the Shelleyan-Wordsworthian communion that failed him, finally, in Canto III. He will seek the desert—where there is no life and nature is barren or dead—in order to "forget the human race" and through a Wordsworthian "ennobling" stir of elements to have, he hopes, a Shelleyan epipsyche accorded him for eternity, "lov[ing] but only her" and "hating no one" (clxxvii). The stanza closes plaintively with the question, "Do I err / In deeming such inhabit many a spot?" As if in answer to himself, and perhaps also in considered revulsion from the idea of the desert, in the immediately succeeding stanzas the poet moves to the pathless woods, where, in Wordsworthian fashion, he will "love not Man the less, but Nature more" (clxxviii). His meditations on the indifference of ocean, in which that hoped-for love of man through nature is turned to contempt, lead him to reject this in turn: "Man marks the earth with ruin" (clxxix), and his "vile strength" is wielded "For Earth's destruction" (clxxx).

Of course what unites all three of these passages is the sense of being happily alone, without man (if we put aside the spirit of the desert), somehow participating in the eternity of nature. Yet we have already seen the vanity of such a wish and the poet's own recognition of it. If he frolicked in youthful sport with the ocean as friend (clxxv), just as Wordsworth's boy bounded over the hills like a roe, the years that bring the philosophical mind bring also the knowledge that nature and man are worlds distinct and that if the ocean in its boundless, endless sublime can go forth "dread, fathomless, alone" (clxxxiii), man cannot. If the boy could lay his hand upon its mane, trusting, delighted, loving (clxxxiv), the man is, as Canto III so eloquently told us, flung like a weed from the rock "to sail / Where'er the surge may sweep, the tempest's breath prevail" (ii). And borne with him upon that tempestuous and vain ocean pilgrimage is the vivid image of the desert, like a sterile track

> *O'er which all heavily the journeying years*
> *Plod the last sands of life,—where not a flower appears.*
>
> *(iii)*

It is appropriate that Canto IV should close abruptly after this uniting of ocean, desert, and woods into a cosmic wasteland,[28] an image cluster that dramatizes the human heart's stirring persistence in living and man's indomitable spirit even amid his ruin and the world's:

> *but I am not now*
> *That which I have been—and my visions flit*
> *Less palpably before me—and the glow*
> *Which in my Spirit dwelt is fluttering, faint, and low.*
>
> *Farewell!*
>
> *(clxxxv–clxxxvi)*

We would be signally remiss here, I think, if we did not catch the distinct echoes of Manfred's dying:

> *'Tis over—my dull eyes can fix thee not;*
> *But all things swim around me, and the earth*
> *Heaves as it were beneath me. Fare thee well,*
> *(III, iv, 146–48)*

and perhaps too his "Give me thy hand" (149).

---

[28] An earlier example of the same equation may be seen in the connection between *Childe Harold* III, iii, and IV, xcii.

It is as wrong, I think, to see Canto IV as pulling together all of the various thematic strands of the first three into a tightly knit whole as it is to consider the one canto as a separate poem. Yet as the culmination of a poem eight years in the making, this final canto does contribute substantially to the multipatterned unity of the whole. If its sporadic carelessness and infelicity of diction and phrasing, its occasionally awkward and apparently arbitrary "stuffing" of a "matrix,"[29] and its only gradual solution of the problem of point of view and tone prevent it from being a great poem, it cannot be considered as anything less than an extraordinary imaginative journey into nothingness and despair and a remarkable feat of mental strength and endurance in the teeth of that stormy and sterile landscape. *Don Juan* will do no more; only the tack will be different.

---

[29] These are T. G. Steffan's terms for describing Byron's associative and accretive habits of composition. See, e.g., his "Byron at Work on Canto I of *Don Juan*," *MP,* XLIV (1947), 141–64, and *Byron's "Don Juan": A Variorum Edition,* Vol. I: *The Making of a Masterpiece.*

Chapter X

BEPPO, POEMS OF 1818–1819, AND THE PLAYS

Canto IV of *Childe Harold's Pilgrimage*, with all its added stanzas finally inserted, was published on April 28, 1818, and *Don Juan* was begun in Venice on September 6 of the same year. This chronological proximity underscores the thematic and structural continuity of Byron's major works, satiric and non-satiric, from *Hours of Idleness* through the tales and *Childe Harold* to *Don Juan* and *The Island*. However, before discussing these last two works, which form the terminus of Byron's career, notice must first be taken of that considerable variety of poetry Byron was writing during the completion of *Childe Harold* and prior to and during the writing of *Don Juan*. While much of it corroborates and solidifies the major lines of development I have been tracing, none of it, I think, contributes dramatically to that development. In one sense, just as Byron throughout his poetic career only gradually became aware of the direction of his own work—and then never so fully aware as to eliminate from it peripheral concerns, arbitrary embellishments, and digressive interests—so here in the penultimate phase of his career his pen started in several directions at once, and his own keen interest in poetry and poetic forms allowed it to proceed with only a modicum of directional control. What is important about some of these works is not so much their intrinsic worth (which varies considerably) as the evidence they provide for studying Byron's imaginative control, almost despite himself, over his erratic and self-willed pen.

I do not propose here to challenge Rutherford's thesis (shared by Marchand and others) that all of Byron's poetry up to late 1817 was in some sense a groping for the vehicle he finally found in *Beppo*, written in "a style completely suited to his genius—one that immediately transformed his work from mediocre competence to assured accomplishment and greatness of a kind."[1] This may or may not be so. More important than Byron's "discovery" of a style is the fact that having "found" it, he still persisted, for reasons Rutherford cannot fathom, in leaving the *ottava rima* of *Beppo* immediately for "other verse forms, other styles," abandoning "the urbane assurance of his new poetic manner for 'romantic' attitudes and histrionic intensities of tone like those which had appeared in former works."[2] The reason, as I have been developing it in this study, is simple: Byron's search was not so much for a style in the sense in which Rutherford uses the term[3] as for a style as Ridenour defines it, which is a way of looking at the world and the deliberate creation of a structure to embody that way of looking. He did not need "urbane assurance" so much as he needed again and again a vehicle which would sustain sanity in despair while it at the same time provided the very images of truth against which he would batter his mind and heart in that continual struggle for expression which was the source of his sanity.

The mode of that expression, from the juvenilia through Canto IV of *Childe Harold*, has become increasingly what must be called "prophetic"—not in the meaner sense of prediction but in the larger sense of a clear and untrammeled vision of the real. This is precisely what Blake meant in the preface to *Milton*, when he quoted from Numbers, "Would to God that all the Lord's people were Prophets"; it is certainly what he had in mind when, fresh from reading Byron's *Cain*, he addressed his own *The Ghost of Abel* "To LORD BYRON in the Wilderness." Yet Keats, too, was right when he said that

---

[1] *Byron: A Critical Study*, p. 123.

[2] *Ibid.*

[3] The limitations of even the most recent Byron criticism are due to this narrow conception of style, which at base still participates in the old-fashioned biographical-critical tradition. Thus Rutherford (and of course he is not the only example), sees Byron's development in terms of a search for "a form and a convention which would enable him to express adequately his own complex nature" (*Byron: A Critical Study*, p. 102). For Ridenour's definition, see his *The Style of "Don Juan,"* (pp. xiff. See also Wolfgang Kayser, *Das Sprachliche Kunstwerk* (Bern, 1948), to which Ridenour is indebted.

Byron copied what he saw instead of copying his imagination—
though we might dispute Keats's conclusion (with which Blake
would certainly agree) that his own task (describing "what I
imagine") was the harder.[4] For Byron "imagination" was neither
Blake's prophetic vision of the eternally real nor Keats's exquisitely refined perception of eternal beauty and truth. It was
rather the clear-eyed recognition of the nature of man and the
world, and, perhaps incidentally, of the God who created both.
Whereas in Blake it is the anti-prophet, Satan, who cries (in
The Ghost of Abel), "O Jehovah! the Elohim live on Sacrifice /
Of Men: hence I am God of Men: Thou Human, O Jehovah!" in
Byron it is the prophet-poet who sees this as the only reality,
who cries, "a Human Victim I wander," and who denies more
vehemently with each new vision of ruin and corruption that it is
"better to believe Vision / With all our might & strength, tho'
we are fallen & lost."[5] Byron's prophecy is the voice of those fallen
and lost, to whom eternity is a myth, Eden an irrecoverable
dream, and life a terrifying succession of horrors. From his
point of view Blake was perfectly right to see Byron among
the lost, crying in the wilderness; but he did not see that that cry
was prophetic in the sense that it articulated the universal
wilderness, in all its myriad detail, for those who would not or
could not hear or see its terrors.

What has put us off is the fact that Byron's prophetic
voice seldom sounds the same from poem to poem. By accepting
varieties of tone as automatically indicative of variety of aim, it
is plain that we have overlooked the fundamental sameness of
the voice's message, befouling ourselves in silly arguments about
whether he is a satiric poet or a romantic poet, a poseur or a
man of sincere heart and good intent, an artist or a supremely
clever dilletante.

I

Beppo is a case in point. Hailed by most Byron critics
as his first notable achievement in his own voice and as the
prelude to the masterpiece *Don Juan*, the poem has never really

---

[4] Ltr. to George and Georgiana Keats, 17–27 Sept. 1819.
[5] A part of one of Eve's speeches in Blake's *The Ghost of Abel*.

been seen for what it is; it is as M. K. Joseph so aptly put it, "like one of the Turkish Tales turned inside-out."[6] More precisely, it *is* one of the Turkish tales turned inside out: if "Beppo's life as slave, renegade and pirate, which would have made the experience of an early Byronic hero, is relegated to the distant background,"[7] it is, nevertheless, there. We merely see it from a different perspective; better still, we see the life of the Turkish tales translated into the civilized life of the everyday modern world. No battles here, or looting, or savagery, or death; instead merely

> *Vile assignations, and adulterous beds,*
> *Elopements, broken vows, and hearts, and heads.*
>
> *(xvi)*

Perhaps more to the point, instead of forcible and often uncertain universalization of the situations and actions of a Giaour, Lara, Conrad, or Alp, Byron now builds on society's very term for itself, "The World" (liv, lix). For the purposes of his story, Venice is the world, but for the purposes of prophecy, "The World" is the world, and "dynasties" of dandies fall into the same massive desolation that claimed Childe Harold, the Turkish heroes, and Napoleon:

> *how*
> *Irreparably soon decline, alas!*
> *The Demagogues of fashion: all below*
> *Is frail; how easily the world is lost*
> *By Love, or War, and, now and then,—by Frost!*
>
> *(lx)*

The tone here, of course, is tongue in cheek, and the capstone last line augurs Byron's frequent use of the bathetic climax in *Don Juan*; but the underlying message is unmistakably the same, and the laughter is merely the mask of despair:

> *methinks the older that one grows*
> *Inclines us more to laugh than scold, though Laughter*
> *Leaves us so doubly serious shortly after.*
>
> *(lxxix)*

---

[6] *Byron the Poet*, p. 135.
[7] *Ibid.*

This is the same deliberate confusion of tones which Byron, with his *Beppo* and *Don Juan* pen in hand, was tempted to introduce at the last minute even into *Childe Harold* IV:

> *Admire—exult—despise—laugh—weep,—for here*
> *Oh, ho, ho, ho—thou creature of a Man!*
> *Thou pendulum betwixt a smile and tear.*
>
> (*cix*)

But he thought better of it and wrote the stanza "straight," crossing out the second of these three lines and substituting "There is such matter for all feeling:—Man!"

Other elements in *Beppo* support a more somber reading of the poem. For example, the speaker advises all not to be caught at the carnival in ecclesiastical costume:

> *Although you swore it only was in fun;*
> *They'd haul you o'er the coals, and stir the fires*
> *Of Phlegethon with every mother's son,*
> *Nor say one mass to cool the cauldron's bubble*
> *That boiled your bones, unless you paid them double.*
>
> (*iv*)

The feminine rhyme of the couplet lightens the tone (as does some of the diction), but the underlying savagery, hypocrisy, and corruption in the literal meaning carries equal weight. Again, of a Giorgione painting, the narrator comments:

> *Love in full life and length, not love ideal,*
> *No, nor ideal beauty, that fine name,*
> *But something better still, so very real,*
> *That the sweet Model must have been the same;*

but her face also

> *recalls some face, as 'twere with pain,*
> *You once have seen, but ne'er will see again;*
>
> *One of those forms which flit by us, when we*
> *Are young, and fix our eyes on every face;*
> *And, oh! the Loveliness at times we see*
> *In momentary gliding, the soft grace,*
> *In Youth, the Bloom, the Beauty which agree,*

> *In many a nameless being we retrace,*
> *Whose course and home we knew not, nor shall know,*
> *Like the lost Pleiad seen no more below.*
>
> *(xiii–xiv)*

The movement from the description of the painting to the intensely personal to the universal sense of loss (not of ideal but real, existing beauty) of the heaven of the past is the movement we have seen again and again in *Childe Harold* and other poems. In the wake of this fleeting though poignant view of lost love and beauty, the narrator's description of the gondola, that scene of modern love, is precisely right in its macabre quality:

> *It glides along the water looking blackly,*
> *Just like a coffin clapt in a canoe,*
> *Where none can make out what you say or do.*
>
> *(xix)*

Again the tone is flip, arch, but the visual image cannot be laughed away. Finally, there is the familiar Byronic lament for a lost and irrecoverable Eden: Venice, the "seat of all dissoluteness,"[8] is hymned by the narrator as still a "Paradise" (xlvi); and the "Mirth and Innocence" of Eden's realm is lamented (and laughed at) as the age of "Milk and Water!"

> *Ye happy mixtures of more happy days!*
> *In these sad centuries of sin and slaughter,*
>   *Abominable Man no more allays*
> *His thirst with such pure beverage. No matter,*
>   *I love you both, and both shall have my praise:*
> *Oh, for old Saturn's reign of sugar-candy!—*
> *Meantime I drink to your return in brandy.*[9]
>
> *(lxxx)*

Once again the confusion of tone and matter produces not merely irony, though the poem certainly has much of that, but a pattern of laughter and seriousness which goes considerably

---

[8] Epigraph to *Beppo*, from Samuel Ayscough's notes to *Dramatic Works of William Shakespeare* (1807), in *P*, IV, 153.

[9] It is quite right, of course, that Byron, in a letter to Moore, associates his facetious Eden with Hobhouse, "who is all clergy and loyalty —mirth and innocence—milk and water" (24 Dec. 1816), in *LJ*, IV, 30.

beyond, let us say, Fielding's idea of the ridiculous and the absurd, or a mere burlesque of human foibles. That those foibles are the targets of Byron's wit and comedy cannot be denied; my claim is only that such comedic "correction" is but a mask for the prophetic voice of doom which underlies the whole.

Of course the accents of that voice have changed considerably from those of the poet of *Childe Harold* or *Manfred* or the tales. No longer the solemn tolling of a bell, the voice has now adjusted itself, as it were, to the very world whose doom it prophesies; it has become the voice of the victim as well as the accuser, in its tones the very corruption and lostness it describes. But, most important, it is still the voice of the poet, who is both subject and object, seer and seen, the epitome of the fragmented world whose panoramic ruin is the burden of his prophecy. Thus, as the poet of *Childe Harold* stood a "ruin amidst ruins" and Manfred sounded the notes of his own fall, here the narrator is "but a nameless sort of person, / (A broken Dandy lately on my travels)" (lii). The tone is that of J. Alfred Prufrock, for Byron's dandy-narrator has also seen them all already, seen them all; but it is mixed with a protective facetiousness that guards his heart through laughter so that he may not weep. The narrator is garrulous, digressive, irreverent, jaded, all-knowing—and he is a poet who is as flippant about his verse as he is about himself and the "world." His periodic pretenses to ignorance are belied constantly by the certainty with which he conveys what he knows in lengthy detail. He "loves" both Italy and England despite the fact that both are shown clearly to be equally corrupt and debased. But underneath the mask is the prevailing sadness of the Byronic poet, who sees where others do not see, who diverts himself from the gloom of his own vision by making it into a joke, who amuses himself at the Ridotto by "guessing at what kind of face / May lurk beneath each mask" (lxiv)—knowing, of course, that they are all the same face—who draws no lesson from it all but leaves us, after our laughter, "doubly serious" after all.

Beppo, then, is a transitional poem; it represents Byron's first attempt to combine in some form the prophetic voice of *Childe Harold* and *Manfred* with the laughter he came more and more to see as essential to his own sanity and well-being. To put it another way, it was his first attempt to combine the tone of the opening of Canto IV of *Childe Harold* (the stanzas on Venice) with the tone of many of his letters from that city. Indeed, even in those letters one can find the same curious confusion of the public-private voice and the private-public voice: the former (in the poetry) reveals his heart and mind while it masks them in public and conventional utterance; the latter (especially in the letters) seems to bare his heart and inner self, yet masks them completely (or almost completely) in the tomfoolery of chattiness and gossip. Thus, in the letters from Venice we can find him writing that Venice "has always been (next to the East) the greenest island of my imagination. It has not disappointed me; though its evident decay would, perhaps, have that effect upon others. But I have been familiar with ruins too long to dislike desolation. Besides, I have fallen in love, which, next to falling into the canal, (which would be of no use, as I can swim,) is the best or the worst thing I could do."[10] The quick movement from the dream of Edenic Venice, green and youthful and beautiful, to decay and desolation, to the steeling of the heart against that desolation, to the half-amused confession of his love, to the macabre parenthetical coupling of drowning and love, to the facetious conclusion is just the sort of movement that *Beppo* essays but does not fully accomplish and that Byron will forge, in *Don Juan*, into a brilliant vehicle for his own peculiar brand of prophecy.

In a remark *en passant* to Augusta, something of this movement toward necessary laughter is evident, here in the context of a humorous jibe at religious hope. What is interesting about it is the clear implication that hope of any sort is vain, and that in lieu of it laughter is man's sustenance and support:

> Your letter of the 1st is arrived, and you have "a *hope*" for me, it seems: what "*hope*," child? my dearest Sis. I remember a methodist preacher who, on perceiving a profane grin on the faces of part of his congregation, exclaimed "no *hopes* for them as *laughs*." And thus it is with us: we laugh too much

---

[10] Ltr. to Moore, 17 Nov. 1816, in *LJ*, IV, 7. Byron seems to have been so taken with his cleverness that he repeated this passage almost verbatim in his ltr. to Murray of 25 Nov. 1816, in *LJ*, IV, 14–16.

for hopes, and so even let them go. I am sick of sorrow, and must even content myself as well as I can. . . .[11]

It is in this light that we can accept, I think, one of Lady Byron's keener insights into her husband's moods: "Beppo," she wrote to her friend Emily Milner, "is just imported but not perused. The greater the levity of Lord Byron's Compositions, the more I imagine him to suffer from the turbid state of his mind. It was always so in his manners."[12] But what Lady Byron read as mere personal "turbidity" was Byron's increasing sense of his own personal fate subsuming that of all men—though this sense, as we have seen, was expressed only through the public-private voice of the poems, not the private-public "confessions" of the letters.

II

Soon after the completion of *Beppo*, Byron went to work on a variety of poems, *Mazeppa*, the "Ode on Venice," the beginning of *Don Juan*, and then, at Teresa Guiccioli's suggestion, *The Prophecy of Dante*. Of these the first two need not detain us long, for from the dearth of comment in the letters Byron himself, quite rightly, thought rather little of them. *Mazeppa* was a return to what was a mode that he had grown far beyond,[13] and the "Ode" was little more than a new version of the beginning of *Childe Harold* IV or *Beppo*. Even given their lack of consequence in the total Byron canon and in his development as a poet-prophet, however, they contain some valuable evidence of the prevailing bent of his thoughts. If one is to find in *Mazeppa* some indication of the mature Byron we have seen

---

[11] Ltr. to Augusta, 19 Dec. 1816, in *LJ*, IV, 22–23. Cf. ltr. to Moore, 10 Mar. 1817, in *LJ*, IV, 72–75, and *Detached Thoughts*, in *LJ*, V, 446.
[12] 19 Mar. 1818, in Marchand, *Byron: A Biography*, II, 735. Cf. Lady Byron's earlier comment in *Detached Thoughts*, in *LJ*, V, 446.
[13] Even so, the simplistic revenge motif is not relieved by any of the larger implications—the death of love, for example—that informed even the less accomplished verse of so early a poem as *The Giaour*. Villemain, however, thought it Byron's masterpiece (*Etudes de littérature ancienne et ètrangère* [Paris, 1855], p. 393).

develop in *Childe Harold* and *Manfred*, one can point to little more than the ending, with Mazeppa's long tale of revenge and his wild ride through a nightmarish wasteland that, ironically, puts his comrades and the defeated, wounded King of Sweden to sleep. Yet if we are tempted to see that denouement as symbolic of the inevitable fate of prophecy in the world (the ravings of Cassandra now modulated into a terrifying verbal portrait of waste and desolation, unheard by man), we must also see immediately that Charles XII is hardly mankind and Mazeppa is no prophet. What is of interest here is the powerful influence of Coleridge's *Ancient Mariner* and *Christabel*, mixed with echoes of Byron's own *Prisoner of Chillon*, which permeates Mazeppa's account of his ride. The older poet's grim and unrelenting vision of evil in the world as a positive and powerful force whose agent is, however unwittingly, man himself, as seen in the Mariner's motiveless crime and in Christabel's transformation, clearly had a profound effect upon Byron's mind. Even though Mazeppa's love for Teresa was engendered not by lascivious eyes or profane touch but by

> *Involuntary sparks of thought,*
> *Which strike from out the heart o'erwrought,*
> *And form a strange intelligence,*
> *Alike mysterious and intense,*
> *Which link the burning chain that binds,*
> *Without their will, young hearts and minds,*
> *(ll. 236–41)*

that love leads inevitably to punishment (in its limited sense of expulsion by the world and society, and in its larger sense of man's descent into his own private doom).

If Mazeppa's story has its fairy-tale ending (he is saved by poor peasants over whom he would soon rule), Byron's evident confusion over his final intention in the poem can lead us to forget that a prominent part of Mazeppa's "moral" is that "we" (that is, all men) still "love even in our rage" and after the lapse of many years; and thus man is "haunted to [his] very age / With the vain shadow of the past" (ll. 228–30). The ride, then, is to be read not as mere punishment but as a horrifying vision of the rewards of man's essential humanity, the feeling heart. Coleridge's *Ancient Mariner* is turned inside out; the Mariner-Mazeppa is "punished" for loving, not for killing; to put it another way, the very human, innocent warmth of Christabel's treatment of Geraldine leads inevitably to her grotesque transformation, from which even "Jesu, Maria" cannot shield her:

> But Christabel in a dizzy trance
> Stumbling on the unsteady ground
> Shuddered aloud, with a hissing sound;
>
> .   .   .   .   .
>
> The maid, devoid of guile and sin,
> I know not how, in fearful wise,
> So deeply had she drunken in
> That look, those shrunken serpent eyes,
> That all her features were resigned
> To this sole image in her mind:
> And passively did imitate
> That look of dull and treacherous hate!
>
> (ll. 583–606)

The parallel is inexact, of course, for Mazeppa is no innocent, and his love for Teresa is hardly the affection of Christabel for Geraldine; but the fact remains that just as Christabel becomes, in effect, a product of the very evil from which her innocence and piety should have shielded her, so Mazeppa steels his mind against his essential humanity to become a vicious avenger, relishing the vision of the desolation he wreaked on the Count far above the delight of his love:

> There is not of that castle gate,
> Its drawbridge and portcullis' weight,
> Stone—bar—moat—bridge—or barrier left;
> Nor of its fields a blade of grass,
>   Save what grows on a ridge of wall,
>   Where stood the hearth-stone of the hall.
>
> (ll. 394–99)

Despite the touches of levity here and there, some anticipating the facetious irreverence of *Don Juan,* the landscape that controls *Mazeppa* is also grim and unrelenting and strik-

ingly similar to that of *The Siege of Corinth*. The poem opens
with a vision of "a slaughtered army,"

> *No more to combat and to bleed.*
> *The power and glory of the war,*
> *Faithless as their vain votaries, men,*
> *Had passed to the triumphant Czar,*
> *And Moscow's walls were safe again—*
>
> *(ll. 3–8)*

but safe only until "A greater wreck, a deeper fall" supersedes
the present (l. 13). And the remainder of the poem is enveloped
by the pall of Mazeppa's wasteland and a vision of "The dying
on the dead" (l. 715) in the "dim waste" (l. 615) that is man's
life on earth.

The "Ode on Venice," completed on July 10, 1818,
was published with *Mazeppa* and serves as a neat comment upon
the apparent tone and temper of *Beppo*, reinforcing my contention of the fundamental despair underlying that seeming *jeu
d'esprit*. In *Childe Harold* IV Byron saw Venice as the epitome
of a paradise now lost, of man's increasing meanness and inevitable defeat at the hands of the world and himself; now in
the "Ode" modern man is compared to "the slime, / The dull
green ooze of the receding deep" (ll. 8–9), as opposed to the
"dashing of the spring-tide foam" (l. 10) which once was. Modern man creeps "Crouching and crab-like, through their sapping
streets" (l. 13) suffering the agony and ignominy of defeat and
despair in a world (Venice) that once evinced

> the busy hum
> *Of cheerful creatures, whose most sinful deeds*
> *Were but the overbeating of the heart,*
> *And flow of too much happiness.*
>
> *(ll. 25–28)*

Now "The weeds of nations in their last decay" (l. 33)—like
the weed flung from every rock with which the poet of *Childe
Harold* identifies himself—flourish in what once was the garden
of Shelley's *Sensitive Plant*:

> *Vice walks forth with her unsoftened terrors,*
> *And Mirth is madness, and but smiles to slay;*

And Hope is nothing but a false delay,
The sick man's lightning half an hour ere Death,
When Faintness, the last mortal birth of Pain,
And apathy of limb, the dull beginning
Of the cold staggering race which Death is winning,
Steals vein by vein and pulse by pulse away;
Yet so relieving the o'er-tortured clay,
To him appears renewal of his breath,
And freedom the mere numbness of his chain;
And then he talks of Life, and how again
He feels his spirit soaring—albeit weak,
And of the fresher air, which he would seek;
And as he whispers knows not that he gasps,
That his thin finger feels not what it clasps,
And so the film comes o'er him—and the dizzy
Chamber swims round and round—and shadows busy,
At which he vainly catches, flit and gleam,
Till the last rattle chokes the strangled scream,
And all is ice and blackness,—and the earth
That which it was the moment ere our birth.

(*ll. 34–55*)

It is an extraordinary passage, which echoes and intensifies the illusory "freedom" of Bonivard, concentering into the image of a dying man the dying of a world. Man, even if he would, is unable to slow the decay; indeed, he seems, paradoxically, to hasten and abet it, for, as Byron writes in the "Ode,"

> *we lean*
> *On things that rot beneath our weight, and wear*
> *Our strength away in wrestling with the air;*
> *For 't is our nature strikes us down.*
>
> (*ll. 60–63*)

From this point on the poem trails off into a paean to the Venice of old with its glory and empire that were somehow better than the glory and empire of other powers and that signify to Byron the freedom from tyranny now enjoyed only, as he says, by "One great clime," America (ll. 133ff.). But the familiar and comfortable rhetoric of these conventional two cheers for freedom and curse upon tyranny cannot quite overshadow the horror of the vision of doom that opened the poem.

That vision, for the first time cast in its proper lineaments as "prophecy," informs the totality of Byron's next con-

311

siderable work, and again we must remind ourselves that the so-called gaiety and fun of *Don Juan* are being created at this same time. *The Prophecy of Dante*, which Byron also called a *"Vision"* and promised Murray to complete with the fire of an Isaiah,[14] is pre-eminently a political poem prophesying the forthcoming unification and "resurrection" of Italy. But it also embodies, like *The Lament of Tasso*, Byron's assumption of the poet-prophet role *in propria persona*—not, as Marshall says, "to demonstrate the ultimate meaningfulness of the universe by asserting the triumph of Self,"[15] but rather to provide once again (though now in an unfamiliar oracular voice) a coherent vision of a fragmented and meaningless universe, whose only potential meaning lies in that very meaninglessness. Byron assumes the poet-prophet role to further establish his poet as symbolic of both that chaos and the agonizing battle of man within his own heart and mind for that coherence.

Dante (as speaker) places before us, in the first three lines, the fallen nature of the world, contrasting it with the paradisaical vision of Beatrice, the "sole pure Seraph of my earliest love" (I, 20). Further, Dante sees himself as the "Cassandra-like" prophet unheard (II, 10), in himself the flaws of all his kind and the hell of his own despair, but also the divine light of the seer:

> Alas! with what a weight upon my brow
>> The sense of earth and earthly things come back,
>> Corrosive passions, feelings dull and low,
> The heart's quick throb upon the mental rack,
>> Long day, and dreary night; the retrospect
>> Of half a century bloody and black,
> And the frail few years I may yet expect
>> Hoary and hopeless, but less hard to bear,

---

[14] Ltr. to Murray, 14 Mar. 1820, in *LJ*, IV, 418. See also ltr. to Murray, 20 Mar. 1820, in *LJ*, IV, 419. In his Preface to the poem, Byron also acknowledges debts to the *Alexandra* of Lycophron (Coleridge suggests also the *Cassandra* of Philip Yorke, published in 1806), Horace's *Prophecy of Nereus*, "as well as the Prophecies of Holy Writ" (*P*, IV, 243–44 and 244n). It should be noted also that Byron's *The Vision of Judgment*, written in October, 1821, is no less a vision or prophecy for its being a comic-satiric anti-visionary poem.
[15] *The Structure of Byron's Major Poems*, p. 125.

> *For I have been too long and deeply wrecked*
> *On the lone rock of desolate Despair,*
>   *To lift my eyes more to the passing sail*
>   *Which shuns that reef so horrible and bare;*
> *Nor raise my voice—for who would heed my wail?*
>   *(I, 130–42)*

Dante is thus the image of Byron as he had come to see himself in his poetry, the seer of "Shapes that must undergo mortality" (II, 7) but a seer unacknowledged:

> *Cassandra-like, amidst the din*
> *Of conflict none will hear, or hearing heed*
> *This voice from out the Wilderness.*
>   *(10–12)*

What is left to the poet is the vitality of his own despair, his own feelings being his "meed, / The only guerdon I have ever known" (13–14). The future holds not hope but unborn earthquakes and "bloody Chaos" (42), yet there is an expectation of creation:

> *all things are disposing for thy doom;*
> *The Elements await but for the Word,*
> *"Let there be darkness!" and thou grow'st a tomb!*
>   *(43–45)*

It is impossible not to hear in this perversion of Genesis the echoes of Byron's nightmare vision and prophecy, "Darkness," the final fall of all into desolation's insatiate maw. And is this the whole of man's "destiny beneath the Sun?" Dante asks (III, 160); must even those of

>   *finer thoughts, the thrilling sense,*
> *The electric blood with which their arteries run,*
> *Their body's self turned soul with the intense*
>   *Feeling of that which is, and fancy of*
>   *That which should be, to such a recompense*
> *Conduct? shall their bright plumage on the rough*
>   *Storm be still scattered? Yes, and it must be;*
>   *For, formed of far too penetrable stuff,*
> *These birds of Paradise but long to flee*
>   *Back to their native mansion, soon they find*

313

Earth's mist with their pure pinions not agree,
And die or are degraded; for the mind
Succumbs to long infection, and despair.

(161–73)

But, for Byron, lost, like Stephen Crane's shipwrecked men of "The Open Boat," amid the indifference of the universe, those native mansions are irrecoverable; and hurling bricks at the temple of the gods who created such chaos is merely a further exercise in futility and despair: there are no bricks and there is no temple. Still, like Prometheus, the poet (and, Byron hopes, man, through his prophecies) "can bear" all (IV, 20); though "chained to his lone rock by the sea-shore" (19), he is sustained by the power of his own despair, the clarity and coherence of his own vision of what *is*, and the implicit hope that the hour will come "When Truth shall strike [men's] eyes through many a tear" (and, for Byron, many a laugh) "And make them own the Prophet in his tomb" (153, 154).

III

Even as Byron's voice was rising more and more confidently in the prophetic laughter of *Don Juan*, it was deepening in another poetic form, the drama. Though a thorough commentary and analysis of all the plays is beyond the scope of this study,[16] it is instructive to examine a few of them in some detail. In general, they rehearse the themes I have been isolating thus far in Byron's work—the fundamental injustice and corruption of the world, the futility of steeling one's mind to revenge, the loss of love, and man's inveterate and repeated fall.

In *Marino Faliero, Doge of Venice*, which Byron apparently planned to write almost immediately after finishing *Manfred* but which he did not begin until the spring of 1820, Faliero's attempt, by way of a treasonable conspiracy, to set right all the ills of Venice is doomed to failure both by the very nature

---

[16] Any full study of Byron's plays must begin with Chew's *The Dramas of Lord Byron*, and there are sensible surveys in the critical books by Rutherford, Marchand (*Byron's Poetry*), Joseph, and Robert Escarpit, all previously cited.

of the world (which will not admit of reform) and by his own reluctance to bury his human affection for the ruling "Forty" in a heartless purge of their power and lives. On the other hand, in his own mind his motive for joining, and thus sanctioning, the treason becomes confused between his lust for personal revenge for Steno's insults to his wife, home, name, and honor and his warm human sympathy for his oppressed people. As a result, beset, Christ-like, "with all the thorns that line a crown" (I, ii, 260) and with a "bold brow" bearing "but the scars of mind" (II, i, 20–21), like so many of Byron's heroes, he accomplishes neither his revenge nor the revolt of the people and is ignominiously decapitated, the somewhat gory symbol of his unregained honor and failure to help his people being his head rolling "down the Giants' Steps" (V, iv, 29) where he was initially crowned.

Clearly, all grand and heroic actions must be at the expense of human ties. In the words of Israel Bertuccio,

> *We must forget all feelings save the one,*
> *We must resign all passions save our purpose,*
> *We must behold no object save our country,*
> *And only look on Death as beautiful,*
> *So that the sacrifice ascend to Heaven,*
> *And draw down Freedom on her evermore.*
> (II, ii, 87–92)

Thus he urges the vacillating Faliero to "Re-man" his "breast" (III, ii, 500) so that, like Bertuccio, he will *"feel not"* and

> *go to this butcher-work*
> *As if these high-born men were steers for shambles:*
> *When all is over, you'll be free and merry,*
> *And calmly wash those hands incarnadine.*[17]
> (506–9)

The Doge's fundamental humanity will not permit such a dehumanization:

---

[17] Although these lines are part of the Doge's speech accusing the fierce Israel Bertuccio of being heartless, my point is substantiated by the whole dialogue. For a similar speech by the Doge, see III, ii, 453–72.

> *But I, outgoing thee and all thy fellows*
> *In this surpassing massacre, shall be,*
> *Shall see and feel.*[18]
>
> (510–12)

Yet Faliero finally agrees to the conspiracy, and his reluctance to man his heart is lost in the equally "manly" desire for revenge, or, as he himself puts it, "all nature" (i.e., human nature) is jarred from his "heart" (540–41).

As a counterpoint to the Doge, Byron creates Bertram, a conspirator whose commitment to pull down the tyrannical rule of the Forty is never in question but whose essential compassion and humanity lead him to betray the conspiracy and thus cause the death of all (including the Doge) who seem to promise the return to Venice of the human values which Bertram himself represents. As always in Byron, man's heart as well as his mind, either separate or in varying combination, tend toward destruction and a perpetuation of man's fall; and paradise—or Venice, everything about which is to Byron "extraordinary" ("her aspect . . . like a dream, and her history . . . like a romance"[19])—not only is not regained but slides further downward toward the doom Faliero envisages:

> *And this proud city, and these azure waters,*
> *And all which makes them eminent and bright,*
> *Shall be a desolation and a curse,*
> *A hissing and a scoff unto the nations.*[20]
>
> (V, ii, 80–83)

In *Marino Faliero*, then (as in the later *The Two Foscari* and *Werner*[21]), there is little that is new either in the

---

[18] Emphasis added.

[19] Preface to *Marino Faliero, Doge of Venice*.

[20] See also the Doge's longer curse and prophecy in V, iii, 26–101.

[21] *The Two Foscari* was written in less than a month (June 12 to July 9, 1821), and *Werner; or, The Inheritance* was completed in a little over a month, on January 20, 1822. In the former, the elder Foscari's conflict is another variation of the mind-heart opposition, for he is both Doge (and hence must uphold the law and punish the enemies of the state) and father (of a son he loves dearly but who is

also such an enemy). The epigraph to the play, from Sheridan's *The Critic*, sets the theme: "The *father* softens, but the *governor's* resolved." Although he does not come to that resolution easily, Foscari finally must fulfill his duty to the state. By so doing, his son dies after undergoing severe torture, he is deposed as Doge, and almost immediately follows his son to the grave. In that place only, Byron indicates clearly, do heart and heart truly join. As in *Marino Faliero* Bertram tragically exemplified the humanness of man, so here Barbarigo, one of the senators, has a heart that fights, vainly, against the endless and increasingly powerful tide of remorseless retribution, death, and desolation (see, e.g., his speech in I, i, 56–67). As in the earlier play, Venice is the hell in which all this takes place, a "crowd of palaces and prisons" almost simplistically presented as "not / A Paradise" (III, i, 147–48); and Byron, perhaps more successfully here than in *Marino Faliero*, builds the city into a symbol of the world, which tramples "on all human feelings, all / Ties which bind man to man" (I, i, 262–63), and which calls forth from the Doge this turgid and bitter epitomization of "That loathsome volume—man":

> *Those black and bloody leaves, his heart and brain,*
>
> . . . . .
>
> > *all the sins*
> *We find in others, Nature made our own;*
> *All our advantages are those of Fortune;*
> *Birth, wealth, health, beauty, are her accidents,*
> *And when we cry out against Fate, 'twere well*
> *We should remember Fortune can take nought*
> *Save what she gave—the rest was nakedness,*
> *And lusts, and appetites, and vanities,*
> *The universal heritage, to battle*
> *With as we may, and least in humblest stations,*
> *Where Hunger swallows all in one low want,*
> *And the original ordinance, that man*
> *Must sweat for his poor pittance, keeps all passions*
> *Aloof, save fear of famine! All is low,*
> *And false, and hollow—clay from first to last,*
> *The Prince's urn no less than potter's vessel.*
> *Our Fame is in men's breath, our lives upon*
> *Less than their breath; our durance upon days,*
> *Our days on seasons; our whole being on*
> *Something which is not us!—So, we are slaves,*
> *The greatest as the meanest—nothing rests*
> *Upon our will; the will itself no less*
> *Depends upon a straw than on a storm;*
> *And when we think we lead, we are most led,*
> *And still towards Death, a thing which comes as much*
> *Without our act or choice as birth, so that*

theme or in Byron's handling of it. *Sardanapalus*, however, aside from its generally neglected impressiveness as a play,[22] claims our special attention because of its unusual reversal of perspective. Unlike the gallery of "heroes" that we have seen, tough-minded and tough-fisted, who are betrayed either by their own efforts to "man" themselves or by a momentary lapse into their essential humanity and feeling heart, Sardanapalus is, at least initially, the unheroic hero, the ruler who prefers love and peace to war, compassion to punishment, trust to suspicion. If he is "a sybarite who defends his life of pleasure as representing a benevolent epicurean pacifism,"[23] he is also, as Joseph says, Byron's "ideal of conduct,"[24] the essential human. "For me," says Sardanapalus, it is "enough"

> *Methinks we must have sinned in some old world,*
> *And* this *is Hell: the best is, that it is not*
> *Eternal.*
>
> (II, i, 335–66)

And if it is Marina, the younger Foscari's wife, who implores heaven, "Oh, thou eternal God! / Canst *thou* continue so, with such a world?" (I, i, 211–12), the question is also Byron's, and the play his affirmative answer.

Werner is far less interesting, hovering uncertainly as it does between a view of the world as "damned" (III, i, 42) and as "indeed a melancholy jest" (II, i, 336); it contains one of Byron's finest passages on time (III, iii, 1–12) but little else except melodramatic claptrap. Even if it does come "closest of all the dramas to the acceptable dramatic form of his time," as Joseph believes (*Byron the Poet*, p. 111), any admirer of Byron would rather be persuaded by T. H. Vail Motter's theory (however tenuous his argument) that the play was written tongue-in-cheek to guarantee the stage success Byron's other dramas had failed to achieve (see "Byron's *Werner* Re-estimated: A Neglected Chapter in Nineteenth Century Stage History," pp. 243–75).

[22] Among its very few champions are E. M. Butler (*Byron and Goethe: Analysis of a Passion* [London, 1956], p. 189) and G. Wilson Knight (*The Burning Oracle*, p. 225).

[23] Joseph, *Byron the Poet*, p. 115.

[24] *Ibid.*, p. 116. In his ltr. to Murray of 22 July 1821 Byron also describes Sardanapalus as "almost a comic character," and then adds, "but, for that matter, so is Richard the third" (*LJ*, V, 324). What he had in mind was certainly something like Horace Walpole's conviction "*that this world is a comedy to those who think, a tragedy to those who feel*—a solution of why Democritus laughed and Heraclitus wept. The only gainer is History, which has constant opportunities

> *if I can make my subjects feel*
> *The weight of human misery less, and glide*
> *Ungroaning to the tomb: I take no license*
> *Which I deny to them. We are all men.*
>
> *(I, ii, 262–65)*

Reminded by the faithful but war-like Salamenes that his "Sires have been revered as Gods," Sardanapalus replies:

> *In dust*
> *And death, where they are neither Gods nor men.*
> *Talk not of such to me! the worms are Gods;*
> *At least they banqueted upon your Gods,*
> *And died for lack of farther nutriment.*
> *Those Gods were merely men; look to their issue—*
> *I feel a thousand mortal things about me,*
> *But nothing godlike,—unless it may be*
> *The thing which you condemn, a disposition*
> *To love and to be merciful, to pardon*
> *The follies of my species, and (that's human)*
> *To be indulgent to my own.*
>
> *(267–78)*

Hating pain, "Given or received" (348–49), not wishing to add to man's "natural burthen / Of mortal misery" (351–52), and seeking to alleviate "The fatal penalties imposed on life" (354), Sardanapalus' whole "life is love" (406), the dream of paradise regained:

> *I thought to have made mine inoffensive rule*
> *An era of sweet peace 'midst bloody annals,*
> *A green spot amidst desert centuries,*
>
> *(IV, i, 511–13)*

a "golden reign," "a paradise" (516, 517). But man cannot tolerate the very paradise toward which his whole soul yearns,

---

for showing the various ways in which men can contrive to be fools and knaves. The record pretends to be written for instruction, though to this hour no mortal has been the better or wiser for it" (ltr. to Horace Mann, 31 Dec. 1769, in *The Letters of Horace Walpole*, ed. Mrs. Paget Toynbee [16 vols.; Oxford, 1904], VII, 346). But also, of course, it is further evidence that Byron's comic and non-comic visions are, at the bottom, always the same vision.

for his very humanness demands empire, war, and his own slaughter, until his world is turned

> *To one wide desert chase of brutes, who* were,
> *But* would *no more, by their own choice, be human.*
>
> (I, ii, 375–76)

Myrrha, the voice of selfless love (IV, i, 524–28), the complement of Sardanapalus, presents the paradox in its most telling and poignant form:

> *earth*[,] *where Peace and Hope,*
> *And Love and Revel, in an hour were trampled*
> *By human passions to a human chaos,*
> *Not yet resolved to separate elements—*
> *And can the sun so rise,*
> *So bright, so rolling back the clouds into*
> *Vapours more lovely than the unclouded sky,*
> *With golden pinnacles, and snowy mountains,*
> *And billows purpler than the Ocean's, making*
> *In heaven a glorious mockery of the earth.*
>
> (V, i, 5–14)

The alternatives presented to Sardanapalus are the familiar ones we have seen in other Byron poems: he must either persist in his humanity or steel his heart against its essential dictates and become a "man"—that is, meet the world on its own terms and succumb to it even while conquering. The pattern was set for him by his royal predecessors, Nimrod and Semiramis; the latter was, as Salamenes says, "a woman only" yet she led the Assyrians even to the "solar shores / Of Ganges" and returned "like a *man*—a hero" (I, ii, 126–29). So Sardanapalus has "remanned" himself (IV, i, 403) and rushes headlong into the fray in defense of the paradise he had hoped to create but which was lost even as he was dreaming of it. To clinch the point, Byron has Myrrha, the emblem of love, send him out to the slaughter with "Go forth, and conquer!" (III, i, 173). What remains is the sentiment of Manfred—"Old man, 'tis not so difficult to die"—and "this blazing palace, / And its enormous walls of reeking ruin" (V, i, 480–81) are left as the noblest monument to man's aspirations and inevitable doom.

This mood of despair, which we have seen deepen and intensify through Byron's career to date, is what gives rise finally to *Cain* and *Heaven and Earth*.[25] It is a mood recorded in a variety of ways in the diary Byron kept while at Ravenna. Late in January, 1821, for example, he writes:

> what sensation is so delightful as Hope? and, if it were not for Hope, where would the Future be?—in hell. It is useless to say *where* the Present is, for most of us know; and as for the Past, *what* predominates in memory?—*Hope baffled.* Ergo, in all human affairs, it is Hope—Hope—Hope. I allow sixteen minutes, though I never counted them, to any given or supposed possession. From whatever place we commence, we know where it all must end. And yet, what good is there in knowing it? It does not make men better or wiser. During the greatest horrors of the greatest plagues, (Athens and Florence, for example—see Thucydides and Machiavelli,) men were more cruel and profligate than ever. It is all a mystery. I feel most things, but I know nothing. . . .[26]

And earlier in the month, fresh from a re-reading of *The Vanity of Human Wishes,* he writes:

> But 'tis a grand poem—and *so true!*—true as the 10th of Juvenal himself. The lapse of ages *changes* all things—time—language—the earth—the bounds of the sea—the stars of the sky, and every thing "about, around, and underneath" man, *except man himself,* who has always been, and always will be, an unlucky rascal. The infinite variety of lives conduct but to death, and the infinity of wishes lead but to disappointment.[27]

The diary continues here with something of the same facetiousness he was employing in *Don Juan* at this time: "All the discoveries which have yet been made have multiplied little but existence. An extirpated disease is succeeded by some new pestilence; and a discovered world has brought little to the old one,

---

[25] Byron "pondered" a play on Cain very early in 1821 but only began it in July. He began *Heaven and Earth* slightly over a month after finishing *Cain,* in September of 1821.

[26] *LJ,* V, 190. This entry in the diary concludes with three lines of poetry he entitled "Thought for a Speech of Lucifer, in the Tragedy of Cain" (*LJ,* V, 191).

[27] *LJ,* V, 162.

except the p[ox] first and freedom afterwards. . . ."[28] He ends one entry with a line from Act IV of Dryden's *Aurengzebe*, "Trust on, and think tomorrow will repay," the context of which betrays the note of apparent hope in the single line:

> *When I consider Life, 'tis all a cheat;*
> *Yet, fool'd with hope, men favour the deceit;*
> *Trust on, and think tomorrow will repay;*
> *Tomorrow's false than the former day.*

On February 2 he is puzzled by the fact that he wakes up "at a certain hour in the morning, and always in very bad spirits—I may say, in actual despair and despondency, in all respects—even of that which pleased me over night"; and he fears, with obvious seriousness, that like Swift he shall "end" by "dying at top."[29]

What is extraordinary about the diary is the fact that amidst this incessant gloom and hopelessness are the very notes of hope which Byron tends to deny to man. The idea of a free Italy is so inspiring to him that his own sacrifice would be "no great matter." "It is a grand object," he writes, "the very *poetry* of politics. Only think—a free Italy!!! Why, there has been nothing like it since the days of Augustus."[30] Thus "it is best to hope, even of the hopeless," for hope "is the grand possession."[31] I see no reason to discount either side of Byron's mood; we have seen the same duality in his earliest voices—the essential Byron, awakening always in despair out of a peaceful sleep induced by escapist pleasures, and Byron the man, whose whole apparent being is thrown somewhat desperately into causes (the most notable being the cause of freedom) without a clear or full awareness of his own essential nature. The constant pain, anguish, and despair of that nature is shouldered aside, as it were, by the public utterance, only to appear, all the more stark and telling, in the "private" utterances of the poetry. Thus it seems

---

[28] *Ibid.*, 163.
[29] *Ibid.*, 194, 198–99.
[30] *Ibid.*, 205. It was with such sentiments as these that he infused the character of Jacopo Foscari in *The Two Foscari*.
[31] *Ibid.*, 205, 211.

to me quite understandable that Byron should never completely see why his writing seemed to have nothing to do with inspiration or imagination or any sort of divine afflatus; and it is also understandable that he should condemn poetry as a serious occupation and regard his own efforts as so much scribbling. Poetry performed for him precisely the kind of service he described so frequently without, again, fully understanding it. Thus he writes to Moore in January, 1821, that the *estro* "comes over me in a kind of rage every now and then, like * * * * [he must have written here, somewhat crudely, as he often did in letters to his friends, a word or phrase describing the sexual urge, which Thomas Moore duly rubbed out], and then, if I don't write to empty my mind, I go mad. As to that regular, uninterrupted love of writing . . . I do not understand it. I feel it as a torture, which I must get rid of, but never as a pleasure. On the contrary, I think composition a great pain."[32] This feeling is nothing quite so crude as West's idea of the need for elimination, but it is the necessary expression of inner torture and despair out of which are created additional craggy images for his mind and heart to break upon.[33]

Whatever theological implications *Cain* has, and whether it is a great play (as Goethe thought[34]) or "some of Byron's worst rubbish" (as H. W. Garrod thought[35]), it must be

---

[32] Ltr. of 2 Jan. 1821, in *LJ*, V, 215.
[33] Cf. Matthew Arnold on Byron's "titanism" and Celticism, in *On the Study of Celtic Literature and on Translating Homer* (New York, 1899), pp. 118–19.
[34] *Goethes Werke* (Weimar, 1887–1919), XLI, 2, pp. 94–99. See also E. M. Butler, *Byron and Goethe, passim.* Goethe also thought highly of *Heaven and Earth* and regretted that Byron did not live "to execute his vocation. . . . To dramatise the *Old* Testament. What a subject, under his hands, would the Tower of Babel have been!" (quoted in *Henry Crabb Robinson on Books and Their Writers*, ed. E. J. Morley [3 vols.; London, 1938], I, 372). Scott and Shelley were also extravagant in their praise of *Cain*; see Scott's ltr. to Murray, 17 Dec. 1821, in *Memoirs of Sir Walter Scott*, ed. J. G. Lockhart (London, 1914), III, 525–26, and Shelley's ltrs. to John Gisborne, 12 and 26 Jan. 1822, in *The Letters of Percy Bysshe Shelley*, ed. F. L. Jones (2 vols.; Oxford, 1964), II, 677, 683.
[35] *Byron 1824–1924*, p. 20n. Garrod included *Heaven and Earth* in this phrase as well.

read as a despairing prelude to the grim prophecy of *Heaven and Earth*. It is probably true, as M. K. Joseph has summed it up, that *Cain* is the combined product of "Byron's early Calvinism . . . blended with Lucretian atomism, and Fontenelle's plurality of worlds [*Entretien sur la pluralité des mondes*]; with the deism of the *Essay on Man* and the cosmology of *Night Thoughts*; with the Pre-Adamites of *Vathek* and with Buffon's giants and 'organic degeneration'; with the spontaneous generation of Erasmus Darwin; and finally with the catastrophism of Cuvier."[36] What is more important is that it is Byron's complete rejection of God in a almost fullblown nihilism. God, like Lucifer, is merely the despair and sorrow of man writ large, carried on into eternity. If it is Lucifer who, in seeking to win over Cain, describes God as "so wretched in his height" and "So restless in his wretchedness" that he "must still / Create, and re-create" (I, i, 161–63), the reader must be struck by the similarity of this description to the portrait of Byron's poet-prophet as we have seen it evolving in the poems. "At least we sympathize," says Lucifer, echoing Sardanapalus,

> And, suffering in concert, make our pangs
> Innumerable, more endurable,
> By the unbounded sympathy of all
> With all!
>
> (157–61)

But under Lucifer's subtle guiding hand God emerges not so much as the archetypal poet as the epitome of man—jealous, destructive, vengeful, hungry for power, the "maker" who only destroys, the "lover" who only extorts or forces obedience, the tyrant who requires blood and decrees for his world endless

> war with all things,
> And death to all things, and disease to most things,
> And pangs, and bitterness.
>
> (II, ii, 149–51)

And though it is Lucifer who conjures up this image, clearly

---

[36] *Byron the Poet*, p. 121.

the image already exists in embryo in Cain's mind, as his first soliloquy so quickly demonstrates:

> *Because*
> *He is all-powerful, must all-good, too, follow?*
> *I judge but by the fruits—and they are bitter.*
> (I, i, 76–78)

That initial bitterness is merely intensified by Cain's guided tour of past worlds and Hades, and the realization, first, that man's stature is infinitesimally small, diminished by the revelation of previous Edens, worlds, and catastrophes, by the awareness of the existences and deaths of beings greater, wiser, more beautiful, and more powerful than himself; second, that "the human sum / Of knowledge" is "to know mortal nature's nothingness" (II, ii, 421–22); and third, that man's choice is, simply, between love, which is slavery, and knowledge, which is the freedom to know one's own nothingness. The heart dictates the lives of Adam and Abel and the others, contentment "with what *is*," and a rejection of the dream of paradise (I, i, 45). Adam is described by Eve as "cheerful and resigned" (51); Adah is hopeful of building a new paradise on earth through love; as the play opens all except Cain give thanks merely for being alive. But Byron's clear intent in the play, it seems to me, is to show that the only final good is death and the ultimate evil, life. To this end he had anticipated in his Ravenna diary, immediately after the passage quoted above on hope eternally baffled, Lucifer's assertion of this truth:

> *Were* Death *an* evil, *would* I *let thee* live?
> *Fool! live as I live—as thy father lives,*
> *And thy son's sons shall live for evermore.*[37]

Byron rejected the lines as too open a confession by Lucifer of his own evil, but they clearly anticipate the sentence of Cain to a life of endless wandering in woe and guilt, branded with the ultimate curse.

On the other hand, to live according to the mind is to live according to Lucifer, to reject both God and man, to make

---

[37] *LJ*, V, 191.

one's self, in Shelley's terms, both the center and circumference of the universe, to

> Think and endure,—and form an inner world
> In your own bosom—where the outward fails;
> So shall you nearer be the spiritual
> Nature, and war triumphant with your own.
>
> (II, ii, 463–66)

This is the prize that Cain ultimately wins; he is triumphant over man and his own mortality, yet doomed to wander defeated, exploring the depths of his own inner hell.

In one sense, I suppose, this is the fate of the poet as Byron sees him—eternally alone, cursing the heart by which his very humanity survives, forming out of his mind an inner world that merely teaches him the lesson of his own nothingness and despair. And out of the visions of Lucifer, of paradise lost, of the death of Abel, and of the vengeance of God comes the truth that must be spoken. What is perhaps most interesting about the play, however, and what makes Cain unlike Byron's poet, is the fact that Manfred's victory in death is not his; he merely suffers the defeat and curse of life, enduring guilt and transformation into the Abel-like man who humbles himself before his God. Cain, as I see it, exits in the very state of slavery he had rebelled against throughout the play;[38] and such a conclusion bespeaks, I believe, the depths of Byron's despair and nihilism at this time. Out of it he created in the poem (as

---

[38] Stopford Brooke, among others, could not be more wrong in interpreting this last scene as Cain's "finding God," learning to love, and thus making his redemption possible (see his "Byron's 'Cain,'" *Hibbert Journal*, XVIII [1919–20], 91–92). Bostetter is the only critic I have read who sees the ending in more nearly proper perspective. He says that Cain, in killing Abel, adopts "the tactics of the tyranny he has defied. Broken and defeated, he is driven into exile. . . . And, at least momentarily, he abandons his right of reason, repudiates his trip with Lucifer as a 'dreary dream,' and intellectually submits to the values of the victor" (*The Romantic Ventriloquists*, p. 288). I cannot agree with Bostetter, however, when he goes on to say that *Cain* is not, therefore, a "drama of despair," but rather "a continuous incitement to defiance, a devastating revelation of the vulnerability of the tyrant God, so that the very manner in which His momentary triumph is presented becomes an ironic prophecy that His ultimate collapse is

he had earlier hinted at it in *Childe Harold*) a "personal myth" of paradise lost endlessly repeated, cosmically as well as personally, each new fall lower than the first, each new creation feebler than the one before. Man, continually struggling against this recurrent doom, only hastens it by his very nature and the force of circumstance. "Men," he writes in Canto IX of *Don Juan*, "are but maggots of some huge Earth's burial" (xxxix), and, as Ridenour has so convincingly shown, cosmos and history, society and art, man and his gods are all finally swept not only into what I have called the general maw of desolation but also into this personal Byronic myth.

Heaven and Earth is in one sense anticlimactic, for it is also a reversion to Byron's poem, "Darkness." The time is just prior to the Deluge, and the spirits of the earth predict that

> *Man, earth, and fire, shall die,*
> *And sea and sky*
> *Look vast and lifeless in the eternal eye.*
> *(I, iii, 105–7)*

"All shall be void" (94), even "the place where strong Despair" endured its infinity of Promethean torture (91). The prophets are not heard, and men "walk darkling to their doom" (279). But Japhet, like Cain, is doomed to live, and he envisages life after the flood in the same imagery of ocean and desert with which *Childe Harold* closed:

> *Aye, father! but when they are gone,*
> *And we are all alone,*
> *Floating upon the azure desert, and*
> *The depth beneath us hides our own dear land,*
> *And dearer, silent friends and brethren, all*

---

inevitable and that the future belongs to the sons of Cain" (*ibid.*). Byron's point here, as in his other poetry, is clearly that there is no future different from the past:

> *for to give birth to those*
> *Who can but suffer many years, and die—*
> *Methinks is merely propagating Death,*
> *And multiplying murder.*
> *(Cain, II, i, 68–71)*

> *Buried in its immeasurable breast,*
> *Who, who, our tears, our shrieks, shall then*
> > *command?*
> *Can we in Desolation's peace have rest?*
> > (696–703)

Byron's answer to this question is perhaps reflected in his inability to bring himself to finish the play,[39] to picture that
agonizing struggle to live in desolation, just as Cain's wandering
never took poetic form; but *Don Juan* was probably his only
answer: "I'd weep,—but mine is not a weeping Muse" (II, xvi).
Thus when, as in *Heaven and Earth*, the Deluge comes and the
poet floats above the chaos of his world, when

> *first one universal shriek there rushed,*
> *Louder than the loud Ocean, like a crash*
> *Of echoing thunder; and then all was hushed,*
> *Save the wild wind and the remorseless dash*
> *Of billows; but at intervals there gushed,*
> *Accompanied by a convulsive splash,*
> *A solitary shriek, the bubbling cry*
> *Of some strong swimmer in his agony,*
> > (*Don Juan*, II, liii)

then the poet will laugh (at all mortal things), so that he may not
weep. For "the sad truth which hovers o'er [his] desk" demands
for sanity's sake that "what was once romantic" (that is, non-
satiric) now be "burlesque" (*Don Juan*, IV, iii–iv).

---

[39] Medwin reports that Byron did talk about a second part to *Heaven
and Earth* (*Conversations*, pp. 234–37), but it too is permeated by
unrelieved despair even as the ark "saves" mankind. Transporting
"the lovers to the moon or one of the planets" occurred to Byron,
Medwin continues, but with that combination of facetiousness and
seriousness that is his trademark, he "did not think they would approve of the moon as a residence. I remember what Fontenelle said
of its having no atmosphere, and the dark spots having caverns where
the inhabitants reside." "Darkness . . . was the Universe" still, for
Byron ("Darkness," ll. 81–82).

Chapter XI

DON JUAN AND THE ISLAND

It requires some temerity for anyone, after the fine work of Steffan and Ridenour, to write again on *Don Juan*. Yet Byron's development as a poet must be seen whole, continuous, and perhaps surprisingly consistent, encompassing all of his poetry. If what I have called (admittedly with a certain looseness in the term) his prophetic voice, which grows in power and conviction through the poems of 1816 and after, modulates itself into the colloquial chatter and banter of the Pulci-Berni mode, we should not be put off. Essentially the voice is still the same; its message has not changed: the various voices heard in *Hours of Idleness*, the tales, *Childe Harold*, and the plays have now, in effect, become one voice, remarkably supple and re-silient and telling.[1] As such, it concentrates all the voices of man into the presentation of a vision of the world, a "vision" in a truer sense than that implied in the only poem he wrote with the word in its title, *The Vision of Judgment*. Whereas there Byron adapts a conventional mode to destroy the efficacy of Southey's idea of vision (and that of others), in *Don Juan* the prophecies of Dante and Tasso are transformed into what is perhaps the only kind of coherent view available to Byron in his time—a fragmented, chaotic, digressive panorama of the world's waste and the unending self-destruction and corruption of man. If one must call it anti-romantic, or negatively romantic, as Morse Peckham might say, in so doing we are only recogniz-ing the inevitability of the form and voice of the poem in Byron's age.

---

[1] Ridenour makes essentially this same point in "The Mode of Byron's *Don Juan*," *PMLA*, LXXIX (1964), 443.

BYRON AND THE RUINS OF PARADISE

I must confess at the outset that I find the poem a grim one—funny, even hilarious at times, irreverent, coarse, moral and immoral at once, but through it all, despairing.[2] It is a poem of endless cycles or, as Ridenour has put it, endless repetitions of the Fall, which form the skeletal framework for the myriad variations Byron plays upon the nature of the fallen. Furthermore, it is a poem written (or narrated) from the point of view of the fallen, and this central fact determines both the form and style of the entire work. It is not written from above, or chanted mysteriously from within the temple of prophecy, or thundered divinely from the mount; the gaze of the poet is level with life, the accents of his voice the very accents of all men. "Byron is caught," as Ridenour says,

and he knows he is caught and he must manage to live in

---

[2] There is still considerable dispute about the final—or overarching—tone of the poem. For many years there were few dissenters from the view that the poem is fundamentally optimistic, a comic masterpiece. Most recently, Alvin B. Kernan argues once again for this reading: "Unfortunately, the majority of readers do not go past the Haidée episode or Juan's Turkish captivity, and for that reason overestimate the pessimistic qualities of the poem. But *Don Juan* as Byron left it ends on an affirmation of the goodness of life, and the entire poem is thus framed by a comic view of experience" (*The Plot of Satire*, p. 199). Still somehow Kernan can also conclude that "the narrator [of *Don Juan*] has no hope of meaningful action because he finds the universe itself ultimately meaningless" (p. 219). Similarly, E. D. Hirsch claims that Byron believed "in the *possibility* of an earthly perfection, and this was a faith that [he] never relinquished"; hence his "melancholy does not lapse into apathy because it is sustained by the hope of future perfection." *Don Juan*, therefore, represents for Hirsch "the victory of faith over experience," a somewhat curious conclusion in view of his admission that all "ideal relationships" in *Don Juan*, "as in all Byron's poems," inevitably "fail" ("Byron and the Terrestrial Paradise," pp. 472, 473, 484, 475).

Harold Bloom, on the other hand, sees the universe of *Don Juan* as "neither Christian nor Romantic, nor yet the eighteenth-century cosmos he would have liked to repossess. . . . What haunts Byron is the specter of meaninglessness, of pointless absurdity" (*The Visionary Company*, p. 258). See also Bostetter (*The Romantic Ventriloquists*, pp. 254–68) and Ridenour (*The Style of "Don Juan," passim*), both of whom emphasize the meaninglessness of Byron's world and the positive note inherent in his reaction to that world; and Brian Wilkie, whose chapter on *Don Juan* in his *The Romantic Poets and Epic Tradition* he entitles "The Epic of Negation" (pp. 188–226).

terms of this awareness. This is what he is engaged in coming
to terms with, and *Don Juan* is the final expression of the
quality of this acquiescence. It is clearly a frightening vision,
and Byron does not try to minimize the terror. In *Don Juan*
at any rate, he wastes little time in feeling sorry for himself
or us. If he has no real answers, the firmness with which he
poses the question is not contemptible, and the poise with
which he manages, for the most part, to keep his fragmentary
world from breaking up is really astonishing. For it is ultimately up to him. It is his attitude alone that can give it what
coherence it is susceptible of.[3]

Though Ridenour is certainly correct here, I should prefer a
somewhat different emphasis. "Caught" in the chaos he envisions, Byron's problem, as I see it, is less to live with his
awareness than to remain sane in the face of it. For it is clearly
an insane world:

> Shut up the World at large, let Bedlam out;
> And you will be perhaps surprised to find
> All things pursue exactly the same route,
> As now with those of soi-disant sound mind.
>
> (Don Juan, XIV, lxxxiv)

His sanity is maintained by the very act of creating as coherent
a vision of incoherence as is possible, not so much in the quality
of his acquiescence as in the quality of his triumph over his own
fallen nature and over the horror of his vision. At the same time,
as we have seen, the very means to the maintenance of sanity—
creation—also gluts the despair out of which that creation comes
—an interaction between poet and poem that Steffan sees but
interprets quite differently.[4] The precarious balance of laughter
and despair in *Don Juan* is a testament to this quest for sanity.
As Maurois says, the poem is the mask for "a strong and bitter
philosophy beneath light-hearted gaiety and whimsical rhymes";[5]
or, as Louise Swanton Belloc put it more tellingly and accurately
a century earlier, the work of *Don Juan* is flowers crowned with
thorns.[6] Victor Hugo was quite right in protesting the identifica-

---

[3] *The Style of "Don Juan,"* p. 148.
[4] *The Making of a Masterpiece,* pp. 52–53.
[5] André Maurois, *Byron,* trans. H. Miles (New York, 1930), p. 404.
[6] *Lord Byron* (Paris, 1824), I, 293–94.

tion of Voltaire and Byron: "Erreur! il y a une étrange différence entre le rire de Byron et le rire de Voltaire: Voltaire n'avait pas souffert."[7]

I should say, then, but for a quite different reason from that which prompted the popular outcry against *Don Juan* in Byron's time and immediately thereafter, that the poem is not moral, despite all of Byron's protestations to the contrary.[8] Fundamentally, it has to do not with morality or immorality but with nothingness, with a world devoid of value and humanity, a world in which even the "good" (in *any* sense) quickly destroys itself in its very effort to be what it is. It was not, as William Blackwood thought, Byron's "grossness or blackguardism," his "vile, heartless, and cold-blooded" attitude, that degraded "every sacred and tender feeling of the human heart"; it was simply that those sacred and tender feelings were no longer a property of man—except in those fleeting and paradoxical moments when he found them again only to die in the act of rediscovery.

I

While I am in almost complete agreement with Steffan's and Ridenour's analyses of *Don Juan*, then, I must add here some further comments in order to cement the relationship between the so-called "romantic" Byron and the satiric Byron and to demonstrate that they are not very different after all. I shall not be concerned with those recurrent patterns of technique and theme the analysis of which makes Steffan's study invaluable, nor, except incidentally, with Ridenour's proof of the extraordinary and elaborate coherence of Byron's vision in terms of the metaphor of the Fall. I should like merely to underscore their readings, and my own analysis of Byron's evolving

---

[7] "Sur Georges Gordon, Lord Byron," in *La muse francaise 1823–1824*, ed. Jules Marsan (2 vols.; Paris, 1909), II, 306–7. Hugo's point is especially interesting in view of Maurois' attempt to see Voltaire's *Candide* in *Don Juan* (*Byron*, pp. 402–4).

[8] E.g., in ltrs. to Murray, 1 Feb. 1819 and 25 Dec. 1822, in *LJ*, IV, 279; VI, 155–56.

career, by commenting briefly on a few of the major themes of the poem.

The most important of these concerns love. Love permeates the entire poem, and upon it is built much of the narrative—from Donna Inez through Aurora Raby and the Duchess of Fitz-Fulke. Equally dominant is the debasement of love to lust, deceit, sexual abandon, jealousy, intrigue, habit. Byron thus provides a constant reminder of man's loss of his essential humanity, "For without hearts there is no home" (III, lii), and even more important, in the look of love is all of that which is best in humankind—the feelings of a

> *friend, child, lover, brother—*
> *All that the best can mingle and express*
> *When two pure hearts are poured in one another.*
> *(IV, xxvi)*

Such love is not of the fallen senses, which have taught us to vulgarize and mechanize human relations into "making love." Rather it is of man's "very Spirit," born with him and in him (xxvii), "A thing, of which similitudes can show / No real likeness" (XVI, x). As in all men, in Juan love had become hardened as the inevitable consequence of his perpetual (and human) steeling of his heart against despair and sorrow so that he might endure the world's ways and triumph over them on the world's own terms. As a consequence of the world's having made love well-nigh impossible, he will tolerate no Haidée-esque idylls long. With the introduction of Aurora Raby into the poem, however, Byron provides what seems to be a hope, for she renews in Juan

> *some feelings he had lately lost,*
> *Or hardened; feelings which, perhaps ideal,*
> *Are so divine, that I must deem them real:—*
>
> *The love of higher things and better days;*
> *The unbounded hope, and heavenly ignorance*
> *Of what is called the World, and the World's ways;*
> *The moments when we gather from a glance*
> *More joy than from all future pride or praise,*
> *Which kindle manhood, but can ne'er entrance*

BYRON AND THE RUINS OF PARADISE

The Heart in an existence of its own,
Of which another's bosom is the zone.

(XVI, cvii–cviii)

Such love Byron, with the typical Romantic nostalgia we have seen as early as the *Hours of Idleness*, associates with the past, home, childhood, innocence, freedom, and the like; and in *Don Juan* this association provides him ample opportunity to identify himself (as the poet in the poem) with his hero and his major theme. For the poet, too, love is lost, the past irrecoverable, the future a vast waste:

I

Remember when, though I had no great plenty
Of worlds to lose, yet still, to pay my court, I
  Gave what I had—a heart; as the world went, I
Gave what was worth a world; for worlds could never
Restore me those pure feelings, gone for ever.

(VI, v)

Similarly, in his address to the critic Jeffrey in Canto X, the verse is easily modulated into a farewell to homeland, childhood, the past, and all that is now only a fond dream:

it may seem a schoolboy's whine,
And yet I seek not to be grand nor witty,
But I am half a Scot by birth, and bred
A whole one, and my heart flies to my head,—

As "Auld Lang Syne" brings Scotland, one and all,
  Scotch plaids, Scotch snoods, the blue hills, and

clear streams,

The Dee—the Don—Balgounie's brig's black wall—
  All my boy feelings, all my gentler dreams
Of what I then dreamt, clothed in their own pall,—
  Like Banquo's offspring—floating past me seems
My childhood, in this childishness of mine:—
I care not—'t is a glimpse of "Auld Lang Syne."

(xvii–xviii)

The confession of the "childishness" of this *recherche du temps perdu* should not deafen us to the solemnity of the voice of loss; the public-private voice of the early lyrics is sounding through the mockery, revelry, and *gaucherie* of *Don Juan*. It is the poet's fate and curse to have his heart fly constantly to his head to melt the armor of cynicism and world-weariness, to revive the dream of all that has been lost with an intensity that demands expression and tramples down the pose of mockery and indifference. The closing "I care not" above is belied by the tone of the whole passage, the flat honesty of "I seek not to be grand nor witty," and the horrible vision of Banquo's unborn children "clothed in their own pall."

Thus the voice that laughs so that it may not weep weeps often in *Don Juan*, for all men and for himself as the constant symbol of suffering and lost humanity.

> *No more—no more—Oh! never more on me*
> *The freshness of the heart can fall like dew,*
> *Which out of all the lovely things we see*
> *Extracts emotions beautiful and new,*
> *Hived in our bosoms like the bag o' the bee.*
> *Think'st thou the honey with those objects grew?*
> *Alas! 't was not in them, but in thy power*
> *To double even the sweetness of a flower.*
>
> (I, ccxiv)

The heart now is steeled by experience to cynicism and to laughter, to the "judgment" of the Augustan satirist rather than the indomitable idealism of the Romantic poet:

> *No more—no more—Oh! never more, my heart,*
> *Canst thou be my sole world, my universe!*
> *Once all in all, but now a thing apart,*
> *Thou canst not be my blessing or my curse:*
> *The illusion's gone for ever, and thou art*
> *Insensible, I trust, but none the worse,*
> *And in thy stead I've got a deal of judgment,*
> *Though Heaven knows how it ever found a lodgment.*
>
> (ccxv)

This is a crucial passage, perhaps even more central to an understanding of *Don Juan* than the one in Canto IV about laughter being necessary to prevent weeping, and the two passages together form a solid basis for understanding the constant fluctuation in tone of the poem.

Kernan interprets that fluctuation in terms of comic, satiric, and tragic modes as they tend to be exemplified in the characters (and "worlds") of Juan, what he calls the "narrator," and "the isolated individual" (the major example of which is Haidée).[9] Kernan's view is important, well argued, and cogent, but it also bifurcates the essential unity that Byron achieves in the poem through the figure of the poet. For Kernan "the onward movement of life," a "constant flow of life leading on from change to change is the essential reality of the world of *Don Juan*"; and Juan himself represents "instinctive and uncodified" life, "spontaneous" and free, a life in which "mind does not intervene between his perceptions of the world and his understanding of it."[10] On the other hand, Kernan defines the narrator not as the poet, as I have been dealing with that emerging figure, but as the man of mind, the disillusioned cynic, who counters the comic vision of life with the conviction that things don't always turn out for the best, that civilized life is a sham, and that meaningful action is impossible because the universe itself is ultimately meaningless. In commenting on the two passages quoted above, Kernan hears in them only the voice of his narrator relating the uncomic facts from his world-weary point of view, with mind dominating heart; but however deep that disillusionment becomes (and Kernan does acknowledge its depth), it is successfully submerged somehow, says Kernan, by the comic life of the poem, flowing "excitedly, bubbling, a surge into which the youthful comic hero flings himself to enjoy the invigoration of being a part of the world's rushing power."[11]

I cannot agree, for whatever else it is (a satire upon society's foibles, man's inhumanity to man, cant and hypocrisy, political tyranny, etc.), *Don Juan* must also be seen as an im-

---

[9] *The Plot of Satire*, pp. 171–222.
[10] *Ibid.*, pp. 178, 182, 201. Kernan goes on to say, quite wrongly I think (although he builds his case quite carefully), that Juan's is in many ways "a beneficent world. He often lands in temporary trouble, but bad luck is only momentary and usually turns out to be good luck in disguise" (p. 191)—thus characterizing the world of the poem as a whole in terms which reflect only the partial view of Juan rather than the all-inclusive view of the poet.
[11] *Ibid.*, p. 212.

mensely compassionate poem. Unlike Kernan's narrator, Byron's poet *does* have a heart. If it can no longer be his sole world, his universe, in a sense the world and universe, shivered into a chaos of feeling elements that brokenly live on, like those of his own heart, have, through the medium of his own experience, loss, and suffering, become *his* heart. As such, the poet's heart is both blessing and curse—blessing in that it represents the essence of his humanity, bruised and beaten yet puissant and warmly breathing, curse in that it leads him to that fundamental sympathy which is the cause of its brokenness and his own despair. The illusion of a world separate, untaintable, and invulnerable, set apart from the slow stain of mundane affairs, is gone forever except in dreams, but in its place is not a heart insensible but a heart whose capacity has been enlarged beyond that of the private, parochial dream. It is this heart that speaks to us in the Haidée episode, which I take to be the fulcrum as well as the symbolic core of the entire poem; it is this heart that envisioned a Haidée, a Dudù, an Aurora Raby, a Leila, that weeps over the carnage of Ismail, that responds to the sparks of humanity, however few, in the characters of Gulbeyaz, Lambro, Baba, and even Suwarrow. But as that heart naturally and inevitably goes out to the essentially human, so it must be constantly restrained for sanity's sake by the laughter of the sophisticate, the sneer of the worldling, the reasoned pessimism of the philosopher, the jokes of the buffoon, and the realism of the prophet-poet. The response of each mask in its own way claims for itself the honesty and clear-sightedness of vision, for in none of them is found the deceit and hypocrisy with which man masks his heart in the world, "Corroding in the cavern of the heart" all feeling,

> *Making the countenance a masque of rest*
> *And turning Human Nature to an art.*
>
> *(XV, iii)*

The structure of the poem, then, whatever coherence it commands through the metaphor of the Fall or patterns of experience or overlapping themes, is built solidly on the thesis and antithesis of the poet's emotional and rational responses to the world. He is constantly being torn by his heart's involvement and restored by his cooler, dispassionate judgment; and both of these dynamic movements cohere in the consistent vision of the universe as a vast sea of desolation and ruin. Again and again the prophet-poet molds the evidence of his eyes into an image of the earth as it is, only to withdraw from it in horror to the safety of his own mind and one of his cerebral masks. He is constantly aware that his prophecy is unheard, his vision vain:

> *This I could prove beyond a single doubt,*
> *Were there a jot of sense among Mankind;*
> *But till that point d'appui is found, alas!*
> *Like Archimedes, I leave Earth as 't was.*
> *(XIV, lxxxiv)*

If he could, he would change it, and in the letters as well as in *Don Juan* Byron hopes (against hope) that this will be the result of his efforts:

> *My Muse by exhortation means to mend*
> *All people, at all times, and in most places,*
> *Which puts my Pegasus to these grave paces.*
> *(XII, xxxix)*

But he is aware throughout that, like Cervantes "in that too true tale," "all such efforts fail" (XIII, viii). What is left is the masquerade which preserves sanity and the unyielding nihilism (VII, vi) of sober vision and prophecy:

> *If I can stave off thought, which—as a whelp*
> *Clings to its teat—sticks to me through the abyss*
> *Of this odd labyrinth; or as the kelp*
> *Holds by the rock; or as a lover's kiss*
> *Drains its first draught of lips,*   *(X, xxviii)*

>   *at least I'll try*
> *To tell you truths you will not take as true,*
> *Because they are so.*   *(lxxxiv)*

Those truths are couched in the comic vision beneath which the heart eternally wails,

Don Juan, The Island

> *A nondescript and ever-varying rhyme,*
> *A versified Aurora Borealis,*
>   *Which flashes o'er a waste and icy clime.*
> *When we know what all are, we must bewail us,*
>   *But ne'ertheless I hope it is no crime*
> *To laugh at all things—for I wish to know*
> *What, after all, are all things—but a show?*
>   *(VII, ii)*

By such means the poet, in the words of Juan in the midst of the siege of Ismail, "At least . . . will endure / Whate'er is to be borne" (VIII, c). In a grimmer, and unduly neglected passage, Byron sees his role as comic poet as analogous to the laughter of a death's head:

> *Mark! how it laughs and scorns at all you are!*
>   *And yet was what you are; from ear to ear*
> *It laughs not—there is now no fleshy bar*
>   *So called; the Antic long hath ceased to hear,*
> *But still he smiles; and whether near or far,*
>   *He strips from man that mantle (far more dear*
> *Than even the tailor's), his incarnate skin,*
> *White, black, or copper—the dead bones will grin.*
>
> *And thus Death laughs,—it is sad merriment,*
>   *But still it is so; and with such example*
> *Why should not Life be equally content*
>   *With his Superior, in a smile to trample*
> *Upon the nothings which are daily spent*
>   *Like bubbles on an Ocean much less ample*
> *Than the Eternal Deluge, which devours*
> *Suns as rays—worlds like atoms—years like hours?*
>   *(IV, xii–xiii)*

What Steffan sees as the manner triumphing over the matter of the poem on occasion, as wit crackling merely "for the sake of isolated jest,"[12] as Byron becoming at times intoxicated with his own brilliance and humor, are not always signs of the poet's loss of his sure grasp of the materials, technique, and structure of the poem. It may be the result of Byron's often expressed determination that the poem, whatever else it might

---

[12] *The Making of a Masterpiece*, p. 295.

be, should not be dull. I take these sallies, however, not merely as an antidote to dullness or, as Steffan suggests, a natural outcome of the "itch for variety and paradox" symptomatic of Byron's "vigorous and boisterous mind."[13] I see them as the result of his mind's constant and fearful attempt to wean him from the sorrows of the heart; from the overflow of compassion that could throw him from the brink of precarious sanity into the abyss of unutterable despair; from the perils of his clear vision of nightmarish darkness to the more comfortable facetiousness of manners within which lurked, ironically, his basic softness and warmth and humanity.

II

The theme of love in *Don Juan* is also related to the metaphor of Eden and the Fall, as Ridenour has noted. Of love, he writes, "the most powerful force undermining the paradisal relationship is the very force that made it a paradise in the first place. . . . love recreates for the individual son of Adam the paradisal state lost by the first Adam. . . ."[14] Although I agree with this idea, once again I would give it a different emphasis. As Ridenour sees it, love for Byron is "the most potent enemy to innocence (as embodied in young love)," and it is also Adam's "experience of such love" which led to the Fall.[15] Perhaps. It is more important that for Byron true love does indeed re-create paradise, indeed *is* paradise regained, but, as the tales and *Childe Harold* have told us, that re-creation is only momentary or illusory: as I have pointed out elsewhere, in the very act of being most human and warm man is betrayed by circumstances or the world (or perhaps even by God) in such a way that his essential humanness is sacrificed or lost the moment it is gained. Once that lesson is learned, man in his new and bitter wisdom thenceforth steels his heart against further loss, sorrow, and despair by "manning" himself through an exercise of will and mind— and in so doing he denies the very humanity whose "loss" was so severe a blow.

---

[13] *Ibid.*, p. 293.
[14] *The Style of "Don Juan,"* pp. 85–86.
[15] *Ibid.*

Love, then, is "Like Adam's recollection of his fall" (I, cxxvii), or, more precisely, Adam's recollection of life before the Fall. Once "The Tree of Knowledge has been plucked" and "all's known," Adam finds that "Life yields nothing further to recall" such an existence (cxxvii).[16] Thus of Juan and Haidée's "marriage" Byron writes:

> on the lone shore were plighted
> *Their hearts; the stars, their nuptial torches, shed*
> *Beauty upon the beautiful they lighted:*
> *Ocean their witness, and the cave their bed,*
> *By their own feelings hallowed and united,*
> *Their priest was Solitude, and they were wed:*
> *And they were happy—for to their young eyes*
> *Each was an angel, and earth Paradise.*
>
> *(II, cciv)*

Alone together, the two lovers found "another Eden" (IV, x), proving Byron's claim that "The Heart is like the sky, a part of Heaven" (II, ccxiv). Dudù is described in precisely the same terms, and in her selflessness, her "perfect innocence" and warmth, she was "kind and gentle as / The Age of Gold" (VI, lx, lv). And Aurora Raby, "a young star who shone / O'er Life, too sweet an image for such glass" (XV, xliii), is described by Byron as a seraph "with an aspect beyond Time":

> *She looked as if she sat by Eden's door,*
> *And grieved for those who could return no more.*
>
> *(XV, xlv)*

Such visions of Eden, seen in the context of love complete and innocent and self-sufficient, are also associated by Byron with childhood, as we have seen. Juan and Haidée

> were children still,
> *And children still they should have ever been;*
> *They were not made in the real world to fill*
> *A busy character in the dull scene,*

---

[16] This point also effectively undercuts Hirsch's argument for Byron's unshakable faith in a "terrestrial paradise" ("Byron and the Terrestrial Paradise," *passim*).

> *But like two beings born from out a rill,*
> *A Nymph and her belovéd, all unseen*
> *To pass their lives in fountains and on flowers,*
> *And never know the weight of human hours.*
>
> *(IV, xv)*

Life and the world, however, will not admit of childhood or of dreams of Eden, "For soon or late Love is his own avenger" (lxxiii), and circumstance, the greater uncreator, demolishes both[17]—sweeps love and childhood and the past into the maelstrom of the present and transforms all into ugliness and waste.

> *In vain the dews of Heaven descend above*
> *The bleeding flower and blasted fruit of Love;*
>
> *(lxx)*

and as in *The Giaour* and other poems, Byron makes the final scene emblematic of the loss:

> *That isle [Haidée's] is now all desolate and bare,*
> *Its dwellings down, its tenants passed away;*
> *None but her own and Father's grave is there,*
> *And nothing outward tells of human clay;*
> *Ye could not know where lies a thing so fair,*
> *No stone is there to show, no tongue to say,*
> *What was; no dirge, except the hollow sea's,*
> *Mourns o'er the beauty of the Cyclades.*
>
> *(lxxii)*

No tongue, that is, save Byron's, no dirge but *Don Juan*, and there is little doubt that the fate of that reincarnation of Haidée, Aurora Raby, would have been the same had Byron lived to continue his fable.[18]

---

[17] Cf. Byron's quotation of the *"Surgit amari aliquid"* passage from Lucretius' *De Rerum Natura* (Bk. IV, 1133) in X, 78.

[18] Kernan interprets these comments on Haidee's death as those of the "narrator" and hence, implicitly, not Byron's (or the poet's). He also sees the last scene of the poem—Juan's sudden confrontation by the Duchess of Fitz-Fulke—as "a climactic image of the comic triumph of life over death. The illusion of a pale, bloodless world moving toward sterility and death is transformed by courage, vitality, and good chance into a living, breathing, and satisfying immediacy" (*The Plot of Satire*, pp. 219, 199). On the contrary, Juan's "union" with the

It is this vision of the archetypal loss of love and the ruins of paradise that gives rise to the variety of tones Byron uses in describing love elsewhere in the poem.[19] As he writes in Canto IV, reminiscent of his use of the same device in *Childe Harold,*

> *But let me change this theme, which grows too sad,*
> *And lay this sheet of sorrows on the shelf;*
> *I don't much like describing people mad,*
> *For fear of seeming rather touched myself.*
>
> *(lxxiv)*

The scene is the aftermath of Haidée's death, and what is "changed" is not so much the theme as the tone—as the passage indicates clearly, the change of tone necessary to preserve sanity. He will laugh at love, rail at love, curse at love, make jokes of it, denigrate it to a game, even revile it and call it "the very God of evil" (II, ccv), but all of these voices are still contained within the voice of despair desperately battling against the further shattering of the heart, a part of which dies "as each fond hope ends" (xxi).

But man, as I have said, and as Byron has so often indicated in his earlier poems, learns from his loss and from the world. Steeling his heart, he becomes more a man and less a human, and thus can survive or even triumph over the world on its own terms. Juan in the court of Catherine the Great, fresh from the slaughter of Ismail, is the symbol of this transformation: in full and gaudy uniform, the obvious hero: "He / Seems Love turned a Lieutenant of Artillery!" (IX, xliv). A variant upon this theme is Lambro, the fisher of men; in a searing parody of Christ, he fishes for wandering merchant vessels only to confiscate their cargoes and sell the crews into slavery or slaughter them in battle (II, cxxv–cxxvi). To clinch his point

---

Duchess will clearly plunge him into the world's ways (the ways of Catherine the Great, for example) on its own terms, thus sealing him off forever from the paradise inherent in the figure of Aurora.

[19] For a quite different discussion on the variety of tones in *Don Juan* see Ernest J. Lovell, "Irony and Image in *Don Juan*," in C. D. Thorpe, C. Baker, and B. Weaver (eds.), *The Major English Romantic Poets* (Carbondale, Ill., 1957), pp. 129–48.

Byron also describes the more civilized piracy, slavery, and slaughter of love amid society in exactly the same phrase, "Fishers for men" (XII, lix).

Such gentlemanly and polite conflict is but the superficial mask for what men truly are once their hearts have been steeled and their bodies and minds manned to do battle. For that truth we must look to the archetypal war and waste which for Byron characterize life when it was not "This paradise of Pleasure and *Ennui*" (XIV, xvii), "that Microcosm on stilts, / Yclept the Great World" (XII, lvi).[20] The Siege of Ismail is his terrifyingly coherent vision of the shattered, violent, bestial world that is left after the death of the heart and the loss of Eden. It is an extended scene introduced, significantly, by a description not of war but of man in the universe, a "scene of all-confessed inanity" which the poet, as prophet, must hold up as the epitome of "the nothingness of Life" (VII, vi):

> Dogs, or men!—for I flatter you in saying
>   That ye are dogs—your betters far—ye may
> Read, or read not, what I am now essaying
>   To show ye what ye are in every way.
> As little as the moon stops for the baying
>   Of wolves, will the bright Muse withdraw one ray
> From out her skies—then howl your idle wrath!
> While she still silvers o'er your gloomy path.
>
> (vii)

And, finally, with grim humor, he prepares for the gore of the battle proper with an image of the new creation, instituted by the fiat of that surrogate god, fallen man:

> "Let there be Blood!" says man, and there's a sea!
> The fiat of this spoiled child of the Night
>   (For Day ne'er saw his merits) could decree
> More evil in an hour, than thirty bright
>   Summers could renovate, though they should be

---

[20] At the same time it should be noted that Byron can at times merge both these images (war and the "great world") with devastating effectiveness:

> Society is now one polished horde,
> Formed of two mighty tribes, the Bores and Bored.
>
> (XIII, xcv)

Don Juan, The Island

Lovely as those which ripened Eden's fruit;
    For War cuts up not only branch, but root.

                                                    (xli)

But war and bloody cruelty, "Hell's pollution" (VIII, li), Byron
sees not merely for what it is but as an emblem of civilization:

Now back to thy great joys, Civilisation!
And the sweet consequence of large society,
    War—pestilence—the despot's desolation,
The kingly scourge, the lust of notoriety,
    The millions slain by soldiers for their ration,
The scenes like Catherine's boudoir at threescore,
With Ismail's storm to soften it the more.

                                                    (lxviii)

Amid the heat of battle and the overpowering bloodlust, even
"War forgot his own destructive art / In more destroying Nature" (lxxxii), the nature of man whose heart has been buried or
destroyed in his cerebrating manhood:

All that the mind would shrink from of excesses—
    All that the body perpetrates of bad;
All that we read—hear—dream, of man's distresses—
    All that the Devil would do if run stark mad;
All that defies the worst which pen expresses,—
    All by which Hell is peopled, or as sad
As Hell—mere mortals who their power abuse—
Was here (as heretofore and since) let loose.

                                                    (cxxiii)

It is *The Siege of Corinth* all over again, or the nightmarish
wasteland ride of *Mazeppa*, or the damp horror of *The Prisoner
of Chillon*, or the visions on the field of Waterloo of *Childe
Harold*, or the mad conflagration of *Sardanapalus*, or any of
the numberless insane slaughters in Byron's poetry—all perpe-
trated by the human mind bereft of the heart's softness and love.
It is visions such as these that call forth from Byron unrestrained
imprecations against the God or gods who permit the carnage.
Cain and *Heaven and Earth* are but the intellectualized versions
of, for example, this passage in the shipwreck scene in Canto II:

'T was twilight, and the sunless day went down
    Over the waste of waters; like a veil,

> *Which, if withdrawn, would but disclose the frown*
>   *Of one whose hate is masked but to assail.*
> *Thus to their hopeless eyes the night was shown,*
>   *And grimly darkled o'er the faces pale,*
> *And the dim desolate deep: twelve days had Fear*
> *Been their familiar, and now Death was here.*
>
> *(xlix)*

Thus man is both destroyer and destroyed, victim and victimizer, and the gods (or God) made in man's image but conspire to sink him in the vast deep of desolation. "The sparrow's fall / Is special providence," he writes in another place, echoing *Hamlet*:

> *though how it gave*
> *Offence we know not; probably it perched*
> *Upon the tree which Eve so fondly searched.*
>
> *(IX, xix)*

In another canto, quoting Wordsworth out of context in a passing attack upon his favorite target among the Romantic poets, Byron turns the passage upon itself to give us a version of the new Trinity overseeing the battle of Ismail:

> *"Carnage" (so Wordsworth tells you) "is God's*
>   *daughter:"*
> *If he speak truth, she is Christ's sister, and*
> *Just now behaved as in the Holy Land.*
>
> *(VIII, ix)*

Byron's prophecy, then, is clearly not based on cause and effect—if you go on so, the result will be so—but rather it is what he refers to facetiously in Canto XV as the prophecy of *is* and *was* (lxxix); of "a plain man" (I, xxii) who "Without, or with, offence to friends or foes" will "sketch" the "world exactly as it goes" (VIII, lxxxix); who makes "addresses from the throne" (III, xcvi) in the guise of merriment because his fundamental humanity "cannot always bring / Itself to apathy" (IV, iv); who denounces "all amorous writing" in a poem dedicated to love and the death of the heart (V, ii); who feigns stoicism only to reveal his hurt more fully; who hates not but knows that he is hated (IX, xxi); who knows that he is unheard yet declaims all the louder for his loneliness; who weeps while knowing that his tears are but the ocean poured into a sieve (XIV, xlix); and whose voice crying in the wilderness, feeding its own despair, is the only hope discernible amid the wreck of all paradises and all worlds.

III

But the masks and voices, the laughter and buffoon-ery, the cynicism and anger of *Don Juan* were not enough for Byron. In the end man must have his visions and his hope, else all is nothingness. Thus at the very time that he was begin-ning to create the stagnant and oppressive boredom of the new Eden of the Amundevilles in Norman Abbey, he had also to create a new Haidée and a new paradise safe from the world's slow stain, and so we have *The Island*, completed early in 1823. The millennial note is sounded immediately: the men of the *Bounty* are all of "Young hearts" languishing not for their home-land but rather "for sunny isle," where "summer years" (I, 27–28) produce

> *The general garden, where all steps may roam,*
> *Where Nature owns a nation as her child,*
> *Exulting in the enjoyment of the wild;*
> *Their shells, their fruits, the only wealth they know,*
> *Their unexploring navy, the canoe;*
> *Their sport, the dashing breakers and the chase;*
> *Their strangest sight, an European face:—*
> *Such was the country which these strangers yearned*
> *To see again—a sight they dearly earned.*
>
> *(42–50)*

It is perhaps appropriate that their return to paradise should be the direct result of their throwing off of the tyranny of Cap-tain Bligh, though this hypothesis is quickly ruled out by Byron's obvious antipathy to the mutineers. What he apparently hoped to exploit, though it is done crudely and awkwardly, is the fact that all men, even the worst and rudest, long for the same thing, "repose," the Edenic retreat from the world's tyranny, the desire to triumph over time and circumstance, the fundamental human desire to follow the heart. (Significantly, Byron notes that verse can do no more "than reach the awakened heart" [II, 102].) Thus

Canto II paints in lavish colors the Edenic existence of the island-
ers, uncorrupted by civilized man, and the aura of love that pervades the whole scene. Neuha, the Haidée of the scene, is
described in precisely the terms Byron lavished upon Lambro's
daughter and upon Dudù. She was "In growth a woman, through
in years a child" (124),

> The infant of an infant world, as pure
> From Nature—lovely, warm, and premature;
> Dusky like night, but night with all her stars;
> Or cavern sparkling with its native spars;
> With eyes that were a language and a spell,
> A form like Aphrodite's in her shell,
> With all her loves around her on the deep.
>
> (127–33)

She was formed, like the gentle "southern seas" (141),

> To bear the bark of others' happiness,
> Nor feel a sorrow till their joy grew less:
> Her wild and warm yet faithful bosom knew
> No joy like what it gave; her hopes ne'er drew
> Aught from Experience, that chill touchstone, whose
> Sad proof reduces all things from their hues.
>
> (143–48)

Her lover is Torquil, also born and bred amid the wilds of nature
and the ocean, a "soaring spirit" destined to lead and rule, but
in this setting merely "A blooming boy" (203, 209). Apparently,
the entire mutineer crew of the *Bounty* falls under the spell of
love and the human heart; for it is

> love which maketh all things fond and fair,
> The youth which makes one rainbow of the air,
> The dangers past, that make even Man enjoy
> The pause in which he ceases to destroy,
> The mutual beauty, which the sternest feel
> Strike to their hearts like lightning to the steel.
>
> (298–303)

Their hearts, in a passage reminiscent of *Sardanapalus* (or

Tennyson's "Lotus Eaters"), "Rapt in the fond forgetfulness of life" (332), were

> *tamed to that voluptuous state,*
> *At once Elysian and effeminate,*
> *Which leaves no laurels o'er the Hero's urn;—*
> *These wither when for aught save blood they burn;*
> *Yet when their ashes in their nook are laid,*
> *Doth not the myrtle leave as sweet a shade?*
> *(312–17)*

Here was "no distracting world to call" them off from love (334–35), no clock time to dole out meagerly "the daily pittance of our span" (350) and to point and mock "with iron laugh at man" (351):

> *What deemed they of the future or the past?*
> *The present, like a tyrant, held them fast.*
> *(352–53)*

This idyll is shattered abruptly by the appearance of a strange sail and "wicked-looking craft" (513). There is a short but fierce battle in which most of the mutineers are either slain or captured, and a few flee "Tracked like wild beasts" (III, 15). The world under the banner of justice and vengeance, has claimed for its own another paradise. The surviving mutineers' "sea-green isle, their guilt-won Paradise, / No more could shield their Virtue or their Vice" (39–40), and "Proscribed even in their second country, they / Were lost" (43–44). But in the world of fairy tale where dreams come true and paradise, though ruined, is regainable, love appears in the form of Neuha, to waft Torquil from the iron death of the invaders into an underwater cave. The archetypal death and rebirth pattern here is too obvious for Byron to have been totally unaware of it, although he does not press the point. The fierce pursuers interpret the lovers' plunge into the ocean (at the foot of a cliff that even Torquil sees initially as his "tombstone") as a mysterious death or transformation:

> *Some said he had not plunged into the wave,*
> *But vanished like a corpse-light from a grave;*

Others, that something supernatural
Glared in his figure, more than mortal tall;
While all agreed that in his cheek and eye
There was a dead hue of Eternity.

(IV, 85–90)

The cave to which Neuha leads Torquil is a cathedral of the sea, architecturally complete, but it is also a world unto itself, something like Zuleika's cave in *The Bride of Abydos*, where "oft in youthful reverie / She dreamed what Paradise might be" (II, 586–87). All within Neuha's cave "Was love, though buried strong as in the grave" (IV, 222)—a simple yet clear image of life, love, and the dominion of the heart amid the strife, desolation, and death of the world:

The waves without sang round their couch, their roar
As much unheeded as if life were o'er.

(227–28)

The poem concludes with the slaughter of Christian and his two remaining comrades, the former shaking his fist in rage against the intrusive and destructive world, and the return of Neuha and Torquil to their island, "No more polluted with a hostile hue" (402). Now "all was Hope and Home" (404) and a reign of love such "As only the yet infant world displays" (420).

This final "surrender to the charms of a utopia," as M. K. Joseph puts it,[21] is, I submit, neither surprising nor illogical in Byron's development as I have been tracing it. Nor is it a surrender to sentiment, a cheap sop to public taste for the romantic. It is rather an extraordinary personal confession as well as the poet's last desperate articulation of hope for man. Throughout the poetry, from *Hours of Idleness* on, man's heart and its loss has been a, if not the, central theme. In *The Island* what I have called the public-private voice of compassion, loss, and wounded humanity simply comes to the fore, nakedly, without embarrassment or mask. For all of Byron's protestations of the invulnerability of the mind, man's last refuge and unrazed citadel of reason, man's only hope for a resumption of pre-

---

[21] *Byron the Poet*, p. 63.

lapsarian life or, to put it less grandly, of happiness, is in love. In the mind's very act of steeling the heart against shock lies the unmanning of the human being, the betrayal of all efforts toward regaining the pristine past, the deadly accommodation of one's being to the world's demands—to what Byron calls in all of his poetry (including *Don Juan*) the irresistible desire for prey.

Yet viewed with unromantic eyes which are hardened to the world that was thrust upon us undesired, the heart is inevitably doomed to destruction and death, or to an eternity of suffering. Thus the poet, paradoxically, must harden his heart to write of what destroys him, only to respond to experience all the more deeply and compassionately through his vivid re-creation of its terror and loss. The desperation inherent in this endless cycle of self-torture and refusal to yield up all humanity is apparent in all phases of Byron's work, lyric, narrative, dramatic, and satiric. Masked continually by the various roles and voices he employs, the human voice, as Robert Frost might say, still comes through, tellingly and poignantly—even as the mental gymnastics of its creator seek to restrain it from leading to total despair and madness.

With no solution to a world so constituted and no balm to heal the wounds of man, or of his own shattered being, Byron's voice seems to me more heroic than that of any of his heroes. It is that of man eternally alive and feeling amidst a universe of death that is eternally bent on perpetuating chaos and nothingness. It sings neither dirge nor triumph, but articulates the enduring agony of a residual humanity to whom the only courage is to endure the heart's continual shattering and to die a man, not an animal. It is the voice of a poet-prophet who has heard, and still hears, "the mermaids singing," but who knows that his vision of a world without mermaids will not be shared by the world's sleepers. They will wake merely to drown; or, to adopt Yeats's terms, they will no longer hear the falconer (if indeed there is a falconer), and all

> *Things fall apart; the centre cannot hold;*
> *Mere anarchy is loosed upon the world,*
> *The blood-dimmed tide is loosed, and everywhere*
> *The ceremony of innocence is drowned.*

BYRON AND THE RUINS OF PARADISE

If for Byron there is no rough beast slouching toward Bethlehem to be born, the very coherence and consistency of his view of the anarchy is itself of value. If in his poetry there is little evidence of a Romantic construct, a world ever created anew, a system of belief however personal, his voice crying out in the accents of the human heart will be, if not so oracular as Shelley's, still a "contagion to the world." For it is upon his ruins of paradise that all future building must take place.

INDEX

INDEX

Fox, Charles James, 119
Francesca (in *Siege of Corinth*), 168, 170, 172–74, 261
Fraser, G. S., 175
Frost, Robert, 351
Frye, Northrop, 48n, 53n, 136n, 203, 204
Fugitive Pieces, xviin

G Galileo (in *Childe Harold*), 281
Garrod, H. W., 210, 323
Geneva, Lake, 181n, 247
Giaffir (in *Bride of Abydos*), 117, 121, 125–26, 129–31, 149, 151–52: as embodiment of mind, 127–28, 141, 159; compared to Claudius in *Hamlet*, 134–35, 137
Giaour, The, 88, 126, 139, 144, 148, 151, 153, 293n, 342: criticism of, 91, 92n, 100, 102n, 111–12, 168n; composition of, 91, 96–98, 101, 103–10 *passim*, 115; B on, 92, 94, 101, 141; analysis of, 94–117; structure of, 97, 111, 113–14, 116–17; compared to *Manfred*, 97, 117, 254–56, 258; point of view in, 97–98, 101, 106, 107–9, 112–17, 121, 191, 256; fisherman-narrator in, 98, 101–2, 105–16 *passim*, 156, 158, 191, 254; poet in, 98–99, 101, 103, 104, 108, 110, 113–17, 191, 256; refrain in, 116; compared to *Bride of Abydos*, 121–22; compared to *Corsair*, 140; compared to *Lara*, 155; compared to *Siege of Corinth*, 167, 172–73; compared to *Parisina*, 177–78; compared to *Mazeppa*, 307n
Giaour, the, 26, 96–98, 101, 106–7, 111–14, 132–33, 141, 145, 170n, 269, 302: compared to Harold, 94–95; nature of heroism, 100, 102–3, 149; compared to Cain, 104, 110, 151; as man, 109, 116; compared to Lara, 156; compared to Alp, 167; compared to Manfred, 253–55, 256–57, 262
Gibbon, Edward, 178–79, 184, 247, 249
Gifford, William, 92, 118, 168n, 171, 174, 177n, 280
Gilfillan, George, 80n
Glover, Richard, 119
Goethe, J. W. von, 122n, 250, 253, 256, 257, 323
Goldsmith, Oliver, 267
Goode, Clement T., 113n, 155n, 187n
Gray, Agnes and May, xix–xx
Greece, 32, 54, 66n, 75, 268: as metaphoric Eden, xx, 33, 86, 101–2, 105–6, 150, 169, 283; as image of slavery, 36,

85, 104, 106, 207; in *Childe Harold*, 70, 75, 82, 84–86, 87, 273; in *Giaour*, 98, 101–8 *passim*, 110, 116, 144; in *Bride of Abydos*, 129
Grey de Ruthyn, Lord, xxii
Grierson, H. J. C., 223n
Guiccioli, Teresa, 52n, 307
Gulbeyaz (in *Don Juan*), 337
Gulnare (in *Corsair*), 145–49, 156, 163–64, 183n

H Haidée (in *Don Juan*), 100, 292, 330n, 336: image of love and paradise, 104, 128, 333, 337, 341–42, 347–48; death of, 219, 342, 343
Hanson, John, xx, xxi, 119
Harley, Charlotte, 88
Haroun (in *Bride of Abydos*), 126
Harrow: B at, xxii, 5, 11, 119, 215
Hassan (in *Giaour*), 98, 106, 107, 112, 113, 114, 116, 122, 132, 156, 170n, 254: compared to Giaour, 102–3, 149, 151; mother of, 106, 107–8, 111, 113, 114; compared to Conrad, 147; compared to Selim, 149
Hazlitt, William, 277n, 283n, 284–85
Heaven and Earth, 321, 323n, 324, 327–28, 345
Hebrew Melodies, 202, 214, 215, 218, 222: analysis of, 204–11, 213; man in, 205, 207–8, 210–11, 213; criticism of, 207n, 209n, 210; unity of, 208, 210; compared to *Hours of Idleness*, 214. *Individual poems:* "'All Is Vanity, Saith the Preacher,'" 210; "A Spirit Passed before Me," 211; "By the Rivers of Babylon," 208; "By the Waters of Babylon," 208; "The Destruction of Sennacherib," 209; "The Harp the Monarch Minstrel Swept," 205–6; "Herod's Lament for Miriamne," 209n; "If That High World," 206–7; "I Saw Thee Weep," 204, 210; "Jephtha's Daughter," 208–9; "My Soul Is Dark," 215–16; "Oh! Snatched Away in Beauty's Bloom," 204, 210; "Oh! Weep for Those," 208; "On the Day of the Destruction of Jerusalem," 208; "Saul," 208; "She Walks in Beauty," 204–5, 210n; "Song of Saul," 208; "Thy Days Are Done," 208; "When Coldness Wraps This Suffering Clay," 211, 213; "The Wild Gazelle," 207
Hemans, Felicia, 92n
Highet, Gilbert, 175
"Hills of Annesley," 19, 22, 24n

Index

INDEX

Robert F. Gleckner
BYRON AND THE RUINS OF PARADISE
Designed by Gerard A. Valerio
Composed in Palatino by Monotype Composition Company, Inc.
Printed offset by Universal Lithographers, Inc., on 60-lb. P&S R B-30
Bound by the Maple Press Company in Holliston Fabrique

A

DIMOSTRAZIONI
DELL'EMISSARIO
DEL LAGO ALBANO

Piranesi F.

Engraving by G.-B. Piranesi